ZaSu Pitts

ZaSu Pitts

The Life and Career

Charles Stumpf

McFarland & Company, Inc., Publishers
Jefferson, North Carolina, and London

Frontispiece: A 1920s studio "glamour" shot of ZaSu Pitts.

Publisher's note: Charles Stumpf died on August 28, 2009, after completing the manuscript for this book.

LIBRARY OF CONGRESS CATALOGUING-IN-PUBLICATION DATA

Stumpf, Charles.
ZaSu Pitts : the life and career / Charles Stumpf.
    p.   cm.
Includes bibliographical references and index.
Includes filmography.

ISBN 978-0-7864-4620-9
softcover : 50# alkaline paper ∞

1. Pitts, ZaSu, 1898 [sic]–1963. 2. Actors —
United States — Biography. I. Title.
PN2287.P55S78 2010 791.4302'8092 — dc22 [B] 2010000272

British Library cataloguing data are available

©2010 Joseph G. Hill. All rights reserved

No part of this book may be reproduced or transmitted in any form or by any means, electronic or mechanical, including photocopying or recording, or by any information storage and retrieval system, without permission in writing from the publisher.

On the cover: ZaSu Pitts publicity photo (courtesy of the author)

Manufactured in the United States of America

McFarland & Company, Inc., Publishers
Box 611, Jefferson, North Carolina 28640
www.mcfarlandpub.com

TABLE OF CONTENTS

Acknowledgments
vi

Introduction
1

Biography
3

Filmography
Shorts
109
Feature Films
113
Television Credits
179
Radio Credits
186
Stage Appearances
188

Bibliography
189

Index
191

ACKNOWLEDGMENTS

Bill Bell
Mike Brotherton
Ed Colbert
Richard Edmunds
Don Gallery
Ross Gibson
Eve Golden
Susan B. Grimes
G.D. Hamann
Luther Hathcock
Lois Laurel Hawes
House and Garden Magazine
Jim King
Bill R. Kizer
Karl Malkames
Cynthia Mathews
Fred McFadden
Andrew Rehak
John Reynolds
Ralf Reynolds
Don Roegge
Robert Rosterman
Melodie Shorey
Jon Guyot Smith
Fredrick Tucker
Raymond B. Wood
E. Ron Wright

INTRODUCTION

Why a book about the life and career of ZaSu Pitts? Any film fan or historian will recognize the name and tell you that ZaSu Pitts was not just one, but *two* of Hollywood's top personalities.

First and foremost, ZaSu Pitts established herself as one of the silent screen's greatest tragediennes. She went on to become one of the finest character actresses in talking film. She was frequently cast as a befuddled, flustered, hand-wringing spinster, and became typecast in that category. ZaSu was a multitalented actress who could project every type of emotion with her large, expressive eyes, her extremely graceful hands, and her general body language. Today she is mainly remembered by Baby Boomers because of the Hal Roach–produced comedy *Oh! Susanna!*, a 1956–1960 TV series starring Gale Storm as the social director on a cruise ship, the S.S. *Ocean Queen*. ZaSu co-starred as Miss Elvira "Nugey" Nugent, the ship's fluttery beautician. But it is unfair to judge the importance of Miss Pitts' 50-plus-year career by only this aspect of her work, no matter how popular the show was.

During her career ZaSu appeared in hundreds of films, in leads and in support, and some popular shorts with Thelma Todd. But, of all her films, it is her work with director Erich von Stroheim which has put her in the history books.

In 1923, the eccentric, Austrian-born filmmaker Von Stroheim set to work on his epic adaptation of Frank Norris's novel *McTeague*. He retitled the film *Greed* and astonished everyone in Hollywood when he announced that he had cast none other than ZaSu Pitts, known for her comedy roles, in the leading role of Trina McTeague. Trina was a young, sweet-natured married woman who wins the lottery; thereafter, her only passion is for the gold coins she has hoarded in a trunk. To add to her treasure, she becomes a shrewish wife and begins to cheat her own husband by skimping on daily household expenses. The very demanding role called for ZaSu to express every facet of her complex character using only her eyes and body language.

The great director had total faith in her talents, despite her multitude of previous comedy roles, and considered her one of the world's foremost dramatic actresses of the silent screen. He was convinced she would give him the performance he needed, and ZaSu did not disappoint him, receiving high acclaim. He nodded knowingly as he declared, "Art must weep when ZaSu Pitts plays a comedy role."

When the realistic drama *Greed* was released in 1924, it was not appreciated or approved of by many (not helped by the studio-enforced cuts), and one critic went so far as to call it "an epic of the sewers." It received limited screenings and was finally withdrawn from exhibition. It took many years for the film to gain the following and reputation it retains to this day.

Most of ZaSu's succeeding film assignments were of a comedic nature, with very few exceptions, such as *Lazybones* and *Mannequin*, both released in 1926, and (again with Von Stroheim) *The Wedding March*. She was so popular and likable in comedy it was only natural that she would be typecast. Von Stroheim was basically the only one to see beyond that, to see the pathos within ZaSu, giving her a chance to stretch as an actress.

In 1929, ZaSu was assigned the comedy role of Rose Gleason, a highly nervous gun moll, in *The Dummy*. She later recalled that fateful role:

> The talkies had only been with us a very short time when the axe crashed down on my head. It was a low-budget gangster film, *The Dummy*, in which I played a scene of heart-rending anguish and I was directed to wring my hands for effect. In disgust, I cupped my hands over my forehead and let out a doleful, "Ooooh, dear!!!" Everyone on the set went into convulsions of laughter, and in my next picture they had me do more of the same.

The funny line and the accompanying gestures became ever after her trademark. She later added, "It was the opening up of a new career for me as a comedienne, but it finished the career I loved most, as a dramatic actress."

ZaSu remained busy in films, starring in Hal Roach shorts with Thelma Todd, appearing on radio, acting on the stage, and venturing into TV starting in 1948. She remained an audience favorite up until her untimely death in 1962.

And she is still remembered today, especially by viewers of TCM, where her films are consistently shown. *Greed* is still regarded as a movie masterpiece, topping many greatest film lists. With its continued appeal and exposure to new generations, ZaSu's brilliant work lives on.

It is my wish that, with this book, those who know Miss Pitts for *Greed* will be introduced to her brilliant comedy — and vice versa. ZaSu was a versatile actress, and it is time for her to finally receive her due. There are numerous reasons why she is remembered — not only for her expressive hands, but also for her kind and generous heart.

In Erich von Stroheim's 1924 silent dramatic masterpiece *Greed*, ZaSu, as Trina McTeague, brushes her long, luxuriant hair.

BIOGRAPHY

In 1900, although the flag of the United States boasted 48 stars, there were only 45 states in the Union. Kansas ranked 22nd in size, with nearly a million and a half residents. Teddy Roosevelt was in the White House, having become the nation's youngest president at the age of 42. There had been no war for almost two full generations. The average American worker earned 22 cents an hour. Most males worked ten hours per day, six days a week, and took home an average $12 for a week's labors.

Business was brisk and taxes were low. Automobiles sold for an average of $1,150, but there were not many around in those days, as there was only a total of 150 miles of paved road in the entire country. The U.S. Treasury showed a surplus of more than $45 million, and the three uppermost things in everyone's life were peace, prosperity and progress.

Parsons, Kansas, was a railroading town through which more than 100 passenger trains passed monthly, as well as more than 1,000 freight trains. The city became known as "the Infant Wonder of the South West." It's no surprise, then, that International Harvester Company chose Parsons as its main distribution point. The official census confirmed a population of 6,808 residents, making it the 12th largest city in the state. Its business district was constantly changing, and its unpaved streets were lined with brick sidewalks. The two main centers of entertainment were Edwards Hall and Russell Hall. Each night at 8:00 P.M. a bell atop the city's firehouse sounded a curfew for all children to get off the streets.

Rulandus Pitts, a New Yorker by birth, enlisted in Company F, 30th Infantry Regiment, on June 1, 1861. Two years later he was transferred to the 76th New York. On June 1, 1863, as part of Cutler's Brigade, he participated in the infamous "Railroad Cut" outside of Gettysburg, Pennsylvania. During the bloody Battle of Gettysburg, Rulandus was shot in the right knee and the right shoulder. When his troop pulled back, he was left behind, badly wounded on the field of battle. Medical help was delayed, and because of this and the seriousness of his injuries, when help did arrive, his leg had to be amputated above the knee. In later years he was also unable to use his right hand. He stayed in the army, however, working in the commissary. He left the service on July 1, 1864, on a medical discharge.

After the war he returned to New York, working the best he could with his disabilities. He married and had a daughter, Clara Belle, but he was widowed after a few years. In 1879 he remarried, moving to Parsons, Kansas, where he lived on his pension and some odd jobs. The bride was the former Nellie Shay (born January 1, 1860, died February 16, 1941), of Irish immigrant parents.

It had been a cold, crisp January 3, 1894, in Parsons, Kansas, when a dark-haired, blue-eyed baby girl was delivered to the Pitts home. The family already consisted of a daughter, Nellie, (born February 2, 1887, died in 1930), and a son, Rulandus, Jr. (born on January 5, 1891, died May 1988).

The parents were in a quandary about choosing a name for the new arrival. Mrs. Pitts had two sisters of whom she was fond, Liza and Susan. Not wishing to slight either one, she came up with a name of her own, ZaSu, using the last two letters of one sister and the first two letters of the second. And so, the unique name of ZaSu came into being. The child would grow up to become a lady as unusual as her quaint name.

Another son, Asa Jennings, was born to the family on April 18, 1897. Asa would pass away on December 19, 1957, in Los Angeles.

In 1903 the Pitts family moved again, to Santa Cruz, California. Mr. Pitts read in the local newspaper about the development of a large new park in Santa Cruz, and he decided it was time to relocate, prompted in part by the harsh Kansas winters. The family packed their meager possessions and headed west.

Santa Cruz was a seacoast town with miles of sandy beaches. Towering redwood trees had once provided ample shade. Little by little, a thriving lumber business had denuded the majestic forestland, and for a time the area's economy had gone into a decline.

Then, in 1883, an enterprising 21-year-old Brooklyn-born college graduate, Fred Swanton, moved to Santa Cruz and changed the course of the area's history. Along with his wealthy father, Swanton built the first three-story hotel on Front Street. Then, in 1890, the younger Swanton formed a partnership with Dr. H.H. Clark to operate an electric light

Parsons, Kansas, circa 1896. The Pitts siblings, Nellie, ZaSu and Rulandus, Jr.

and power company. Within a two-month period the electric company installed more than 18 miles of power lines.

The adventurous young businessman then took some time off to venture to the Alaskan gold fields. After experiencing some moderate success, he returned to Santa Cruz to organize an electric streetcar line. With his keen foresight, he soon realized the potential of the sandy beaches and wisely purchased a huge abandoned bathhouse and refurnished it to accommodate the many bathers for changing into their bathing attire.

In 1904, Swanton acquired another business partner, wealthy John Martin, and together they opened another enterprise, a massive structure they named Neptune's Casino. In addition to a casino, it included a café, grill and a grand ballroom, as well as a "roof garden." To attract business, Swanton installed hundreds of electric lights to illuminate the 400-foot pier that faced the Casino. Business thrived, but after only twenty-two months of operation, tragedy struck—Neptune's Casino burned to the ground, a loss of more than a half-million dollars. Undaunted, Swanton quickly convinced his partner, Martin, to invest yet another million dollars and erect a second, larger casino. The new casino had its grand opening in June of 1906.

It was into this thriving area that Rulandus Pitts moved his family in early 1903. They settled into a sizable home, located at 208 Lincoln Street. All of the family members enjoyed the much warmer climate. Mr. Pitts immediately began to feel much better. ZaSu and her younger brother were delighted to be near the beach, with its large boardwalk and many amusements. Unable to afford the admission for the amusement rides, the youngsters contented themselves with simply enjoying the excitement of seeing the large crowds and listening to the band organ of the carousel.

That fall, when the school term started, ZaSu, who was nine years old, was thrilled to be enrolled in the first grade. She applied herself to her lessons and made rapid advancement. Although the awkward girl with the melancholy blue eyes enjoyed school, her family's financial condition was such that she had to wear hand-me-down dresses, sturdy shoes and cotton stockings. She still retained her Kansas accent, but most pointedly, her unusual first name prompted the other students to make fun of her, calling her "Zoo-Zoo," "Zoo-Loo," "Zay-Zoo," "Jazz-Su," "Hey You," and even "ZuZu Gingersnaps." The poor girl endured their cruel taunts with quiet reserve.

When school let out for the day, the serious-minded girl rushed home to help her mother with the housework. She scrubbed the floors, washed the stacks of dishes, and helped with the laundry. She also hauled groceries in a basket attached to her bicycle—not only for her mother, but for several neighbors as well. The sight of sad-eyed ZaSu, with her spindly legs vigorously working the pedals, became a familiar sight around town.

Her Santa Cruz friend Dorothy Fargo recalled years later, "I always thought ZaSu had talent, but she was so very reserved and quiet. She had no boyfriends; she simply had no time for them. She had to help at home and worked very hard. When she had some rare free time, she liked to play tennis. The high school we attended had no courts, so ZaSu went over to the Casa del Rey."

Her father stayed active in veteran affairs, being a member of the GAR, the Grand Army of the Republic. However, he went blind in his final years and needed much assistance. He died on February 26, 1908, and was buried at the Odd Fellows Cemetery in Santa Cruz (now Santa Cruz Memorial Park). His passing added extra hardship to the family.

His plucky widow, Nellie, who was 24 years his junior, made ends meet by renting out their extra bedrooms to visiting tourists during the summer season. ZaSu pitched in and did all she could, helping with the cleaning, laundry, and cooking. She spent hours in the kitchen carefully observing her mother cook. The dutiful daughter soon became a very good cook herself, specializing in desserts. When not busy in the kitchen, ZaSu liked to putter with flowers in the garden, and even mowed the lawn.

In 1911 ZaSu enrolled at Santa Cruz High School. She was especially excited when she learned that the school had a drama department. Secretly, she wanted to join but was too timid, so she lingered in the auditorium watching the other students rehearse. For a time she gave serious thought of training to become a nurse, but two of her classmate friends, Dorothy Fargo and Lois Neilson, encouraged her to take part in school plays. They urged her to try a comedy monologue, such as "Mrs. Smart Learns How to Ice Skate." Reluctantly, she consented, and with her doleful accent and much fluttering of her nervous hands she raised more than a few laughs.

Mr. Bond, the school principal, took notice of her brave efforts and also offered encouragement. As recounted in the *Santa Cruz Sentinel*, the principal "happened to see ZaSu defending herself in a fist fight with some boys who had ridiculed her."

At his suggestion she agreed to try a dramatic recitation of the serious poem "The Midnight Ride of Paul Revere." Under her mother's guidance she rehearsed diligently. Filled with apprehension, ZaSu stood up in front of her classmates, but midway through her recitation a few of the students began to laugh. Thoroughly humiliated, ZaSu put her hands to her face and rushed offstage. Mr. Bond was standing in the wings; he comforted her and urged her to go back on. "Laughter is God's hand upon a troubled world," he told her. Summoning her courage, she went back out, took a deep breath, and began the piece all over again. Mr. Bond smiled encouragement from the wings, and, little by little, the audience began to feel her sincerity. At the end of the poem a hearty round of applause greeted the startled young performer. In that moment cold fear melted away in the warmth of applause, and she hurried home to tell her mother. Thereafter, young Miss Pitts was welcomed into the once forbidding drama department. "Years later she remembered that as one of the turning points in her life," Dorothy said.

"She took some part in most of the high school plays, although she didn't have much time," Dorothy Fargo told the *Santa Cruz Sentinel* in 1985. "She had to help at home, and she worked very hard."

In her senior year at Santa Cruz High School, the class yearbook, *The Trident*, contained a formal pose of ZaSu looking quite mature, with her long dark hair, done up in braids, framing her pale face. Beneath the picture was the comment: "Rarely is a class so fortunate as to have such a brilliant leading lady as ZaSu Pitts. Even the solemnest, most awe-like member of her class loses their dignity at her comedy interpretations. Can you imagine what future high school plays will be without her? Moreover, she possesses that unusual quality, common sense, and lots of it."

Her mother, who had been wondering if ZaSu had the potential to be a professional actress, needed no further proof. She began to see her daughter as a stage actress and possibly even a star in motion pictures.

Local entrepreneur Fred Swanton also took notice of the young lady's potential and decided to help her raise money for a trip to the film capital. He arranged to stage a benefit for her, and she was starred in a production of the comedy *Fanchon the Cricket*, which was well suited to her special talents. A performance was staged at Knight's Opera House on Thursday evening, July 15, 1915. General admission was set at 25 cents, with reserved seats at 35 cents and front row seats at 50 cents.

On opening night her heart was beating wildly as the curtains rose and she stepped out into the bright lights. She was speechless for a moment and tugged nervously at the folds of her costume. Carefully, she mouthed her first line, and then the words began to come more easily. She had rehearsed thoroughly and believed that her future hung in the balance. When she got her first laugh, it was music to her ears. Tensions relieved, she began to use some of the hand gestures which would later make her famous. She found she actually enjoyed being in front of an audience. That night, on the stage of the opera house in Santa Cruz, an actress was born.

The next morning Mrs. Pitts took her youngest daughter on a frugal-minded shopping spree. They picked out a plain but pretty print dress, some sensible, sturdy shoes, black cotton stockings and other practical undergarments. They also selected a sturdy tin suitcase and then hurried home as they made excited plans for the coming trip to Hollywood.

A few days later ZaSu was bundled into her mother's best coat and a large-brimmed hat, and anxiously boarded the train. The lonely ride seemed endless as the clickety-clack of the rails echoed in her ears. Unwrapping the sandwich her mother had packed for her, she tried to imagine what the fates had in store for her.

Alone in Los Angeles, with no friends or contacts of any kind, ZaSu must have been a pathetic sight as she toted her tin suitcase down the street in a drab part of town in search of the least expensive boarding house.

The January '36 issue of *Collier's* magazine featured an article by Kyle Crichton entitled "Mr. Woodall's Wife — The Story of Miss ZaSu Pitts, Whose Diffidence Amounts to Genius." The article commented on the actress's early days in the film capital: "ZaSu had a room in Hollywood with some other girls and made the rounds of the studios every morning and got looking more pathetic every day. The casting offices were cluttered up with beauties, and ZaSu felt like a peg-legged lady who had wandered into a harem." Minus the benefit of flashy clothes and glamorous looks, the young hopeful began to make endless daily rounds of casting agents. Finally, one day a casting agent asked for her résumé, but she was such an amateur she wasn't sure what he meant. She seemed, at this point, a very unlikely candidate for success as an actress in Hollywood.

Remembering her mother's words of encouragement, she worked at overcoming the nervous habits she had developed during her childhood. To complicate matters even further, she still had a Kansas twang and spoke hesitantly in tremulous tones. ZaSu was reed-like, with a thin upper lip and a slightly drooping mouth. Fidgeting hands gave her a look of constant dismay. Her large wistful eyes were her most appealing feature.

One rainy afternoon, while riding on a crowded streetcar along Hollywood Boulevard, the young would-be movie star with the unusual name nervously clutched the wide brim of her hat and struggled to keep from jabbing other passengers with her dripping umbrella. She was totally unaware that her every movement was being carefully observed by a fellow passenger. He, too, had an unusual name — King Vidor — and was also a relative newcomer to the film capital. Another coincidence — he was just a little more than a month younger than she was.

Vidor remembered the incident vividly in his autobiography, *A Tree Is a Tree*:

> The next heaven-sent gift came to me while I was riding on a Hollywood Boulevard streetcar. A strange angular young girl sat opposite me watching anxiously for her destination. Each time she turned she managed by weird gesticulation to accidentally bump the passenger on either side of her. When the conductor announced that hers was the next stop, she showed her delight and appreciation with a good backhand slap on his stomach. She retreated down the aisle, knocking hats, heads, and newspapers in grand confusion. Most of the passengers were at the windows to watch her get off, but I just couldn't sit there and let this interesting creature go out of my life forever. I bounded out of the car and caught up to her as she reached the corner of Hollywood and Gower.
>
> "What is your name, please?"
>
> "ZaSu. Last of Eliza, first of Susie.... I was named after two maiden aunts, Eliza and Susie. Do you think I should change my name? ... I hope they let me stay at the Hollywood Studio Club. It's a nice place, isn't it?" As an accent to this last remark, I got a surprising blow on the chest.

King Vidor had been born in Galveston, Texas, and at a very young age became interested in photography. "I was interested in photography and movement even before I started photographing things with a camera," Vidor recalled to Nancy Dowd. "Various kinds of movement held my attention, and, of course, when motion pictures came to Galveston, it was only natural that I would jump on this means to recording the things that I felt." He eventually got himself a job as a ticket-taker in a local nickelodeon, soon working himself up to becoming the stand-by projectionist. He started to record local events, going to work for a newsreel company, Mutual Weekly. Vidor then set up his own company in Houston.

He met a pretty girl, Florence, from Houston, who had ambitions of becoming a screen actress. A romance blossomed, and shortly after, they married. "We lived in Houston for six or eight months before we decided to come to California, where the action was," Vidor remarked. So, in 1915, the young couple set out for Hollywood in an old Model-T Ford. They both found work as extras in films.

The ambitious cameraman and screenwriter was disappointed with what he observed when he arrived. He later recalled, "When I first arrived I immediately noticed that there was a sort of unreality about films. The acting was overdone and the make-up was even worse. I soon decided that I would change all that."

That rainy afternoon, as he observed the vulnerable young woman with a body language which bespoke both insecurity and a lanky kind of style, King Vidor vowed that when he achieved a position of power in films, he would write a picture for her to star in. At that particular point in time, neither Vidor nor Miss Pitts could possibly imagine the degree of success they would both find in filmmaking.

Another newcomer to the film capital that ZaSu met and befriended was future director Byron Haskin. She consented to go on a date with him. He was worldlier than the girl from Kansas, and he good-naturedly tried to introduce her to Hollywood nightlife. He later told interviewer Joe Adamson that he "took her to the first nightclub she ever went to in Los Angeles," although they were not romantically involved because, said Haskin, "I had never thought of her as a female — you know, for any lecherous dalliance." But, Haskin was quick to point out, he had tremendous respect for her. "She turned out to be a hell of an actress, as well as a wonderful person." Their paths crossed again in 1952 when Haskin directed her in *Denver and Rio Grande*.

As she kept up her daily quest for work in films, someone she met suggested that perhaps she needed a different name. Reluctantly, for a short time, she was known as "Zona Parker," thereby retaining her true initials — Z.P. "She had a terrible time staying in Hollywood, and she thought she'd have to give up," related her hometown friend Dorothy. "Her mother sent her a pittance to live on — she rented a room."

Finally, in 1917, she obtained some extra work at the Paramount Pictures lot in the Douglas Fairbanks film *A Modern Musketeer*. Next, she was used in a circus scene in *Rebecca of Sunnybrook Farm*, with Mary Pickford. While filming was underway, screenwriter Frances Marion visited the set, and her attention was called to ZaSu's rather pathetic look. She saw before her a thin, awkward girl with enormous eyes, fluttering hands, and a pinched face that gave her the look of a trapped animal. She approached ZaSu and introduced herself. After some hesitant conversation, the famous screenwriter promised the apprehensive actress that she'd help her obtain more work in films.

In the spring of 1917, ZaSu learned that Universal Pictures was producing a series of one-reel comedies called *Joker Comedies*. In a salary dispute, they had lost the series' leading lady, Gale Henry (1893–1972). ZaSu applied, was tested, and was hired to fill the vacated position.

Finding herself alone in a studio dressing room for the first time, she had little idea how to prepare herself for the camera. Betty Compson, one of the studio's top blonde stars, came to her rescue by extending some costume and make-up tips. ZaSu was eternally grateful.

ZaSu's first appearance in the *Joker* series came in *Uneasy Money*, and she worked with the comedy team of Bobbie Mack and William Franey, under the direction of William Beaudine. The short was released to theaters on June 2 and met with much audience favor. Other shorts quickly followed, at an average of one short each week in 1917: *A Desert Dilemma* (June 23), *His Fatal Beauty* (June 25), *He Had 'Em Buffaloed* (July 21), *Canning the Cannibal King* (July 28), *The Battling Bellboy* (August 2), *O-My the Tent Mover* (August 11), *Behind the Map* (August 25), and *Why They Left Home* (August 27). For Mutual, she did the short *Tillie of the Nine Lives*, released on June 19. Two more of the *Joker* shorts were released in 1918, *Who's Your Wife?* (May 27) and *The Pie Eyed Piper* (August 19). Eddie Baker, Milburn Moranti and Lillian Peacock were some of the other performers that appeared in the series. Gale Henry returned to the studio in 1918, and ZaSu appeared in one short with her, *Who's Your Wife?*

"In His First Million Dollar Picture" (as publicity boasted), Charles Chaplin wrote and directed his first short for First National, *A Dog's Life*, released on April 14, 1918. ZaSu was cast by an impressed Chaplin, but her scenes were ultimately cut from the final print. Chaplin apparently felt bad about this. When it came time to film his next project for First National, *Shoulder Arms*, the June 1918 issue of *Picture-Play* magazine reported:

> Charley Chaplin has chosen the plot for his second starring vehicle at the head of his own company, and the majority of those who appeared in his first screen offering since he severed his connection with Mutual will support him. Fred Starr, the gigantic figure who replaced the late Eric Campbell in Chaplin's company, and ZaSu Pitts, formerly with the Mary Pickford Company, but also seen in the first Chaplin offering, are in the cast.

Alas, when *Shoulder Arms* was released on October 20, 1918, ZaSu was not in it.

ZaSu did a small uncredited bit as a party guest in *'49-'17*, a Western directed by Ruth Ann Baldwin (from her own scenario), starring Joseph Girard.

True to her word, Frances Marion arranged a private introduction for ZaSu with Mary Pickford, "America's Sweetheart," during which Frances slyly suggested to the star that the waif-like young hopeful would be ideally suited for a small role in Pickford's next film, *The Little Princess*.

Miss Pickford took a closer look at the young woman before her and let her fertile imagination picture her as Becky, a young char-girl at a private school for girls. "Yes," she thought, "she is just right for the role." The role, while brief, gave ZaSu an excellent opportunity to prove her acting abilities. She gave a very touching and convincing performance that won the favor of both audiences and critics alike.

The studio's costume department provided her with appropriate attire, but ZaSu added her own personal touch by substituting a pair of old high-button shoes that had been given to her by high-school chum Dorothy Fargo in Santa Cruz.

Years later, in an interview, Fargo recalled:

> My mother often invited [ZaSu] to our house for dinner. One time, when she was visiting, she spotted a pair of old high-button shoes that had been discarded on our back porch. She admired them very much, so we gave them to her. She wore those shoes in her first picture with Mary Pickford. ZaSu always said it was those old shoes that brought her luck and made the picture a success. She later wore them in a number of other pictures she made.

The Little Princess premiered at the Strand Theatre in Los Angeles on November 11, 1917, and was greeted by an enthusiastic audience. A reviewer for *Moving Picture World* wrote, "Watch for ZaSu Pitts—for she is a coming star."

Following this success, ZaSu suffered a setback. The great director D.W. Griffith was giving serious thought to casting her in his forthcoming epic *The Greatest Thing in*

In one of her first silent comedy shorts, circa 1918, ZaSu wore a pair of old high-button shoes that she brought to Hollywood with her.

Life (1918), but changed his mind when he decided that she bore too close a resemblance to the film's star, Lillian Gish. ZaSu's scenes were cut from the release print. Director King Vidor clarified years later:

> She was very eccentric and Griffith had her over to rehearse.... He used to have his cast, his stock company, watch people who came in to rehearse. She had such strange individual movements with her arms, hitting people with them as they swing about, that they stole her movements and gestures and used them in their films. In those days you didn't have to pay someone to come for rehearsals, and they would make people rehearse all day long. I think it was Dorothy Gish who they used with the Pitts mannerisms.

ZaSu had a smallish role in the 50-minute farce *Good Night, Paul* (1918). It starred the "first" Harrison Ford (as Paul), Constance Talmadge and Norman Kerry. Then Frances Marion came through again. Pitts appeared as a servant girl (and Larry Peyton's sweetheart) in *How Could You, Jean?* starring Mary Pickford in a William Desmond Taylor–directed comedy written by Marion.

Universal then cast her as a character known only as "Just Mary" in the five-reel production of *A Society Sensation*, which was shot on location in Balboa. Exotic Carmel Myers was also in the cast, as was the then-relatively unknown Rudolph Valentino, billed then as Rudolpho De Valentina. When the studio re-released this in 1924 to coincide with Valentino's success, it was cut to two reels, emphasizing just Valentino's scenes. The original is thought to be lost. In later years ZaSu delighted in relating that it was Valentino who first taught her how to dance.

Also at Universal, ZaSu had an uncredited bit in *The Talk of the Town*, a comedy about infidelity, which also included Lon Chaney in its cast. It starred Dorothy Phillips and George Fawcett. For Select Pictures, ZaSu was seen as Emily in *A Lady's Name*, with Constance Talmadge and Harrison Ford.

In 1919, at Metro, she played Sal Sue in the Western *As the Sun Went Down*, as well as Katie Jones, a dressmaker's assistant, in *Men, Women and Money*. Her bit in the film *Sunnyside*, however, was cut from the release print.

As her prospects brightened, ZaSu moved from her drab room at a boarding house to the famed Studio Club, where many budding actresses lived. ZaSu recalled her Santa Cruz High School chum, Lois Neilson, who was a very pretty blonde with dancing abilities. ZaSu wrote her and encouraged her to come to Hollywood and seek work in motion pictures. Neilson made the move, and the pair shared an apartment. ZaSu was instrumental in obtaining some extra work for her friend.

In 1919 Universal would sign Neilson to a contract for a series of comedy shorts, in

An early publicity portrait of a budding young actress.

which she was sometimes billed as "Lois Nelson." Through her film work she met comedy great Stan Laurel, whom she wed in August of 1926. The following year the couple had a daughter, Lois, and in 1930 a son, Stan, Jr., who, sadly, succumbed within a few days. The Laurels divorced in 1936, but ZaSu and Lois would remain lifelong friends.

Dorothy Fargo, too, became a movie extra because of her friend — as a socialite in one

Lois Neilson, a girlhood friend from Santa Cruz, was encouraged by ZaSu to come to Hollywood. She became a dancer and actress, and married silent screen comedian Stan Laurel (courtesy Lois Laurel Hawes).

of ZaSu's films: "A banquet scene in the old Alexandra Hotel in Los Angeles. We sat around at small tables, and we were all dressed up in evening gowns — it was a lot of fun."

While still in Hollywood, Dorothy went with ZaSu to visit a Harold Lloyd set where he was being chased by a lion. "He fell off a balcony into the street below — but the balcony was really only three feet above the 'street'— it was fun to see how they faked some things."

Meanwhile, King Vidor had achieved success in Hollywood as both a screenwriter and a director (after working for a time as an actor and assistant director). With the picture of the awkward young woman that he had seen on the streetcar on that rainy afternoon still in his mind, Vidor wrote a screenplay called *Better Times*. The script was sold to the Robertson-Cole Distributing Corporation, and Vidor was hired to direct. He insisted on ZaSu for the role of Nancy Scroggs, an awkward, unpopular student at an all-girl school. The wallflower is constantly taunted by the other students. To fend off their torment, Nancy invents a make-believe romance by mail with a top athlete at a nearby school (future director David Butler). In reality, she sent herself a series of gushy love notes, all of which turn the others green with envy. As the wallflower, ZaSu was completely believable, and audiences empathized with her.

King Vidor was very pleased that his instincts had proven correct; ZaSu was a natural. The star and her director developed mutual admiration and respect for each other, and a lifelong friendship was formed.

Their next film together was a comedy, *The Other Half*, and Vidor further tapped her versatility by casting her as a rebellious flapper, Jennie Jones, known to her fun-loving pals as "the Jazz Kid." Again, audiences approved, and ZaSu next portrayed Daisy Perkins in a comedy, *Poor Relations* (1919), also written and directed by King Vidor.

In 1920, at Robertson-Cole, she was featured in *Seeing It Through*, as Betty Lawrence.

With *Bright Skies*, the studio teamed her with a new leading man, the very handsome, dark-haired and highly personable Tom Gallery (born Thomas Patrick Sarsfield Gallery on November 27, 1898, in Chicago, Illinois), who was making his film debut after serving as a private in the United States Army

After ZaSu was signed to a movie contract, the studio's make-up department began to alter her appearance, altering her lip line while adding false eyelashes and mascara.

during World War I. Off the set, there was a strong attraction between the pair, and they began to see a lot of each other. They re-teamed in a romantic comedy, *Heart of Twenty*, in which the role of Katie Abbott, a very single young lady, had been written by Sarah Y. Mason especially with ZaSu in mind.

The couple surprised all of their acquaintances when they eloped to Santa Ana on July 23, 1920. There was barely time for a honeymoon. They both immediately reported back to the studio to work.

Films in which Gallery appeared without ZaSu were *The Chorus Girl's Romance* (1920), based on an F. Scott Fitzgerald story, with Lawrence Grant and Viola Dana; *Dinty*, with Wesley Barry, Colleen Moore and Noah Beery; *The Son of Wallingford*, in which he played the lead (one of his best parts, in the role of a minister); *Bob Hampton of Placer*, (with James Kirkwood in the leading role); *Home Stuff*, with Viola Dana; *A Parisian Scandal*, with Marie Provost; *Grand Larceny*, with free-spirited Claire Windsor; and *The Wall Flower*, with Richard Dix and Colleen Moore.

ZaSu and Tom were together onscreen in *Patsy* in 1921. She played the title role, an orphan who disguises herself as a boy. In the cast were Wallace Beery, Marjorie Daw, John MacFarlane and Fanny Midgley. ZaSu's old Santa Cruz booster, entrepreneur Fred Swanton, had a hand in the production. In 1923 he was instrumental in encouraging film production in Santa Cruz, and two small studios were erected, both of which were short lived. *Patsy* seems to be his only Hollywood movie credit. Swanton became mayor of Santa Cruz from 1927 to 1933, and passed away in 1940.

Mrs. Gallery's screen work was curtailed during the latter part of 1921 as she awaited the birth of her only child, daughter Ann, born on April 17, 1922. A family source has said that the girl's given name at birth was "ZaSu," but she later insisted on being called simply Ann.

ZaSu and Tom Gallery were reteamed in the prophetically titled *Is Matrimony a Failure?* (1922). Directed by James Cruze, the cast included Lila Lee, Tully Marshall, T. Roy Barnes, and, in smaller roles, Adolphe Menjou and Lois Wilson. ZaSu appeared as a married lady, Mrs. Wilbur. Arthur Hoyt played her husband.

Also in 1922 she was happy to be cast in the role of Jennie Dunn, a troubled young woman accused of murdering a lecherous hypnotist while in a fit of jealous rage in *For the Defense*. She then reported to Metro, where she played the role of Emily in *Youth to Youth*. Directed by Emile Chautard, the film starred Billie Dove, Edythe Chapman, and Noah Beery.

In 1922, ZaSu and Tom's next joint appearance came in Paramount's *A Daughter of Luxury*. She appeared as heiress Mary Cosgrove, and he was a playboy, Blake Walford, who loses his heart to the glamorous Agnes Ayres. *A Daughter of Luxury* marked the last time the couple would appear together on film.

The year 1923 was a very busy time for the ambitious actress, and the roles she was assigned gave her ample opportunity to display the many facets of her versatility. For Preferred Pictures she essayed a brief but impressive character role as Apple Annie in *Poor Men's Wives*. Then, for P. Schulberg Productions, she portrayed an Irish lass, Anastasia Muldoon, in *The Girl Who Came Back*. For Goldwyn she appeared as a character known only as Mickey in *Three Wise Fools*, directed by friend King Vidor. Then, in a definite change of pace, she was cast as Brainy Jones in the oddly-titled comedy *Tea: With a Kick!* released through Associated Exhibitors. Publicity for the film called it "a 27 Star Dramatic Treat with 10 Prize-Winning Beauties and a Ballet of 100 Hollywood Heartbreakers." Creighton Hale and Doris May starred, supported by the comedy talents of Louise Fazenda as Birdie Puddleford, Dot Farley, Hank Mann, and Chester Conklin. Also in the cast were her pals from the Universal comedy shorts, Billy Franey and Gale Henry. For Paramount ZaSu was seen as demure Dessie Arnhalt in *West of the Water Tower*.

She had now become a well-known screen personality, as evidenced by brief appearances as herself in *Mary of the Woods*, along with 23 other celebrities, and *Hollywood*. The latter was a Paramount all-star spectacle in which the studio made use of all its contract

ZaSu married actor Tom Gallery on August 20, 1920. Daughter Ann was born on April 17, 1922. The couple divorced in 1932.

A smiling ZaSu enjoys browsing through the latest issue of *Vanity Fair* in this photograph from the 1920s (courtesy Lois Laurel Hawes).

players. It was directed by James Cruze, whose talents gave the film great panache, and it became a big hit.

While on the sets of Goldwyn's *Souls for Sale* and Preferred Picture's *Poor Men's Wives* in 1923, ZaSu forged a very significant friendship. Barbara La Marr, the star of both films, was Hollywood's most beautiful and glamorous star. La Marr was frequently referred to as "the Girl Too Beautiful For Her Own Good" and "the Girl Who Is Too Beautiful." Pitts and La Marr were worlds apart in appearance and personality, but they found enough in common to form a friendship. ZaSu was a little more than four years Barbara's senior.

La Marr had been born Reatha Dale Watson on July 26, 1898. There is some confusion as to the place of her birth, but at one month of age she was adopted by newspaperman William Wright Watson and his wife. The Watsons claimed the child was born in North Yakima, Washington, while La Marr herself always insisted that she was born in Richmond, Virginia. The family was constantly on the go because of Mr. Watson's work. In 1904, in Tacoma, Washington, La Marr was said to have made her acting debut as Little Eva in a stock company production of *Uncle Tom's Cabin*. Relocating to Los Angeles in 1913, the dark-haired, fun-loving and carefree beauty began to dance professionally. She was experiencing much beyond her young years. At the age of 14 she was arrested for dancing in a burlesque show. The juvenile court judge prophetically remarked that she was "too beautiful to be in a big city alone and unprotected."

Arizona rancher Jack Lytell became her first husband when she was only 16. A few months later she was widowed. She and Lytell reportedly had a fight. He took to riding his horse in the rain, the story goes, mourning her absence by spending hours riding around his ranch. He died of pneumonia.

La Marr moved to Los Angeles, where she married a handsome attorney, Lawrence Converse. Much to her horror, however, she soon learned that he didn't know his law; he was already married and a father of three children. He was jailed on bigamy charges the day after their wedding. When he was arrested, newspapers across the country reported that he screamed he "had to have her, to possess her magnificent beauty." In prison, Converse banged his head against his cell bars incessantly, reportedly screaming La Marr's name in repeated anguish. Knocked unconscious, he died two weeks later from a blood clot caused by his self-induced injury.

She continued to support herself by dancing in Chicago, New Orleans, the World's Fair in San Francisco, and at the famous Lincoln Hotel on 52nd Street and Broadway in New York City. Everywhere she went, Barbara collected new lovers. She once commented, "I take lovers like roses — by the dozen."

In 1916 she entered into a third marriage with musical-comedy actor and ballroom dancer Phil Ainsworth. It was an ill-fated union. According to the *New York Times*, "He soon began forging checks, sold her car out from under her and spent time in prison." He forged checks to purchase clothes and jewelry for Barbara. He was arrested and sent to prison in San Quentin. Upon his release, he tried to resume his career. At Paramount in 1918 he appeared with Wallace Reid in *The Man from Funeral Range*. At Metro he was seen in *The Chorus Girl's Romance* (1920), which, interestingly, featured Tom Gallery. While her husband was in the Big House, Barbara sued for divorce in 1917. One of her lovers at this time was reportedly writer Ernest Hemingway.

In 1918 she unwisely entered into her fourth marriage — to her much-older dancing partner Ben Deely (born 1878). Their relationship was marked by their mutual excessive drinking and his gambling problem. For a time she was billed as Barbara La Marr-Deely.

She had a talent for writing, and in 1920 she turned to screenwriting. She doctored up troubled screenplays, and turned out six original scripts at Fox and United Artists: *The Mother of His Children, Rose of Nome, The Little Grey Mouse, Flame of Youth, The Land of Jazz* (all 1920) and *My Husband's Wives* (1924). When Mary Pickford saw her at the writers' building at United Artists, she embraced her and said, "My dear, you are too beautiful to be behind a camera. Your vibrant magnetism should be shared by film audiences."

La Marr entered films in 1920 when Louis B. Mayer cast her in a secondary role in *Harriet and the Piper*, billed as Barbara Deely. She stole the notices from the film's star, Anita Stewart, and she was on her way. She played the vamp in *The Nut* and was in John Ford's *Desperate Trails*. Her biggest splash came playing the juicy role of Milady de Winter in *The Three Musketeers* (1921).

During the filming of *The Three Musketeers*, Barbara separated from Ben Deely. Deely (also billed as "Deeley") returned to New York, where he made appearances in vaudeville, acted in some films and wrote songs. He died of pneumonia in 1924. La Marr rode the crest of her newfound popularity in such films as *Arabian Love, The Prisoner of Zenda* (1922), and *Trifling Women. Moving Picture World* raved, "Barbara La Marr is one of the most beautiful women on screen and an actress of uncommon ability."

Barbara had a secret she did not share with the press and her friends. On July 28, 1922, while on a trip to Dallas, Texas, she gave birth to a son. As it happened, she was not married at the time, and Ben Deely was not the father. The clever Barbara arranged an elaborate cover-up. She had named her son Marvin Carville La Marr, and when he was seven months old she placed him in a Dallas orphanage, Hope Cottage. In an article in the *Los Angeles Times* (September 30, 2007), her son related that "through contacts, she made sure she got a tour of the orphanage. A Dallas newspaper reported how this one particular baby touched her heart." La Marr then "adopted" him.

La Marr never disclosed who the father of her child was, but many years later her son, now named Don Gallery, told the *Los Angeles Times*, "I have no idea who my real father was, but I can guess—Paul Bern. He was my godfather and visited me every Sunday," up until Bern's death in 1932. Don told Jimmy Bangley in 1996 that "Mr. Bern used to bring me wonderful gifts. I especially remember a battery-operated boat that was about three feet long."

Paul Bern was a screenwriter, producer and director, and became Irving Thalberg's top assistant at MGM. One of his claims to fame was having supervised a number of Garbo's films. In 1932 he married platinum blonde bombshell Jean Harlow. In one of Hollywood's most notorious scandals, Bern reportedly committed suicide two months after the wedding. The details of his death remain a mystery to this day.

In May 1923, La Marr entered into her fifth marriage. This time the groom was a handsome, red-haired actor named Virgil "Jack" Dougherty (born in Missouri in 1895). He starred in a number of silent Westerns.

Whilst filming *Souls for Sale* at Preferred Pictures in 1923, La Marr sprained her ankle during the filming of a dance sequence. So as to avoid production delays, the studio nurse was instructed to administer morphine, cocaine, and heroin to dull La Marr's pain so she could resume filming. La Marr would soon become an addict. "For the pain, studio doctors gave her all sorts of drugs, including ... heroin," Don Gallery remarked. "It was important to keep filming and not let her hold up production."

ZaSu genuinely liked the actress and was very sympathetic to her plight, and they became close friends.

Although La Marr was newly married, she continued to lead a wild life. While filming *The Eternal City* in Italy with Lionel Barrymore, Bert Lytell, Richard Bennett and Ronald Colman, rumors arose that Barbara had a romantic fling with Fascist dictator Mussolini, who made a cameo appearance in the film.

According to La Marr authority Jimmy Bangley, by 1924,

> over-indulgence in food, alcohol, and drugs had begun to show their ill effects. Barbara reacted by going on a starvation diet of cocaine and liquids (including those potent Barbara La Marr highballs). She quickly lost the pounds but ruined her health, and she never fully recovered. It was even rumored that she digested sugar-coated tape worms because she was so desperate to lose weight.

Lack of sleep wasn't helping the situation, and she told the press, "I cheat nature. I never sleep more than two hours a day. I have better things to do."

She began her last film, *The Girl from Montmartre* (a.k.a. *Spanish Sunshine*), for First National in 1925. Her friend Paul Bern begged her to turn the movie down and go away for a rest-cure. Bern was said to be in love with Barbara and had even attempted suicide when Barbara married Jack Dougherty. "Many said that Barbara was the great love of his life," Don Gallery remarked. "She didn't feel the same about him romantically, but she was very fond of him."

Unfortunately, she did not heed Paul Bern's loving advice.

In late 1925, La Marr, who had been indulging in heroin, cocaine, and alcohol in her dressing room during the shoot, collapsed on the set. As the studio scrambled to finish the movie, Barbara went into a coma. She regained consciousness long enough to entrust her son, whom she affectionately called "Sonny," to the Gallerys. She arranged for the Gallerys to have legal adoption rights, and, in gratitude, bequeathed a large sum of money for his care. She seemed to rally after that, but she soon contracted tuberculosis. Her devoted friend Paul Bern bought her a small house in Altadena, California, where she died, at the age of 28, on January 30, 1926.

Where her widower, Jack Dougherty, was during this time is anyone's guess. After starring in films such as *Chain Lightning* (1922), *The Burning Trail* (1925) and *The Runaway Express* (1926), Dougherty's career began to wane. Some attributed this to alcohol. After the ten-chapter serial *Haunted Island* (1928) at Universal, his name pretty much faded into obscurity. He appeared mostly in bit parts thereafter. He was briefly married to his *The Body Punch* (1929) leading lady, Virginia Brown Faire. In 1933, he made an unsuccessful suicide attempt. On May 16, 1938, he died after locking himself in his car with the motor running. He left four suicide notes, one explaining that he had recently passed several bad checks.

Leatrice Gilbert Fountain, daughter of actors John Gilbert and Leatrice Joy, told Jimmy Bangley in 1996:

> The too beautiful Barbara La Marr was fascinating, of course. I wasn't quite two years old when she died, but I was always told how gorgeous she was. She was also considered a great actress, quite an accomplishment for a movie vamp. Father made two movies with Barbara, *Arabian Love* and *St. Elmo*. They also had a torrid affair that was on and off. It's interesting, even though my mother was jealous of Barbara, she liked her very much, so she must have been very charming. I wish someone could find *St. Elmo* because it was highly successful and respected in its day. Bessie Love was also in the cast with John Gilbert and Barbara La Marr. What a tragedy Barbara died so young, she was so beautiful and gifted. Now, Barbara La Marr's son, Don Gallery, and I have been very, very close all of our lives. I can't remember not knowing Don! He was a big part of my early years and school life. I remember he had this beautiful apricot-colored, cotton, two-piece suit he used to wear when we attended kiddie parties. Don was and is so very handsome, he's such a dear.

Continued Leatrice:

> I adored ZaSu Pitts. Everyone did. She had so many friends — close friends like Thelma Todd, Frances Marion, Barbara La Marr, and, of course, my mother, Leatrice Joy. ZaSu and Tom Gallery adopted Don Gallery after Barbara La Marr died. Barbara entrusted the care of little Don to ZaSu. Really, ZaSu was a brilliant, brilliant dramatic actress in silent film. Did you ever see her incredible performance in Erich von Stroheim's *Greed*? She was remarkable. Her face was so mobile and expressive. Those unforgettable eyes of hers.... I think she was beautiful in a waif-like way when she was young, not classically beautiful, but her eyes and hair. She was lovely in a unique way. After talking pictures came in, she was restricted to spinsters and fluttery old maids and eccentric character types mostly in comedies. What a misuse of her great talents! Mother and I were very close with ZaSu until her death in the early 1960s.

When the Gallerys adopted La Marr's son, they changed his name from Marvin to Don Gallery. He was practically the same age as their daughter Ann. Don was raised knowing full well the identity of his real mother. In a 1996 interview, he stated, "Mama ZaSu always told me that Barbara was a wonderful mother, and we loved each other very much. Her last wishes were that I would always be taken care of by ZaSu Pitts because she was such a very good woman."

In 1924, ZaSu had a full dozen roles. She had a bit in *Sunlight of Paris*. For Selznick, she was seen as Lorena in *Daughters of Today*, which starred Patsy Ruth Miller and Ralph Graves. It had first been released a year earlier with the more marketable title *What's Your Daughter Doing?* ZaSu appeared as Amelia Pugsley in *The Goldfish*, with Constance Talmadge, Jack Mulhall and Jean Hersholt, for Associated–First National. She was seen briefly as a factory worker in Cecil B. DeMille's epic *Triumph*, with Leatrice Joy and Rod La Rocque. Again with Leatrice Joy, ZaSu appeared as Delia in *Changing Husbands*.

For Producers Distributing Corp., in 1924 she essayed the important role of moviestruck Mary Brown in *Legend of Hollywood*. Mary falls in love with a young screenwriter (Percy Marmont), who, when he fails to find success, decides to commit suicide in an unusual manner. He fills seven glasses with wine and then places poison in one of the glasses. He mixes them up so that he does not know which glass contains the poison. Each day he drinks one glass of wine. After he has finished drinking all seven glasses and has not died, only then does he realize that Mary, his true love, has removed the poison, and that "true love" is much more important than success.

Inexplicably, her scenes, as Lucy, were deleted from King Vidor's *Wine of Youth* (1924) at Metro.

An unusual assignment came ZaSu's way via Paramount when she portrayed a prostitute named Mona in *The Fast Set*. William C. de Mille directed Betty Compson and Adolphe Menjou in this adaptation of the play *Spring Cleaning* by Frederick Lonsdale.

At Universal she played Celia Stebbins in *Secrets of the Night*, starring James Kirkwood and Madge Bellamy. The highlight for many who've been lucky enough to see this "Universal Jewel" is the sight of ZaSu, as the maid, falling down a flight of stairs with a full tray of tea, but spilling absolutely nothing!

The zany screen persona of ZaSu Pitts was about to receive a jolt, however, from a very unlikely person.

Prior to — and after — gaining Hollywood stardom, ZaSu portrayed many awkward household drudges.

Erich Oswald von Stroheim was born on September 22, 1885, in Vienna. Much later, von Stroheim would construct elaborate lies about his early life, even claiming that his father, in reality the owner of a hat store, was a count and his mother a baroness.

This very colorful, very talented man came to Hollywood in 1914. He began acting and was an assistant director for a time until his first film as full-fledged director, *Blind Husbands* (1919), which he also wrote, starred in and designed the sets for. *Foolish Wives* (1922) was a big moneymaker for Universal, but Von Stroheim was gaining a notorious, troublesome reputation. His obsession with detail, his excessive shooting of film, and his seemingly oblivious non-concern for the money being wasted was becoming a problem. Added to this was his fixation on seamy subjects — more specifically, sexual fetishes — which often got him into hot water with not only his bosses but also the censorship boards.

As early as 1920 Von Stroheim had announced plans to make a film version of Frank Norris' intriguing "realistic fiction," the 1899 novel *McTeague; A Story of Old San Francisco*. Norris, a 25-year-old writer, finished his work in 1895, but it took another four years for him to interest a publisher. He wrote of ordinary middle-class people who develop an absolute compulsion for money. He related, in great detail, the disintegration of their characters and their ultimate destruction. "The function of the novelist," Norris once said, "is to comment upon life as he sees it." Of his unique literary work, he commented, "I never truckled; I never took off the hat to Fashion and held it out for pennies. By God, I told them the truth."

The story was adapted first for the screen by director Barry O'Neil, who also wrote the scenario. Entitled simply *McTeague* (1916), it starred Holbrook Blinn in the title role, with Russian-born Fania Marinoff as Trina.

But to accurately bring the novel's brutal truths to the screen was unthinkable to everyone except Von Stroheim. The director believed the tale and its subject was timeless and universal.

At last he convinced the Goldwyn studios to finance his great undertaking. Shooting of the stark drama began in 1923, and Von Stroheim had an obsessive commitment from the beginning to follow the author's every detail of plot and character. He was in charge of the screenplay, now retitled *Greed*, and gave the book many more layers of context than the author had originally intended. Wrote Arthur Lennig in *Stroheim*:

> Many of Stroheim's commentators seem to suffer from the delusion that he slavishly presented every scene of the book and altered nothing. His detailed script (which has been published and runs over three hundred pages, almost the length of the novel) shows that he did not merely translate *McTeague* into visual terms but rethought it. Stroheim *renders* the book. At times, he substantially adds; occasionally, he subtracts. The film is by no means just a dogged copy of the original.

The tale of desire for wealth above and beyond anything else was depicted with unparalleled ferocity. There would be no hero, no knight in shining armor ... and no happy ending.

To head his cast, Von Stroheim chose British actor Gibson Gowland (1877–1951), who was nearing his 50th birthday. He began in films in 1915 with a bit role in *The Birth of a Nation*. With the significant exception of his lead role in *Greed*, Gowland's career was made up largely of secondary or bit parts. Gowland had previously worked with Von Stroheim on *Blind Husbands*. The director knew Gowland would be well-suited to the role of McTeague, an unsuccessful gold-miner-turned-dentist in *Greed*.

For the role of Trina, McTeague's wife, Von Stroheim surprised everyone when he chose ZaSu Pitts, who had previously been noted for her comedic performances. She was more than twenty-two years younger than her leading man, and many thought she would not be credible in the role of the dentist's wife.

But Von Stroheim was confident he had made the right choice. He stated:

> It is difficult to explain why I consider ZaSu Pitts a great emotional actress. There is an elusive something that is the secret of her personality, and therein lies her greatness. Mystery — she breathes it! A woman of sweet gentle moods, capable of tenderness — a woman of fire, capable of conflicting emotions, smoldering within her. One looks at ZaSu Pits and sees pathos, even tragedy, and a wistfulness that craves for something she has never had, or hopes to have. Yet she is one of the happiest and most contented women I have ever known.... Art must weep when ZaSu Pitts played a comedy role.

Author and historian Arthur Lennig believes Von Stroheim chose ZaSu because of her resemblance to Lillian Gish, and that ZaSu's "plaintive, yet spiritual, quality in her face ... appealed" to him.

Director Bryon Haskin, who knew ZaSu, had mixed feelings regarding Von Stroheim's casting choice. "She wasn't even conventionally good-looking. I think originally Stroheim was attracted to her because of her innocence and vulnerability. He cast her in *Greed*. It must have been some sadistic impulse on his part, judging by the kind of part she played."

For the second male lead, Marcus, one of Trina's previous suitors, the director chose Danish-born Jean Hersholt (1886–1956), who was eight years older than Miss Pitts. He had migrated to the United States in 1914, distinguishing himself on both the stage and in films. Hersholt is perhaps best remembered today for having portrayed the kindly Dr. Christian on radio and in a series of films for RKO.

The perfectionist and taskmaster Erich von Stroheim drove his cast and crew relentlessly. He had no consideration for anyone's personal comfort (or lack of it) and made many demands. ZaSu later commented, "There was little time for sleep, between takes we napped on cots." The director, knowing that she was a dedicated wife and mother of two young children, insisted that ZaSu have no contact whatsoever with her family during the nine long months of filming. He strongly felt that if the ties with her loved ones were eliminated, it would remove all warmth from her characterization. The actress was greatly dismayed by this edict but gave in to the director's unwieldy demands.

The opening title of *Greed* reads:

> Gold, gold, gold, gold,
> Bright and yellow, hard and cold,
> Molten, graven, hammered, rolled,
> Hard to get and light to hold,
> Stolen, borrowed, squandered, doled.

The opening scenes were practically a documentary-like depiction of gold mining, shot at the Big Dipper Mine in Placer County, California. As a most unique feature of the harshly black-and-white silent film, Von Stroheim ordered that any object of a golden hue depicted in the film be painstakingly hand-tinted a bright golden yellow — everything from a vein of gold in rock, golden coins, an elaborate bedspread, a gilt birdcage, a canary, even a gold tooth!

The complex role of McTeague's wife, Trina, called for much versatility and was a real challenge to Miss Pitts. She starts out as a sweet-natured, attractive young woman whose foolish suitor, Marcus, introduces her to a dentist friend of his, McTeague. Later, when she goes to the dentist's office to have a tooth repaired, the dentist becomes enamored of her beauty. He administers sleeping gas to make the needed repairs, and while she's unconscious, he steals a kiss. Soon after the office visit, she becomes attracted to him. He courts her, and they wed.

Trina is at first an obediently devoted wife, and strives to keep their humble home clean and neat. She purchases a lottery ticket and becomes the lucky winner of $5,000 in gold coins. The windfall brings about a complete change in her personality. She hides the coins in a chest and refuses to discus her newfound fortune with her husband. Marcus, her previous suitor, of course regrets that he has lost out on sharing in her good fortune. She begins to deceive her husband by skimping on groceries and other small necessities of life. She refuses to spend a cent, no matter how dire their circumstances become.

Little by little, Trina's youthful beauty begins to fade as her face hardens. She develops a gesture that reveals her avarice — holding a finger to the corner of her mouth, slightly squinting one eye, her thin lips forming a sardonic smile. Often she gives her husband "the look." Before they had married, she was aware that her dentist-husband had yearned to have a large sign in the form of a huge gold tooth to hang in his office. She had one made for him as an engagement present.

Her only passion becomes her golden coins. At night, when she is alone in the house,

After winning the lottery, Trina (ZaSu Pitts) becomes a shrewish miser, obsessed with hoarding gold coins in *Greed* (1924).

she takes them out of the chest and spreads them upon the bed. She disrobes and crawls into bed; her long hair flowing, she luxuriates among her treasures.

When the time arrived for this scene to be shot, ZaSu became reluctant and tried to talk the director out of doing it. He persisted, however, and eventually convinced the actress that the scene was vital to convey the totality of Trina's lust for gold. He assured her that it would be done with complete discretion. The bedroom setting was placed in a remote section of the studio, the lighting was dimmed, and only the lighting man and the director remained on the set.

ZaSu's hair hung below her waist, and hair pieces were attached to it and flowed over her shoulders, concealing her nudity. Von Stroheim's camera covered every little detail. Although the scene was shot at length, only a brief glimpse remained in the edited print, and it was totally cut from the release print. Nonetheless, it was an incident the actress chose to forget entirely.

To earn extra income that she could add to her hidden treasure, Trina turns out handmade miniature wooden animals for her uncle to sell in his toy shop. She spends long hours feverishly toiling at her intricate artifacts. Her once fragile hands become blistered and swollen. The cheap paint she uses to decorate them has a high content of lead, causing some disfigurement. Still, she labors on...

One fateful day a letter arrives in the mail informing them that it has been discovered that McTeague has been practicing dentistry without an official license, and that his business will have to cease. Trina is aghast at the loss of income, insisting that he seek immediate employment elsewhere. Even though there is a great deluge of rain falling outdoors, she refuses to give him the meager amount of money for carfare. In a fit of rage, he seizes her hand and bites it, forcing the coins she had been grasping to fall upon the floor. He hastily retrieves them and heads for the door. Because of the bite, infection sets in and Trina has to have several of her fingers amputated, bringing to an end the use of her artistic talents. With no other recourse, she obtains a low-paying job as a scrubwoman at a kindergarten. Although it is very difficult for her to hold onto a scrub-brush with the remaining stumps of her fingers, she toils on.

On a Christmas Eve, as Trina is laboriously scrubbing the floors at the kindergarten, with a pained look on her hardened face, McTeague appears and demands money. She pleads but knows she is helpless. The brutal husband knows she has the gold coins on her person and begins to strangle her, forcing her to give him the coins. With her last breath she refuses to give up her treasure. He brutally murders her, finds the gold and tries to escape.

When her former beau Marcus learns of the murder and realizes that McTeague now has the treasure, he sets out in hot pursuit. The murderer flees to Death Valley, where Marcus eventually tracks him down and demands that he turn the treasure over to him. A great struggle ensues, and they roll about in the scorching sand. The coins are released from their hiding place and spill into the desert. McTeague draws a gun and aims it at Marcus' head, who, with one last burst of strength, manages to clasp a pair of handcuffs onto his nemesis' wrist and snaps them shut, locking them together for eternity. McTeague realizes he is now doomed. His horse had died of thirst, his own throat is now parched, and the dead weight of his ex-friend is now permanently attached to his arm. The gold coins gleam in the blazing sun, and McTeague squints as he looks to the sky — knowing that death is imminent.

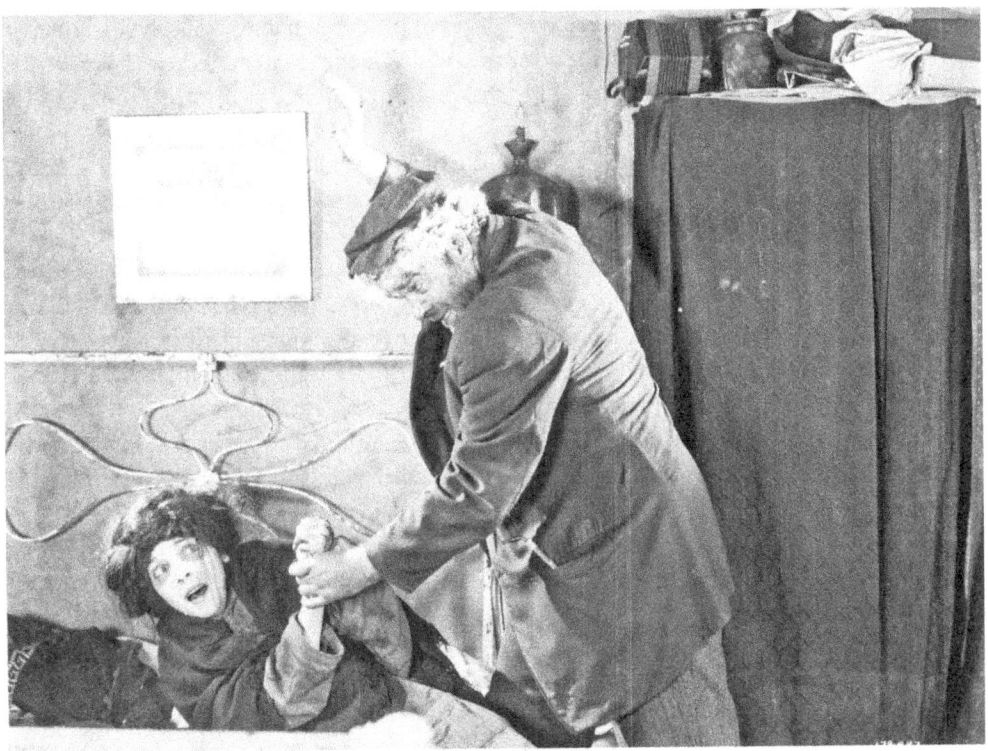

In *Greed* (1924), the brutal McTeague deals harshly with his miserly wife.

Many of the early scenes for *Greed* had been shot on location in and around San Francisco. For the climactic desert scenes, the director sent the cast and crew to Death Valley, where the temperatures rose to as high as 140 degrees; in addition, they were exposed to the added dangers of tarantulas, scorpions, the blazing sun and the scorching sands. Fortunately, ZaSu was spared this ordeal, as her character of Trina was dead before these desert sequences were shot.

All three of the film's stars gave extraordinary performances, in addition to a strong supporting cast that was headed by Dale Fuller.

With an obsessive commitment to detail, Von Stroheim shot a massive amount of film. When the director began the monumental task of editing the 47 reels of footage he shot, he found it extremely difficult to eliminate any part of the complex story and situations. But what he had in the cans would require a full nine hours of viewing. (Among the cuts are sequences involving Trina's family, and ZaSu's gradual breakdown and transformation.)

Meanwhile, while Von Stroheim was on location, Goldwyn was being sought by Marcus Loew, who owned Metro Pictures. Goldwyn at that time was being "supervised" by June Mathis, who had replaced Samuel Goldwyn himself. (Goldwyn went on, of course, to have his own company, with much success.) Goldwyn Studio was in trouble financially, not helped by the costly productions of *Ben-Hur* and *Greed*. To replace Mathis, Loew brought in Louis B. Mayer, who had his own independent company at the time. "Mayer was offended by the haphazard way Goldwyn was being run and wanted to show everybody how it should be done," wrote Scott Eyman in *Lion of Hollywood: The Life and Legend of*

Louis B. Mayer. Irving Thalberg was Mayer's head of production and would be included in this new venue. (Von Stroheim's past relationship with Thalberg was extremely shaky. When Thalberg was over at Universal in 1922, he had Von Stroheim fired as director from the film *Merry-Go-Round* after three months.)

On May 16, 1924, Loew's Metro Pictures, Goldwyn and Louis B. Mayer Productions were fatefully merged. MGM was born. (*Greed* would be credited as a Metro-Goldwyn Picture, "produced by Louis B. Mayer.")

One of the reasons that Marcus Loew was so adamant about bringing in Mayer was that Louis B. was certainly no pushover. He wouldn't take anything from anyone. He was more than a match for Erich von Stroheim and his extreme shooting rituals.

Mayer was aghast with the director's excessive filming and demanded severe cuts. Reluctantly, Von Stroheim whittled away at what he considered his masterpiece. Finally, the film was cut to twenty-four reels, but the studio continued to insist that it was much too long. Naturally, the studio demanded drastic editing in order to have a marketable product. Secretly, the director sent an edited copy to his famed filmmaking friend Jack Ingram, requesting suggestions as to further cutting. Ingram obliged, and after performing some very careful pruning, he returned eighteen reels to his friend and sent a telegram, stating, "If you cut one more foot, I'll never speak to you again."

In desperation, Von Stroheim begged to have the film released in two parts, to be shown on a single day, with an intermission for a dinner break. The studio would have none of his suggestion. He then pleaded to have the separate halves shown on two different nights. No deal. They removed the project from his hands and turned it over to June Mathis for final editing, but she turned it over to writer/editor Joseph Farnham. Farnham would be the sole editor credited.

The devastated director felt totally defeated. As reel after reel was cut, he felt the film had been debased. He had only been paid for the nine-month duration of filming, not for any of his other services as editor, etc. Those fifteen months of dedication had been a labor of love. To go on with the work he had to hock his home, his car and even his life insurance. He sadly stated, "I received a certain sum of money for nine months of shooting, which would have been the same had I made the picture in two weeks." The studio claimed that it had spent more than a half-million dollars on the production due to the director's excessiveness. They more or less wrote the film off as a loss and did very little to advertise or further promote it.

In addition to the studio-dictated cuts, the New York Censorship Board had their say on November 25, 1924. Among other items, the scene in which McTeague bit Trina's fingers was ordered to be eliminated.

A world premiere was held at the Cosmopolitan Theater at Columbus Circle in New York City in December. There were two screenings daily for six weeks. Some of the critics' reviews were quite favorable. The *New York Times* reported, "ZaSu Pitts throws herself into the role with vehemence. She is a natural as the woman counting her golden horde and makes the character truly live, when she slyly robs her husband of trifling amounts." Others were even more lavish in their praise. Film historian/author Herman Weinberg called her portrayal of Trina, "the greatest performance with the widest range any actress ever was called on to give on the screen." Years later, Deems Taylor, the well-known film authority, noted, "Miss Pitts has always had a touch of Chaplin's genius for combining comedy with pathos. The picture [*Greed*], dealing with lust for money and the destruction it causes, had considerable power and was one of Von Stroheim's best."

The majority of critics agreed with him, with one noting: "The complicated role of McTeague's wife, Trina, called for much versatility and was a demanding challenge for Miss Pitts." Everybody marveled at ZaSu's never-before-seen fearlessness. Here was a lady, seen mostly as a comedic actress, digging in her heels and playing a very unsympathetic, shrewish miser. Playing off her established screen image, Von Stroheim first has her playing an engaging, attractive young woman. When her character's demeanor changes, it's all the more shocking onscreen. It was a meaty role for Miss Pitts, one that still continues to impress viewers into the 21st century.

Greed, with all of its intense, realistic drama about avarice and human degradation, was not fully appreciated or approved of by many others. Some critics termed it "an epic of the sewer." The film had limited screenings in other cities and some smaller towns, without much success at the box office, and it was finally withdrawn completely from exhibition.

Its heartbroken creator sadly stated, "I consider I have made only one real picture in my life and nobody ever saw that. The poor, mangled, mutilated remains shown as *Greed*."

Louis B. Mayer's daughter Irene married David O. Selznick, son of Mayer's former business associate, film magnate Lewis J. Selznick. Irene was a highly opinioned individual and hastened to defend Von Stroheim's vision for a lengthy masterpiece. She also pleaded his case for no more cutting of the film. But after she sat through a private screening of the ten-hour film, she changed her mind:

> Ten hours in a concrete box in MGM. I wish everybody who talks about a ruined masterpiece could be condemned to spend ten hours in a concrete box watching it. It was masterful in ways, and parts of it were riveting, but it was an exhausting experience; the film in conception was a considerable exercise in self-indulgence, and a testament to the incompetence of the previous regime [at Goldwyn who okayed the script].

For years many have pondered the fate of an uncut print of the film. Rumors have surfaced about its existence. Many of the rumors were as extravagant as Von Stroheim was reputed to be. One Texas millionaire claimed that he had once owned an uncut version but sold it to a museum in Paris. Another implausible tale involved a wealthy South American eccentric who kept an uncut print in a vault, and every year on New Year's Eve he screened it for an exclusive, invited audience. Another claim had an ex–GI finding a full print amid the rubble of postwar Berlin, bringing it to the States, and turning it over to the Boston Film Society for screening. A socialite from Redwood City, California, professed that she owned "the longest existing version of *Greed*," which she had reportedly purchased "somewhere in Europe." There have also been reports that MGM had preserved not one, but two complete prints in a vault built into a salt mine in Utah. None of these foolish fancies have ever been confirmed.

One *confirmed* report stated that Von Stroheim had been shown a copy of the released, edited version at the *Cinémathèque* in Paris in 1950. It was a very painful experience for him, and he wept later, describing the viewing as "an exhumation":

> It was like opening a coffin in which there was just dust, giving off a terrible stench, a couple of vertebra and a piece of shoulder bone.... It was if a man's beloved was run over by a truck, maimed beyond recognition. He goes to see her in the morgue. Of course, he still loves her,

but it is only the memory of her that he can love—because he does not recognize her anymore.

In recent years the film's reputation has grown, and it has been partially restored to a four-hour version, with the inclusion of many production stills to fill in the gaps created by the cut footage that has been lost.

After the completion of her scenes for *Greed*, ZaSu was free to accept other screen assignments, which she did with a vengeance. At Metro in 1925, ZaSu was seen as Polly Jordan in *The Great Divide*, with Alice Terry, Conway Tearle, and Wallace Beery. At Principal Studios, she was a servant girl named Judy in *The Re-Creation of Brian Kent*, directed by Sam Wood and starring (as Brian Kent) Kenneth Harlan, Helene Chadwick and Mary Carr. She also made a drama about child abuse, *Old Shoes*, written and directed by Frederick Stowers, and featuring Noah Beery as the abusive stepfather of Johnny Harron.

Pretty Ladies, also at Metro, boasted a great cast of future stars. A top-billed ZaSu appeared as Maggie Keenan, a star comedienne in the *Follies* who is lonely. Director Monta Bell guided ZaSu in one of her best early dramatic performances as a loveless, uncertain woman who falls for drummer Tom Moore but must fight *femme fatale* Lilyan Tashman for his affections. Norma Shearer appeared in a supporting part, and the film boasted two up-and-comers in bits who, in future years, would prove valuable to MGM—Myrna Loy and a young unknown chorus girl named Lucille Le Sueur, later to become Joan Crawford.

The wide-eyed blonde with ZaSu in *Pretty Ladies* (1925, MGM) is Joan Crawford, a relative unknown at the time. She was billed as Lucille LeSueur.

At Universal, ZaSu played the role of Blanche in *A Woman's Faith*, with Alma Rubens, Percy Marmont and Jean Hersholt. ZaSu was also seen with Edward Everett Horton in *The Business of Love* for Astor Pictures. At Fox she played Mandy Couiter in the Western *Thunder Mountain* (1925), directed by Victor Schertzinger, and also starring Madge Bellamy, Leslie Fenton, Alec B. Francis, Russell Simpson, Arthur Housman and Paul Panzer. The movie, based on the story *Howdy, Folks* by Elia W. Peattie, and the play *Thunder* by Pearl Franklin, contained some location shots near ZaSu's girlhood home of Santa Cruz, at sites in Felton, Mt. Hermon and Paradise Park. "You know," Dorothy Fargo remarked wistfully, "she was always loyal to Santa Cruz until the day she died."

In 1925 ZaSu had another very fine dramatic role at Fox, cast as Ruth Fanning in *Lazybones*, a non–Western starring Charles "Buck" Jones. As Ruth, she portrayed a tragic young woman who strayed from home and married a seaman. His ship went down, and he was not rescued. She gave birth to a child and, unable to provide a proper home for herself and her baby, returns to her hometown. Her hardened and embittered mother does not believe her story and refuses to accept the baby into her home. Ruth turns to her old friend Steve Tuttle, who is withdrawn and slow-moving, and whom everybody calls "Lazy Bones." He and his kindly mother take the child to live with them. Because, as a baby, the girl had made the sound of a mewing kitten, her adopted parents call her Kit. She grows into a beautiful young woman, and her real mother is never able to reveal their true relationship. Ruth withers away from heartache and loses her will to live. In her final hour, a frail and

Lazy Bones, 1925. In the silent drama *Lazy Bones* (1925), ZaSu shares an emotional scene with Charles "Buck" Jones, who later became a star of western films.

sickly Ruth manages to visit Kit and finally holds her in her arms as she dies. ZaSu gave a beautifully subdued performance, keeping in check her famous animated hands. As directed by Frank Borzage, the death scene was extremely poignant. Others in the stellar cast were Madge Bellamy, Leslie Fenton, Jane Novak, Edythe Chapman, and Emily Fitzroy.

Both ZaSu and Borzage next moved on to the Fox studios, for *Wages for Wives*, based on the play *Chicken Feed*. She appeared as Luella Logan, while the leads went to Jacqueline Logan, Creighton Hale and Earle Fox. ZaSu also appeared as Nancy in *The Great Love*, an atypical love story about an elephant.

ZaSu and Tom Gallery enjoyed entertaining guests in their Brentwood home, and occasionally took part in social activities. They became active members of the Catholic Motion Picture Guild, which organized in 1923. Rather than act in the capacity of screen censorship, the Guild provided moral support to build and defend the reputation of the profession, and promoted the best interests of the industry. Each year the organization staged a lavish stage "Gambol" to raise funds for their cause. For its third anniversary, the Guild staged a star-studded spectacle at the Los Angeles Philharmonic Auditorium on Wednesday, February 23, 1925. A large number of top personalities appeared in the presentation, including such illustrious names as Fanny Brice, Eddie Cantor and child star Jackie Cooper (sporting his first short haircut). Also participating in the festivities were Trixie Friganza, the Quillian Family, Lilyan Tashman, and Ben Turpin. Joan Crawford danced in the chorus. The Gallerys also took part, with Tom serving as business manager and ZaSu as chairlady of the Hostess Committee. To further aid the cause, many of Hollywood's top celebrities sponsored full-page ads in the program.

The March 1925 issue of *Photoplay* included a news item stating, "Tom Gallery, husband of ZaSu Pitts, and himself a corking good actor, has become the Squash Champion of the Hollywood Athletic Club." In addition, on March 24, 1925, Gallery succeeded movie actor Tom Kennedy as the arranger of boxing matches at the Hollywood Legion Stadium. He held this job until the Depression cut into the Legion's profits, and he resigned in late 1931. Tom had also handled boxing matches at the Dreamland Arena in San Francisco, as well as the Olympic Auditorium in Los Angeles.

Meanwhile, Gallery's film career seemed to be going nowhere. He appeared in the Westerns *The Limited Mail* (1925) and *Home Struck* (1927). In 1927 he appeared in the boxing drama *One-Round Hogan*, with Monte Blue, Leila Hyams, James Jeffries, and Tom Kennedy. His final screen appearance came in *A Dog of the Regiment* (1927), starring canine star Rin-Tin-Tin. Gallery played a pilot who crashes his plane and is rescued by Rinty. Gallery's film career was sporadic at best, with many of his twenty-some films including him in mere featured (or lower) roles. Some implied that his failure to click as an actor, and ZaSu's own rising star, contributed to their eventual martial discord.

Meanwhile, ZaSu's most important screen role in 1926 came in the dramatic *Mannequin*, a Paramount feature directed by James Cruze. In this she portrayed Annie Pogani, a mentally disturbed nursemaid who kidnaps the child she is supposed to care for. Warner Baxter, Dolores Costello, Alice Joyce, and Walter Pidgeon rounded out the cast. For Universal, ZaSu was seen as Hilda in *What Happened to Jones?* a comedy billed as a "Laughing Whirlwind" and a "Laugh Riot." The Jones of the title, played by Reginald Denny, got himself into all kinds of mix-ups on the night before his wedding to Marian Nixon, including running from the police and hiding out in a Turkish bath in drag.

Back at MGM, ZaSu appeared as Hope Durant in *Monte Carlo*, directed by Christy Cabanne, and starring Lew Cody and Gertrude Olmstead. She joined Matt Moore, Kathryn Perry and director Frank Borzage at Fox for *Early to Wed*, where she played Mrs. Dugan.

For Producers Distributing Corp., ZaSu played Evelyn in *Sunny Side Up*, which was directed by actor Donald Crisp and starred Vera Reynolds, Edmund Burns and George K. Arthur, with famed fan dancer Sally Rand in a small role. Based on the novel *Sunny Ducrow* (Reynolds' character's name) by Henry St. John Cooper, it shouldn't be confused with the like-titled, more popular Charles Farrell/Janet Gaynor movie of 1929.

Also for Producers Distributing Corp. was *Risky Business*, with ZaSu playing Agnes Wheaton. The star was Vera Reynolds again, supported Ethel Clayton, Kenneth Thomson and Louis Natheaux as ZaSu's husband Lawrence. Based on a story ("Pearls Before Cecily") by later Hitchcock favorite Charles Brackett, it was adapted by Beulah Marie Dix and directed by actor Alan Hale.

In her last 1926 release, ZaSu played Laura La Plante's roommate, Gladys Smith, in the "Universal Jewel" *Her Big Night*. The farcical story focuses on shop girl La Plante being mistaken for a lookalike movie star and the routine complications that ensue.

After a decade in Hollywood, Miss Pitts had established herself as a first-rate dramatic actress, as well as a reliable comedienne who could be counted on to turn in a sterling per-

ZaSu gave an impressive performance, along with Alice Joyce (left), in the silent drama *Mannequin* (1926).

ZaSu owned an extensive collection of antique candy molds that she proudly displayed. As a hobby she collected candy recipes, and her book *Candy Hits by ZaSu Pitts* was published posthumously in 1963.

formance—no matter what the role. The proof came in the form of her non-stop work load; she was in demand at almost all the studios.

Throughout her long career, many of ZaSu's co-workers became close friends. ZaSu always extended a friendly warmth, and often treated the cast and crew of her films to batches of handmade candies that she brought from home. She also collected candy recipes, and enjoyed testing them and sharing the results with friends and co-workers. She became known for her fudge, caramels, marshmallows, and nougats, as well as innovative concoctions such as candied grapefruit peels, candied flowers and mint leaves. A good cook since she was a girl, she studied the art of candy making and employed a special technique for hand dipping chocolates. According to Dorothy Fargo, when ZaSu heard that Frazier Lewis, the well-known local Santa Cruz candy maker, had died, she sent Dorothy to buy his famous "secret recipe" for his Victoria candy bar. Lewis had left it to the local Native Sons of the Golden West. "I approached them, but they said they'd never sell it," Dorothy recalls. Dorothy laughingly adds that the "secret" ingredient in Lewis' candy bar was "probably real brandy," but "ZaSu really wanted that recipe." A 93-page book of her candy recipes, *Candy Hits by ZaSu Pitts—The Famous Star's Own Candy Recipes*, compiled by Edi Horton, was published posthumously in 1963 by Duell, Sloan & Pearce. The first edition sold out, and a second printing was issued in March of 1964.

In her book she wrote:

> Many people have asked me how I happened to choose candy making for a hobby. It really began in my childhood, and if I close my eyes, I can still see the kitchen in our Santa Cruz home, smell the fragrant odor of spice cookies baking in our old iron stove and molasses candy bubbling in the iron frying pan that we called a "spider." ... I stood by, all eyes, waiting for that exciting moment when my mother would give me a piece of taffy to pull into sticky strings.... Oh, those were big moments in a little girl's life, until she grew old enough to make the candy herself.

She further recalled:

> When I arrived in Hollywood, I could make four different kinds of candy. They were basic candies. In that day every schoolgirl had her own special fudge, which she used to whip up on a Sunday afternoon with friends. I could make divinity, panocha (a non-chocolate type of fudge), and I finally remembered my mother's taffy recipe.

One day ZaSu wandered into the famous Farmers Market in Los Angeles. After purchasing some produce, she glanced across the street and noticed a glass booth enclosing a candy kitchen. Inside were two candy dippers, a woman and a man, busily at work. She had thought that all chocolate dippers were male, and the sight made her smile. The woman was intent on her task, her capable hands repeating the swirling motion, round and round in the chocolate. Then she gently flipped the piece and dabbed a bit of chocolate on top. As ZaSu watched, the male dipper repeated the motions, but when he flipped the candy over to add a dab of chocolate on top, he formed the letter "Z"—for he had recognized the curious actress and knew her name. They exchanged smiles, and she scribbled a note on her shopping list: "Will you teach me?" Thereafter, Miss Pitts was a frequent visitor to the shop. She befriended the woman, Mrs. Littlejohn, who gave her some instruction in chocolate dipping and introduced her to Susie Ribardier, who came to ZaSu's kitchen for further instruction.

ZaSu had only one film in release in 1927, Paramount's *Casey at the Bat*. Wallace Beery played the baseball hero, she played Camille, the demure village milliner, and funnyman Sterling Holloway was seen as the villainous village barber.

Playing Mathilde, a fluttery housekeeper, ZaSu joined Jean Hersholt (playing a cat burglar posing as deacon) and Alice Joyce at Universal in the screen mystery *13 Washington Square* (1928). At Paramount she appeared with Wallace Beery, Raymond Hatton and Sally Blane in the World War I comedy *Wife Savers*, where she played the gentle-mannered Germaine. At Universal, she shared the comedy antics in *Buck Privates*, with Lya De Putti and Malcolm McGregor.

Back in 1926, ZaSu had been elated to learn that her favorite director, Erich von Stroheim, wanted her for a leading role in his lavish production *The Wedding March*. As Cecelia Schweisser, the lame daughter of the wealthy magnate of the Red Raven Corn Plaster Co., she would have many dramatic opportunities. Originally budgeted at $300,000, the film's shooting schedule was set at four months; but, of course, with Von Stroheim at the helm, those figures proved unrealistic.

After a great deal of pre-production preparation, shooting began on June 2, 1926, backed by producer Pat Powers. The director held to his well-known extravagant routine. Filming went on and on, the budget was soon exhausted, and nearly a million dollars more was invested. Eventually filming was called to a halt by Powers in January 1927. Although Von Stroheim had 60 reels of film in the can, only two-thirds of the story had actually been

Burly Wallace Beery tips his hat in greeting to the shy village seamstress, played by ZaSu, in *Casey at the Bat* (1927).

13 Washington Square (1928). This melodrama starred Jean Hersholt and Alice Joyce (right), along with ZaSu Pitts.

shot. After editing down his nearly eight hours of footage, von Stroheim requested that the film be released in two different halves. This suggestion was met with strong resistance. After his initial cutting of just the first half of the film, Von Stroheim had over four hours. More cutting, of course, was required.

While all this editing was taking place, Pat Powers secured distribution with Paramount. The studio, however, was not keen on the length or the idea of releasing the film in two parts. A shortened print was prepared and previewed in March 1928. When that didn't go well, they decided the footage should be cut into two separate features. *The Wedding March* was released in October 1928, running fourteen reels. The second feature, titled *The Honeymoon*, was, according to author Arthur Lennig, "severely mutilated and released in eight reels. In order to do this, the first part's story was reprised and condensed into three reels, leaving room for only four and one-half reels (4,588 feet) of new material, one-fifth of Stroheim's first." Von Stroheim bluntly refused to allow *The Honeymoon* to be shown in the United States. Instead, it received some limited screenings in Europe, but was never viewed by American audiences.

Despite its many artistic merits, *The Wedding March* was considered far too sophisticated for most audiences and did not succeed at the box office. The lengthy, convoluted story became even more complex under Von Stroheim's "minute-detail obsession." Additionally, he employed much subtle symbolism. There was much more to his "masterpiece" than meets the eye.

The opening sequence of *The Wedding March* contained some Technicolor shots of Old Vienna. Three-dozen elaborate sets depicted various parts of the Austrian city. No expense was spared, and costuming was equally lavish. All of the story's complex characters were fully established by much exposition.

Prince Nicki, as portrayed by von Stroheim himself, was an eccentric, womanizing, penniless member of nobility. Fay Wray appeared as Mitzi Schrammell, a beautiful young harpist with a symphony orchestra. Matthew Betz portrayed Johann "Schani" Eberle, a burly butcher in love with Mitzi. George Nichols (in his last film) was seen as Fortunat Schweisser, a wealthy corn-plaster magnate and father of shy, innocent and lame Cecelia (ZaSu). The father fears that his crippled daughter might never find a husband, and so arranges a marriage to the prince. He breaks the news to the prospective bride, without concern for her fragile feelings, and with callous candor:

FORTUNAT: I was with His Highness Prince von Wildeliebe-Rauffenburgand. We have arranged for you and his son, Prince Nicki, to get married.
CECELIA: But I have never even met the Prince.
FORTUNAT: You will — soon.
CECELIA: How could he be in love with me?
FORTUNAT: You are heiress to $20,000,000!
CECELIA: Money could not make a man feel love.
FORTUNAT: Don't be a silly goose. Love will come — in time. Princess Cecelia — doesn't that sound nice?
CECELIA: A lame princess?

The marriage ceremony in the film was shot at the actual St. Stephen's Cathedral, with its vast sanctuary filled with fragrant apple blossoms. When Von Stroheim viewed the results, he was not satisfied by the way the altar appeared on film and ordered an expensive replica constructed at great expense.

Von Stroheim also demanded thoroughbred stallions for his Calvary soldiers to mount. He further insisted on blue-ribbon St. Bernard dogs for the hunting scenes. He also ordered little leather casings to protect the dogs' feet. He was even able to borrow the Royal Coach of the Emperor from the Vienna State Museum. If that were not enough, he demanded monogrammed silk underwear for the soldiers to wear underneath their elaborately-detailed uniforms. Studio officials insisted that audiences would never know the difference, but Von Stroheim retaliated with, "But *I* will!" The director's creative genius was wrecked by his willful, wasteful ways.

As the intricate tale unfolded onscreen, the philandering Prince Nicki is attracted to the fresh young beauty of harpist Mitzi. Despite the fact that she is engaged to marry the butcher Schani, Nicki arranges a romantic tryst with her in an apple orchard, fully in blossom. As the couple embraces, a virtual "blizzard" of apple blossoms tumbles overhead.

Later, when Schani learns of the encounter, he plots to shoot Nicki as he leaves the cathedral after the Prince's marriage to Cecelia. Schani takes careful aim with his revolver, but Mitzi thwarts his vengeful scheme.

As the newlywed couple drive off in an elaborate carriage (one once used by Austria's real-life emperor), Cecelia clutches her large bouquet of apple blossoms to her bosom and innocently asks, "Who was that sweet girl in tears outside the church?" Unfazed, the groom calmly lies, "I have no idea." The bride brushes her bouquet with her lips. "How beautiful these apple blossoms are ... will they always remind you?" With a cold stare in his eyes, her husband utters ironically, "Yes ... *always!*"

It was at this point that *The Wedding March* came to an abrupt close, leaving many things unresolved.

For *The Honeymoon*, the second half of the film, ten minutes from *The Wedding March* recapped the storyline in order to refresh the audience's memory. *The Honeymoon* then continued as the coach with the wedding couple journeyed on to the baronial chateau for a brief vacation.

Several events occur symbolic "omens of bad luck," that herald the ill-fated couple's future life together. First, one of the wheels on the carriage becomes dislodged. Second, as the couple arrives at the chateau, a fierce downpour of rain descends upon them. And third, as the lame Cecelia crosses the threshold, she trips and stumbles. Finally, three hags, much like the three witches in *Macbeth*, gather and chant, "Grief — Sickness — and Death!"

Later, when the couple is in their bedchamber, Nicki pours a glass of champagne for his bride ("A toast!"). Shyly, Cecelia holds the glass to her lips. She is unaccustomed to wine, and it tickles her nose, making her giddy. Her bouquet of wilting apple blossoms lay nearby; she glances at them as Nicki begins to remove her gown. Modestly, she places her hands before her face. "Nicki," she whispers, "please don't hate me — that you had to marry me, just to get some of my father's stupid money — to be here, just with me — alone — poor little limping me," she sobs. Then, to distract him, she points to the bouquet. "They're still fresh ... if only they would last forever." The mention of the flowers reminds him of his secret love, Mitzi. He brushes her cheek with his lips and tells her she must be very tired. He then informs her that he will be leaving to go off to his private hunting lodge in the morning. She tells him she will miss him and then makes the fatal mistake of wishing him "good luck." He departs, and she sobs silently. Alone, she glances down at her honeymoon nightgown. Then, in anguish, she rips it to shreds and cries herself to sleep.

The Honeymoon (1928), the second half of Von Stroheim's *The Wedding March*, was only screened in Europe. ZaSu plays the anguished bride who realizes her husband loves another.

ZaSu at her large home in Brentwood with her daughter Ann and adopted son Don, along with family pets.

Unfortunately, Cecelia remains loyal to the lout right up to the end of the two-hour saga. When a jealous rival tries to shoot him, she shields his worthless body with hers and dies for her valiant effort.

Miss Pitts was elated to have the opportunity to work with her favorite director once again. It was von Stroheim who gave her the emotional roles she craved.

Her last film of 1928, though in a lesser way than *The Wedding March*, still gave her a terrific acting opportunity. She essayed the dramatic role of Mother Spengler, the sickly, overworked, loyal and deceived wife of Emil Jannings in *Sins of the Fathers*. Restaurant owner Jennings becomes a bootlegger to please Ruth Chatterton (in her only silent), but things go terribly wrong. Jean Arthur and Barry Norton play ZaSu's children.

ZaSu's very busy work schedule kept her away from home quite often. Whatever free time she had at her disposal she spent with her children. It distressed her that she had to be absent so often, and candidly told an interviewer, "I'm not a very good mother. I rarely get to see them." Her many friends were quick to disagree, stating, "ZaSu is a very good mother. If she had a million dollars, she would probably take over two or three complete orphanages. She's just that kind of girl."

A fan magazine reported:

> Whether tragedienne or comedienne, ZaSu is raising her children sensibly. Her home in Brentwood is nearly ten miles from Hollywood, and on this three-acre estate her children are

being taught how country people live. They have a cow which her young son milks and cares for; and chickens which are fed and looked after by her little daughter.

All was not smooth sailing in the Gallery household, however. Tom, in his free time, was often seen at sporting events and nightclubs, openly escorting quite glamorous young ladies. One blonde, a former stage star newly arrived in Hollywood, caught his attention, and the relationship appeared to be more than casual. Rumors began to spread, and some eventually reached ZaSu's ears.

The December 1928 issue of *Photoplay* magazine stated:

A pitiful fight to hold her husband's love is being made by a certain Hollywood actress. The wife has given her husband years of devotion. She is well loved in the industry and not only has a child of her own, but adopted a boy, one who was left orphan by a world-famous star. She is not as beautiful as many of her more fortunate sisters, but her charm is undenied. Now Hollywood discovers that her husband is more interested in an ex–Broadway favorite. The wife displays a gallant bravery. She has invited the other woman to her home, has entertained for her and has even appeared in public with the other two, but her eyes have taken on the look of tragedy.

The "other woman" was a beautiful blonde more than a dozen years ZaSu's junior. As a young child, beautiful Madge Evans had modeled nude for Fairy Soap advertisements. At the age of five she made her Broadway debut, billed as "Baby Madge," in the drama *The Highway of Life*. Her early silent films include *Shore Acres* (1914), *Sudden Riches* (1916), *The Power and the Glory* (1918), *Home Wanted* (1919), *Heidi* (1920), and *The Little Match Girl* (1921). Strangely, and coincidentally, she also was seen in a film titled *Zaza* (1915).

Evans continued to appear in films produced in the East until 1928, when she ventured to Hollywood, did a few Vitaphone shorts and was signed to a contract by MGM. Her first talking feature film was *Son of India*, opposite the dashing Ramon Navarro. Studio publicity hailed her as a "new face — and a lovely one." In 1931 she was leading lady to Clark Gable in *Sporting Blood*, and John Gilbert in *West of Broadway*. Her 1933 films included *Hell Below*, and she was also part of the all-star cast of *Dinner at Eight* and the aptly-titled *Broadway to Hollywood*. In 1934, Evans was loaned to 20th Century–Fox to portray Shirley Temple's mother in *Stand Up and Cheer!* After the low-budget *Army Girl* (1938), she returned to the Broadway stage in 1939 to appear in *Here Comes the Clowns*, written by playwright Sidney Kingsley (of *Dead-End* and *Detective Story* fame), whom she would marry in July of that year. She never returned to the movies, but did return to acting — via television — in 1949, making over a dozen episodic appearances until her last, *The Alcoa Hour*, in 1956. Her final Broadway appearance was in Kingsley's *The Patriots*, after which she retired. Madge would pass away on April 26, 1981, at the age of 74, of cancer.

After the great financial success of Al Jolson's *The Jazz Singer*, in 1928 the motion picture industry underwent a drastic change. No longer was it enough that the movies could move and walk; the time had come when they were going to have to begin to learn how to talk.

Miss Pitts had eight important film roles in 1929.

At Paramount she was given a role that changed the course of her movie career. It was the gangster yarn *The Dummy*, starring Fredric March, Ruth Chatterton, and Jack Oakie (as Dopey Hart). ZaSu played Rose Gleason, a nervous gun moll. The actress was up to the challenge, and her personal characteristics proved to be perfectly suited to the material.

Her ever-moving hands were a virtual fountain of liquid motion, with one emotional gesture cascading into the next. She was also given the line "Oh, dear!" and made it into one of her trademark expressions.

As she once recalled:

> The talkies had not been with us very long when the axe crashed down on my head. I was "typed," and — of all things — I was typed as a comedienne. It was a low-budget gangster film, *The Dummy*, in which I played a scene of heart-rending anguish, and I was directed to wring my hands for effect. In disgust, I cupped my hands over my forehead and let out a doleful "Oh, dear!" Everyone on the set went into convulsions of laughter, and in my next picture they had me do much more of the same things. It was opening up a new career for me as a comedienne, but it finished the career I loved, as a dramatic actress.

The Squall, based on the 1926 Broadway play, was another of ZaSu's dramatic characterizations, and British producer-director Alexander Korda's first talking picture. The melodrama was set in a Hungarian village and told the tragic tale of a humble family that gives shelter to a young gypsy woman during a raging storm. Little do they know that Nubi, the gypsy, is trying to escape a very jealous husband. Miss Pitts was seen as Lena, a hard-working servant girl who wore her long hair in braids. Once Nubi is taken into the family, she sets out to attract the romantic interest of both the father and the son. And, not content with her conquests, Nubi sets her eyes on Lena's fiancé, another servant, Peter (Harry Cording). To further complicate matters, the son steals Lena's life savings to buy a ring for the gypsy. The household is in a complete shambles by the time Nubi's jealous husband arrives on the scene and drags her back to their camp. Myrna Loy gave a fine performance as the gypsy wench.

The Squall was a failure at the box office; it had been released through First National, a branch of Warner Brothers. The studio had a total of eighty-nine features in release that year, and netted a profit of more than 14 million dollars. The studio's major profit-making celebrity was canine star Rin-Tin-Tin, who appeared in three features.

ZaSu's other features for Warner–First National included the comedy *Twin Beds*, also starring Jack Mulhall and Patsy Ruth Miller. She played Tillie, of which a reviewer wrote, "ZaSu Pitts does her surefire stuff as the unconsciously funny maid." In the whodunit *The Argyle Case*, ZaSu appeared as talkative Mrs. Wyatt, a murder suspect. In *Her Private Life*, she portrayed Timmins, the discreet wife of a vulgar, self-made millionaire. This marked the first time ZaSu would work with beautiful blonde Thelma Todd. The stars, Billie Dove, Walter Pidgeon, Holmes Herbert and Montagu Love, were directed by Alexander Korda.

Then, for Pathé, ZaSu was teamed with Robert Armstrong and funnyman James Gleason in *Oh, Yeah!* Gleason also co-directed the film with Tay Garnett, and ZaSu appeared as an awkward waitress at a railroad lunch counter, where customers referred to her as "the Elk."

Next she was seen in a musical, *Paris*, featuring international entertainers Irène Bordoni and Jack Buchanan. For this, the studio shot a few scenes in Technicolor.

The 1929 murder mystery *The Locked Door* starred Barbara Stanwyck (in her talkie debut), William "Stage" Boyd, and Rod La Rocque. It was based on the 1919 Channing Pollock play *The Sign*, and had been filmed before, in 1921, with Norma Talmadge. ZaSu was seen as a dumb telephone operator, of which one reviewer reported, "Every word she utters is a laugh." The film was released through United Artists. The movie, however, has not aged well; it was creaking even in 1929. The *New York Herald Tribune* reviewer noted that the actors "should be playing *The Locked Door* in powdered wigs and crinoline." A more succulent appraisal came from Stanwyck herself when she told the *Los Angeles Times* in 1958, "They never should've unlocked the damned thing."

For Pathé, ZaSu was seen as Clara Bertrand, with Constance Bennett and Edmund Lowe, in *This Thing Called Love*. Roscoe Karns played her husband, Harry.

There were also some color sequences in the movie version of the stage musical hit *No, No, Nanette* (1930), starring early musical film favorites Bernice Claire and Alexander Gray. Pitts was seen as the maid Pauline, who constantly threatens to quit. Again she attracted the attention of a critic, who noted, "ZaSu Pitts is a capable comedienne. She has some of the choice lines, and moreover she does right by them."

In his 1974 book *They Had Faces Then*, John Springer wrote that ZaSu was "one of the superlative dramatic actresses of the silent screen":

> Then came talkies, and that flat woebegone accent of ZaSu's voice, plus the already established mournful face, added up to laughter, not tears. The eyes grew wider, the voice more doleful, the hands even more waving. Even so, she usually could stir up amusement, even in the most thankless roles."

Another author, Ethan Morden, commented, "An actress of great power was thrust into comic bits and never allowed to escape. She was not a great beauty, having no qualifications other than a wild desire to do it, she crashed the movies."

Meanwhile, in her private life, ZaSu did everything she could to save her marriage, but nothing could change her husband's philandering ways. The situation grew worse, and he moved out of their Brentwood home near the end of November 1929. She hoped that he would return, but he did not. She threw herself into her screen work to keep her mind occupied.

In 1930 at Paramount ZaSu supported the studio's most popular star — pretty, perky, blue-eyed, red-haired Nancy Carroll — in the sparkling musical *Honey*. ZaSu was seen as the maid Mayme. One of the highlights of the film was Lillian Roth singing "Sing, You Sinners."

The actress was thrilled to have been cast in Universal's dramatic screen production of *All Quiet on the Western Front*, with Lew Ayres, based on Erich Maria Remarque's novel of the horrors of World War I, *Im Westen nichts Neues*. One of the film's stars, William Bakewell, explained in an interview with John Gallagher in 1989 what happened:

> I loved ZaSu. There's a sequence where Lew comes home on furlough and his mother is dying of tuberculosis, and he has a nice scene with her. She was known primarily for comedy, but ZaSu had done *Greed* (1924) for Stroheim, and [director Lewis] Milestone remembered that and cast her as Lew's mother. They shot the scene, and when it was previewed in San Bernardino, I was at the preview, and the main feature was a Nancy Carroll picture called *Honey* (1930), a comedy with Stanley Smith, and ZaSu played a silly comedy maid. When the preview picture came on, *All Quiet on the Western Front*, and ZaSu's scene appeared, the audience laughed just at the sight of her, those wispy hands, that character that she did. So they had to reshoot it, and Beryl Mercer did it.

"The audience sat with rapt attention as the latter unfolded until I appeared on the screen," ZaSu remembered in *Candy Hits*. "A gale of laughter greeted me."

In any event, the audience reaction had been devastating, so studio executives unfairly withheld the film until ZaSu's scenes could be reshot. "The following day the studio snipped off a piece of my heart when they snipped my entire role out of the picture," was how ZaSu put it. ZaSu's scenes were retained in the silent version of the picture, which was shown only in Europe.

The director, Lewis Milestone, was not pleased that ZaSu was replaced. "Despite my pleading that this was a one-in-a-million coincidence, the studio insisted on replacing ZaSu Pitts with someone else," Milestone told authors Charles Higham and Joel Greenberg in 1969. "So we looked around and eventually found Beryl Mercer; and although her speech wasn't ideal, we couldn't do anything about it and were stuck with her."

Interestingly, when ZaSu was a guest on the radio show *The Baker's Broadcast*, on November 7, 1937, a show sponsored by Fleischmann's Yeast, she got to reenact the scene that was cut from *All Quiet on the Western Front*. This time, though, she did it to great applause.

All Quiet on the Western Front went on to become a classic, winning the Best Picture Oscar; but for ZaSu it was one of the biggest disappointments of her long career. Thereafter, casting agents were reluctant to consider her for important dramatic roles.

Again with Nancy Carroll (as a gold-digging manicurist), ZaSu was seen as another comical phone operator, this one named Ethel, in Edmund Goulding's *The Devil's Holiday*. There was another comedy at Universal, *Little Accident*, in 1930, starring Douglas Fairbanks, Jr. as Norman Overbeck, who postpones his second marriage after he learns that his

Lanky Slim Summerville was a frequent co-star. Their first pairing came in *Little Accident* (1930). Theirs was a special combination of screen magic, and they went on to make nearly a dozen films together.

ex-wife has given birth to a baby. ZaSu played a wet nurse named Monica. Others involved in these hijinks included Anita Page, Henry Armetta, Sally Blane, Slim Summerville, and Roscoe Karns.

For Columbia she worked with Jack Holt in a crime melodrama, *The Squealer*, about bootleg gangsters. She played yet another comic maid, Bella. Also appearing in the cast was Matthew Betz, the actor who essayed the role of Schani the butcher in *The Wedding March*. Then, under the direction of Ernst Lubitsch, ZaSu appeared as Jeanette MacDonald's maid, Bertha, in *Monte Carlo*.

Actress Lucile Webster, the wife of James Gleason, served as the president of a charitable organization known as the Dominoes. The Gleasons were longtime friends of Miss Pitts, and in September of 1930 Lucile persuaded ZaSu to participate in an entertainment to be staged at the group's clubhouse. It was in the form of a variety show, and Nancy Carroll danced in the opening number. Thelma Todd took part in the playlet titled *His, Hers and Theirs*. ZaSu had the leading role in another playlet, "Scarlet," which was written and directed by Maude Fulton. ZaSu welcomed the opportunity to perform onstage, and a good time was had by all.

At MGM, ZaSu appeared as a student nurse named Cushie in the stark Edgar Selwyn–directed World War I drama *War Nurse*, furnishing the somber film with some much-needed lighter moments. The atmosphere on the set was very tense. The wartime story was heavy and the lines highly dramatic. ZaSu worked alongside an old acquaintance, comedy star Marie Prevost. Despite the grave material, while they were filming, the pair had a difficult time holding their composure, especially when Miss Pitts was called upon to be dramatic. A reviewer of the film wrote:

> Some delicious comedy is furnished by ZaSu Pitts. She does some of her best work in this picture. *War Nurses* is often devastating in its horror, and it would have been very trying without the portrayal of Miss Pitts. Judging from audience reaction, she could have appeared twice as often with still better results.

The film starred Robert Montgomery and Anita Page.

For United Artists, ZaSu joined Jeannette MacDonald, John Garrick and Joe E. Brown in the comedy *The Lottery Bride*. The setting was a logging camp in which ZaSu was seen as Hilda, the proprietress of the Viking Ship Café. Based on an old Norwegian custom, the lonely miners hold an annual lottery to gain a wedding partner. ZaSu was paired with Brown (as Hoke Curtis), resulting in some rather silly dialogue:

HILDA: Do you know the meaning of spring?
HOKE: Yes. It means...
HILDA: Yes...?
HOKE: ... that you can take off your winter underwear.

At Warner Brothers, in *River's End*, she supported Charles Bickford, who, through the magic of the split-screen process, played dual roles as a Royal Mounted policeman and his lookalike prisoner. Directed by Warner reliable Michael Curtiz, it was an adaptation of James Oliver Curwood's famous story. ZaSu played the village gossip, Louise.

On May 7, 1930, she signed a $5,000 contract with Pathé to play another maid, Anna, in the pre–Code *Sin Takes a Holiday*, starring Constance Bennett and Basil Rathbone, and released in November.

Another romantic drama over at MGM was *Passion Flower*, with Kay Francis, Charles Bickford, and Kay Johnson. ZaSu played the role of the landlady, Mrs. Harney, of which one critic noted: "ZaSu Pitts scores heavily with another of her wistful pathetic comic roles, by which her value to Hollywood is rapidly expanding."

Universal did release another of her films this year, *Free Love*, a romantic comedy about a psychoanalyst and his wife, starring Conrad Nagel and Genevieve Tobin. ZaSu appeared as Ada, a dumb housemaid. A reviewer noted: "ZaSu Pitts acts as a sort of modern Greek chorus to the amorous monkeyshines of Nagel and Tobin."

Miss Pitts' work schedule in 1931 was a heavy one. At Paramount she co-starred with rubber-legged comedian Leon Errol in *Finn and Hattie*, based on Donald Ogden Stewart's novel, *Mr. and Mrs. Haddock Abroad*, with a screenplay by a young Joseph L. Mankiewicz. They appeared as a Midwestern couple, Mr. and Mrs. Haddock, who, along with their spoiled-brat daughter, go on a trip to Paris. Mrs. Haddock becomes seasick before they even board the boat, and the family encounters many misadventures during their trip abroad. Child star Mitzi Green, as the daughter, stole most every scene she was in. A female reviewer wrote:

> *Finn and Hattie* is billed as a comedy, but don't believe it. It's a tragedy. And the tragedy is that ZaSu Pitts, who is certainly one of the most capable and popular comediennes on the screen today, has, for her first really big part since the advent of talkies, one of the most stupid roles ever written for anyone. But the remarkable thing about the situation is that Miss Pitts, in spite of her role, manages to be almost amusing.

However, Louella Parsons wrote in her Hollywood column:

> Time some of the producers were getting some sense. Every time you go into theaters and ZaSu Pitts comes into the scene, the whole house roars. Just one look at her and they laugh expectantly.... I think she is one of the greatest comedy bets in pictures.

Parsons was always most positive in her comments about ZaSu.

At Universal, Pitts played the role of Minnie in the drama *The Bad Sister*, which was based on a Booth Tarkington story (*The Flirt*). Also in the cast were Sidney Fox, Charles Winninger, Emma Dunn, Humphrey Bogart, and Slim Summerville, a tall, lanky, dry-witted comedian with whom ZaSu would later frequently appear opposite. In her first film, Bette Davis plays a member of the Madison family, but hers was not the bad sister; that honor goes to bad-to-the-bone Miss Fox in one of her best performances. Later that same year, Bette Davis had another small role, in *Seed*, a drama about birth control concerning a budding author who deserts his wife and five children. Stars of that film were John Boles, Frances Dade and Genevieve Tobin, with ZaSu appearing as the nursemaid Jennie. In her review of the film, Louella Parson noted, "Keep an eye on Bette Davis, that girl has something worth developing"—a gross understatement, to say the least.

At RKO Pathé, ZaSu again worked with James Gleason, this time in an anti-war drama, *Beyond Victory*. The story and the screenplay were written by Gleason and Horace Jackson, but the production ran into censorship problems and had to be re-cut. Bill Boyd, Lew Cody and Marion Shilling were also in the cast, and ZaSu appeared as a famous knife-thrower, Mlle. Fritzi Mobley, and wore a fanciful costume with large bows on her shoes. A reviewer said of her characterization, "ZaSu Pitts is her usual dependable, very likeable self."

Beginning in 1931, Hal Roach, Sr., producer of many comedies, decided to team ZaSu

Real-life friend and frequent co-star Thelma Todd (right) appeared in 16 two-reel comedies for Hal Roach from 1931 to 1933. She and ZaSu were a perfect combination.

Pitts and blonde Thelma Todd in a series of comedy shorts, to be released through MGM. The first of the series was the three-reeler *Let's Do Things*, released on June 6, 1931. Both actresses basically portrayed themselves: ZaSu the zany, awkward and insecure proponent of perpetual problems, and Thelma the cool, beautiful blonde who sedately smoothes things over. The pair were surrounded by many of Hollywood's top supporting players, prominent among them Billy Gilbert. The shorts were hurriedly made, with scripts that were thin on plot but long on slapstick and physical comedy, with both ladies winding up in some very undignified positions. The plucky pair risked life and limb, and after scuffling with various other actors, they usually wound up with mussed-up coiffures, torn dresses, and bruised knees and elbows. They were frequently up-ended and tousled about, so both wore dark-colored gym-type bloomers beneath their skirts to keep their undergarments from being on constant display. ZaSu and Thelma were both willing to do most anything to get a laugh. Various directors were employed to referee the madcap antics. One who managed to do best by the ever-willing comediennes was Gus Meins, although several others, including Hal Roach, Marshall Neilan, George Marshall and Charley Chase, all gave it a try. Movie audiences howled with laughter and clamored for more.

A Woman of Experience, from RKO-Pathé, was yet another World War I melodrama. Helen Twelvetrees starred as a seductive female spy who has to ply her wiles on a German agent. She is "wounded in action," and a gallant young officer volunteers his blood for a transfusion. The male stars were Lew Cody and William Bakewell. H.B. Warner and funny

Franklin Pangborn were also in the cast. ZaSu played a hapless innocent, Katie. Future movie director John Farrow adapted his own play, *The Registered Woman*, for the screen, while Harry Joe Brown directed.

For Fox studios, Dorothy Mackaill and Warner Baxter played the romantic leads in a semi-comedy, *Their Mad Moment*. There wasn't much ZaSu could do with her role as the inconsequential maid Miss Dibbs.

The second of the Pitts/Todd series, *Catch as Catch Can*, was released on August 22, and was one of their best. ZaSu has a boxer boyfriend, Strangler Sullivan (played by Guinn "Big Boy" Williams), who gives her a new hat and then takes her out to a boxing match. She becomes greatly annoyed when her new hat is knocked off, thrown into the ring and tossed from one corner of the arena to another.

At RKO-Pathé, *The Big Gamble* was an unusual, suspenseful yarn of a gambler who has grown weary of life and allows a nefarious mobster to insure his worthless hide for $100,000, with the plan that he will be dead within the year. The gambler also enters into a marriage with a woman he hardly knows but later falls in love with. The film's director, Fred Niblo, worked some honest suspense into the plot. The lead male roles were played by Bill Boyd, who would later gain film immortality as Western hero Hopalong Cassidy, and mysterious Warner Oland. Oland, a Swedish-born actor, achieved screen stardom by his portrayal of Oriental characters such as Dr. Fu Manchu and Charlie Chan. Comedy relief for the film was furnished by tough-talkin' "dese, dose and dem" James Gleason. As for Miss Pitts' character, Nora Dugan, one critic commented, "You've guessed it, she plays the maid. She's grand, but it's getting so I wouldn't recognize the girl unless she had an apron on."

The Pajama Party was Pitts and Todd's third series entry, released on October 3. The girls are invited to spend the weekend at a swanky mansion. On the way there they get into a car accident and end up in a lake. The concerned other driver asks, "Please tell me you're not hurt," to which a frazzled Thelma replies, "Who says we're not hurt? I can't find one of my legs." Once at the mansion, each is assigned a French maid. In one of the best scenes in the short, ZaSu becomes highly indignant when her maid tries to undress her, and the elegantly-gowned Thelma trips and falls into a sunken swimming pool. Glancing directly into the camera she coyly coos, "Imagine my embarrassment!"

Also for Warners, ZaSu had a very good role in the remake of another Booth Tarkington story, *Penrod and Sam*, which followed the adventures of two juveniles, played by Leon Janney and Junior Coghlan. Pitts appeared as Mrs. Bassett, the overly protective mother of a sissified son, Georgie (Billie Lord). When other boys refuse to let her son join their secret society, called "the Independent Order of Infidelity," she is all a-flutter, with her famous hands constantly tugging at her collar, readjusting her hat and twisting her handkerchief.

When stage greats Alfred Lunt and Lynn Fontanne made their only sound motion picture, *The Guardsman*, they personally chose Miss Pitts for the role of the vague, melancholic but loyal maid Liesl. Also adding to the sophisticated comedy were Roland Young, Maude Eburne and Herman Bing.

ZaSu Pitts' and Thelma Todd's fourth short, *War Mamas*, released on November 14, had the girls driving an ambulance during World War I. The gals are spies who entertain two German officers, played by Charles Judels and Stuart Holmes. One of the funniest scenes in the short had the girls, making the rules up as they went along, playing strip poker with the two dense Germans.

For Columbia Pictures, ZaSu co-starred with Una Merkel in *The Secret Witness*. Merkel was an amateur lady detective investigating a series of murders in a penthouse who foolishly rules out the major suspect "because he has such nice eyes." Once again ZaSu appeared as a telephone operator, and drew considerable praise for her work. One reviewer was quite lavish, stating:

In one of her early talkie timid-maid roles, an unidentified fellow player holds ZaSu's hands to keep them from fluttering.

> What mystifies me is why some bright producer doesn't snatch up ZaSu Pitts and really do something with her. She is one of the funniest people on the screen, and audiences begin to chuckle the moment her plaintive countenance appears (seems somebody else had already said that). She plays the apartment house telephone operator, and wails lugubriously throughout the excitement of a suicide and two murders, for fear her employer will forget to pay her overtime.

Another writer termed the film "an under-nourished pot-boiler." Audiences, however, enjoyed ZaSu's comedy efforts.

The fifth and final entry of the year in the Pitts/Todd series was *On the Loose*, released on December 26. The girls become bored after being frequently taken to Coney Island on dates. They meet a couple of British gentlemen (John Loder and Claud Allister) who, in an effort to please them, take them to the exact same place of amusement. After experiencing a harrowing time in the funhouse and on various violent rides, they demand to be taken home. A few moments later their doorbell rings. They open it to find two new suitors—Stan Laurel and Oliver Hardy in a surprise, unbilled cameo appearance. The duo asks the girls for a date and suggests a trip to Coney Island, which results in a violent response.

The year 1932 was Miss Pitts' most prolific period, with well over thirty different pictures in release. At Universal she played Polly Perkins in *The Unexpected Father*, opposite Slim Summerville. He is a shy lad from Oklahoma named Hick who unexpectedly strikes oil. Shortly thereafter, through no particular fault of his own, he becomes the custodian of a cute four-year-old girl. Out of desperation, he hires a nursemaid for the child in the person of Monica, sweetly played by Miss Pitts. Naturally, she and Slim fall in love. Little Cora Sue Collins was most effective as the child, and the usually-cast-as-society-matron Alison Skipworth also had a choice role.

In January, Hedda Hopper hosted an afternoon tea for Tallulah Bankhead; among the invited guests were Marie Dressler, Roland Young, ZaSu and Madge Evans.

At Paramount in 1932 there was yet another maid role for ZaSu in *Broken Lullaby*, a most unlikely title for a basically anti-war tale. (In England, it was retitled the more-appropriate *The Man I Killed*.) The film was helmed by German director Ernst Lubitsch, renowned for his ultra-sophisticated comedies. This tragic and humane story told of a young French soldier in World War I who is haunted by the fact that he killed an American serviceman. He later meets the dead man's fiancée and, ironically, falls in love with her. Phillips Holmes played the Frenchman, and lovely Nancy Carroll was the hapless heroine. Lionel Barrymore co-starred as a kindly German doctor. Comedy relief was offered by ZaSu Pitts and Lucien Littlefield.

The first ZaSu Pitts/Thelma Todd short of the year was released on February 6, *Seal Skins*, in which Thelma and ZaSu hear that the royal seal of a foreign country has been stolen. In their attempt to regain the royal seal, they become involved with a sea lion.

Child actor Buddy MacDonald, who was in *Seal Skins*, told silent movie historian Richard W. Bann in 2001:

> *Seal Skins* was funny because Mr. Roach let the gals use their own nicknames—one was Toddy and the other was Pittsy. That's what they really called each other, too. Those were two great friends, it seemed to me. They played girl reporters on a newspaper, and I was a "printer's devil," which meant an office boy. Billy Gilbert was in that. He liked to smoke big cigars, and he was as big as Oliver Hardy.

Added MacDonald, "Thelma Todd was a gorgeous, gorgeous woman, and sweet, both of them were; ZaSu Pitts was as nice as could be."

On February 27, 1932, to promote the Pitts/Todd comedies, the pair began a series of daily radio broadcasts heard over station KNX at 6:45 P.M. The locale was a Hollywood boarding house; Miss Todd was heard as an ambitious young lady newly arrived in Tinseltown and hoping to land in the movies. ZaSu played a sympathetic maid. The broadcasts marked Miss Pitts' debut on radio airwaves. The show aired only on the West Coast.

In *Steady Company*, a boxing drama over at Universal, starring Norman Foster and June Clyde, ZaSu played her typical role—that of a flustered spinster named Dot.

Red Noses, with Thelma Todd, was released on March 19. It dealt with the zany girls' misadventures in a Turkish bath ("No Turk's gonna give *me* a bath!" ZaSu says dimly), where they go to seek a cure for head colds.

At Columbia Pictures, in *Shopworn*, ZaSu's character was known simply as Dot. The drama starred Barbara Stanwyck as a waitress from the wrong side of the tracks who falls in love with a man way above her station in life. His mother offers fierce objections to the romance. Fine support was offered by Regis Toomey as the suitor and Clara Blandick as his mother. Miss Blandick is best remembered today as the kindly Auntie Em in *The Wizard of Oz* (1939). ZaSu added a touch of levity to the domestic drama that was "a dynamic story that will make you think twice before you call yourself 'decent.'" Or at least that's what the ads said.

It was, however, a movie that no one associated with it particularly liked. Regis Toomey called it an "undistinguished little effort." He recalled to writer Ella Smith how "unhappy" Stanwyck was during the making of the picture, surmising, perhaps, that the reason for her dissatisfaction was the "B" movie director assigned to the film, Nick Grinde—or even himself. Smith asserts that it was the script, written by Sarah Y. Mason, that Stanwyck was displeased with. Stanwyck called *Shopworn* "one of those terrible pictures they sandwich in when you started." Nevertheless, *Shopworn* did well at the box office.

With Tom Mix in *Destry Rides Again*, ZaSu added a few laughs as a timid temperance worker riding on a stagecoach. This was the first film version of the Max Brand Western classic. Brand's story was originally serialized in six parts as *Twelve Peers* in Street & Smith's *Western Story Magazine*, from February 1, 1930, to March 8, 1930; later that year it appeared in novel form as *Destry Rides Again*. There was little similarity between Brand's original story and the movie versions to follow. (For one thing, Brand called his hero "Harry" Destry; on film the character is always named Tom.) Because of the success and classic status of the second adaptation of the story (starring James Stewart and Marlene Dietrich), from 1939, the 1932 version has been renamed *Justice Rides Again* for television. (A later remake, 1954's *Destry*, starred Audie Murphy; and a one-season television program ran in 1964, with John Gavin as Tom's son, Harrison. Again it was called *Destry*.)

April 30's entry in the Roach/Pitts/Todd series was *Strictly Unreliable*. This one found Thelma appearing solo at a vaudeville theater to pay her back rent. ZaSu, a maid, visits and inadvertently stumbles onstage, destroying the other acts, clumsily dancing a ballet, and "playing the piano."

For Fox, ZaSu appeared as Miss Fairweather, a troubled sob sister taking courtroom notes in *The Trial of Vivienne Ware*, starring Joan Bennett, Donald Cook and Skeets Gallagher. Then, for Tiffany Pictures, she had a showy role in *Strangers of the Evening*, adapted from Tiffany Thayer's book *The Illustrious Corpse*, which was a strange mixture of mystery, melodrama, suspense and broad farce. The locale was a morgue, and the villain of the piece was the owner of an undertaking establishment. There were plenty of close-ups of corpses on slabs and caskets being unearthed from graves. Fortunately for the audience, there were brief interludes of comedy provided by Lucien Littlefield ("Snookie") and pompous Eugene Pallette as a cocksure detective. Once again, Louella Parsons offered words of praise for a favorite character player: "Looks as if ZaSu Pitts has been hiding her light under a bushel all these years. Her performance as Sybil is so good, you realize what a fine comedienne ZaSu is, and what a great addition she is to any comedy."

Any moviegoer who expected RKO-Pathé's *Westward Passage* to be a Western adventure was sadly disappointed. Instead, it was a domestic drama about a struggling author, played by Laurence Olivier, and his sophisticated wife, Ann Harding. They squabble, separate, divorce, and later remarry. ZaSu played an inquisitive innkeeper, Mrs. Truesdale. Unfortunately, she had very little footage to establish her character. She was on the screen only long enough to quiz "Who?" and "Why?" and to wring her weeping-willow hands and utter a soulful, "Oh, dear!"

Adding a touch of comedy to *Westward Passage*'s proceedings were Edgar Kennedy and Florence Lake, seen as a romantic couple on a dance floor. Back in '31 they had appeared as the quarrelsome couple in *The Average Man* series for RKO. Kennedy was a former film director who became a comedian, famous for his "slow burn" routine.

The Old Bull, released on June 4, found the girls, ZaSu and Thelma Todd, stranded on a farm out in the country where a lion, escaped from a circus, is on the loose. We are also treated to ZaSu driving around the farm in the car Thelma foolishly allowed her to drive, crashing, bumping into and literally destroying everything in her path.

Also at RKO in 1932, ZaSu was seen as a telephone operator in *Is My Face Red?* with Helen Twelvetrees, Ricardo Cortez, Jill Esmond, and Robert Armstrong. At Paramount she was seen briefly as the landlady Mrs. Scudder in *Make Me a Star*, a remake of *Merton of the Movies*. Stuart Erwin starred and was given excellent support by Joan Blondell and Ruth Donnelly. Silent screen star Ben Turpin also appeared in a brief scene. The locale for *Roar of the Dragon*, starring Richard Dix, was Manchuria. Miss Pitts appeared briefly as a chatty tourist. Also featured was Danish actress Gwili Andre, as well as Edward Everett Horton, who helped furnish what little comedy there was. In *The Vanishing Frontier*, about homesteaders in the Old West, ZaSu was kindly Aunt Sylvia. Johnny Mack Brown, Evalyn Knapp, Raymond Hatton and Ben Alexander also starred in this Western.

In *Show Business*, released on August 20, ZaSu and Thelma Todd are two girls in a vaudeville troupe traveling by train with their pet monkey, which gets them into too many monkeyshines. The short was directed by Jules White, who said years later, "I don't think I ever heard greater laughter than at the preview of that one picture I made for Hal Roach. It was really very funny." His brother, Sam White, concurred: "When the preview was held, the audience just got hysterical, and ZaSu Pitts was never funnier."

At MGM ZaSu played Gertie in *Blondie of the Follies*, starring Marion Davies and Billie Dove as two shop girls seeking stardom on Broadway. Both fall in love with the same man, Robert Montgomery. ZaSu is a married sister with a baby. Her complacent husband is played by Sidney Toler. (In 1938 Toler would take over the role of Oriental detective Charlie Chan from the late Warner Oland. He would play the sleuth in twenty-two pictures.) Also adding to the merriment were Jimmy Durante and Douglass Dumbrille. ZaSu's showy part was written especially for her by old friend Frances Marion, with an assist from Anita Loos. Marion Davies did some intricate dancing and a very amusing take-off on the Great Garbo. James Gleason appeared as ZaSu's father!

Alum and Eve, released on September 24, revolved around ZaSu and Thelma Todd being stopped for speeding in their car. They use the excuse that they are on their way to the hospital because ZaSu is ill. The cop, for some reason or another, thinks ZaSu is pregnant. The wildness continues with a hilarious scene in which ZaSu, Thelma and some others accidentally ingest alum and water, then can't talk properly. George Marshall directed the mayhem.

ZaSu was reunited with James Gleason in the comedy-mystery *The Crooked Circle* for Sono Art-World Wide productions. He played a typical hard-boiled, dumb cop, and she was the shuddering, scared-silly servant. Rounding out the cast were Ben Lyon, Irene Purcell, and Roscoe Karns.

One of the best roles of her career came in the very funny *Once in a Lifetime*, in which she was cast as Miss Leyton, the absent-minded secretary at a fictional film studio. She was at her fussy, fidgety best. A reviewer for *Time* stated, "She utters genteel moans, so sad, they are almost yodels." Also contributing to the laughter were Jack Oakie, Louise Fazenda, Sidney Fox, Aline MacMahon, and Gregory Ratoff as a tempestuous director.

She and Thelma Todd were door-to-door salesgirls in *The Soilers*, released on October 29. A fine slapstick moment occurs when poor ZaSu gets tangled up in a ladder.

Harry Joe Brown directed the prizefight drama *Madison Sq. Garden*, with Jack Oakie as a boxer and William Collier as his fight manager. Thomas Meighan, who had played romantic leading men in silent films, was seen as the manager of the well-known sports arena in New York City. A few scenes were shot on location at the famous site. Also in the cast were Marian Nixon, William Boyd and Lew Cody. Adding to the authentic atmosphere, a number of former sports champions made brief appearances, including Jack Johnson, Tommy Ryan, Tom Sharkey, Billy Papke, Stanislaus Zbyszko, and baseball player Mike Donlin. Also appearing were sportswriter Grantland Rice, Westbrook Pegler, Damon Runyon and others. ZaSu was seen as a news reporter named Florrie.

ZaSu Pitts was one of the best

In *Once in a Lifetime* (1932), ZaSu gave one of her best early comedy performances as the absent-minded secretary at a down-and-out film studio.

known and beloved screen personalities of her day. Max Fleischer's brother, Dave, directed the Betty Boop cartoon *Popeye the Sailor*, released on July 14, 1933, which introduced the Popeye character to the screen. Bonnie Poe was the first actress to voice Olive Oyl. But to supply the voice of Olive on a regular basis, Max Fleischer selected versatile, Bronx-born actress Mae Questel (1908–1998), who was also the voice of Betty Boop. It was she who modeled the seaman's scrawny sweetheart on Miss Pitts' screen personality, basing her vocal characterization of Olive on the woebegone style of ZaSu. From 1938 and 1944, Margie Hines (married at the time to "Popeye" Jack Mercer) voiced Olive, accentuating the ZaSu connection, but then Questel took over again, remaining fixed and identified in the role.

Olive Oyl had been introduced in 1919 by cartoonist Elzie Segar (1894–1938) in his *Thimble Theater* strip. Among the first featured characters were the Oyl twins, Olive and her brother, Castor Oyl. Originally, the scrawny Miss Oyl had a boyfriend named Ham Gravy. Popeye did not appear in the strip until January 17, 1929. As everyone remembers, the muscle-bound sailor developed his spectacular biceps by guzzling enormous amounts of spinach. In later cartoons he battled the brawny Bluto for Olive's affections. From 1935 to 1938 there ran a three-times-a-week radio series on which an actress named Olive LaMoy played the role of Olive. Some sources claim that Mae Questel also did Olive's voice at some point.

As further proof of the effect ZaSu's zany image had on the public during the 1930s, Cab Calloway, the "Hi De Ho" man and the great showman of jazz music, frequently used the unusual expression "Zah-Zuh-Zaz" in his scat style of singing.

In *Back Street* (1932), ZaSu comes to the door of the home of Irene Dunne to borrow a cup of sugar — or is it to return the cup she had borrowed sugar in?

ZaSu and Thelma Todd's last short for the year was also one of their best. *Sneak Easily* was released on December 10 and offered ZaSu plenty of opportunity to display her unique talents. She appeared as an addlepated juror in a most peculiar trial. Among her zany antics was a bit where she accidentally swallowed "Exhibit A," a time bomb in liquid form, leaving everyone expecting her to explode before their very eyes. Her groans, grimaces and gyrations were captured mainly in close-ups.

In *Back Street*, a domestic tearjerker starring Irene Dunne and John Boles, ZaSu was seen as the landlady, Mrs. Dole. Based on the romantic novel by Fannie Hurst, it was the sad saga of a woman in love with a married man, destined to remain on the "back streets" of his life. (Said the dramatic publicity, "Waiting — always waiting — in the shadows of the back streets ... longing for the man she loves ... asking nothing, receiving nothing — yet content to sacrifice all for him. WHY?") The narrative's action took place over a period of twenty-five years, and the actors required aging make-up, which was most effective.

ZaSu was elated when she learned that Erich von Stroheim was planning to make a Fox drama to be called *Walking Down Broadway*, and that he wanted her for the important role of Millie, a neurotic, sexually-aggressive girl with suicidal tendencies. Von Stroheim would direct and write the screenplay.

On September 2, 1931, Winfield Sheehan, Fox's vice president, had okayed the project on several conditions. One important stipulation was that the famously excessive and difficult Von Stroheim had to limit the amount of footage he would shoot; no more than 85,000 feet of film, or 95 minutes of screen time.

Shooting on the project was delayed because of several unforeseen incidents within the studio, through no fault of Von Stroheim's. Finally, the production started shooting in August of 1932. All went relatively smoothly, and the film was completed in October. Incredibly, Von Stroheim brought the film in within 48 days, at a cost of $300,000, with no problems — and on time. A rare occurrence, indeed.

Everything seemed to be going extremely well. Fox wanted Von Stroheim for another project, overjoyed at the easy, trouble-free relationship they shared with the director on *Walking Down Broadway*.

Then they viewed the footage.

"Suddenly the sexual obsessions, neuroses, and other grim aspects of the film were noticed by the Fox executives," wrote Arthur Lennig. Sol Wurtzel, who was involved in a power struggle with Winfield Sheehan at Fox, used *Walking Down Broadway* as a pawn. Sheehan, in a precarious position at a studio having financial troubles (this is before the merger with Darryl F. Zanuck and 20th Century Pictures), finally agreed that the film should be reshot. To protect itself, according to Arthur Lennig, the studio sent out false reports of Von Stroheim's work on the set. Therefore, *Variety* quoted a "Fox insider" as claiming that Von Stroheim had done excessive shooting, and that another director, Alfred L. Werker, would have to come in to cut the film down to a normal, average length. It simply wasn't the truth, but because of the director's notorious reputation, it was accepted as such.

On November 22, *Variety* reported that:

> [Fox] decided to remake about 50% of the picture.... Impossible story plus miscasting of Zasu Pitts and Boots Mallory are the reasons. Raoul Walsh will handle the retake. In spite of Miss Pitts' ability, audience refused to accept her in a strongly emotional role. Figured it must

be comedy since she's always cast for humorous bits. She will probably be replaced by some other actress not so definitely identified with comedy parts. James Dunn and Terrance Ray, other two members of the cast, gave poor performances with the direction rather than their ability blamed for the result. Boots Mallory in her initial screen effort utterly failed to impress.

Fox called for five weeks of reshooting, directed by Alfred L. Werker, Raoul Walsh, and Edwin Burke. (No director was credited on the final film.) Finally released in 1933, it was retitled *Hello, Sister!* The just-under-one-hour disfigurement bore little resemblance to what it had started out to be. Ironically, and almost comically, the movie was retitled *Clipped Wings* in England.

Erich von Stroheim never directed another film. He concentrated on acting, most notably in the classics *La Grande Illusion* (1937), directed by Jean Renoir, and *Sunset Blvd.* (1950), with Gloria Swanson. He died in 1957.

Although ZaSu would not be replaced as *Variety* mentioned, the experience was another crushing blow to her dramatic career, and she was devastated. But she bravely shouldered on.

Nevertheless, trade papers reported that the busy actress' earnings for the year totaled nearly half a million dollars, a very impressive sum during the depths of the Depression.

Hello Sister! (1933) was a drama that misfired. It started out under the direction of von Stroheim, who was replaced. ZaSu's part was greatly altered, with disastrous results. The film co-starred Boots Mallory and James Dunn.

She disputed the reports, but it was quite clear to everyone that this awkward girl from a poor family was doing very well in motion pictures, to say the least.

It was through her avid interest in sports that ZaSu first became acquainted with ex–tennis champion John E. Woodall, now a real estate broker. He was tall and handsome, with a sedate nature. The pair found much in common and began to keep steady company. In April 1932 she finally filed for divorce from Tom Gallery, who had been seen frequently in public escorting beautiful young women, mostly aspiring actresses. The divorce decree became final on May 2, 1933.

Gallery stayed out of film, where he had little or no success, and after World War II he became an important television executive at both the DuMont and NBC networks. He would be inducted into the World Boxing Hall of Fame for his importance to the sport of boxing. He would eventually remarry, to Lillian Fette, and have a daughter, Michelle. He passed away on August 25, 1993, in Encino, California.

The year 1933 was another extremely busy one for ZaSu. In addition to four more comedy shorts with Thelma Todd, there were eight more features.

At Universal, ZaSu teamed with dour-faced comedian Slim Summerville in a series of comedy features. *They Just Had to Get Married* was not nearly as racy as the title implied. ZaSu was seen as Molly Hull, another flustered housemaid, this time secretly in love with butler Sam Sutton (Summerville). When their rich employer dies, he leaves his fortune to the pair, and they are free at last to marry.

Slim Summerville and ZaSu pause to kiss as they play cards in *They Just Had to Get Married* (1933).

On January 21, *Asleep in the Feet*, with ZaSu and Thelma, was released. This short has often been listed as *Asleep in the Fleet*, although neither title makes a great deal of sense. In this entry, one of the girls' neighbors is about to be evicted. To keep this from happening they accept jobs at a dime-a-dance emporium. ZaSu is not successful at attracting dance partners, however, so one of the regular dancers decides to "doll her up" in order to make her more appealing to the clientele. Very heavy make-up is applied to her face, with disastrous results, as her mascara smears from forehead to chin.

Early in the year the results of a poll to determine the Ten Biggest Money-Making Stars of 1932–33 found ZaSu receiving 18.4 percent of all votes cast by participating motion picture exhibitors. Her name surpassed such screen personalities as Marlene Dietrich, Greta Garbo, Tom Mix, Clara Bow, and Laurel and Hardy.

In *Maids a la Mode*, released on March 4, ZaSu and Thelma cause no end of problems when, instead of delivering dresses to a customer, they wear them to a party. Never ones to go unscathed anywhere, ZaSu actually loses her underwear in this one and has the back of her dress ripped off. Thelma "fixes" this situation by sewing a piece of drapery across the revealing area.

Bargain of the Century, released on April 8, is considered by many to be the best of the ZaSu Pitts/Thelma Todd comedy shorts. Directed by comedian Charley Chase, the highly amusing episode finds ZaSu coyly flirting with a traffic cop (James Burtis) to keep Thelma from getting a parking ticket. The pair then convinces him to accompany them to a sale of bed sheets, which are in short supply. The trio engages in a tug-of-war with a number of stout customers. The policeman's uniform is torn to shreds in the fracas, and, as a result, he is fired from the force. The girls feel responsible for his predicament and hire him on the spot to be their personal cook. On the way back to their apartment, ZaSu faints and is carried home by the grateful policeman. The cop-cook whips up a meal, and ZaSu decides to make ice cream for dessert in a hand-cranked freezer. The police chief stops by for a visit. In an attempt to appease him, the ex-cop does some magic tricks and tries to make the chief's expensive pocket watch disappear. It winds up in the ice-cream mixer and is ground to fragments. Thereupon, the captain flies into a fit of rage and smashes every timepiece in the girls' apartment, including Thelma's wristwatch, a cuckoo clock, and even the alarm clock ZaSu attempts to conceal under her clothing. In the closing shot, ZaSu is on the receiving end of a knock-out punch.

In *Out All Night*, ZaSu appeared as Bonny, a nursemaid at a department store daycare center. She is madly in love with bachelor Ronald Colgate (Slim Summerville), who is firmly tied to his mother's (Laura Hope Crews) apron strings. They eventually wed, but the meddling mother-in-law accompanies them on their honeymoon. Friends try to intervene by staging a fake kidnapping of the bride. The groom finally proves his manhood. Also in the cast was an adorable tyke—a very young Shirley Temple. As Shirley recalled in her 1988 autobiography *Child Star*, "Universal gave me two and a half days work in a comedy titled *Out All Night* replacing Cora Sue Collins, who was judged too big to be carried around like a baby, so I got to hear ZaSu Pitts recite [the story about] the big bad wolf eating up Red Riding Hood. It was a sad story, so I cried on cue, then went home."

The final short the girls made together for Hal Roach was released on May 20, 1933, *One Track Minds*. Thelma wins a screen test and takes a train to Hollywood, accompanied, naturally, by ZaSu. Also aboard the train is the very young child star Spanky McFarland

In *Out All Night*, ZaSu, as department store kindergarten attendant Miss Bonnie, supervised as well as entertained the customers' children (unidentified).

(*Our Gang*), as well as a flamboyant and hammy German screen director named Von Sternheim (played by Lucien Prival), head of the Roaring Lion studios. Miss Pitts must have felt embarrassed satirizing her favorite director.

More than fed up with all the strenuous slapstick antics required by the shorts, she asked Hal Roach for her release. Attempting to fill her shoes was a difficult task. On a trip to New York City, Roach attended a Broadway show, *Flying Colors*, and took special notice of Brooklyn-born Patsy Kelly's raucous style of comedy. She was promptly signed to a contract to replace Pitts. The studio retained ZaSu's services to coach Kelly, who had only one previous screen experience, the Vitaphone short *The Grand Dame* (1931), and to "tone her down a few notches" on the volume dial. The new pair's first entry was titled *Beauty and the Bus*, and was released on September 16, 1933.

At RKO, ZaSu was seen as gullible gossip columnist Elmerada de Leon in *Professional Sweetheart*. It was a yarn dealing with the behind the scenes shenanigans at a radio station, focusing on a program sponsored by the Ippsie Wippsie Washcloth Company. Ginger Rogers appeared as "Glory—the Ippsie Wippsie Washcloth Girl." She is advertised as the "ideal of American womanhood," which she rebels against until she meets Norman Foster in this pre–Code comedy. Elmerada delivers the punch line: "Just because a washcloth and a dish rag got together—it's a clean up." Also in the cast were Franklin Pangborn, Allen Jenkins, Frank McHugh, Edgar Kennedy and Lucien Littlefield.

In *Her First Mate*, ZaSu plays Mary Horner, who buys a ferryboat. Slim Summerville is her humble hubby who yearns to be a sea captain but has to content himself as a peanut vendor on a night boat. It includes a hilarious scene wherein the henpecked husband flies into a rage and smashes all of his mother-in-law's dishes. Una Merkel also took part in this funny, William Wyler–directed comedy.

In *Love, Honor and Oh, Baby!* ZaSu appeared as Connie Clark, a filing clerk. When her wealthy boss makes amorous advances toward her, she launches a sexual discrimination suit against him for $100,000. Slim Summerville is seen as a struggling lawyer who takes her case, and blustery George Barbier is the boss, Jasper B. Ogden. Publicity blurbs claimed, "He was the best lawyer that ever sent a client to jail. She was the best Jill that ever tried to frame a millionaire out of his jack."

Following the kidnapping and subsequent murder of the Lindbergh baby in 1932, many celebrities began to receive similar threats. Among the Hollywood celebrities to fall victim were famed comedian Stan Laurel and ZaSu Pitts. She was at the peak of her film career and a very likely candidate for some form of extortion.

ZaSu received a threat by mail demanding a huge sum of money to prevent a similar fate for her beloved children. The letter insisted that she drive alone to a secluded spot where she would see a red flag along the road, at which point she would receive further instructions. Her heart pounded wildly in her chest, but she kept a level head and promptly

In *Professional Sweetheart* (1933), ZaSu and a group of fellow "sob sisters" (unidentified) jointly interview "star" Norman Foster.

informed the police. The lawmen advised her that she should follow the instructions to the last detail.

Bravely, she got behind the steering wheel of her car and set out for the designated spot. Minutes seemed like hours as her eyes scanned both sides of the road for a red flag. None could be seen, so she retraced her route several times. No flag could be found. In

Because of kidnapping threats in the 1930s, ZaSu's children Ann and Don were rarely photographed with her.

desperation, she returned to her Brentwood home. Within a few moments her phone rang, and she anxiously snatched up the receiver. "Hello," she said in more tremulous tones than she had ever used on the screen. "Hello," she repeated, "is someone there?" After a long pause a thug-like voice began to speak, informing her, in very persuasive terms, that it would be very wise to hire some security guards to protect her brood. Then, with a heated, "Take warning, Miss Pitts," she heard the other party hang up the phone.

The wise Miss Pitts once again informed the police of the phone call urging her to employ security guards. She had friends, like Stan Laurel, who had also received similar threats—and she felt it best to keep police headquarters fully informed.

As it later developed, the letter and the phone call urging ZaSu to hire security guards were all a part of an elaborate scheme of some ruthless racketeers hoping to force celebrities into hiring fake guards at exorbitant wages to keep their children from coming to possible harm. It was yet another of the many devious measures taken by desperate men to secure profitable employment during those hard times of the Depression era. Thereafter, all famous people took every precaution for the safety of their children.

Meanwhile, her screen work continued. In 1933 at RKO, *Aggie Appleby, Maker of Men* was a very confusing matter. Wynne Gibson starred as a woman of strong will who attempts to make over a number of her male acquaintances, trying to turn Charles Farrell from a softie into a tough guy and William Gargan from a hardboiled type into a pansy. ZaSu played an innocent bystander with the ridiculous name of Sybby or "Sib." Also seen were Jane Darwell and Betty Furness.

At MGM she had a featured role as "ZaSu" in the comedy *Meet the Baron*, starring radio star Jack Pearl as "Baron Munchausen," famous for the line "Vas you dere, Sharlie?" and as a teller of tall tales. Also cast was Jimmy Durante, Edna May Oliver and the Three Stooges.

Also released by Fox was *Mr. Skitch*, starring Will Rogers, with ZaSu as his wife. Also appearing were Rochelle Hudson (as their daughter) and Eugene Pallette. During filming, Rogers gave ZaSu an unusual nickname, "Bazzoo."

Fox released a three-minute short, *Mother's Helper*, to aid President Franklin D. Roosevelt's NRA (National Recovery Administration), which was established to regulate wages and working hours. ZaSu appeared as a wife complaining that the NRA wasn't much help to her, as she had to work eighteen hours a day at home. Her husband, played by comedian El Brendel, tells her that he is willing to get help for her by hiring a shapely chorusgirl type. The wife firmly states that she doesn't need that kind of help, and the chorus girl is not hired. The skit may not have been any real aid to the NRA, but it *was* amusing.

In August 1933, Louella Parsons' columnist daughter, Harriet, wrote a "Keyhole Portrait" of the actress, stating in part:

> ZaSu Pitts of the woeful eyes ... the never-still hands ... symbol of comic-tragic futility ... portrayer of humor and pathos and human frustration ... has created a character whom all the world knows, laughs at, and loves ... a bewildered little pawn of destiny ... like Chaplin..., but unlike him, she uses no costume tricks ... is the movies' prize picture stealer ... without meaning to be.... ZaSu lives quietly, with dignity ... wrapped up in her home and her two children.... You'd never think it, but she's one of Hollywood's best dressed women ... wears a great deal of blue, which matches her eyes ... was so thrilled over her first thousand-dollar check, she had it photographed.... Which proved ironic ... because it bounced.... [There's] something wistful about ZaSu.... You have to admire her for her tireless devotion to her chil-

dren ... and her work, and home.... There's a simple dignity and lack of artificiality about her personality, and her life.... When she wants something to worry about, besides her kids or her career ... there's always Guinevere, her canary.

In 1933 Warner Brothers released a *Merrie Melody* cartoon, *I've Got to Sing a Torch Song*, featuring animated caricatures of such diverse personalities as Greta Garbo, Mae West, Ed Wynn, and ZaSu Pitts. The parody of her image and voice was quite good.

On October 23, 1933, ZaSu took ill while working on a film and was rushed by ambulance to the Lutheran Hospital, where her physician, Dr. Edwin Larson, performed an operation for acute intestinal obstruction. She remained in serious condition for two weeks, but as soon as she was able she returned to filming.

A news item of January 12, 1934, stated:

> ZaSu Pitts has been taking time off to become a judge of cows. She advertised for a cow and found that they could be had in a price range from $5 to $500. Being essentially cautious, she finally bought a cow that cost $103 and is sending it to her small country home where her two children consume prodigious amounts of milk, so that now they can have a daily fresh supply, without worry of milk strikes.

The Meanest Gal in Town matched ZaSu, as Tillie Prescott, the owner of a dry goods store, with Pert Kelton as a saucy showgirl in fishnet stockings named Lulu. Kelton, stranded in town, goes after the town barber (El Brendel), who happens to be Tillie's beau. Along comes a wiseacre, played by James Gleason, and the showgirl begins to pursue him, too. Also in the cast was "Skeets" Gallagher as a fast-talking salesman.

The stars of *Two Alone* were Jean Parker, as an orphan mistreated by Arthur Byron and Beulah Bondi, and Tom Brown, a reform school runaway who rescues her. It was a rather aimless affair, but offered roles to a number of fine character people, including Charley Grapewin, Nydia Westman, and ZaSu as a spinster named Esthey Roberts, who occasionally wanders off to get drunk on applejack.

West Coast newspapers carried this message on February 12,

ZaSu possessed a keen sense of fashion and always appeared well-dressed off-screen, though she sometimes expressed her whimsical nature, as with this zebra-striped affair.

1934: "The secret marriage of ZaSu Pitts, screen comedienne, and Edward Woodall, tennis instructor, was reported by friends here today. They were said to have been married last October 8th at Minden, Nevada, by a justice of the peace, while she was on location filming a picture." The new bride had refused to have any wedding photographs made, and informed Universal studios not to release any publicity about it. While this formal announcement to the public was made, the couple left on a delayed honeymoon in New York City. They took in all the sights. When she returned to Hollywood, however, RKO rushed her through four features.

In the low-budget comedy *3 on a Honeymoon* at Fox, ZaSu played the spinsterish Alice Mudge. The stars were Sally Eilers and Charles Starrett.

Pitts and Pert Kelton were together again in *Sing and Like It.* The movie offered ZaSu one of her best roles, as Annie Snodgrass, a timorous bank clerk who absurdly dreams of becoming a famous singer. When she is rehearsing her awkward rendition of a sad ballad about mother love, she is overheard by a gangster, T. Fenny Sylvester (beefy Nat Pendleton), who, even though he is in the midst of a heist, becomes captivated by her singing. He strong-arms a theatrical producer into giving the pathetic Annie the leading role in a forthcoming Broadway musical. Hilarious scenes abound, especially when Fenny's hard-boiled moll (hip-swinging Pert Kelton) imagines that her boyfriend is stuck on his plain Jane protégée, Annie. The moll induces Annie to take a steaming hot bath and then has her sit in front of an open window—hoping she will catch pneumonia and lose her voice. The show, entitled *Silver Threads—A Fantasy in Music,* opens, and Annie is a smash hit with her heart-wrenching ballad "Your Mother" (an original number, written specially for the film by Dave Dreyer and Roy Turk). Nat Pendleton was excellent as the gangster, and John Qualen played Annie's timid beau, Oswald. Years later Qualen recalled one of ZaSu's quirks. "ZaSu Pitts was terrific, but she had a habit of whacking fellow actors on the chest when she forgot her lines." This same idiosyncrasy was also confirmed by other co-workers. "She

In *Sing and Like It* (1934), ZaSu was a perfect comedy foil for brassy showgirl Pert Kelton.

did the whacking out of her frustration with herself for not being able to remember her lines."

Love Birds again reunited her with Slim Summerville, this time at Universal. ZaSu, as schoolmarm Araminta Tootle, decides to retire from teaching and settle down on a nice, quiet little chicken farm. Along with her nephew, Gladwyn, played by a young Mickey Rooney, she applies to a crooked real estate agent and is sold a worthless stretch of land in the desert, compete with a dilapidated shack. The agent sells the exact same property to Henry Whipple (Summerville), a countrified bachelor whose only interest in life is a scruffy bunch of molting chickens. A modest war breaks out between the mousey pair, and the feathers begin to fly. The young nephew plays cupid and brings the henpecked Henry and the mother-hen Araminta together to settle down and form a happy roost.

At Paramount she appeared as Miss Coates, a secretary, in the mystery-comedy *Private Scandal*. It offered a confused plot about an embezzling financier who is found dead. At first, suicide is suspected, but eventually everything points to murder. The plot had many loose ends that were never tied up. Also in the cast were Phillips Holmes, Mary Brian, Lew Cody and Ned Sparks as a defective detective.

ZaSu then reported to Warners Brothers for a featured role in the lavish musical *Dames*. Dick Powell starred as an ambitious young songwriter with a sweetly understanding dancer girlfriend, played by Ruby Keeler ("I'm free, white, and 21. I love to dance *and* I'm going to dance"). Busby Berkeley staged the intricate song-and-dance numbers; Ray Enright

Private Scandal found ZaSu on the opposite side of the telephone switchboard for a change.

directed the actors. Hugh Herbert is the president of the Ezra Ounce Foundation for the Elevation of American Morals who becomes the "angel" financing Powell's stage production. Also involved in the backstage banter and bickering were Keeler's parents, the battling Hemingways, Horace and Matilda, excellently played by Guy Kibbee and ZaSu.

At RKO, the comedy-mystery *Their Big Moment* re-teamed ZaSu with Slim Summerville. It dealt with the expose of a fake spirit medium by a stage magician and his addlepated assistant, Tillie Whim (ZaSu). Summerville played a stooge named Bill who was unknowingly involved in some pickpocket activities. Stage star William Gaxton portrayed the magician, the Great La Salle, who stages a few fake séances, placing Tillie in a trance and thereby debunking the real fakers. Also involved in the shenanigans were Ralph Morgan, Bruce Cabot and Julie Haydon.

One of Miss Pitts' most notable roles came along in 1934 when she played Miss Tabitha Hazy, the shy, spinster neighbor in *Mrs. Wiggs of the Cabbage Patch*, directed by Norman Taurog. Mrs. Wiggs was the mother of a brood of five: two sons with normal names, Billy and Jimmy, but three daughters named after continents — Asia, Australia, and Europena. Stage actress Pauline Lord portrayed the title character, and Donald Meek was her shiftless husband. Villainous Charles Middleton was skinflint Bagby who holds the overdue mortgage on their humble shantytown house. The film viewed the Wiggs' dismal poverty through rose-colored glasses, with an ample dose of levity. Miss Hazy, in the hopes of landing a husband, replies to an ad in a matrimonial catalogue. This results in a visit from Mr. C.

Dames (1934), with Guy Kibbee (left), ZaSu and Hugh Herbert, was lots of laughs.

Ellsworth Stubbins, in the person of W.C. Fields. At the sight of him, Miss Hazy flings aside all her maidenly reserve and begins a fervent wooing.

W.C. Field, a number of years older than ZaSu, had a reputation for being difficult to work with. However, ZaSu gained his respect, and they worked well together. For unknown reasons he took a dislike to the star, Pauline Lord. When they filmed a scene together in which the Wiggs' sway-backed horse drops dead, Fields leaned close to the horse laying on the ground and said, "Good morning, Pauline, my darling. Never saw you looking better."

Child actress Virginia Weidler played the role of bratty Europena Wiggs who often threatened her kindly mother with, "I'll hold my breath 'til I turn blue in the face!"

Helen Lowell, a character actress who had played Mrs. Wiggs on the stage for seven years, was very interested to learn that ZaSu had been cast in the second-lead role of Miss Hazy. The gracious stage actress kindly sent her a copy of the original script from the play, some stills from the production and some of the original costumes.

In 1934's *Mrs. Wiggs of the Cabbage Patch*, ZaSu had the featured role of the Wiggs' neighbor, the spinsterish Miss Hazy, who searches for a mate in the pages of *Cupid's Matrimonial Guide*.

W.C. Fields was the unlikely answer to Miss Hazy's prayers in *Mrs. Wiggs of the Cabbage Patch* (1934).

On November 15, newspapers reported, "ZaSu Pitts came to court today, and in hurt tones, told Municipal Court Judge Wilbur C. Curtis that she did not owe $275 for the services of a nursemaid who, she insisted, never served her." The maid, Lula Woollesen, claimed that in October 1933 the actress had employed her as a companion to her children. ZaSu informed the judge that the claim was incorrect, stating, "I met Mrs. Woollesen through my masseuse and she asked me for a job. I told her that when and IF I needed anyone to care for my children, I would telephone her; but I did NOT hire her!" The judge then inquired, "How did you happen to pay Mrs. Woollesen $25?" Miss Pitts explained, "My masseuse told me that she was in financial need, so I sent her a check." The understanding judge ruled that the actress did not have to pay the claimant anything, and ordered the woman to pay court costs. End of matter.

On December 8 the *Motion Picture Herald* published its annual report of movie exhibitors' choices of "Top Ten Stars" of the year. Will Rogers came in first (by a large margin), followed by Clark Gable, Janet Gaynor, Wallace Beery, Mae West, Joan Crawford, Bing Crosby, Shirley Temple, Marie Dressler, and Norma Shearer. Former top star Greta Garbo had fallen to the 29th spot. Incongruously, Gary Cooper and ZaSu Pitts tied for number 35. Audiences' tastes were changing.

ZaSu then ventured over to MGM, where she appeared with Carole Lombard in *The Gay Bride*, a romantic comedy. Lombard appeared as gold-digger "Merry Widow Mary,"

The Ruggles of Red Gap (1935): Gathered at the bar is a quartet of colorful characters — wistful ZaSu, a perplexed Charles Laughton, a reflective Charlie Ruggles, and feisty Maude Eburne (as Ma Pettingill).

who becomes engaged to and marries three different petty gangsters, each of whom is quickly bumped off by the mob. ZaSu was the misdirected Mirabelle, the Merry Widow's misguided accomplice. Others in the cast were Leo Carrillo, Chester Morris and Nat Pendleton. During the course of filming, Miss Pitts struck up a friendship with Lombard. Well known for her keen sense of humor, glamorous Carol borrowed one of ZaSu's spinsterish dresses to wear to a masquerade party.

Miss Pitts experienced some personal embarrassment during 1934. *Ballyhoo*, a magazine of so-called "Hollywood humor," ran a composite photograph of Jean Harlow, Clark Gable, Edward Everett Horton and ZaSu Pitts "frolicking nude." The celebrities' faces had been superimposed atop some other nude bodies. All four stars threatened to sue, but in order to avoid any further adverse publicity, the matter was instead dropped.

One of ZaSu Pitts' best screen roles came along in 1935 with Paramount's rollicking tale of the Old West, *Ruggles of Red Gap*, directed by Leo McCarey. Charles Laughton appeared as Marmaduke Ruggles, a very prim and proper "gentlemen's gentlemen." His English employer loses his services to an American rancher in a poker game. The butler is transported to a tank town in the West. There he encounters the lonely widow Prunella Judson (ZaSu), and a most unlikely romance begins. The admirable cast of funsters included Roland Young, Charlie Ruggles, Mary Boland (as the socially-ambitious grande dame), and Maude Eburne (as Ma Pettinggill). ZaSu played, of course, a twittering widow, but director McCarey allowed her to be not only wistful but utterly charming. The fun was briefly interrupted when Laughton performed a very serious, dramatic recitation of Lincoln's Gettysburg Address.

ZaSu looked particularly pretty in her period costumes. In speaking of her role as Prunella Judson in *Ruggles of Red Gap*, she laughed, "I played the love interest in it. Imagine that. It's the first time I've played the love interest for as long as I can remember. Me — the love interest! I'm telling you, I was thrilled!"

At Fox she made a quickie low-budget production with Evelyn Venable, Lew Ayres, Claire Trevor and Jack Haley. The shooting title was *Man Eating Tiger*, but when the picture was released, it was called *Spring Tonic*. ZaSu's character name was Maggie Conklin. Evelyn Venable once recalled:

> I was in a picture with ZaSu Pitts and Lew Ayres. I adored ZaSu, and Lew is a marvelous man. But when we all saw the picture we got together and said, "Let's combine our money, buy the picture and *burn* it." We could not believe how bad it was.... I loved ZaSu. I had seen her in *The Wedding March* where she played a crippled princess, and she was great as a tragedienne, and here she was playing comedy just as well. I'll never forget those hands that she used to such great effect, twisting her fingers, and all that.

At Warners, ZaSu was once again teamed with portly Guy Kibbee. Together they played Cora and Matt Upshaw, a nouveau rich, social-climbing couple from out West in *Going Highbrow* (aka *Goin' to Town*). They contact an incompetent business manager about the best and easiest way to crash high society. He advises them to stage a lavish party to introduce their debutante daughter. Trouble is, they do not have any offspring, so they hire an awkward waitress named Annie, played by Judy Canova, to pose as their daughter. Other funsters involved in the hijinks were Edward Everett Horton, Ross Alexander, June Martel, and Arthur Treacher.

At Universal, ZaSu appeared as a naive waitress, Esmeralda Smith, who inadvertently

Spring Tonic (1935), which started out at Fox as ***Man Eating Tiger***, left audiences confused. The picture co-starred Lew Ayres, Claire Trevor, Jack Haley and Evelyn Venable, who here looks like a young Lucille Ball.

helps capture a bank robber in *She Gets Her Man*. An overambitious press agent attempts to make a national heroine out of her by forming a "Crush Crime Club." Others involved in this merry mix-up were Hugh O'Connell, Helen Twelvetrees and Lucien Littlefield.

At RKO ZaSu re-teamed with James Gleason for *Hot Tip*. He played Jimmy McGill, a sucker for horseracing, and she was Belle McGill, his wife, who loathes and abominates all forms of gambling. Gleason co-directed the film (with Ray McCarey), and his son Russell also had a role.

ZaSu was seen in the romantic comedy *The Affair of Susan* at Universal. She played a candy factory worker, Susan Todd, longing for romance. By chance, one day at Coney Island she meets a lonely auto factory worker who has been living in the same apartment building, across the hall from her. They are just getting to know each other when a thunderstorm separates them. Then, back in her lonely room, she hears him playing the radio in his room, and they are happily reunited. Hugh O'Connell was seen as her heartthrob, and Walter Catlett was also in the cast.

In April 1935 ZaSu and her husband took a six-week vacation in the East, but they bypassed New York City.

Radio was another medium that put her special talents to frequent use. On October 28, 1935, the *Lux Presents Hollywood* dramatization of the comedy classic "Dulcy" showcased ZaSu in the zany title role.

In *Going Highbrow* (Warner Bros., 1935), ZaSu and Guy Kibbee, as nouveau riche couple Cora and Matt Upshaw, attempt to crash the "blue book crowd" by hiring a hillbilly waitress to pose as their debutante daughter in order to give her a coming-out party — with hilarious results.

All of Hollywood was saddened by the news that vivacious Thelma Todd had been found dead on December 16, 1935. Her body was discovered in her automobile in the garage of her residence. The coroner determined that the cause of death was carbon monoxide poisoning. The circumstances were very mysterious. She had attended a party in her honor the night before and had been driven back home by her chauffer. She instructed him to drop her off in the driveway, and then climbed the long stairway to her home. Later the next day her dead body was discovered inside another of her cars. Adding to the baffling mystery was the fact that one of her satin slippers was missing. The case was never solved. Several friends testified that the day before her death she had been seen driving around town with an unidentified man. His identity was never determined. The late actress had lunched with ZaSu and her husband only four days prior to her death.

On December 17 the *Los Angeles Examiner* reported:

There was never any jealousy in Thelma's heart. Her inseparable and dearest friend had always been ZaSu Pitts, with whom she appeared in Roach pictures. It was while the girls worked together that they grew to know each other, and she [Thelma] often sacrificed her own scenes if her friend could get a laugh.

On December 25 the newspaper reported, "It was announced yesterday that ZaSu Pitts, premiere comedienne, and her husband J.L. Woodall, former tennis champion, who had lunched with Miss Todd on the Wednesday preceding her death at Perino's fashionable Wilshire Boulevard restaurant, are to be questioned on the possibility that Miss Todd may have confided something to them about the un-named man who has figured so prominently in the probe." The following day the Woodalls stated that they "were ready to appear before the grand jury if they are called when the official inquiry is resumed tomorrow.... Miss Pitts declared she could disclose to the inquisitors only what is already known — that she and her husband had lunch with Miss Todd on December 11, four days before she died."

Miss Todd's maid had testified, "I believe that Miss Todd must have told Miss Pitts, who was one of her very closest friends, the same thing she told me; that she was 'pulling out' of the arrangement under which she was living, and that she probably would be 'broke' as a result." Some witnesses testified behind locked doors. The full circumstances remain a mystery to this day.

On January 8, 1936, the *Los Angeles Evening Herald Express* reported on the wages earned by top Hollywood celebrities. The top moneymaker was glamorous blonde Constance Bennett, followed by Marlene Dietrich and Gary Cooper. ZaSu's name was also on the list, with her earnings reported as $60,416.57. In May of that year she asked the Board of Tax Appeals to review an income tax deficiency for a period in 1932 and 1933 when she had been married to Tom Gallery, requesting the amount in question be considered "community property."

ZaSu had only four films in release in 1936, but she turned in some fine characterizations. In *13 Hours by Air*, she played Miss Harkins, a nervous governess for a bratty boy traveling by air to the opposite coast. Several of the fellow passengers are anxious to touch down at San Francisco. Fred MacMurray is the handsome pilot attracted to a mysterious passenger, Joan Bennett. Complications ensue when Fred suspects that she is involved in a jewel theft. In reality — made-up reality, that is — she is an heiress. Brian Donlevy is a detective posing as a doctor, and young Benny Bartlett is the brat. A crook attempts to highjack the plane, and later it is forced to land during a blinding snowstorm. Director Mitchell Leisen kept the action lively in this Paramount quickie.

Back in 1932, while filming *Out All Night* at Universal, ZaSu had been quite impressed with four-year-old moppet Shirley Temple, and predicted a bright future for the youngster. In future years, ZaSu and the dimpled-darling Shirley would become neighbors and friends.

On May 12, 1936, the *Los Angeles Herald Express* announced, "Perhaps it is just a coincidence, but when Shirley Temple's new house started to rise up next to her, ZaSu Pitts began a program of remodeling. Now she has torn her whole house down and will build an entirely new place."

Temple's parents purchased a four-acre property in Brentwood, adjacent to the home of Miss Pitts. They built a very comfortable home and a large, life-size dollhouse for their famous daughter, big enough to live in.

As the years rolled on, Shirley became close friends with ZaSu's son and daughter. When, as a blossoming teenager, Shirley required an escort when seen in public, handsome Don Gallery was only too happy to oblige. Said Don:

> I always adored Shirley and still do today. We were always close. I loved her family, and they loved and trusted me. I used to take Shirley to movie premieres, and we used to go out and have a lot of fun at parties, the beach, skating. We were not a romantic couple, but we had many friendly dates, and I was like "the boy next door"— that rascal Shirley Temple still has my Stanford varsity jacket to this day! Shirley is a wonderful person.

ZaSu's daughter also became a pal of Shirley's, and it was at the Woodall home that the former child-star first met the dashing Air Corps Sergeant John Agar (1921–2002), who had been a beau of Ann's. Although Agar was seven years older, he was greatly attracted to the pretty teenager. The attraction was mutual, and in 1945 they wed, with ZaSu being one of the few invited guests. The happy couple took up residence in the life-sized dollhouse, while Temple's family lived in the main house. (John Agar also had acting aspirations, in addition to being an avid golfer. He enrolled in a drama school and made his film debut in 1948 in John Ford's *Fort Apache*, opposite his wife. The following year they made a joint appearance in *Adventure in Baltimore*. The couple would have a daughter, Susan, before they divorced in 1949. Agar would continue to act until his death.)

When the time arrived for ZaSu to have her new house built, she chose famed designer Paul Williams (1894–1980) for the job. Williams was the first African American to become a member of the American Institute of Architects (AIA). "In the moment that they met me and discovered they were dealing with a Negro, I could see many of them freeze," he wrote in *American Magazine* about his other clients. "My success during those first few years was founded largely upon my willingness — anxiety would be a better word — to accept commissions which were rejected as too small by other, more favored, architects." He was renowned for his use of oval windows, arched doorways, fluted columns, as well as long, theatrical passageways. One of his most famous designs was the Los Angeles International Airport. Said one admirer, Paul was "the last word in elegant traditionalism." ZaSu noted, "Paul Williams uses everything that is romantic and picturesque in Georgian and Regency architecture." The landscaping was also outstanding, with terraced gardens. The interior of the home combined elements of sophistication and elegance, while retaining a welcoming warmth.

In addition to the spacious dining room and bedrooms, there was a wood-paneled library with a secret stairway leading to the master bedroom. Entrance to the stairway was gained by selecting a certain book from one of the bookcases, which opened the secret door.

The living room had floor-to-ceiling windows that overlooked the blue Pacific Ocean. For many years ZaSu had been collecting antiques to furnish her home. She placed a high antique pipe organ between two living room windows. In her attractive garage she kept two vintage electric automobiles, one from 1903 and another from 1906. Dorothy Fargo, in a 1985 interview, said that she vividly recalled two things about the house:

> The kitchen — ZaSu was a fabulous cook! And a pipe organ set into the wall between two floor-to-ceiling windows overlooking the Pacific Ocean. Those were two-storey windows in the huge living room. ZaSu gave an engagement party in that house for my daughter, Abbie Mae.

The kitchen was something that ZaSu was extremely proud of: The heart of my Brentwood home at 241 Rockingham Road was its kitchen. It was not square or oblong or L-

ZaSu Pitts was an antique automobile enthusiast and kept two early models of electric cars in the garage of her Brentwood home.

shaped, it was ROUND — completely round. It was my dream come true. Everything was so conveniently located. There were special shelves to hold my large collection of cookbooks. I also collected rare food-molds to decorate the walls — and there was a large brick oven built into one wall."

For the June 1944 issue *The American Home* magazine, the cover featured a full-color picture of ZaSu at her brick oven, her nimble fingers clutching a long-handled fork in one hand, while the other drooped in her trademark pose.

In the article on the inside of the magazine, ZaSu raved about her circular kitchen and made other homey comments:

> Now take aprons. Some folks think of aprons as a homely drudgery garment — I think of them as homey, not homely. When I've got one on I think of glistening pots and pans, of pantries and cookie jars, and of buttercup-yellow batter in a mixing bowl. But, I guess an

The architect who designed ZaSu's Brentwood mansion complied with her wishes and included a circular kitchen.

apron means more to me than it would to other folks.... There's been only one trouble about my career — it's kept me out of the kitchen too much.

On September 22 the *Los Angeles Evening Herald Express* reported, "ZaSu Pitts is writing a cookbook and you can count on some tasty recipes.... The Pitts hands may look fluttery and helpless on the screen, but they are very capable in the kitchen."

Miss Pitts' Brentwood home became a showplace. She greatly enjoyed having guests in her home, many of them celebrities. Through the years her Brentwood neighbors included not only Shirley Temple, but Mary Astor, Claudette Colbert, Joan Crawford, Clark Gable and Barbara Stanwyck. When Colbert moved out, the elusive Greta Garbo moved in next door. Don Gallery recalled in 1996:

> She was really beautiful. I mean *really* beautiful. This may come as a surprise to some people, but she was very nice and friendly. I liked her a lot, but her Swedish accent was so thick I had trouble understanding her. She was very kind to my sister Ann and me. She always smiled and waved to us, and she let us use her tennis court. Garbo used to laugh and talk to us through this metal fence that separated our yard from hers. It had cypress trees and vines growing up it, and I can still hear her voice and see her gorgeous face.... She was always nice and friendly and childlike with me and my sister Ann.

When Garbo filmed *Love* in 1927, ZaSu had been cast in a minor role, one that would require her to ice skate in a scene with the reclusive Swedish star. Dutifully, Miss Pitts learned to ice skate; but, alas, her only scene was cut from the release print of the film. In later years the Woodalls began to feel that the Brentwood mansion was much too big for them. They would sell it and move to a smaller home in Pasadena.

ZaSu fondly recalled:

> Money is good for taking care of your needs and responsibilities. But it is no guarantee of happiness. I had plenty of money in the old days, but I can not in all honesty say that I was truly happy.... That came later when I met "Pops" [Woodall]. He filled my world with goodness, the way the sun fills our universe with light.

In *Mad Holiday*, at MGM, ZaSu was seen as not-so-bright Fay Kinney, an innocent aboard a ship on the high seas. It was a delightful murder mystery-comedy and dealt with the theft of a famous diamond known as "the White Dragon," remarkable for its size, shape and value. Suave Edmund Lowe portrayed a movie actor who grows tired of playing detectives on the screen. Elissa Landi was a sultry blonde heroine-type screenwriter, of whose performance one reviewer wrote, "This is Miss Landi's least ambitious but most successful picture in several years, albeit she retains a distressing habit of lunging at a cue as if she were going to bite its head off." Edgar Kennedy played a dumb detective, and the usually lovely character actor Edmund Gwenn had a dual role playing a valiant valet and ... the malicious murderer. A dubbed-in voice was employed to help effect Gwenn's dual characterization.

In 1932 RKO had bought the rights to Stuart Palmer's novel *Penguin Pool Murder*, which introduced to the world the schoolmarm-sleuth Hildegarde Withers. An enjoyable comedy-mystery series was fashioned, with Edna May Oliver ideally cast in the lead of the amateur sleuth, and James Gleason on board as police inspector Oscar Piper. The first film, *Penguin Pool Murder* (1932), was followed by *Murder on the Blackboard* (1934) and *Murder on a Honeymoon* (1935). Unfortunately, Oliver left RKO and was replaced in the role by character actress Helen Broderick for *Murder on a Bridle Path* (1936). For the next, *The Plot Thickens* (1936), ZaSu Pitts was tapped to play Hildegarde, while James Gleason continued on as her partner, Oscar Piper. The plot dealt with a band of international jewel thieves out to steal a valuable gem from a local museum. This was yet another picture for Miss Pitts dealing with the theft of a jewel.

In 1937, at Warner Brothers, ZaSu joined Metropolitan Opera tenor James Melton and Patricia Ellis for *Sing Me a Love Song*. Melton had enjoyed great popularity singing on the radio, and the studio attempted to establish him as a musical film star. He appeared as Jerry

Sing Me a Love Song (Warner Bros., 1937): Fussy floorwalker Walter Catlett checks up on ZaSu, playing a clumsy clerk in the music section of a posh department store, where she constantly rips apart sheet music and breaks stacks of records.

Hanley, the grandson of a department store owner who poses as a worker in the store to launch new concepts in store sales — one of these concepts being a traveling store, pulled by a train. ZaSu was seen as Gwen Logan, a timid and awkward employee in the store's music department. The overeager saleslady frequently breaks phonograph records she sets out to sell, accidentally crumples sheet music, and, at one point, even falls into and breaks a bass drum. ZaSu gets to sing a duet with Melton, "Carry Me Back to the Lone Prairie." The strong comic supporting cast included Allen Jenkins as Criss-Cross, her elevator-operator boyfriend, Walter Catlett as a fussy floorwalker and Hugh Herbert as a clumsy kleptomaniac with plans for shoplifting a grand piano. In the final scene the elevator operator finally proposes marriage to Gwen; she joyfully accepts and deliberately proceeds to smash a whole counter full of phonograph records.

As was often the case, ZaSu struck up a friendship with Melton. She invited him to be her houseguest. The pair discovered a mutual interest in antique automobiles. ZaSu showed him her two antique electric autos, and they went for a drive. Years later, when he had his own show on television, he invited ZaSu to be his guest a number of times.

Someone else interested in ZaSu's vintage electric autos was Clark Gable. Says her son Don:

> He resided across the street and was always very pleasant. Momma owned two very rare electric automobiles from 1903 and 1906. They were very beautiful and unusual. I remember that

they had leather fenders. Anyway, Mr. Gable always pestered Momma and tried to purchase them from her, but she would not sell them to Clark.

Early in 1937 Miss Pitts accepted an offer to appear in two film productions in England, both produced and directed by George King. In the first, *Wanted!* she appeared as Winnie Oatfield, a shipping clerk mistaken for an American jewel thief. The film was released in April and featured popular character actress Norma Varden.

The second film was released in May. In *Merry Comes to Town*, ZaSu plays Susannah Merridew, a Miss-Fix-It who inherits a small legacy that her relatives believe to be a fortune. Hermione Gingold appeared as one of the greedy relatives, Iva Witherspoon. Neither film received a wide release in the United States.

While in London, ZaSu stayed with friends from California, art dealer Howard Taylor and his former actress wife Sara. Temporarily located in London, the couple were the parents of an adorable five-year-old daughter with dark hair and violet-colored eyes. Miss Pitts would later appear with young Elizabeth Taylor in *Life with Father* (1947). In 1939, with war looming, the Taylors would move back to Hollywood with their daughter. The Taylors would become ZaSu's neighbors when they took up residence in Shirley Temple's former home.

After completing her two film assignments, ZaSu returned home.

In 1937, Pitts and Gleason repeated their roles in another Hildegarde Withers comedy-mystery, the misleadingly titled *Forty Naughty Girls*. The picture concerned the double murder of a show's leading man and press agent. Detectives Withers and Piper ignore the obvious clues and ferret out the real evidence. ZaSu instigated some zany antics backstage while seeking clues. Regrettably, this movie marked the end of RKO's short-lived Hildegarde Withers series.

For United Artists ZaSu was seen as Letitia Rondell in the semi-musical *52nd Street*. The story dealt with a swanky mansion on 52nd Street in New York City which is converted into a nightclub, with Leo Carillo as the chef. Others in the film were Scottish singer-comedienne Ella Logan, who would later gain Broadway fame in *Finian's Rainbow* (1947), singer Kenny Baker and pop-eyed funnyman Jerry Colonna.

On March 24, 1938, ZaSu was heard over the airwaves as a guest of horticulturist James Bateson, whose show was broadcast from radio station WFWB in San Bernadino. The broadcast was heard only on the West Coast.

During the summer of 1938, ZaSu set out on a cross-country vaudeville tour. Special material was written for her by Wilkies Mahoney, and appearing with her in the act was comedian Cliff Hall. Her many film fans welcomed the opportunity to see her perform in person. As part of the act she performed a devastatingly funny impression of an impersonator doing an impression of ZaSu Pitts, with flailing, fluttering hands, as well as a heart-wrenching moan of "Oh, myyyy!" She later recalled modestly:

> I don't know why I was a big hit. I wasn't good, I know. I had a straight man and he fed me the laughs. The laughs were all mine — that's why it was terrible. I didn't do anything, really. Maybe it was the films that played with the act, or maybe it was the stage bands. I don't know.

On August 17, Miss Pitts was a guest on Rudy Vallee's network program heard over NBC. She presented a comedy sketch entitled "Miss Pringle Gets a Ticket." She also got

Biography 77

to participate in a comic take-off on Svengali called "Swing Ally," playing, of all people, Trilby! On October 4 she was a special guest on NBC's *Fibber McGee and Molly* program. And on October 29 she guested on the air with Al Jolson and Martha Raye.

Independent film producer Jed Buell announced plans for a Western musical film to be entitled *Follies on Horseback*. He began negotiations with ZaSu, Edward Everett Horton

In the mid–1930s, *Stage Magazine* ran a series of full-page photographs of film personalities dressed as a favorite historical character. ZaSu chose to appear as Marie Antoinette.

and singer Herb Jeffries to star (Harry Langdon was also mentioned briefly), but the plans did not work out.

When MGM studios launched a massive, country-wide talent search to cast the colorful characters in its planned screen production of Margaret Mitchell's *Gone with the Wind* (1939), among the names mentioned was ZaSu Pitts. Of course, it would have been ludicrous to think of her in terms of the fiery Scarlett O'Hara, but she would have made a very fine, fussy Aunt Pitty-Pat.

One of her biggest screen role disappointments came in the 1938 casting of Frank Capra's classic comedy *You Can't Take It with You*. ZaSu had actively campaigned for the role of the awkward ballerina Essie VanderHoff, and had even gone so far as to take some ballet lessons to prepare for the part. Later, the disappointed actress told the press:

> Essie was a perfect role for me, except that I had never danced ballet. I went to a ballet professor and said that I wanted to learn. Furthermore, I wanted to be able to whirl on my toes, in a week. So we started to work, and after a week arrangements for my screen test was made. I could get up on my toes, alright, but the only way I could get off them was to fall flat on my face, and, oh dear, I usually did. So they gave the role to Ann Miller, that Texas girl who is such a good dancer, and has glamour, too!

In 1939, at Paramount, ZaSu appeared as Dulcey Lee in *The Lady's from Kentucky*, a comedy about horseracing. George Raft played a gambler, with Ellen Drew as his love interest. Dulcey Lee's main interest is Hugh Herbert, who plays Mousey Johnson. To add some

In *The Lady's from Kentucky* (1939), romantically inclined ZaSu wraps her loving arms around Hugh Herbert's neck.

authenticity to the film's atmosphere, three thoroughbreds appeared — one named Mickey O'Boyle, who starred as race horse "Roman Son"; a colt named Mike Arnold as "Cantankerous"; and a foal named "Kentucky Lady." The foal had been born on the set during filming.

Also that year, Paramount filmed a musical called *Zaza*, directed by George Cukor; but Miss Pitts was not in it. The star was Claudette Colbert, who was coached for her musical numbers by none other than Fanny Brice.

At Warner Brothers, ZaSu was seen as Aunt Penelope Hardwick in the comedy musical *Naughty but Nice*. It was singer Dick Powell's last film for the studio, and he was cast as a young college professor-turned-songwriter accused of plagiarizing the musical masters, such as Bach, Liszt, Mozart and Wagner, for his compositions. His trio of spinster aunts comes to his rescue. They also formed a musical trio specializing in the classics, with ZaSu's famously flaccid fingers floridly floated amongst the vacillating harp strings. She did an excellent job of pantomiming playing the instrument. Character-wise, ZaSu's Aunt Penelope also had the very annoying habit of correcting everyone's sentences for them. Also in the cast were Gale Page, Helen Broderick, Allen Jenkins, Maxie Rosenbloom, Jerry Colonna, a young Ronald Reagan, and the "Oomph Girl," Ann Sheridan, playing a vampish singer.

For Republic Studios, ZaSu appeared in the low-budget feature *Mickey the Kid*. It was a 68-minute drama about a criminal trying to raise his young son in the slums. During a

Naughty but Nice **(1939) was Dick Powell's last film for Warner Brothers. He played a young composer supported by a doting trio of spinsterish aunts: Vera Lewis, ZaSu Pitts and Elizabeth Dunne.**

robbery he kills a bank teller, and he and his son take to the road. He then hijacks a school bus that runs into a snowdrift. The police arrive, and the criminal is shot and killed. Meanwhile, his son has saved the school kids from freezing to death by building a bonfire and thereby becomes a hero. ZaSu appeared as a kindly neighbor named Lilly. Bruce Cabot was the criminal, and Tommy Ryan played the boy. Others in the cast were Ralph Byrd, June Storey, J. Farrell MacDonald, John Qualen, and Jessie Ralph.

In April 1939 ZaSu was the first Hollywood player signed to appear in Herbert Wilcox's production of *Nurse Edith Cavell*. It was the first British film to be shot in the United States. It was a true tale of a British nurse who, with the help of several influential women from German-occupied Brussels, establishes an underground system to help refugees and escaped prisoners of war escape across the border to Holland. It was a prestigious anti-war drama with a very tense performance from British star Anna Neagle. The real-life Cavell was later executed for her bravery. ZaSu's role as Mme. Moulin, a patriot canal boat drudge who also aided Allied soldiers escaping from Belgium, was of a dramatic nature, and she won the praise of critics. The role presented her an opportunity to exhibit her dramatic abilities, and she impressed critics with her excellent performance. Others who gave very fine performances were Edna May Oliver, May Robson and George Sanders.

For the United Artists release *Eternally Yours* she appeared as Mrs. Bingham, the gullible wife of business tycoon Raymond Walburn. The plot deals with a purveyor of prestidigitation and his wife, from whose marriage the magic has disappeared. David Niven and Loretta Young starred, along with Eve Arden, Billie Burke, Broderick Crawford, Virginia Field, Hugh Herbert, and C. Aubrey Smith.

ZaSu had only two films in release in 1940. She had a very good role at Warner Brothers in the comedy *It All Came True*, playing a flighty seamstress Miss Flint who lives in a rundown boarding house. The spinster imagines that mysterious men are following her home every night. Humphrey Bogart, in a rare comedy role, appeared as a gangster hiding out in the same boarding house, with plans to turn it into a successful nightclub. On the night of the club's gala opening, Miss Flint sips a champagne toast and immediately becomes inebriated. The club is raided, and she is hauled off to court to testify as a character witness. The part offered ZaSu a delightful drunk scene. Jeffrey Lynn appeared as a struggling songwriter, and sultry Ann Sheridan played a songstress.

In the remake of *No, No, Nanette*, ZaSu repeated her 1930 role of the disgruntled maid Pauline. The film starred Anna Neagle, supported by Richard Carlson, Victor Mature, Eve Arden, Helen Broderick and Roland Young. Directed by Neagle's husband, Herbert Wilcox, the remake was not as successful as its predecessor. Nor did it equal the 1971 Broadway revival, which starred Ruby Keeler, and featured Patsy Kelly, still sounding as loud as ever, in the role of Pauline.

Uncle Joe started the new year of 1941. It looked and felt like a Hal Roach comedy, but apparently it wasn't. It starred ZaSu (as Aunt Julia) with Slim Summerville (as Uncle Joe) and her future television co-star Gale Storm (as their niece).

In the spring of 1941 ZaSu toured movie houses, appearing on stage with Patsy Kelly.

Hal Roach had decided to try the innovation of releasing shorter films running only half the time of a usual feature. He called them "Streamline Comedies." ZaSu's first was with Patsy Kelly, *Broadway Limited*, released through United Artists. The film found Miss Pitts portraying a lovelorn clubwoman, Myra Prottle, traveling by train from Chicago to

New York, determined to interview a young starlet aboard the train. Instead, she winds up auditioning for an extremely hammy actor-director, played by Leonid Kinskey. Patsy Kelly is seen as the inept secretary to the starlet, played by Marjorie Woodworth. Traveling incognito, the starlet poses as a young mother with an infant, but finds herself innocently implicated in a kidnapping. Also in the cast were Dennis O'Keefe and Victor McLaglen.

The second of ZaSu's "Streamline" short comedies was *Niagara Falls*, again with Slim Summerville. This time ZaSu was seen as Emmy Sawyer, who, after waiting twenty years to marry her beau, is finally headed to Niagara Falls for a honeymoon. ("Funny things happen at Niagara Falls!" said the ads.) En route, they encounter a bickering couple who are having car problems and mistake them for newlyweds. Both couples wind up staying at the same honeymoon resort, and many mishaps ensue. The young couple was played by Marjorie Woodworth and Tom Brown.

A 1939 RKO publicity photograph of ZaSu.

At RKO, ZaSu was seen as Anna the maid in the comedy *Weekend for Three*, starring Dennis O'Keefe and Jane Wyatt as young marrieds whose romantic weekend is interrupted by pest-guest Phillip Reed. Although famous wit Dorothy Parker had a hand in the writing of the screenplay, it did not contain many laughs. Miss Pitts, Edward Everett Horton and Franklin Pangborn supplied the film's few moments of hilarity.

Her last Roach "Streamline" comedy was entitled *Miss Polly*. It starred ZaSu as Pandora Polly, a prim and proper spinster from the small town of Midville, somewhere in rural America. Life in Midville moved at a snail's pace; in fact, the speed limit was a mere twelve miles per hour. Miss Polly has a secret crush on handyman Slim Wilkins (played by Slim Summerville), who spends much of his time tinkering with highly impractical inventions. He is employed by Minerva Snodgrass (Kathleen Howard), head of the town's Civic League, and someone with very puritanical notions about love and romance. The League deems it immoral for young lovers to kiss in public (or anywhere else). Miss Polly does not agree with them and goes to bat for a young couple she feels are perfectly matched. By mistake, ZaSu drinks some of Slim's homemade "love potion" and finds herself in a very romantic mood. She dolls herself up in a flimsy organdy gown and attends one of the League's meetings. While testifying on behalf of the young couple, she inadvertently stands in front of a sun-drenched window; the bright sunlight shines through her gown, revealing much of her anatomy. All's well that end's well, however, and the couple are finally able to kiss. Adding to the fun were Brenda Forbes, and Elyse Knox and Dick Clayton as the young couple.

Also at RKO, ZaSu appeared as Miss Emily Pepper in *Mexican Spitfire's Baby*, with

Beginning February 12, 1940, ZaSu played the role of Aunt Mamie Wayne on the daily CBS radio soap opera *Big Sister*.

fiery Lupe Velez, Leon Errol, Charles "Buddy" Rogers, and blonde vamp Marion Martin. It was the fourth entry in a series that had begun in 1939. The action took place on an ocean liner headed for Hawaii. ZaSu would reprise her role as Emily Pepper in *Mexican Spitfire at Sea* (1942), the very next entry in the series.

The studio also launched a film series based on the highly popular radio program *Lum and Abner*, starring Chester Lauck and Norris Goff. The first entry was entitled *The Bashful Bachelor*, relating the tale of Lum's long-running romance with spinster Miss Geraldine, played, of course, by ZaSu Pitts. Hoping to convince Miss Geraldine to finally marry him, Lum attempts to make himself into a hero by tying Abner to the railroad tracks and rescuing him just before the train strikes. Failing in that attempt, Lum stages a kidnapping of his Jot-em-Down store partner. Again foiled, the wedding bells do not ring. The picture was directed by Malcolm St. Clair, a very successful comedy director in the early days.

Miss Pitts also made a low-budget film for Monogram, *So's Your Aunt Emma*, also called *Meet the Mob*, which has always been a big favorite of her fans. She appeared as Emma Bates, a spinster who had once been engaged to a famous boxer, Jim O'Banion; but her family voiced strong objections, and the marriage plans were called off. Later, when Emma learns that O'Banion's son, also a boxer, is going to fight in the city, she makes the journey to see him. By the wildest stretch of the imagination, she is mistaken for a notorious female gang-

At RKO in 1941, ZaSu joined the stars of radio's *Lum and Abner* (Norris Goff, left, and Chester Lauck) in a feature film, *The Bashful Bachelor*. She had also been part of the radio show's regular cast.

ster, Ma Parker. Others involved in the merry mix-up were Roger Pryor, Douglas Fowley, Elizabeth Russell, Warren Hymer and Tristram Coffin.

At MGM, ZaSu joined Marjorie Main and Aline MacMahon in *Tish* to play a trio of spinsters caring for an infant. The studio had planned for a series of films starring the three, but audience reaction was poor, so plans were abandoned. ZaSu appeared as Aggie Pilkington, a spinster whose fiancé had fallen off a tin roof to his death. She never married. For the role she wore a pince-nez perched on the end of her nose, and she went bear hunting with a bow and arrow. She encounters a dancing bear, escaped from the circus, and is chased up a tree. The script was based on a novel by famous mystery writer Mary Roberts Rinehart. Also in the film were Guy Kibbee as a judge, Susan Peters, Lee Bowman, and Richard Quine.

For British War Relief she joined a number of other Hollywood personalities for a stage appearance of Noël Coward's *Tonight at 8:30*.

In the early fall of 1942 ZaSu set out on a Midwestern stage tour in the mystery farce *Her First Murder*. The story revolved around two sisters who take over their late brother's office, finding it is a detective agency. In late October she performed the play in Hershey, Pennsylvania, and the *Lebanon Daily News*, which headlined their review "ZaSu Pitts Gets Laughs at Hershey," reported that it was "a mirth-provoking performance that furnished plenty of laughs." The reviewer further added, "Miss Pitts, by the way, played her part, which was tailor made for her, up to the hilt without being hammy, and her gestures and pantomiming, which have made her famous in the movies, were very much in evidence, to the great delight of the audience."

In Toronto, Canada, on November 12, 1942, it was reported that ZaSu was made an honorary, full-fledged member of the Canadian Army. She had entertained the troops at the Salvation Army service canteen there.

ZaSu's only film in 1943 was Paramount's *Let's Face It*, starring Bob Hope and Betty Hutton. Based on the 1925 stage comedy *Cradle Snatchers*, and the then-recent Cole Porter Broadway show (also called *Let's Face It*), it told the tale of three matrons taking revenge on their unfaithful spouses by hiring three young men as their "escorts." ZaSu appeared as one of the wives. Other funsters in the cast were Raymond Walburn, Andrew Tombes and Joe Sawyer. The movie retained a few musical numbers by Porter, including a frenetic rendition of "Let's Not Talk About Love" by Hope and Hutton.

Eve Arden, who played Maggie Watson, another of the wives, recalled ZaSu in her 1985 autobiography as "a great lady," adding that, with their respective husbands away (Arden's hubby was in the Army), the two of them "spent a lot of time together, mostly in her fantastic kitchen, making date-nut cookies for the cast and crew."

In the fall of 1943 Miss Pitts set out on a Midwestern stage tour with the mystery-drama *The Bat*. Co-starring with her was character actress Jane Darwell, who had won a Best Supporting Actress Oscar for her role as Ma Joad in the classic *The Grapes of Wrath* (1940).

With no film work in the offing, ZaSu set her sights on more stage work. She made her Broadway debut on January 5, 1944, in the mystery-melodrama *Ramshackle Inn*, a play

Gun moll ZaSu gets the drop on Tris Coffin in *So's Your Aunt Emma*.

that had been specially written for her by her playwright friend George Batson (1918–1977). She starred as Belinda Pryde, a librarian from East Ipswich who, after twenty years of being surrounded by dusty books, invests her life savings to buy a rundown tavern, Ye Olde Colonial Inn. She takes possession during a raging thunderstorm, not knowing that the Inn has a shady past. No sooner has she unpacked than all kinds of strange things begins to take place. Weird noises are heard in the night, and moans and groans emanate from the gloomy, dark, bat-infested cellar, which she bravely investigates with her plumed-hat perched firmly on her head. Throughout the course of the play the mild-mannered Miss Pryde either witnesses or participates in more crime, violence, mystery, gunplay and outright skullduggery than she ever believed possible. But thanks to stout-hearted Belinda's flustered ruses and stratagems, the guilty are trapped and the innocent vindicated. Others in the cast were Joe Downing, Cora Witherspoon, Maurine Alexander, Richard Rober, William Blees, and Margaret Callahan.

In *Tish*, ZaSu, as spinster Aggie Pilkington, goes hunting bear with a bow and arrow. Instead of bagging the bear, she winds up perched on a tree branch.

The show's producer, Robert Rued, hailed it as a "melodramatic farce. Dedicated to both chills and laughter. It has no message, argues no cause, tests no theories. It simply provides a hilarious evening in the theatre, with an occasional scare thrown in shrivel the spine of the beholder."

In one suspense-tinged scene some armed gangsters return to the scene of one of their earlier crimes, Ye Olde Colonial Inn, and Miss Pryne, with her plumed hat fixed firmly on her noble noggin, fights them off with a pick-axe!

Prior to opening on Broadway, in December 1943, the show played some previews in Norfolk, Virginia, after having rehearsed in New York. On December 2, en route to Norfolk, the only available transportation was a troop train crowded with young soldiers. ZaSu recalled:

> The train was so crowded we took turns sitting down, and it wasn't possible to walk in the aisle without warning the standees to hold their breath. We shared seats and fruit and books.

ZaSu made her Broadway debut in January 1944 in the mystery-comedy *Ramshackle Inn*, written especially for her.

> All those fine lads had stayed with their families until the last possible minute of their furloughs. They had to get back to camp. We [the cast] were just en route to put on a show.

While touring with the show, ZaSu took her daughter Ann along with her. One morning, before a performance, ZaSu was interviewed by one of New York's leading newspapers. She told the interviewer, "My goodness, I'm tired out. I can certainly understand why people like President Roosevelt and Mr. Churchill get tired, with all the work they have to do. Now, Eleanor Roosevelt, she never seems to get tired with all the traveling she does."

ZaSu's many long-time film fans were anxious to catch a glimpse of their favorite and flocked to the theater to see her perform. The opening night audience at the Royale Theatre gave her a standing ovation.

Robert Garland, critic for the *Journal-American*, wrote:

> ZaSu Pitts, a natural born comedienne, received a genuine ovation when the curtain fell on the opening performance of *Ramshackle Inn* at the Royale. A genuine ovation, mind you; no picayunish imitation of the real thing. Having concluded her Broadway debut as an honest-to-goodness off-screen actress, Miss Pitts was taking one curtain call after another. There was no doubt about it. The folks out front were genuinely glad to see her.

Critic Brooks Atkinson reported that her performance was "consistently funny." However, other critics were not so enthusiastic, although it didn't matter at all to audiences. The play ran for 216 performances on Broadway, closing there on July 8, then moving on to Chicago for an extended run. The play remained one of Miss Pitts' favorites, and in succeeding years, whenever her busy schedule allowed, she toured in various productions of it around the country.

ZaSu's pretty daughter Ann, after attending college, decided to give acting a try. She spent a season with a summer stock company, along with young actress Nancy Davis. Nancy's mother, Edith Davis, was also an actress, and both families became close friends. Ann eventually decided that acting was not for her and sought other pursuits.

In late 1944, 22-year-old former child star Jackie Cooper, then serving in the United States Navy, had become innocently involved in an incident while on a weekend pass with several other young sailors. They met three teenage girls and invited them to a party. The girls later testified that they had been offered alcohol. The young sailors were brought before Juvenile Court and charged with contributing to the girls' delinquency. When Miss Pitts learned of the charges, she attended the trial and, on her own volition, appeared as a "character witness" for Cooper. She testified, "I have known Cooper since he was seven years old, and his reputation as to morality is spotless."

In August 1946, ZaSu set out on tour in another play written specially for her by George Batson, called simply *Cordelia*. She starred as spinster Cordelia Tuttle, who lives in a shack at the end of a wharf in a New England fishing village in the early 1900s. Cordelia, who has no means of visible support, is raising two children who had been left in her care by an errant mother who went off to see the world.

The unusual play gave ZaSu ample opportunity to display her dramatic abilities, as well as her unique comedic gift. Publicity blurbs for the production hailed Miss Pitts as "the Funniest Woman in the World." She looked very elegant in the charming costumes that had been designed for her by Edith Head. The play was directed by Russell Fillmore, who had enjoyed a long-time affiliation with the El Capitan Theatre in Los Angeles. He had directed many top names, such as Billie Burke, Joe. E. Brown, Jane Cowl, Charlotte Greenwood, and Edward Everett Horton.

In the cast of *Cordelia* was ZaSu's protégé, Nancy Davis. She had been influential in having Davis cast in the role of Millicent. During the tour, Miss Pitts graciously shared her hotel accommodations with the young actress.

Both the playwright and the show's star were greatly disappointed with the lukewarm reactions of critics and audiences alike. After a two-month tour, the show closed. Batson revised the script and gave it a new, perhaps more marketable title, *A Dangerous Woman!* It was completely re-staged and set out on tour on January 24, 1947, continuing though February 15. ZaSu had invested some of her own money in the production, and its financial failure was another big disappointment to her. Although she did experience some disappointments in her career, she stayed optimistic. "Am I bitter? Heavens, no!" she insisted to columnist Hal Humphrey in 1957. "I'm working, and I'm just glad to be alive." She wryly told Humphrey, "I never could sing, dance or jig. I really don't know how I made it at all."

She made only one film in 1946, *Breakfast in Hollywood*, released in February that year. It was based on a popular radio program of the same name that was broadcast live daily from a restaurant in Hollywood. The show was presided over by Tom Breneman, a genial host who was a great favorite with a large female audience. With microphone in hand, he wandered among the tables, chatting and flattering femme egos. He commented on the ladies' headgear, and if a hat caught his fancy, he would put it on his head and model it, to the audience's delight. It was buttered-up, pure corn, and the ladies ate it up. The eldest lady in attendance would be presented with an orchid and a kiss on the cheek from chivalrous Tom. The unique show enjoyed a long run, lasting until April 1948, when Breneman died suddenly of a heart attack just hours before a broadcast.

The film version of *Breakfast in Hollywood* introduced Tom Breneman to the movie screen. Produced on a low budget, it was a hodge-podge of sentimental vignettes about elderly female radio fans, mixed in with a varied assortment of musical numbers. ZaSu appeared as Elvira Spriggens, one of Breneman's more ardent fans. Because of the whimsically tall, three-tier chapeau she wore, with three bows in the front and a large plume in the back, she is referred to as "the Mad Hatter." Others in the cast were Beulah Bondi, Billie Burke, Raymond Walburn and Bonita Granville. The musical fare included Nat "King" Cole, Latin heartthrob Andy Russell, Frances Langford, and the musical depreciation of Spike Jones and His City Slickers.

At Paramount, ZaSu rejoined former co-stars David Niven and Loretta Young, with whom she had appeared in *Eternally Yours* back in 1939. The new picture was inaptly titled *The Perfect Marriage*

ZaSu had a short run on tour in *Cordelia*. A Broadway opening had been hoped for, but the show closed before it could reach the Great White Way. The show had been written for ZaSu Pitts and featured lavish costumes designed by Edith Head.

ZaSu Pitts was a frequent guest star on many radio programs. She's seen here at the April 30, 1946, CBS broadcast of *By Request*, along with Cornel Wilde, Ed Gardner (Archie of *Duffy's Tavern*) and the musically brilliant Oscar Levant.

(1947). It was all about an over-privileged couple who, after ten years of wedded bliss, have a simple quarrel and decide to divorce. The husband is an amateur magician, but it seems the magic of their happiness has suddenly vanished like a rabbit out of a hat. Family and friends try to intervene, but it comes together in the last reel when the couple kiss and make up just in time for a happy ending.

During the summer of 1947, ZaSu toured in a stock production of *The Late Christopher Bean* with one of her former co-stars, the portly and baldpated Guy Kibbee. ZaSu played Abby, an ordinary-looking and devoted housekeeper who had once posed for an unknown portrait artist who never received any degree of fame until after he died. One day, merely by chance, Abby's portrait is seen by a traveling art critic who takes one look and declares it a masterpiece. He offers to purchase the painting, but Abby's employer greedily claims ownership. The dilemma is happily resolved when it is learned that the artist, who was secretly in love with his model and painted her with such genuine love that her true beauty shone through, had willed the valuable painting to her.

During the production's stay in Chicago, drama critic Ashton Stevens wrote in his column that he far preferred ZaSu's interpretation of the role over that of the play's original star, Pauline Lord. Incidentally, back in 1934, Miss Pitts had appeared in the film version of *Mrs. Wiggs of the Cabbage Patch,* a play that had been originally performed onstage by

Miss Lord. Critic Stevens went on to call ZaSu's performance as Abby "the best projected characterization of her too-limited stage career."

In June 1947 a young actress named Madge Meredith was accused of causing the beating and kidnapping of her former business manager, Nicholas Gianaclis, and his bodyguard. Meredith, who was born Marjorie Massow in Iowa Falls, Iowa, in 1921, had done a few uncredited parts at Fox and Paramount. Things looked like they were picking up when she was signed to an RKO contract in 1946, appearing in *Child of Divorce* (1946), *The Falcon's Adventure* (1947), and *Trail Street* (1947).

Unbeknownst to the girl, the business manager she had hired was tied in with mobsters. After she refused his romantic advances, he made a complaint to the police that she had had thugs beat him up and then attempt to kidnap him and his bodyguard. The police, for whatever reason, believed his story, and Miss Meredith's name was placed on the "Most Wanted" list. When she learned about it, she went to the police, denying the accusation and declaring her innocence. She testified that Gianaclis had harassed her and even forced his way into her home and held her family at gunpoint. Her story was not believed, and she was confined to the county jail.

An assembly sub-committee called her trial "a frame-up," as well as "a mockery of investigation, procedure, and justice." Yet all appeals on her behalf were ignored, and in May 1949 she was transferred to the California Institution for Women at Tehachapi.

When ZaSu Pitts learned what was happening, she tried valiantly to intervene. She began a campaign, making phone calls and writing letters to various judicial departments, including the governor. She spoke with Miss Meredith and was convinced that she was innocent of the charges. Dorothy Fargo, ZaSu's childhood friend, noted in 1985, "[ZaSu] was a soft touch for anyone in trouble."

It was a long struggle, but, finally, in July of 1951, an inmate confined to San Quentin confessed that it had been Gianaclis himself who had hatched the plot to falsely implicate Miss Meredith. When word reached Governor Earl Warren, he commuted her sentence, and after more than two years of imprisonment, Miss Meredith was declared innocent and released.

Sometime later, when Meredith appealed to the Los Angeles courts for the return of her home, ZaSu accompanied her and offered testimony as a character reference. The shady Gianaclis later had his citizenship revoked because of reasons of "poor character." Madge Meredith and ZaSu Pitts remained friends.

Madge Meredith would get back to acting after she was cleared of the charges. She appeared mostly on television on such shows as *Racket Squad, Cowboy G-Men, Fireside Theatre, The Adventures of Kit Carson, The Lone Ranger, Judge Roy Bean*, etc. Movie work consisted mainly of uncredited bits, such as playing a slave in Cecil B. DeMille's *The Ten Commandments* (1956). Her last known acting job was on 1961's *The Best of the Post*, in the episode "Off the Set."

Meanwhile, ZaSu Pitts had the showy role of Cousin Cora Cartwright in the Technicolor production of the long-running stage hit *Life with Father* (1947). With William Powell and Irene Dunne in the leads, not to mention youngsters like Elizabeth Taylor and Jimmy Lydon, it was a big draw at the box office.

From late December 1947 into January of 1948 ZaSu once again toured in *The Late Christopher Bean*.

During the years of touring with stage productions, Miss Pitts preferred to dine in her

In *Life with Father* (1947), young Elizabeth Taylor is startled by the news that one of her relatives has not been baptized. ZaSu Pitts looks on in utter mortification. Pitts was a longtime friend of Taylor's parents.

hotel room rather than go out to public restaurants. Musical stage star Mary Martin, in her autobiography *My Heart Belongs*, recalled having met ZaSu while on a stage tour in 1945:

> ZaSu was one of the greatest ladies I ever knew. Years before I met her I had learned to imitate her famous fluttery hands and squeaky voice from watching all her pictures. Now, when I met her, I discovered how much talent she really had. That amazing woman would entertain five or six people in her hotel room, and could carry on a conversation on the telephone, while at the same time preparing hot biscuits and crisp bacon on an electric grill she kept in the tub in her bathroom. The grill was concealed there because cooking was against hotel rules, and she had to keep the smells from getting into the hall. Fortunately, she liked to use the shower, because she could never use the bathtub — because it was full of grills, pots and pans, etc.

Frances Marion, ZaSu's dear friend, after having been one of Hollywood's favorite and highest paid screenwriters for more than thirty years, decided to leave the film capital and move to New York City in 1948. Miss Marion had won an Oscar for her script of the prison yarn *The Big House* in 1930. The following year she wrote the original story for the boxing ring drama *The Champ*, again winning the Oscar. Both films had starred Wallace Beery, and he won an Oscar for his performance in *The Champ*. She was the first woman to win an Academy Award for Best Original Screenplay.

Marion was born in San Francisco on November 18, 1888, and was nearly six years ZaSu's senior. She had four marriages and two sons. A former advertising illustrator, model and silent film actress, she began her writing career for the *San Francisco Examiner*. During the First World War she was one of the first female war correspondents to cover actual battles in Europe. In Hollywood she directed a few films and wrote more than two hundred scripts. She served as the first vice president (and the only woman board member) of the Writers' Guild. She also spoke several languages, painted, sculpted and played "concert-caliber" piano. She painted a very life-like portrait of ZaSu.

In New York, Marion joined with Anita Loos to write a play expressly for Miss Pitts. Originally titled *Mother Was a Lady*, it was later changed to *Red Lamp in My Window*. Producer George Abbott became interested, and a pre–Broadway opening was planned for Boston on December 27. During rehearsals, Abbott, who also served as director, wanted to make some script changes in the third act. Frances Marion was willing, but Anita Loos flatly refused any alterations. She had nothing to lose, as she was already committed to working on the musical version of *Gentlemen Prefer Blondes*. Greatly disappointed, Abbott lost interest, and *Red Lamp in My Window* was cancelled, causing more sad frustration for ZaSu. When *Gentlemen Prefer Blondes* opened at the Ziegfeld Theatre on December 8, 1949, it made a star of a statuesque, wide-eyed blonde with a most unusual voice, Carol Channing (not to mention the song "Diamonds Are a Girl's Best Friend").

While in New York, ZaSu went to Madison Square Garden with Frances Marion to attend a gala "Night of Stars." When she stood to take a bow as the audience applauded, the famed screenwriter thought to herself, "The Hollywood studios had been fools not to keep ZaSu on the screen. They had a valuable asset within their grasp. Typical of how they do things out there."

The intriguing new medium of television then beckoned, and ZaSu made her debut on November 22, 1948, on *The Chevrolet Tele-Theatre* in a playlet called "The Flattering Word." Her second television appearance came on *The Philco Television Playhouse* on January 2, 1949, in an adaptation of her stage success *Ramshackle Inn*.

Radio broadcasting was making a desperate effort to maintain its popularity, and, beginning in March 1949, ZaSu became a regular member of the cast of the *Lum and Abner* program. When the television version of the series was being planned, she would guest star in the pilot, with Andy Devine. It aired on November 2, 1949, on CBS. ZaSu played Miss Pitts of the Eureka Moth-Spraying Company.

In February of 1950, ZaSu appeared in a stock production of *The Late Christopher Bean* in El Paso, Texas, with the El Paso Star Repertory Theater. ZaSu told reporters as she got off her plane:

> My coming to El Paso to take the lead in *The Late Christopher Bean* is due to the efforts of the "fabulous" Mr. [Charles] Deane [director of the repertory company].
> Mr. Deane contacted me at the Watkins Glen Summer Theater in New York and asked me to star in the opening play of a new stock theater he was forming. I told him I'd be delighted to. So, here I am.

Following ZaSu's commitment, the theater was able to attract John Loder, Jean Parker, Edward Everett Horton, and others to appear in their plays.

In 1950 she was once again back on the big screen, this time with Donald O'Connor in a comedy about a talking mule (voiced by Chill Wills), *Francis*, made at Universal. ZaSu was seen as flighty nurse Valerie Humpert in a psychiatric hospital ward. Based on a book by David Stern, *Francis* was the first entry in a seven-movie series cranked out by Universal, lasting until 1956. It would prove to be a great training ground for their up-and-coming actors (Mamie Van Doren, Julie Adams, Piper Laurie, David Janssen, Lori Nelson, Martha Hyer, and Clint Eastwood among them). ZaSu would repeat her characterization in the fifth entry (and stole the show), 1954's *Francis Joins the WACS*, this time as *Lieutenant* Humpert.

During the summer of 1950, ZaSu set out on an East Coast tour with the comedy *Post Road*. In early August, when she got off a plane at Boston's Logan International Airport with bags in hand, she hailed a cab and informed the driver, "Take me to the playhouse, please." Only she did not mention which playhouse. As the cab entered Boston's business district, the passenger suddenly inquired if the driver would mind if they stopped so she could run some errands. After completing said errands, the lady got back into the cab, calming saying, "Thank you very much. Now, please, let's go to the playhouse."

"Where to, lady?" the bewildered cabbie asked.

The lady fussed with her hat before replying, "Oh ... it's about fifty miles ... somewhere, up in New Hampshire."

So, off they drove, finally arriving at their destination, the Lakes Region Playhouse in Gilford, New Hampshire. As the driver unloaded her bags, the flustered actress thought to herself, "I hope he doesn't think I'm a little odd to take a cab for such a long trip.... But, after all, it was really the easiest and most sensible way to get from the airport to the theater, particularly since I had some shopping I needed to do."

The 105-mile trip cost a mere $45, and as she paid him, she demurely inquired if he would like to drive her to Skowhegan, Maine, the following week, to her next engagement. It is not known if he took her up on the offer.

ZaSu guested, along with Hugh Herbert, on Milton Berle's *Texaco Star Theater* on November 7, 1950. Performer Harold "Stumpy" Cromer explained in 2001 to Nancy Rosati what it was like working on Berle's show:

In *Francis* (1950), a movie about a talking army mule, ZaSu portrayed nurse Valerie Humpert, a role she repeated in 1954's *Francis Joins the WACS*.

That was a madhouse because everything was live then. It was like, "You sing and dance. Then we'll have some dialogue. When I say this, you say that." You had to remember what it was, and improv, because there was such a limited amount of time between sketches. Even if you weren't ready to end the sketch, the live Texaco commercial would come on and cut you off. That was wild. We had the pleasure to work with ZaSu Pitts, who was a wonderful comedienne, and lots of other people on the Milton Berle Show.

The year 1951 was an exciting time for the aging actress, as her daughter Ann, who had become the wife of John Reynolds, gave birth to son Ralf on October 12, making ZaSu an elated grandmother.

ZaSu had only one film released in 1952, a Western about railroading, *Denver and Rio Grande*. Her character was named Jane Dwyer, the camp cook who keeps trying to get Paul Fix, the train engineer, to propose to her. At one point she escapes a train wreck by crawling out of a coach window. Filmed in Technicolor, the cast included Sterling Hayden, Dean Jagger, and Edmond O'Brien. It was directed by her old friend Byron Haskin.

In the summer of 1952 she set out on another stock tour of *Ramshackle Inn*, along the East Coast. The advance director for this production was Miss Charva Chester, who had acted in *There Shall Be No Night* (1940). Chester was the stage manager on the shows *There Shall Be No Night*, *The Pirate*, *O Mistress Mine*, and *I Know My Love*, among others.

On January 20, 1953, ZaSu decided to give the Broadway stage another try with the comedy-mystery *The Bat*. She played an easily frightened maid, Lizzie Allen, to an aristocratic dowager, Miss Cornelia Van Gorder (played by Lucile Watson). Shepperd Strudwick also starred. Some of the funniest moments of the play occurred when ZaSu and Miss Watson consult a Ouija board. Perhaps the material was too dated for the time, but the show lasted only 23 performances, ending on February 7, 1953. It was another disappointing experience for Miss Pitts. During the show's brief run, she took up residence at the Hotel Pierre on 5th Avenue and remained in her hotel room much of the time, reading mystery novels, as the wintry weather raged outdoors.

Any sadness she may have been feeling quickly

An autographed photograph from the early 1950s.

turned to joy when she became a grandmother for the second time with the birth of John Stanford Reynolds II on May 28, 1953. Regarding her adored grandsons, she said at the time, "I'm the best babysitter in Hollywood."

During the summer months she toured in a third play written especially for her by George Batson, *Miss Private Eye*. The setting for the mystery-comedy was an antique shop. It opened at the Somerset Playhouse in Somerset, Massachusetts, and toured the East Coast.

ZaSu had returned to her home on the West Coast by the time Hollywood was celebrating its Golden Anniversary in 1953 (Hollywood had been incorporated as a sixth-class city on November 14, 1903). ZaSu was a special guest at a luncheon sponsored by the Hollywood Chamber of Commerce held at the Hollywood Roosevelt Hotel. Among other Hollywood pioneers of the silent screen present were Theda Bara, Mack Sennett, Jesse Lasky and Frances Marion. Missing was Louise Fazenda, who had been invited but was absent because of illness.

On April 3, 1954, television beckoned once again, and ZaSu guest-starred on *The Spike Jones Show*, appearing in the comedy sketch "The Charity Bazaar." The next day, on the April 4, she was seen as Aunt Laura on *General Electric Theater*'s "Pardon My Aunt," a comedy starring Richard Carlson and Claudia Barrett. On August 4 she starred on *Kraft Television Theatre* in a production of "The Happy Touch."

For many years the very versatile character actress Virginia Sale (1899–1992) performed monologues that she had written herself. She presented more than 25,000 performances onstage in theaters, before women's clubs, and in auditoriums, both large and small. She frequently gave performances with as many as two dozen different characters, and made the various costumes herself. In 1927 she ventured to Hollywood and began an illustrious film career. She appeared with ZaSu in two films, *The Lady's from Kentucky* (1939) and *Miss Polly* (1941).

Miss Sale committed most of the routines to memory and rarely wrote them down. Her husband, Sam Wren, was able to write shorthand and set down on paper a number of her most popular monologues. In 1952 the Samuel French play-publishing company released a collection of her monologues, *Virginia Sale's Americana*. The last sketch in the booklet was titled "An Imaginary Personal Appearance Act for ZaSu Pitts" and concerned the plain-looking comedienne's "private beauty secrets." In part, it ran:

> We owe it to ourselves and to our friends, to be beautiful.... I am going to demonstrate to you a new method toward beauty — my own discovery — a beautifier more vulgarly known as "mud." This mud, applied to the skin, removes blotches, blemishes, freckles, crow's-feet and wrinkles — and also purifies the breath! ... Rub it well into the face — always rub outward and upward.... Rub the mud into the face starting at the hair-line, passing the bridge of the nose, and down to the tip of the double chin. Then, from the lobe of the left ear to the lobe of the right ear. Be careful to keep your tongue in. Smear it on all parts of the face. Don't rub, ladies and gentlemen, just *smear*.... Allow it to dry, all the while fanning with a palm leaf.... With a damp towel, briskly remove the mud.... And, now, ladies and gentlemen, the final and most important step of the "ZaSu Pitts' Beauty Treatment" — the toning-process, with the violet ray.

Miss Sale's book of monologues remained one of the most popular of its type. Virginia Sale was the youngest sister of famed comedy monologist Charles "Chic" Sale. He was renowned for his routine called "The Specialist," concerning the expert building of an outdoor privy (outhouse). He appeared in full make-up as a bewhiskered old codger. He toured the country on the vaudeville stage, and eventually appeared in a number of full Broadway revues. He also forged a career in films as a character actor in both comedy shorts and features. In 1929 Mr. Sale published his monologue "The Specialist," which became a popular bestseller. One reviewer stated that Mr. Sale "seeks to portray generally known, but seldom mentioned, incidents in every day life." Charles Sale died at the age of 51 on November 7, 1936. His sister, Virginia, continued to perform until shortly before her death, at the age of 82, on August 23, 1992.

ZaSu's most outstanding appearance on television that year came on October 13 in "The Man Who Came to Dinner," on *The Best of Broadway* telecast. Bearded Monty Woolley recreated his 1939 Broadway star-making role of Sheridan Whiteside, the arrogant and vitriolic invalid confined to a wheelchair. A dinner guest, he falls and breaks his leg and becomes a permanent house guest. A stiff-backed nurse, Miss Preen, is hired to care for him. Miss Pitts was ideally cast as the much put-upon female member of the medical profession. Sarcastic Whiteside refers to her as "Miss Bedpan." In time, she begins to stand up for her profession. Typical of his insults to her was "My great-aunt Jennifer lived to be 102 and the day before she died, she looked better than you do now." Finally, Miss Preen has had enough and retorts, "I am not only quitting you, Mr. Whiteside—I am leaving the nursing profession. If Florence Nightingale had met you, she would have ended up marrying Jack the Ripper instead of founding the Red Cross." The telecast boasted an all-star cast, including Joan Bennett, Reginald Gardiner, Sylvia Field, Merle Oberon, Margaret Hamilton, Buster Keaton, Bert Lahr, and Howard St. John.

Miss Pitts was diagnosed with cancer, and her acting career was temporarily interrupted. As soon as she was able, she returned to work. On April 8, 1956, she gave a delightful performance as Miss Appleton, a snooping neighbor, on *The 20th Century Hour of Stars* program, supporting haughty Reginald Gardiner in an adaptation of "Mr. Belvedere."

It was around this time that ZaSu entered another phase of show business—recordings. She joined Reginald Gardiner and Nancy Walker for a musical parody of the great Broadway success *My Fair Lady* entitled *My Square Laddie*. The satire dealt with the hilarious misadventures of two Brooklynese taxi cab drivers trying to teach a proper Englishman how to speak with a New York accent. The clever recording was released on the Foremost label, with music by actor Max Showalter, and arrangements by Billy May and Eddie Dunstedter. The delightful parody was dubbed "one of the wackiest wax sessions ever recorded," and ZaSu and Nancy Walker were perfectly and hilariously matched.

The recorded musical parody was the closest that ZaSu ever came to fulfilling her longtime dream of appearing in a Broadway musical. If she had still been alive in the 1970s, when Broadway was presenting the revival of the 1925 hit *No, No, Nanette*, one can only speculate how wonderful she would have been had she reprised the role of Pauline, the constantly-complaining maid, which she played twice onscreen—for First-National in 1930 and for the 1940 RKO version. In the 1970 revival the role of Pauline was played by comedienne Pasty Kelly.

In the fall of 1955, members of the Screen Directors Guild joined forces to direct TV adaptations on a half-hour dramatic anthology series for NBC. On December 21, the *Screen Directors Playhouse*'s weekly episode was "The Silent Partner," co-starring ZaSu (as Selma), Joe. E. Brown and Buster Keaton. George Marshall, wearing his customary baseball cap, directed the episode. Marshall had directed four Thelma Todd/ZaSu Pitts comedy shorts for Roach in 1932.

A very intriguing credit almost came ZaSu's way in 1955. Charles Laughton, her old co-star in *Ruggles of Red Gap* (1935), thought of her for the highly dramatic role of Rachel Cooper in the movie he was about to direct, *The Night of the Hunter*. The role, that of the guardian/protector of two children being stalked by the murderous phony preacher Harry Powell (Robert Mitchum), would have been a late-in-life triumph for her, something she could have pulled off easily. She could have proved to her past naysayers that she could act if given the proper chance — and here was the chance. Unfortunately, Laughton's wife, Elsa Lanchester, nixed the idea and suggested Lillian Gish. This was Charles Laughton's (1899–1962) only directorial effort for the screen.

ZaSu's many fans may not have noticed that she was long past her 50th birthday, as she maintained her youthful figure and appearance and kept very active in films, stage, radio and television. Always on the go!

At the famed Pasadena Playhouse, which had been founded by Gilmor Brown in 1925, ZaSu starred in a production of *The Solid Gold Cadillac* in 1956.

On September 29, 1956, CBS-TV introduced a weekly half-hour sitcom, *Oh, Susanna!*, starring Gale Storm as Susanna Pomeroy, a social director on a cruise ship. The series was created by Lee Karson and produced by Hal Roach, Jr. ZaSu was featured as Elvira "Nugey" Nugent, the fluttery-fingered ship's beautician. Together they caused the ship's captain, Captain Huxley, constant aggravation. Huxley was portrayed by character actor Roy Roberts, and the mix of temperaments led to many hilarious situations. The sprightly Miss Storm was an irresistible one-woman tornado — singing, dancing, and using her many comedic talents. She and ZaSu made a delectable combination. Susanna, with the hectic help of her beauty-parlor pal, made life aboard the mythical cruise ship S.S. *Ocean Queen* highly amusing for the passengers, and immensely annoying for the captain.

Storm and Pitts' madcap misadventures presented ample opportunity to don diverse disguises, and they appeared as everything from old ladies to harem girls. At one point, all dressed up for a masquerade ball, ZaSu appeared in full regalia as Marie Antoinette. Occasional guest stars also appeared, including Boris Karloff playing a dual role.

ZaSu's regular appearances on television brought her a whole new legion of fans. Her TV work also won her the admiration and affection of her fellow cast members. It was a very satisfying time for the aging actress. At the time she told an interviewer:

ZaSu's weekly television appearances on the CBS sit-com (*Oh, Susanna!* aka *The Gale Storm Show*) during the 1956–59 seasons earned her a legion of new, younger fans. The series starred Gale Storm (right) and featured ZaSu as the cruise ship's addled manicurist, Elvira "Nugey" Nugent.

Gale Storm is as dear to me as my own daughter. And Hal Roach, Sr. still drops by the lot for a chat about the old days. He likes to tease me by saying I have not changed a bit. And I come back at him by asking if he would like to star me in one of his old bathing-beauty Keystone Kop series.... And the way they all take care of me.

The sparkle returned to her deep-blue eyes as she fondly recalled:

Oh, I am so lucky! My family, and my dear friends, all of whom stood by me so loyally when my acting seemed limited to playing maids, when I was so sick. And my dear husband, who, when we sold our big home in Brentwood and moved into a small apartment, put his arms around me and softly said, "Moms, the smaller the place, the closer we'll be." I'm a lucky, happy woman.

ZaSu often supplied her own transportation to the lot. She purchased an old car with a standard shift in order to exercise her weakened arm and side. Her co-workers recalled that she was sometimes an hour or so late for appointments when she drove herself. One noted, "She can't stand heavy traffic, and, like it or not, she'll pull up to the side of the road and patiently wait until the rush is over."

ZaSu appears to be mildly frightened by two fugitives in front of a cigar store in this scene from *The Gale Storm Show*.

One of the series' assistant directors, Bill Seider, recalled stories of how ZaSu flailed her arms about whenever she fluffed a line. "I'd worked with ZaSu before, so I was prepared, but poor Roy Roberts, he didn't know. So when I heard her blow a line during rehearsal, I yelled, 'Look out!' and ducked. Roy often got it square on the chest."

Co-star Gale Storm smilingly added, "We're all on to her now, and the second she fluffs a line, which she seldom does, we all begin ducking out of range. Imagine, she's the gentlest of people, but when she goofs, ZaSu Pitts starts swinging!"

ZaSu's co-workers took notice of the fact that she hardly ate a thing, and usually brought only a pint of buttermilk for her lunch. So Roy Roberts often took a sandwich to her dressing room. Others in the cast and crew would offer her a sandwich or a piece of homemade cake or pie. The series' star, Storm, commented, "We're only paying her back for all of the mothering she's given us. How she hovered over me when I was pregnant."

Oh, Susanna! was an audience pleaser and aired for 99 episodes during the 1956-57 seasons. In the fall of '58, the series switched networks, moving to ABC, and began daytime reruns. In addition, 26 first-run episodes aired in primetime on ABC during the 1959-60 seasons. A later name change found the series being called *The Gale Storm Show*. ZaSu would be nominated for an Emmy Award in 1959 for Best Supporting Actress (Continuing Character) in a Comedy Series.

During a hiatus from taping the television series, ZaSu found time to do another film, *This Could Be the Night*, for MGM in 1957. It was a black-and-white comedy directed by Robert Wise, and starring Anthony Franciosa (his film debut), Jean Simmons and Paul Douglas. ZaSu's role was Mrs. Katie Shea. Also in the cast were Joan Blondell and J. Carrol Naish.

Back at the Pasadena Playhouse, ZaSu portrayed the leading role in the comedy *The Curious Miss Caraway*. This play is noteworthy for being future Oscar-winner Gene Hackman's stage debut.

In 1958 Miss Pitts became active with the Republican Party and helped campaign for Senator Joseph Knowland in his race for the position of governor of California. During her campaign speeches, she alluded to the misuse of union dues of automotive workers. The United Auto Workers Union threatened a lawsuit, and she backed off. In 1960 she actively campaigned for Richard Nixon.

ZaSu spent much of her free time with her two grandsons, Ralf and John. She babysat for them and enjoyed making homemade candy for them. On occasion she took the boys to the set with her. Both boys displayed musical abilities, and grandma ZaSu encouraged them.

Ralf and John Reynolds grew up to become professional musicians, playing in several jazz groups. Ralf had the rare ability to play a musical washboard. At one time he headed a jazz band at Disneyland in Anaheim, California. Brother John handled similar duties at Disney's Florida location. They are both very capable at handling vocals, and both have taught music. Among the various groups they were associated with were the Palm Springs Yacht Club and Mora's Modern Rhythmists.

Miss Pitts could be justly proud of her talented grandsons. In her honor they formed a group known as the Reynolds Brothers Rhythm Rascals. They formed a recording company and released recordings on the "ZaSu" label, which also bore her picture.

ZaSu always had a loving relationship with her adopted son, Don. As a boy he attended the prestigious Webb School and graduated from Stanford in 1942. Said Gallery in 1996:

In *This Could Be the Night* (1957), ZaSu demonstrates her famous "fluttering fingers" technique.

In 1957, ZaSu returned to the stage. At the Pasadena Playhouse, she starred in a production of *The Curious Miss Caraway*. The young actress with her is Annette Milton.

> All my classmates were the children of movie stars, very wealthy parents or famous folks such as writers, directors, producers, and that sort of thing. We also had classes on Catalina Island, which I loved and where I now reside. When I was real young, I thought everyone was brought up like me. I was a lucky young man!

Living amongst the Hollywood colony, he developed close friendships with Shirley Temple and Elizabeth Taylor, among others. ZaSu was very proud when he served in the armed forces, and he looked very handsome in his uniform. He trained as a fighter pilot, transferring into the Counter Intelligence Corps, forerunner of the CIA. In Europe, from 1944 to 1947, he hunted war criminals.

It was inevitable that handsome Don Gallery would have a try at moviemaking. In a 1996 interview with Jimmy Bagley, he recalled, "Well, I never had much of a career, but I have been in more than 25 films. My first wife, Joyce Reynolds, was an actress under contract to Warner Brothers." They would appear together in *Janie* (1944), *Always Together* (1947) and *Wallflower* (1948). With Joan Leslie, he appeared in *Janie*'s follow-up, *Janie Gets Married* (1946), which is among his several bit parts; Don also did stints on the soap operas *The Young and the Restless* and *The Bold and the Beautiful*.

Don and Joyce later divorced. After his second marriage, to a lady named Patricia, they moved to Catalina and operated a jewelry business.

In 1959, although ZaSu's health was failing, she reported to MGM for the small role of Mrs. McGruder in *The Gazebo*. The film, a very funny black comedy, was directed by George Marshall, and starred Glenn Ford and Debbie Reynolds. In strong support were Carl Reiner, John McGiver, Doro Merande and Mabel Albertson. ZaSu's character of Mrs. McGruder has a problem of being tipsy most of the time. She is the wife of the wealthy prospective buyer of the mysterious gazebo. Coincidentally, Erich von Stroheim's son worked as assistant director on the film.

In 1960 Miss Pitts returned to the stage of the Pasadena Playhouse in a revival of John Patrick's heartwarming play *The Curious Savage*. ZaSu appeared as kindly Ethel Savage, a wealthy widow who decides to turn her inherited fortune into a "happiness fund" to assist people who could not afford to do the foolish things they had always dreamed of doing. The widow's benevolent plan meets with much objection from her three greedy stepchildren. The play's theme expressed the view that the greatest values in life are love and kindness to other human beings. It also made the point that being slightly eccentric can be healthy and downright enjoyable. When the play had originally opened on Broadway, critic Brooks Atkinson noted, "The leading character represents the female counter-part of philanthropic Mr. Deeds, the bucolic hick who gives away $20 million in *Mr. Deeds Goes to Town*," which starred Gary Cooper and was directed by Frank Capra.

On September 29, 1960, ABC premiered a new weekly half-hour sitcom, *Guestward Ho!* The series was based on a book by John Patrick. It told of a prosperous young couple from New York City, Bill and Babs Horton. The series starred Joanne Dru and Mark Miller, with Earle Hodgins as the ranch foreman, Lonesome. On May 11, 1961, ZaSu guest starred in an episode entitled "Lonesome's Gal."

In 1961 ZaSu returned to films in a low-budget production, *Teen-Age Millionaire*, released through United Artists, in which she was seen as Aunt Theodora to teenaged rock 'n' roll singer Jimmy Clanton.

A wistful portrait of ZaSu Pitts, painted by her grandson John Reynolds, a talented artist and musician.

A gallant trouper — ZaSu continued with her acting work even as her health worsened and her energy ebbed.

During her final years there were recurring bouts with cancer. "At first she refused treatment, then she changed her mind and finally took cobalt treatments," her friend Dorothy Fargo said in 1985. "She also went back to acting, but she didn't work as hard as she had before. And she moved to San Marino to be nearer her daughter." ZaSu subsequently underwent a number of serious surgeries.

In frail health, with her energy waning and in severe pain, she graciously agreed to star in a benefit for the Pasadena Playhouse, a production of the comedy *Everybody Loves*

Opal in 1962. The Playhouse was going through financial difficulties, and ZaSu wanted to help. It was a very demanding role, and taxed her determination and physical strength. Opal was a befuddled and kindly recluse who lived in a shack at the edge of the town's dumping ground. Daily, she rescued "treasures" that has been discarded and took them back to her shack in a little wagon.

The valiant Miss Pitts continued her acting work. With her health in rapid decline, it is amazing that she was able to appear in two more films. Her well-honed comedic skills were very much in evidence in her role of Olivia, a lovelorn and frustrated spinster housekeeper for a doctor and his wife. The spinster sleeps with a baseball bat under her pillow to ward off any would-be suitors. The comedy, *The Thrill of It All!* (1963), starred Doris Day and James Garner.

For the television detective series *Burke's Law*, ZaSu guest starred as Mrs. Bowie, another housekeeper, in an episode entitled "Who Killed Holly Howard?" The episode was not aired until September 20, 1963, more than two months after her death.

When Stanley Kramer began to round up every surviving classic screen comic to appear in his Cinerama spectacle *It's a Mad Mad Mad Mad World*, he prevailed upon the frail and ailing Miss Pitts to make a cameo appearance in a police station scene as a harried switchboard operator, Gertie. The prolific actress appears seated at the switchboard with only a few words of spoken dialog. The scene was shot in one day and marked her final screen appearance.

Her old Santa Cruz classmate and friend Dorothy Fargo phoned her almost every day. Then, one day, ZaSu's voice faltered as she softly said, "I won't be talking to you much longer. I think my menace has got me."

At her home in Pasadena, the pain became excruciating, and she was admitted to Good Samaritan Hospital on June 6, 1963, where she quietly passed away the following day.

Her many friends and fans mourned her loss. On Tuesday, June 12, ZaSu was laid to rest in the Our Lady of the Grotto section of Holy Cross Cemetery in Culver City, in a grave adjoining that of her friend Gary Cooper. About 100 friends and associates were present as the Rev. James P. Colberg celebrated a requiem mass for the beloved actress. Those in attendance, in addition to her family, were ex–co-workers Patsy Kelly, Gale Storm, and Virginia Grey, as well as Mr. and Mrs. Ronald Rea-

Though frail and ill, ZaSu Pitts delivered some very fine comedic moments in *The Thrill of It All*. Released in 1963, it was her last featured role in a film.

gan and Madge Meredith. Pallbearers were Admiral Robert Berry, John Dye, Cornwall Jackson, LeRoy Prinz and Hal Roach, Sr.

At the time of her passing, most of ZaSu Pitts' obituaries listed her age as 63. Actually, she was six years older, having been born in 1894, not 1900 as her studio biographies had reported through the years.

In April 1998 her hometown of Parsons, Kansas, under the assumption that the year marked the centennial of her birth, staged a two-day film festival in her honor. The event was under the joint sponsorship of the Labette Community College and the Parsons Art and Humanities Council. At the Henderson Gallery there was a special memorabilia display on her life and career. A very attractive program, containing a number of photographs of the honored guest, was distributed to those in attendance. Local historian Randy Roberts thoroughly researched and published a thirty-page booklet, *ZaSu Pitts in Parsons, Kansas*. Souvenirs of the festival included pin-on buttons and T-shirts bearing her likeness. There was also a candy-tasting party featuring several of ZaSu's favorite recipes. Another unique feature of the event was the handing out of special ZaSu Pitts masks for all to wear.

At the evening festivities on Friday, April 24, the silent feature *The Little Princess*, with Mary Pickford, was screened. On Saturday afternoon one of ZaSu's early silent screen comedies was viewed, and in the evening there was a screening of the 1924 classic silent screen drama *Greed*. The audience also had an opportunity to view Paramount's 1934 comedy *Mrs. Wiggs of the Cabbage Patch*, in which ZaSu romantically sparred with W.C. Fields.

The Pitts Film Festival was a resounding success and became an annual event through 2002.

The second annual celebration of the life and work of Miss Pitts was staged during April 23 and 24, 1999. On Friday evening there was a discussion of her work with Erich von Stroheim, followed by a screening of *The Wedding March*. The following day ZaSu's two musician grandsons, Ralf and John Reynolds, presented a musical program. In addition, an episode of the television series *The Gale Storm Show* was shown. Two of Miss Pitts' feature films were also screened: *Dames* (1934) and *The Ruggles of Red Gap* (1935).

The third annual Pitts Film Festival was planned for the weekend of April 28 and 29, 2000. A week before the festival,

ZaSu's final film appearance came in Stanley Kramer's spectacular all-star madcap comedy *It's a Mad Mad Mad Mad World*. As Gert, she appeared seated at the switchboard in the busy police station.

however, a tornado struck Parsons and destroyed 700 homes. The plucky Kansans persevered, and the festivities went on as scheduled. Special guest star Gale Storm was on hand and unveiled a ZaSu Pitts "Star of Fame" award at the Parsons Theater. During the celebration, three of Miss Pitts' films were screened: *Life with Father* (1947), *Francis Joins the WACS* (1954) and *It All Came True* (1940).

For the fourth annual film festival, staged on April 27 and 28, 2001, the emphasis was not only on ZaSu but another Kansas-born actress, Louise Brooks. Brooks had been born in Cherryvale on November 14, 1906, and was a dozen years younger than ZaSu. Brooks became a silent screen beauty noted for her bobbed hair and jet-black bangs. After much success onstage as a dancer, including appearances in both *George White's Scandals* and *The Ziegfeld Follies*, her film debut came in 1925 with *The Street of Forgotten Men*. Later she appeared in several films shot in Germany and created a sensation when she portrayed a vamp named Lulu. The 2001 festival was entitled "Lulu and ZaSu: Lust and Laughter."

Three of Brooks' most successful films were exhibited—*A Girl in Every Port* (1927), with live piano accompaniment by John Tibbets, *Beggars of Life* (1928) and *Pandora's Box* (1929). Three comedy shorts made by ZaSu and Thelma Todd also screened: *Catch as Catch Can* (1931), *Sneak Easily* (1932) and *One Track Minds* (1933). A live fashion show highlighted "Fashions of the Twenties."

The fifth film festival at Parsons was staged on April 26 and 27, 2002. This time the subject was "Screwball Comedy," and several features were screened. A number of Pitts/Todd comedies were shown, as well as the feature *Broadway Limited* (1941), co-starring ZaSu and Patsy Kelly.

Interest appeared to be waning, and, due mainly to a lack of volunteers to organize and stage the event, the festivities at Parsons were discontinued.

In the spring of 1994 the United States Postal Service announced the release of a set of ten commemorative postage stamps under the heading "Stars of the Silent Screen." Miss Pitts was one of the ten stars to be honored, with the others being Theda Bara, Clara Bow, Lon Chaney, Sr., Charles Chaplin, John Gilbert, Buster Keaton, the Keystone Kops, Harold Lloyd and Rudolph Valentino. Face value was set at 29 cents, and the caricatures of the ten honorees were supplied by theatrical artist Al Hirschfeld (1903–2003). He depicted ZaSu in a typical pose, with her hands prominently featured.

The site of the first-day issue was designated as San Francisco. The city of Santa Cruz, where Miss Pitts had spent her girlhood, applied as the site of the first-day issue of the stamps, but it was awarded to San Francisco. Though Santa Cruz's request was declined, residents there decided to conduct their own two-day festival in ZaSu's honor. The sponsors of the event were the City of Santa Cruz, the Downtown Association, the city's post office, and the History Museum of Santa Cruz County. It followed the release of the set of ten "Stars of the Silent Screen" stamps on April 27 in San Francisco by commencing the following day at 10:30 A.M.

From the steps of the post office, Santa Cruz mayor Scott Kennedy issued a proclamation declaring it "ZaSu Pitts Day." There were special first-day covers and cachet envelopes available, and more than 50,000 sheets of the stamp sets and nearly 7,000 envelopes were sold. The post master announced, "I didn't realize there were that many stamp collectors in town."

At 5:00 P.M. further festivities got underway in front of the post office on Front Street.

The emcee introduced special guests Don Gallery, the adopted son of Miss Pitts, as well as both her grandsons, Ralf and John Reynolds. All three were presented with copies of the special commemorative stamps. At 5:30 there was a free concert by a San Francisco band known as "the ZaSu Pitts Memorial Orchestra," with dancing lining the streets. (Formed in 1984 in San Francisco, the ZaSu Pitts Memorial Orchestra was a unique Big Band organization that featured female singer/dancers. They recorded several LPs, applying their Big Band sound to Motown and other contemporary pop songs.)

At 7:30 the crowd gathered at the nearby McPherson Center for Art and History for a screening of Von Stroheim's *Greed*. Musical accompaniment was supplied by Phil Collins, and Morton Marcus provided the commentary.

The festivities continued the following day. There was a ZaSu Pitts lookalike contest — with only two entrants. Santa Cruz horticulturist John Ghio presented his most recent variety of irises, which he named "the ZaSu Iris." It was a glorious bloom with salmon-colored petals and black cherry-colored edges. Miss Lori Holland, the winner of the ZaSu lookalike contest, was presented with a bouquet of ZaSu Irises. Local candy makers the Burkhart Co. prepared ZaSu Crème Bars, as well as ZaSu Peanut Brittle, both made from Miss Pitts' own recipes.

At 7:30 P.M. the group reassembled at the McPherson Center for Art and History for a screening of *Mrs. Wiggs of the Cabbage Patch*. As a special attraction, Ron Fields, the grandson of W.C. Fields, was present and introduced to the audience.

Santa Cruz historian Ross Gibson gave an address and also composed two musical selections in Miss Pitts' honor: "ZaSu's Lullaby — or the Jazz Baby's Dream," which was based on a dance routine she had done in a 1920 comedy short, and "ZaSu Pitts — The Girl with the Gingersnap Name." The lyrics for the latter song were:

> Hey you!
> Say, have you seen Zay-Zoo
> Or heard her say
> Oh, dear! Oh, my!
> I die from laughter
> And say why I'm after her
> Zay-Zoo Pitts
> Gives me the fits,
> The girl with the gingersnap name.
> Showing no mercy
> She'll drive me to the brink
> And worry too, when I am blue
> Until she strikes me — pink!
> She's just so dandy
> I crave her, like candy.
> The flavor of Zay-Zoo Pitts
> Gives me the fits,
> The Girl with
> The Gingersnap name!

A handout for the festival was a cut-out mask of ZaSu's familiar image. The event was a rousing success and created new fans for the long-deceased celebrity.

During the years of exhaustive research conducted in preparation for this book, including interviews with Miss Pitts' relatives, friends and co-workers, not a single negative comment was encountered—discounting one lone paragraph that appeared in a 1992 book authored by ex-sports announcer Guy LeBow. The supposed exposé book was titled *Are We on the Air? The Hilarious, Scandalous Confessions of a TV Pioneer*. In his text, LeBow related many awkward and embarrassing happenings he alleged had occurred to various celebrities.

After ZaSu divorced Tom Gallery, Tom moved to New York City and did some sports announcing during the early days of television. LeBow and Gallery were competitors in the field. LeBow accused Gallery of being anti-Semitic and made some disparaging remarks about ZaSu, whom he had never met. LeBow wrote:

> [Gallery's] only special distinction was that he had been married to the only screen actress actually barred by President Franklin D. Roosevelt from visiting Veteran's Hospitals during the war. This was ZaSu Pitts. Before she stopped, she had already traumatized injured veterans, lying blinded, maimed, and forever emotionally scarred, by telling them that their injuries had been for nothing—the United States should not be fighting the Germans.

The book was published by an obscure New York firm. All efforts to contact them, as well as the author, met with no success. The veracity to these absurd accusations remains doubtful. If it had been true, there certainly would have been some kind of report to the press, considering that the author claims that ZaSu was "the only screen actress barred" by Franklin Delano Roosevelt himself. That certainly would have been newsworthy if true, and would have been mentioned at least in some of the many biographies on the president. Readers of LeBow's book were given a vindictive, distorted image of ZaSu Pitts' loving and patriotic spirit.

When legendary stage and screen actress Dame Judith Anderson was asked who she considered to be the most "feminine" actress, without hesitation she replied, "ZaSu Pitts!" Actress Esther Muir, musing about the effects of stardom and her own lack of starring roles, said before her death in 1995, "A superstar is only as good as his or her last film, but character players like ZaSu Pitts could have gone on forever."

Although typecasting mainly limited her screen career to comedy, ZaSu Pitts still managed to perform some important dramatic roles. It is, however, her comic roles that most still remember, thanks to the pathos which she so perfectly expressed. In her personal life she was a caring and giving person, so it is fitting that ZaSu Pitts will long be remembered not only for her expressive hands, but also for her generous heart.

FILMOGRAPHY

Shorts

Uneasy Money (1917). **Director:** W.W. Beaudine [William Beaudine]. **Writer:** Jack Cunningham. **Cast:** William [Billy] Franey, Milburn Moranti [Morante], Lillian Peacock, ZaSu Pitts. Universal Film Manufacturing Company (Joker Comedy). **Release Date:** June 2, 1917.

Tillie of the Nine Lives (1917). Mutual Film Corporation. **Release Date:** June 19, 1917.

A Desert Dilemma (1917). **Director:** William Beaudine. **Cast:** ZaSu Pitts, Milburn Morante. Universal Film Manufacturing Company. **Release Date:** June 23, 1917.

His Fatal Beauty (1917). **Director:** William Beaudine. **Writer:** Jack Cunningham. **Cast:** William [Billy] Franey, ZaSu Pitts, Lillian Peacock, Milburn Moranti [Morante]. Universal Film Manufacturing Company (Joker Comedy). **Release Date:** June 25, 1917.

He Had 'Em Buffaloed (1917). **Director:** William Beaudine. **Writer:** C.B. Hoadley (scenario). **Cast:** William [Billy] Franey, ZaSu Pitts, Lillian Peacock, Milburn Moranti [Morante], Bobbie Mack. Universal Film Manufacturing Company (Joker Comedy). **Release Date:** July 21, 1917.

Canning the Cannibal King (1917). **Director:** William Beaudine. **Writers:** C.B. Hoadley (scenario), Charles J. Wilson (story). **Cast:** William [Billy] Franey, ZaSu Pitts, Lillian Peacock, Milburn Moranti [Morante], Bobbie Mack. Universal Film Manufacturing Company (Joker Comedy). **Release Date:** July 28, 1917.

The Battling Bellboy (1917). **Director:** William Beaudine. **Writer:** Jack Cunningham (scenario). **Cast:** William [Billy] Franey, ZaSu Pitts, Lillian Peacock, Milburn Moranti [Morante], Johnnie Cooke [John Cook], Bobbie Mack. Universal Film Manufacturing Company (Joker Comedy). **Release Date:** August 2, 1917.

O-My the Tent Mover (1917). **Director:** William Beaudine. **Writers:** Tom Gibson (scenario), E.M. McCall (story). **Cast:** William [Billy] Franey, ZaSu Pitts, Lillian Peacock, Milburn Moranti [Morante], Eddie Baker. Universal Film Manufacturing Company (Joker Comedy). **Release Date:** August 11, 1917.

Behind the Map (1917). **Director:** William Beaudine. **Writers:** William Beaudine (story), Tom Gibson (scenario). **Cast:** William [Billy] Franey, ZaSu Pitts, Lillian Peacock, Eddie Baker, Milburn Morante. Universal Film Manufacturing Company (Joker Comedy). **Release Date:** August 25, 1917.

Why They Left Home (1917). **Director:** William Beaudine. **Writer:** C.B. Hoadley (scenario). **Cast:** William [Billy] Franey, ZaSu Pitts, Lillian Peacock, Milburn Morante, Burton Law, Bobby Mack. Universal Film Manufacturing Company (Joker Comedy). **Release Date:** August 27, 1917. **Notes:** This short's original title was *Why Harry Left Home.*

A Dog's Life (1918). **Director/Writer/Producer:** Charles Chaplin. **Cinematography:** R.H. [Roland] Totheroh. **Editing:** Charles Chaplin (uncredited). **Production Design:** Charles D. Hall. **Assistant Director:** Charles Reisner. **Second Camera Operator:** Jack Wilson. **Cast:** Charles Chaplin (Tramp), Edna Purviance (Bar Singer), Syd Chaplin (Lunchwagon Owner), Henry Bergman (Unemployed Man/Dancehall Lady), Charles Reisner (Employment Agency Clerk), Albert Austin (Crook), Tom Wilson (Policeman), M.J. McCarthy (Unemployed Man), Mel Brown (Unemployed Man), Charles Force (Unemployed Man), Bert Appling (Unemployed Man), Thomas Riley (Unemployed Man), Slim Cole (Unemployed Man), Ted Edwards (Unemployed Man), Louis Fitzroy (Unemployed Man), Dave Anderson (Unemployed Man), Granville Redmond (Dancehall Proprietor), Minnie Chaplin (Dancehall Dramatic Lady), Alf Reeves (Man), N. Tahbel (Hot Tamale Man), Rob Wagner (Man), L.S. McVey (Musician), J.F. Parker (Musician), Bud Jamison (Crook), Park Jones (Man), James T. Kelley (Man at Hot Dog Stand), Janet Miller Sully (Woman), Loyal Underwood (Man), Billy White (Man), Dog (Scraps, a Thoroughbred Mongrel), ZaSu Pitts (bit part, scenes deleted). First National Pictures. **Release Date:** April 14, 1918. **Notes:** This was Chaplin's first short for First National. Advertised as Chaplin's "First Million Dollar Picture," it was also the first time Chaplin worked with his brother Syd onscreen.

Who's Your Wife? (1918). **Director:** Allen Curtis. **Writer:** Tom Gibson (scenario). **Cast:** Billy Franey, ZaSu Pitts, Gale Henry, Milton Sims, Charles Haefeli. Nestor Film Company/Universal Film Manufacturing Company. **Release Date:** May 27, 1918.

The Pie Eyed Piper (1918). **Director:** William Beaudine. **Writer:** C.B. Hoadley (scenario). **Cast:** ZaSu Pitts, William [Billy] Franey, Milburn Moranti [Morante], Lillian Peacock, Bobbie Mack. Universal Film Manufacturing Company/Nestor Film Company. **Release Date:** August 19, 1918.

Let's Do Things (1931). **Director/Producer:** Hal Roach. **Song:** "Them There Eyes" (Maceo Pinkard, William Tracey, Doris Tauber), performed by Thelma Todd and Male Sextet, including Donald Novis. **Cast:** ZaSu Pitts (ZaSu Pitts), Thelma Todd (Thelma Todd), George Byron (Milton), Jerry Mandy (Doctor Mandy), Charlie Hall (Waiter), Maurice Black (Nightclub Manager, uncredited), Baldwin Cooke (Nightclub Patron, uncredited), Mickey Daniels (Nightclub Bellhop, uncredited), Edward Dillon (Music Store Manager, uncredited), Bill Elliott (Music Store Customer, uncredited), Dorothy Granger (Nightclub Dancer, uncredited), Mary Kornman (Nightclub Cigarette Girl, uncredited), Gertrude Messinger (Nightclub Dancer, uncredited), Donald Novis (Singer, uncredited), Charley Rogers (Drunk Nightclub Customer, uncredited), David Sharpe (Dancer, uncredited), Leroy Shield (Singer, uncredited). **Release Date:** June 6, 1931. Hal Roach Studios Inc./Metro-Goldwyn-Mayer (MGM). 27 min.

Catch as Catch Can (1931). **Director:** Marshall Neilan. **Writer:** H.M. Walker. **Producer:** Hal Roach. **Music:** Leroy Shield. **Cinematography:** Art Lloyd. **Editing:** Richard Currier. **Recording Engineer:** Elmer Raguse. **Cast:** ZaSu Pitts (ZaSu), Thelma Todd (Thelma), Guinn Williams (Strangler Sullivan), Reed Howes (Harry), Billy Gilbert (Ring Announcer, uncredited), Bud Duncan (Drunk, uncredited), Sammy Brooks (Little Wrestling Match Referee, uncredited), Edward Dillon (Wrestling Match Spectator, uncredited), Frank Alexander (Fat Man in Audience, uncredited), Ivan Linow (Strangler's

Wrestling Opponent, uncredited), Kit Guard (uncredited). **Release Date:** August 22, 1931. Hal Roach Studios Inc./Metro-Goldwyn-Mayer (MGM). 20 min.

The Pajama Party (1931). **Director/Producer:** Hal Roach. **Writer:** H.M. Walker. **Music:** Leroy Shield. **Cinematography:** Walter Lundin. **Editing:** Richard Currier. **Recording Engineer:** Elmer Raguse. **Cast:** ZaSu Pitts (ZaSu), Thelma Todd (Thelma), Elizabeth Forrester (Mrs. Van Dyke), Eddie Dunn (Eddie), Donald Novis (Jimmy), Lucien Prival (the Baron), Billy Gilbert (Butler, uncredited), Sydney Jarvis (Party Guest, uncredited), Charlie Hall (Drunk Party Guest, uncredited). **Release Date:** October 3, 1931. Hal Roach Studios Inc./Metro-Goldwyn-Mayer (MGM). 20 min.

War Mamas (1931). **Director:** Marshall Neilan. **Producer:** Hal Roach. **Music:** Leroy Shield. **Cast:** Thelma Todd (Thelma), ZaSu Pitts (ZaSu), Charles Judels (German Major), Allan Lane (Doughboy), Guinn "Big Boy" Williams (Doughboy), Stuart Holmes (German General), Carrie Daumery (Countess), Harry Schultz (German), Charlie Hall (Doughboy), Blanche Payson (Head Nurse), Adrienne D'Ambricourt (Countess's Maid, uncredited), William J. O'Brien (Heinrich, uncredited), William Yetter Sr. (German Guard, uncredited). **Release Date:** November 14, 1931. Hal Roach Studios Inc./Metro-Goldwyn-Mayer (MGM). 21 min.

On the Loose (1931). **Director/Producer:** Hal Roach. **Writers:** Hal Roach (story), H.M. Walker (writer). **Music:** Leroy Shield. **Cinematography:** Len Powers. **Editing:** Richard C. Currier. **Cast:** ZaSu Pitts (ZaSu), Thelma Todd (Thelma), John Loder (Mr. Loder), Claud Allister (Mr. Loder's Friend), William [Billy] Gilbert (Pierre), Gordon Douglas (Fun House Worker, uncredited), Otto Fries (Bully, uncredited), Oliver Hardy (New Suitor, uncredited), Stan Laurel (New Suitor, uncredited), Charlie Hall (Shooting Gallery Attendant, uncredited), Jack Hill (Fun House Worker, uncredited). **Release Date:** December 26, 1931. Hal Roach Studios Inc./Metro-Goldwyn-Mayer (MGM). 20 min.

Seal Skins (1932). **Directors:** Morey Lightfoot, Gil Pratt. **Writer:** H.M. Walker. **Producer:** Hal Roach. **Music:** Leroy Shield. **Cinematography:** Len Powers. **Editing:** Richard Currier. **Recording Engineer:** Elmer Raguse. **Cast:** ZaSu Pitts, Thelma Todd, Charlie Hall (uncredited), Leo Willis, Billy Gilbert (uncredited), Buddy MacDonald (Office Boy), Frank Austin (uncredited), Charles Gemora (Jocko the Boxing Gorilla, uncredited), Tiny Sandford (Jocko's Keeper, uncredited), Clifford Thompson (uncredited). **Release Date:** February 6, 1932. Hal Roach Studios Inc./Metro-Goldwyn-Mayer (MGM). 21 min.

Red Noses (1932). **Director:** James W. Horne. **Writer:** H.M. Walker. **Producer:** Hal Roach. **Music:** Leroy Shield. **Cinematography:** Art Lloyd. **Editing:** Richard Currier. **Recording Engineer:** James Greene. **Cast:** ZaSu Pitts (Miss Pitts), Thelma Todd (Miss Todd), Blanche Payson (Dr. Payson), Wilfred Lucas (Mr. Lucas), Billy Gilbert (Customer), Lyle Tayo (Physical Therapist), Bobby Burns (Secretary, uncredited). **Release Date:** March 19, 1932. Hal Roach Studios Inc./Metro-Goldwyn-Mayer (MGM). 21 min.

Strictly Unreliable (1932). **Director:** George Marshall. **Writer:** H.M. Walker (dialogue). **Producer:** Hal Roach (uncredited). **Music:** Leroy Shield (uncredited). **Cinematography:** Len Powers. **Editing:** Richard Currier. **Recording Engineer:** James Greene. **Cast:** ZaSu Pitts (Pitts), Thelma Todd (Miss Thelma Todd), Charlotte Nemo (Mrs. Hawkins), Bud Jamieson [Jamison] (Bud), Billy Gilbert (the Actor), Charley [Charlie] Hall (the Stage Manager), Symona Boniface (the Actress, uncredited), Charles Williams (Billy Freeman, uncredited). **Release Date:**

April 30, 1932. Hal Roach Studios Inc./ Metro-Goldwyn-Mayer (MGM). 20 min.

The Old Bull (1932). **Director:** George Marshall. **Writer:** H.M. Walker (dialogue). **Producer:** Hal Roach (uncredited). **Music:** Leroy Shield (uncredited). **Cinematography:** Art Lloyd. **Editing:** Richard Currier. **Recording Engineer:** James Greene. **Cast:** ZaSu Pitts (ZaSu), Thelma Todd (Thelma), Otto Fries (Mr. Bailey), Bobby Burns (Farmhand, uncredited). **Release Date:** June 4, 1932. Hal Roach Studios Inc./Metro-Goldwyn-Mayer (MGM). 19 min.

Show Business (1932). **Director:** Jules White. **Producer:** Hal Roach. **Music:** Leroy Shield. **Editing:** Richard C. Currier. **Cast:** Thelma Todd (Thelma), ZaSu Pitts (ZaSu), Anita Garvin (Anita Garvin), Monte Collins (Collins), Paulette Goddard (Blonde Train Passenger, uncredited), Bobby Burns (Train Passenger, uncredited), James P. Burtis (Policeman, uncredited), Charlie Hall (Train Passenger, uncredited). **Release Date:** August 20, 1932. Hal Roach Studios Inc./ Metro-Goldwyn-Mayer (MGM). 20 min.

Alum and Eve (1932). **Director:** George Marshall. **Writer:** H.M. Walker (uncredited). **Producer:** Hal Roach (uncredited). **Music:** Leroy Shield (uncredited). **Cinematography:** Hap Depew. **Editing:** Richard Currier. **Recording Engineer:** James Greene. **Cast:** ZaSu Pitts (ZaSu), Thelma Todd (Thelma), James Morton (Policeman), Almeda Fowler (Nurse), Otto Fries (Doctor, uncredited), Bobby Burns (Hospital Patient, uncredited), Ernie Alexander (Intern, uncredited). **Release Date:** September 24, 1932. Hal Roach Studios Inc./Metro-Goldwyn-Mayer (MGM). 19 min.

The Soilers (1932). **Director:** George Marshall. **Producer:** Hal Roach (uncredited). **Music:** Leroy Shield (uncredited). **Cinematography:** Hap Depew. **Editing:** Richard Currier. **Sound Engineer:** James Greene. **Cast:** ZaSu Pitts (ZaSu), Thelma Todd (Thelma), James C. Morton (Judge J.A. Morton), Bud Jamieson [Jamison] (Detective Jamison), Charlie Hall (Elevator Operator, uncredited), William J. O'Brien (Bald Juror, uncredited), Ernie Alexander (Maintenance Man, uncredited), Sam Lufkin (Courtroom Policeman, uncredited), George Marshall (Helpful Bystander, uncredited). **Release Date:** October 29, 1932. Hal Roach Studios Inc./Metro-Goldwyn-Mayer (MGM). 18 min.

Sneak Easily (1932). **Director:** Gus Meins. **Producer:** Hal Roach. **Cinematography:** Art Lloyd. **Editing:** Richard C. Currier. **Recording Engineer:** James Greene. **Stock Music:** Leroy Shield (uncredited). **Cast:** Thelma Todd (Miss Thelma Todd, Attorney for the Defense), ZaSu Pitts (Miss ZaSu Pitts, Woman of the Jury), Billy Gilbert (Attorney for the Prosecution), James C. Morton (Presiding Judge), Bobby Burns (Professor Austin), Rolfe Sedan (Juryman), Harry Bernard (Courtroom Guard), Charlie Hall (Page), Billy Bletcher (Police Radio Announcer, uncredited). **Release Date:** December 10, 1932. Hal Roach Studios Inc./ Metro-Goldwyn-Mayer (MGM). 17 min.

Asleep in the Feet (1933). **Director:** Gus Meins. **Producer:** Hal Roach. **Music:** Leroy Shield. **Editing:** Louis McManus. **Cast:** Thelma Todd (Thelma), ZaSu Pitts (ZaSu), Billy Gilbert (Mr. Gilbert), Eddie Dunn (Sailor), Anita Garvin (Dance Hall Hostess), Kay Lavelle (Landlady), Nelson McDowell (Police Officer, uncredited), Julia Griffith (Female Police Officer, uncredited), Nora Cecil (Female Police Officer, uncredited), Tiny Ward (Dance Hall Patron, uncredited). **Release Date:** January 21, 1933. Hal Roach Studios Inc./Metro-Goldwyn-Mayer (MGM). 19 min.

Maids a la Mode (1933). **Director:** Gus Meins. **Producer:** Hal Roach. **Music:** Leroy

Shield. **Editing:** Louis McManus. **Cast:** ZaSu Pitts (Miss Pitts), Thelma Todd (Miss Todd), Billy Gilbert (Von Smaltz), Cissy Fitzgerald (Mrs. Von Eckterhorse), Charlie Hall (Party Guest, uncredited), Mary Kornman (Model, uncredited), Harry Bernard (Cop, uncredited), Kay Deslys (Dolores Deslys, uncredited), Marvin Hatley (Pianist, uncredited), Sydney Jarvis (Furniture Man, uncredited), Leo White (Andre, uncredited). **Release Date:** March 4, 1933. Hal Roach Studios Inc./Metro-Goldwyn-Mayer (MGM). 18 min.

The Bargain of the Century (1933). **Director:** Charles Parrott [Charley Chase]. **Producer:** Hal Roach. **Music:** Leroy Shield (uncredited). **Cinematography:** Art Lloyd. **Editing:** Jack Ogilvie. **Recording Engineer:** James Greene. **Cast:** ZaSu Pitts, Thelma Todd, Billy Gilbert (Captain Schmaltz), James Burtis (Officer Butterworth), Frank Alexander (Elmer, uncredited), Fay Holderness (Elmer's Wife, uncredited), Harry Bernard (Lieutenant Finnegan, uncredited), May Wallace (Bargain Shopper, uncredited). **Release Date:** April 8, 1933. Hal Roach Studios Inc./Metro-Goldwyn-Mayer (MGM). 20 min. **Notes:** This short's working title was *The Island of Lost Heels.*

One Track Minds (1933). **Director:** Gus Meins. **Producer:** Hal Roach. **Music:** Leroy Shield. **Cinematography:** Hap Depew. **Editing:** Louis McManus. **Cast:** ZaSu Pitts, Thelma Todd, Billy Gilbert (Train Conductor), Lucien Prival (Von Sternheim), Jack Clifford (Deaf Beekeeper Passenger), Sterling Holloway (Salesman), Billy Bletcher (Train Passenger, uncredited), George "Spanky" McFarland (Spanky, uncredited), Charlie Hall (Train Passenger, uncredited), Eddie Tamblyn (Train Passenger, uncredited). **Release Date:** May 20, 1933. Hal Roach Studios Inc./Metro-Goldwyn-Mayer (MGM). 20 min.

Feature Films

Rebecca of Sunnybrook Farm (1917). **Director:** Marshall Neilan. **Writers:** Frances Marion (writer), Charlotte Thompson, Kate Douglas Wiggin (play), Kate Douglas Wiggin (novel). **Cinematography:** Walter Stradling. **Assistant Director:** Dudley Blanchard. **Cast:** Mary Pickford (Rebecca Randall), Eugene O'Brien (Adam Ladd), Helen Jerome Eddy (Hannah Randall), Charles Ogle (Mr. Cobb), Marjorie Daw (Emma Jane Perkins), Mayme Kelso (Jane Sawyer), Jane Wolff [Wolfe] (Mrs. Randall), Josephine Crowell (Miranda Sawyer), Jack McDonald (Reverend Jonathan Smellie), Violet Wilkey (Minnie Smellie), Frank Turner (Mr. Simpson), Kate Toncray (Mrs. Simpson), Emma Gordes (Clara Belle Simpson), Milton Berle, Wesley Barry, ZaSu Pitts (uncredited bits). Mary Pickford Company/Artcraft Pictures Corporation. **Release Date:** September 22, 1917. 78 min. **Notes:** This feature was filmed on location in Pleasanton, California. *Rebecca of Sunnybrook Farm* has been filmed at least three other times — in 1932, 1938 (starring Shirley Temple) and 1978 (for television). Edith Taliaferro starred as Rebecca in the first Broadway production in 1910.

'49-'17 (1917). **Director:** Ruth Ann Baldwin. **Writers:** William Wallace Cook (story "The Old West Per Contract"), Ruth Ann Baldwin (scenario). **Cinematography:** S.S. Norton [Stephen S. Norton]. **Cast:** Joseph Girard (Judge J.R. Brand), Leo Pierson (Tom Reeves, a.k.a. Tom Robbins), William J. Dyer (J. Gordon Castle), [Mattie] Martha Witting ("Ma" Bobbett), George Pearce (Ezra "Pa" Bobbett), Jean Hersholt (Gentleman Jim Raynor), Donna Drew (Peggy Bobbett), Harry L. Rattenberry (Colonel Hungerford), Bud Osborne (Cowboy Pitchman), Phyllis Haver (Young Bee Adams), ZaSu Pitts (Party Guest), Lon Poff (Bald-Headed Wrangler).

Universal Film Manufacturing Company (A Butterfly Picture). **Release Date:** October 15, 1917. 61 min. **Notes:** This is acknowledged as the first Western to be directed by a woman. Baldwin, who was married to '*49-'17* star Leo Pierson, directed eleven other films in 1917 before concentrating exclusively on her writing.

The Little Princess (1917). **Director:** Marshall Neilan. **Writers:** Frances Hodgson Burnett (novel), Frances Marion (writer). **Producer:** Mary Pickford. **Cinematography:** Charles Rosher, Walter Stradling. **Production Design:** Wilfred Buckland. **Assistant Directors:** Nat G. Deverich, Howard Hawks (uncredited). **Cast:** Mary Pickford (Sara Crewe), Norman Kerry (Captain Richard Crewe), Katherine Griffith (Miss Minchin), Ann Schaefer (Amelia Minchin), ZaSu Pitts (Becky), William E. Lawrence (Ali-Baba), Theodore Roberts (Cassim), Gertrude Short (Ermigarde), Gustav von Seyffertitz (Mr. Carrisford), Loretta Blake (Lavinia), George McDaniel (Ram Dass), Josephine Hutchinson, Edythe Chapman, Joan Marsh (uncredited bits). Mary Pickford Company/Artcraft Pictures Corporation. **Release Date:** November 11, 1917. 62 min. **Notes:** There have been at least seven other versions of *The Little Princess*, the most popular being Shirley Temple's 20th Century–Fox vehicle in 1939. In that version, Sybil Jason played Becky. Burnett's novel was adapted first as a play, *The Little Princess*, which opened in New York on January 14, 1903. Burnett is also the author of the classics *Little Lord Fauntleroy* and *The Secret Garden*.

A Modern Musketeer (1917). **Director:** Allan Dwan. **Writers:** Allan Dwan (writer), F.R. Lyle Jr. (story "D'Artagnan of Kansas"). **Producer:** Douglas Fairbanks. **Cinematography:** Victor Fleming. **Cast:** Douglas Fairbanks (Ned Thacker), Marjorie Daw (Dorothy Dodge, a.k.a. Moraine), Kathleen Kirkham (Mrs. Dodge, a.k.a. Moraine), Frank Campeau (Chin-de-dah), Eugene Ormonde (Forrest Vandeteer, a.k.a. Raymond Peters), Tully Marshall (James Brown, a.k.a. Philip Marden), Edythe Chapman (Mrs. Thacker), ZaSu Pitts (uncredited). Douglas Fairbanks Pictures Corp./Artcraft Pictures Corporation. **Release Date:** December 30, 1917. 35 min./65 min. **Notes:** Filmed on location at Canyon de Chelly National Monument, Chinle, Arizona, and Grand Canyon National Park in Arizona, the picture's original running time was 65 minutes. All that remains today, released on Grapevine Video, is half— about three reels.

Good Night, Paul (1918). **Director:** Walter Edwards. **Writers:** Charles Dickson (story), Julia Crawford Ivers (adaptation), Roland Oliver (story). **Cinematography:** James C. Van Trees. **Cast:** Constance Talmadge (Mrs. Richard), Norman Kerry (Richard Landers), Harrison Ford (Paul Boudeaux), John Steppling (Batiste Boudeaux), Beatrice Van (Rose Hartley), Rosita Marstini (Madame Julie), ZaSu Pitts. Select Pictures Corporation (Select Star Series). **Release Date:** June 20, 1918. 50 min.

How Could You, Jean? (1918). **Director:** William Desmond Taylor. **Writers:** Eleanor Hoyt Brainerd (novel), Frances Marion (scenario). **Producer:** Mary Pickford. **Cinematography:** Charles Rosher. **Assistant Director:** Frank Richardson. **Cast:** Mary Pickford (Jean Mackaye), Casson Ferguson (Ted Burton Jr.), Spottiswoode Aitken (Rufus Bonner), Herbert Standing (Burton Sr.), Fanny Midgley (Mrs. Bonner), Larry Peyton (Oscar), ZaSu Pitts (Oscar's Sweetheart), Mabelle Harvey [Maie B. Havey] (Susan Cooper), Lucille Ward (Mrs. Kate Morley), Emma Gerdes [Gordes] (Morley Child), Wesley Barry (Morley Child), Burwell Hamrick (Morley Child), Althea Worthley (Morley Child), Dorothy Rosher [Joan

Marsh] (Morley Child), Jack Herbert (Morley Child), Valeria Traxler (Morley Child). Mary Pickford Company/Artcraft Pictures Corporation/Famous Players–Lasky Corporation. **Release Date:** June 30, 1918.

A Society Sensation (1918). **Director:** Paul Powell. **Writers:** Perley Poore Sheehan (story "The Borrowed Duchess"), Hope Loring, Paul Powell (scenario). **Cinematography:** E.G. Ullman. **Cast:** Carmel Myers (Sydney Parmelee), Rudolpho De Valentina [Rudolph Valentino] (Dick Bradley), Lydia Yeamans Titus (Mrs. Jones), Alfred Allen (Capt. Parmelee), Fred Kelsey (Jim), ZaSu Pitts (Mary), Harold Goodwin (Timmy). Universal Film Manufacturing Company (Bluebird Photoplays). **Release Date:** September 23, 1918. 24 min./50 min. **Notes:** This was a Universal "Bluebird" production. At Universal, a Red Feather production was for low-budget programmers, then came Bluebirds, which were for mainstream audiences, followed by the prestige pictures, called Jewels. *A Society Sensation* originally ran as a feature at 50 minutes; when it was re-released in 1924, it had been cut down to 24 minutes, emphasizing Valentino's role. By that time, however, director Paul Powell had been blacklisted (for trying to organize a directors' union), so his name was replaced on the reissue prints with that of actor/director Edmund Mortimer, who had nothing to do with the film.

The Talk of the Town (1918). **Director:** Allen Holubar. **Writers:** Allen Holubar (scenario), Harold Vickers (story "Discipline of Ginevra"). **Cinematography:** Fred Granville. **Cast:** Dorothy Phillips (Genevra French), George Fawcett (Major French), Clarissa Selwynne (Aunt Harriet), ZaSu Pitts, William Stowell (Lawrence Tabor), Lon Chaney (Jack Lanchome), Gloria Joy (Genevra, age 5), Norman Kerry, Una Fleming (Dancer), George Lewis, Charles Hill Mailes, William Burgess. Universal Film Manufacturing Company (A Universal Special Attraction). **Release Date:** September 28, 1918.

A Lady's Name (1918). **Director:** Walter Edwards. **Writers:** Cyril Harcourt (play), Julia Crawford Ivers (scenario). **Cinematography:** James C. Van Trees. **Cast:** Constance Talmadge (Mabel Vere), Harrison Ford (Noel Corcoran), Emory Johnson (Gerald Wantage), Vera Doria (Maud Bray), James Farley (Flood), Fred Huntley (Adams), John Steppling (Bird), Truman Van Dyke (Bentley), Lillian Leighton (Mrs. Haines), ZaSu Pitts (Emily), Emma Gerdes (Margaret). Select Pictures Corporation. **Release Date:** December 10, 1918. 50 min. **Notes:** Harcourt's *A Lady's Name* played on Broadway in 1916, running 56 performances. The cast included Ruth Draper, Beryl Mercer and W. Graham Brown.

The Greatest Thing in Life (1918). **Director/Producer:** D.W. Griffith. **Writers:** Lillian Gish (story), Captain Victor Marier [D.W. Griffith, Stanner E.V. Taylor] (writer). **Cinematography:** G.W. Bitzer. **Editing:** James Smith. **Special Effects:** Hendrik Sartov. **Camera Operator:** Karl Brown. **Still Photographer:** Hendrik Sartov. **Cast:** David Butler (Mr. Le Bebe), Lillian Gish (Jeannette Peret), Robert Harron (Edward Livingston), Peaches Jackson (Miss Peaches), Adolph Lestina (Leo Peret), Elmo Lincoln (the American Soldier), Edward Peil Sr. (the German Officer), Kate Bruce (Jeannette's Aunt), Carol Dempster (uncredited dancer), Ernest Butterworth, Lucille Young, Fred Malatesta (uncredited), ZaSu Pitts (scenes deleted). Artcraft Pictures Corporation. **Release Date:** December 22, 1918. 70 min. **Notes:** This film's working title was *The Cradle of Souls*. ZaSu's scenes were reportedly cut because of her resemblance to star Lillian Gish.

As the Sun Went Down (1919). **Director:** E. Mason Hopper. **Writer:** George D. Baker (play/screenplay). **Cinematography:** William Thompson. **Cast:** Edith Storey (Col. Billy), Lewis J. Cody [Lew Cody] (Faro Bill), Harry S. Northrup (Arbuthnot), William Brunton (Albert Atherton), F.A. Turner (Gerald Morton), Frances Burnham (Mabel Morton), ZaSu Pitts (Sal Sue), F.E. Spooner (Gin Mill Jack), Alfred Hollingsworth (Pizen Ike), Vera Lewis (Ike's Wife), George W. Berrell (Piety Pete), Pop Taylor (Miner), Cal Dugan (Miner). Metro Pictures Corporation. **Release Date:** February 10, 1919.

Men, Women, and Money (1919). **Director:** George Melford. **Writers:** Beulah Marie Dix (scenario), Cosmo Hamilton (story). **Cinematography:** Paul P. Perry. **Assistant Director:** Louis Howland. **Cast:** Ethel Clayton (Marcel Middleton), James Neill (Parker Middleton), Jane Wolfe (Sara Middleton), Lew Cody (Cleveland Buchanan), Sylvia Ashton (Aunt Hannah), Irving Cummings (Julian Chadwick), Winifred Greenwood (Noel Parkton), Edna Mae Cooper (Miss Cote), Leslie Stewart Jr. [Leslie Stuart] (Toto), Mayme Kelso (Madame Ribout), Lillian Leighton (Mrs. Weeks), Lallah Hart (Miss Dunston), ZaSu Pitts (Katie Jones), Fay Holderness (Mrs. Parkton), Helen Dunbar (Mrs. Channing), Charles Ogle (Dr. Malcolm Lloyd), Marie Newell (Cora). Famous Players–Lasky Corporation/Paramount Pictures. **Release Date:** June 15, 1919. 50 min.

Better Times (1919). **Director/Writer:** King W. Vidor. **Cinematography:** William Thornley. **Cast:** ZaSu Pitts (Nancy Scroggs), David Butler (Peter Van Alstyne), Jack McDonald (Ezra Scroggs), William De Vaull (Si Whittaker), Hugh Fay (Jack Ransom), George Hackathorne (Tony), Georgia Woodthorpe (A Young Old Lady), Julianne Johnstone. Brentwood Film Corporation/Robertson-Cole Distributing Corporation/Exhibitors Mutual Distributing Company. **Release Date:** July 13, 1919. **Notes:** *Better Times* offered ZaSu her first starring role. Scenes at the finishing school were shot in the private Oak Knoll district of Pasadena, California. David Butler had over sixty acting credits before becoming a successful director at 20th Century–Fox, Paramount and Warner Bros.

The Other Half (1919). **Director/Writer:** King W. Vidor. **Cinematography:** Ira H. Morgan. **Assistant Director:** Roy H. Marshall. **Cast:** Florence Vidor (Katherine Boone), Charles Meredith (Donald Trent), ZaSu Pitts (Jennie Jones, the Jazz Kid), David Butler (Cpl. Jimmy), Alfred Allen (J. Martin Trent), Frances Raymond (Mrs. Boone), Hugh Saxon (James Bradley), Thomas Jefferson (Caleb Fairman), Arthur Redden (the Star Reporter). Brentwood Film Corporation/Robertson-Cole Distributing Corporation/Exhibitors Mutual Distributing Company. **Release Date:** August 18, 1919. 50 min.

Poor Relations (1919). **Director/Writer:** King Vidor. **Cinematography:** Ira H. Morgan. **Assistant Director:** Roy H. Marshall. **Cast:** Florence Vidor (Dorothy Perkins), Lillian Leighton (Ma Perkins), William Du Vaull (Pa Perkins), Roscoe Karns (Henry), ZaSu Pitts (Daisy Perkins), Charles Meredith (Monty Rhodes). Brentwood Film Corporation/Robertson-Cole Distributing Corporation (A Superior Picture). **Release Date:** November 1, 1919. 50 min.

Seeing It Through (1920). **Director:** Claude Mitchell. **Cinematography:** Joe Morgan [Ira H. Morgan]. **Cast:** W.H. Bainbridge (Mr. Allen), Hughie Mack (Mr. Tweeney), Anna Hernandez [Anna Dodge] (Mrs. Tweeney), Fannie Midgley (Mrs. Lawrence), Frank Hayes (Bolter), ZaSu Pitts (Betty Lawrence), Fred Mack (Sandy MacPherson), Julanne Johnson (Janice Wilson), Frankie Raymond [Frances Raymond] (Mrs. Allen), Edwin Stevens (Ichabod Borgrum), Henry Woodward (Jim Carrington), Mayme Kelso (Bogrum's Housekeeper). **Release Date:** February 8, 1920. Brentwood Film Corp./Robertson-Cole Distributing Corp. 50 min.

Bright Skies (1920). **Director:** Henry Kolker. **Writers:** Burke Jenkins (story), Sarah Y. Mason. **Cinematography:** John W. Leezer. **Cast:** ZaSu Pitts (Sally), Tom Gallery (Billy), Jack Pratt (Carnsworth), Kate Price (Mrs. Cassidy), Edward Delavanti (Tonio), Jack Braughall (Durkin). Brentwood Film Corporation/Robertson-Cole Distributing Corporation. **Release Date:** April 4, 1920. 50 min.

Heart of Twenty (1920). **Director:** Henry Kolker. **Writer:** Sarah Y. Mason. **Cinematography:** John W. Leezer. **Cast:** ZaSu Pitts (Katie Abbott), Jack Pratt (J.W. Wiseman), Percy Challenger (Henry Higginbotham), Hugh Saxon (J. Dale Briggs), Tom Gallery (Nice Young Man), Aileen Manning (Aunt Lucy), Billie Lind (Alma Dale Briggs), Verne Winter (Rusty Higginbotham). Brentwood Film Corporation/Robertson-Cole Distributing Corporation. **Release Date:** June 20, 1920.

Patsy (1921). **Director:** John McDermott. **Writers:** Ed Lawshe (play), John McDermott. **Cast:** ZaSu Pitts (Patsy), John MacFarlane (Pops), Tom Gallery (Bob Brooks), Marjorie Daw (Margaret Vincent), Fannie Midgley (Mrs. Vincent), Wallace Beery (Gustave Ludermann), Harry Todd (Tramp), Milla Davenport (Matron), Henry Fortson (Bones). Fred Swanton/Truart Film Co. **Release Date:** February 1, 1921.

Is Matrimony a Failure? (1922). **Director:** James Cruze. **Writer:** Walter Woods. **Cinematography:** Karl Brown. **Cast:** T. Roy Barnes (Arthur Haviland), Lila Lee (Margaret Saxby), Lois Wilson (Mabel Hoyt), Walter Hiers (Jack Hoyt), ZaSu Pitts (Mrs. Wilbur), Arthur Hoyt (Mr. Wilbur), Lillian Leighton (Martha Saxby), Tully Marshall (Amos Saxby), Adolphe Menjou (Dudley King), Sylvia Ashton (Mrs. Pearson), Charles Ogle (Pop Skinner), Ethel Wales (Mrs. Skinner), Sidney Bracey (Bank President), William Gonder (Policeman), Lottie Williams (Maid), Dan Mason (Silas Spencer), W.H. Brown [William H. Brown] (Chef), Robert Brower (Marriage License Clerk). Famous Players–Lasky Corporation/Paramount Pictures. **Release Date:** April 16, 1922.

For the Defense (1922). **Director:** Paul Powell. **Writers:** Beulah Marie Dix (adaptation), Elmer Rice (play). **Cinematography:** Hal Rosson. **Cast:** Ethel Clayton (Anne Woodstock), Vernon Steele (Christopher Armstrong), ZaSu Pitts (Jennie Dunn), Bertram Grassby (Dr. Joseph Kasimir), Maym Kelso (Smith), Sylvia Ashton (Signora Bartoni), Mabel Van Buren (Cousin Selma). Famous Players–Lasky Corporation/Paramount Pictures. **Release Date:** June 4. 1922. 50 min. **Notes:** Richard Bennett and Louise Closser Hale starred in the original Broadway production in 1919–20.

Youth to Youth (1922). **Director/Producer:** Emile Chautard. **Writers:** Hulbert Footner (story "Country Love"), Edith Kennedy (adaptation/screenplay). **Cinematography:** Arthur Martinelli. **Art Direction:** J.J. Hughes. **Cast:** Billie Dove (Eve Allinson), Edythe Chapman (Mrs. Cora Knittson), Hardee Kirkland (Taylor), Sylvia Ashton (Mrs. Jolley), Jack Gardner (Maurice Gibbon), Cullen Landis (Page Brookins), Mabel Van Buren (Mrs. Brookins), Tom O'Brien (Ralph Horry), Paul Jeffrey (Everett Clough), Carl Gerard (Howe Snedecor), ZaSu Pitts (Emily), Lincoln Stedman (Orlando Jolley), Gertrude Short (Luella), Noah Beery (Brutus Tawney), Esther Ralston. Metro Pictures Corporation. **Release Date:** October 16, 1922.

A Daughter of Luxury (1922). **Director:** Paul Powell. **Writers:** Beulah Marie Dix (adaptation), Leonard Merrick, Michael

Morton (play "The Imposter"). **Executive Producer:** Adolph Zukor. **Cinematography:** Bert Baldridge. **Cast:** Agnes Ayres (Mary Fenton), Tom Gallery (Blake Walford), Edith Yorke (Ellen Marsh), Howard Ralston (Bill Marsh), Edward Martindel (Loftus Walford), Sylvia Ashton (Mrs. Walford), Clarence Burton (Red Conroy), ZaSu Pitts (Mary Cosgrove), Robert Schable (Charlie Owen), Bernice Frank (Winnie), Dorothy Gordon (Genevieve Fowler), Muriel McCormac (Nancy). Famous Players–Lasky Corporation/Paramount. **Release Date:** December 4, 1922. **Note:** *The Imposter* ran on Broadway in 1910–11 for 31 performances.

Poor Men's Wives (1923). **Director:** Louis J. Gasnier **Writers:** Frank Dazey, Agnes Christine Johnston (adaptation/screenplay), Eve Unsell (titles). **Producer:** B.P. Schulberg. **Cinematography:** Karl Struss. **Cast:** Barbara La Marr (Laura Bedford/Laura Maberne), David Butler (Jim Maherne), Betty Francisco (Claribel), Richard Tucker (Richard Smith-Blanton), ZaSu Pitts (Apple Annie), Muriel McCormac (Twin), Mickey McBan (Twin). B.P. Schulberg Productions/Al Lichtman Corporation/Preferred Pictures Corporation/States Rights Independent Exchanges. **Release Date:** January 28, 1923. 70 min.

The Girl Who Came Back (1923). **Director:** Tom Forman. **Writer:** Evelyn Campbell. **Cinematography:** Harry Perry. **Cast:** Miriam Cooper (Sheila), Gaston Glass (Ray Underhill), Kenneth Harlan (Martin Norries), Fred Malatesta (Ramon Valhays), Joseph Dowling (Old 565), Ethel Shannon (Belle Bryant), Mary Culver (Mayme Miller), ZaSu Pitts (Anastasia Muldoon). B.P. Schulberg Productions/Al Lichtman Corporation/Preferred Pictures Corporation/States Rights Independent Exchanges. **Release Date:** April 14, 1923.

Three Wise Fools (1923). **Director:** King Vidor. **Writers:** King Vidor, June Mathis (writers), John McDermott, James O'Hanlon (adaptation), Winchell Smith, Austin Strong (play). **Cinematography:** Charles Van Enger. **Cast:** Claude Gillingwater (Theodore Findley), Eleanor Boardman (Rena Fairchild/Sydney Fairfield), William H. Crane (Hon. James Trumbull), Alec B. Francis (Dr. Richard Gaunt), John Sainpolis [John St. Polis] (John Crawshay), Brinsley Shaw (Benny, the Duck), Fred Esmelton (Gray), William Haines (Gordon Schuyler), Lucien Littlefield (Douglas), ZaSu Pitts (Mickey), Martha Mattox (Saunders), Fred J. Butler (Poole), Charles Hickman (Clancy), Craig Biddle Jr. (Young Findley), Creighton Hale (Young Trumbull), Raymond Hatton (Young Gaunt). Goldwyn Pictures Corporation. **Release Date:** August 19, 1923. 70 min. **Notes:** Harry Davenport and Claude Gillingwater starred in the original 1918-1919 Broadway production. It was filmed again in 1946, by MGM, starring Margaret O'Brien and Lionel Barrymore.

Tea: With a Kick! (1923). **Director:** Erle C. Kenton. **Writer:** Victor Hugo Halperin (story). **Cinematography:** William Marshall, Philip Rand. **Cast:** Doris May (Bonnie Day), Creighton Hale (Art Binger), Ralph Lewis (Jim Day), Rosemary Theby (Aunt Pearl), Stuart Holmes (Napoleon Dobbings), ZaSu Pitts (Brainy Jones), Gale Henry (Hesperis McGowan), Dot Farley (Mrs. Juniper), Louise Fazenda (Birdie Puddleford), Dale Fuller (Kittie Wiggle), Edward Jobson (Editor Octavius Juniper), Spike Rankin [Caroline Rankin] (Mrs. Bump), Harry Lorraine (the Rev. Harry White), Sidney D'Albrook (Pietro), Tiny Ward (King Kick), Earl Montgomery (Convict Dooley), Hazel Keener (Hazel), Julanne Johnston (Gwen Van Peebles), William De Vaull (Napoleon), Hank Mann (Sam Spindle), Chester Conklin (Jiggs), Snitz Edwards (Oscar Puddleford), William Dyer (a Businessman), Harry Todd

(Chris Kringle), Bill Franey (Convict Hooney), Victor Potel (Bellboy 13). Victor Halperin Productions/Associated Exhibitors. **Release Date:** August 26, 1923. 60 min.

West of the Water Tower (1923). **Director:** Rollin Sturgeon. **Writers:** Homer Croy (novel), Lucien Hubbard (adaptation), Doris Schroeder (writer). **Cinematography:** Harry B. Harris. **Cast:** Glenn Hunter (Guy Plummer), May McAvoy (Bee Chew), Ernest Torrence (the Rev. Adrian Plummer), George Fawcett (Charles Chew), ZaSu Pitts (Dessie Arnhalt), Charles Abbe (R.N. Arnhalt), Anne Schaefer (Mrs. Plummer), Riley Hatch (Cod Dugan), Allen Baker (Ed Hoecker), Jack Terry (Harlan Thompson), Edward Elkas (Wolfe), Joseph Burke (Town Drunk), Gladys Feldman (Tootsie), Alice Mann (Pal). Famous Players–Lasky Corporation/Paramount Pictures. **Release Date:** January 6, 1924. 80 min.

Daughters of Today (1924). **Director:** Rollin S. Sturgeon. **Writer:** Lucien Hubbard. **Cinematography:** Milton Moore. **Cast:** Patsy Ruth Miller (Lois Whittall), Ralph Graves (Ralph Adams), Edna Murphy (Mabel Vandegrift), Edward Hearn (Peter Farnham), Philo McCullough (Reggy Adams), George Nichols (Dirk Vandegrift), Gertrude Claire (Ma Vandegrift), Phillips Smalley (Leigh Whittall), ZaSu Pitts (Lorena), H.J. Herbert (Calnan), Fontaine La Rue (Mrs. Mantell), Truman Van Dyke (Dick), Dorothy Wood (Flo), Marjorie Bonner (Maisie). Sturgeon-Hubbard Company/Selznick Distributing Corporation. **Release Date:** February 2, 1924. **Notes:** This was originally released in May 1923 as *What's Your Daughter Doing?*

The Goldfish (1924). **Director:** Jerome Storm. **Writers:** C. Gardner Sullivan (writer), Gladys Unger (play). **Producer:** Joseph M. Schenck. **Cinematography:** Ray Binger. **Costume Design:** Clare West. **Cast:** Constance Talmadge (Jennie Wetherby), Jack Mulhall (Jimmy Wetherby), Frank Elliott (Duke of Middlesex), Jean Hersholt (Herman Krauss), ZaSu Pitts (Amelia Pugsley), Edward Connelly (Count Nevski), William Conklin (J. Hamilton Powers), Leo White (Casmir), Nellie Bly Baker (Ellen), Kate Lester (Mrs. Bellmore), Eric Mayne (the Prince), William Wellesley (Mr. Crane), Jacqueline Gadsden (Helen Crane), Percy Williams (Wilton), John Patrick (Reporter). Constance Talmadge Film Company/Associated First National Pictures. **Release Date:** March 30, 1924. 70 min. **Notes:** *The Goldfish*, with Marjorie Rambeau, Wilfred Lytell, Lucille La Verne, and Norma Mitchell, ran for three months on Broadway in 1922.

Triumph (1924). **Director/Producer:** Cecil B. DeMille. **Writers:** May Edginton (novel), Jeanie Macpherson (adaptation). **Music:** James C. Bradford. **Cinematography:** Bert Glennon. **Editing:** Anne Bauchens. **Assistant Director:** Frank Urson. **Cast:** Leatrice Joy (Ann Land), Rod La Rocque (King Garnet), Victor Varconi (William Silver), Charles Ogle (James Martin), Theodore Kosloff (Varinoff), Robert Edeson (Samuel Overton), Julia Faye (Countess Rika), George Fawcett (David Garnet), Spottiswoode Aitken (Torrini), ZaSu Pitts (a Factory Girl), Raymond Hatton (a Tramp), Alma Bennett (a Flower Girl), Jimmie Adams (a Painter), William Boyd (uncredited). Famous Players–Lasky Corporation/Paramount. **Release Date:** April 27, 1924. 80 min.

Changing Husbands (1924). **Directors:** Paul Iribe, Frank Urson. **Writers:** Sada Cowan, Howard Higgin. **Cinematography:** Bert Glennon. **Costume Design:** Paul Iribe. **Supervisor:** Cecil B. DeMille. **Cast:** Leatrice Joy (Gwynne Evans/Ava Graham), Victor Varconi (Oliver Evans), Raymond Griffith (Bob Hamilton), Julia Faye (Mitzi), ZaSu Pitts (Delia), Helen Dunbar (Mrs. Evans Sr.), William Boyd (Conrad Bardshaw), Guy

Oliver (Director, uncredited), Monte Collins (Stagehand, uncredited). Famous Players–Lasky Corporation/Paramount Pictures. **Release Date:** June 22, 1924. 70 min.

Legend of Hollywood (1924). **Director:** Renaud Hoffman. **Writers:** Alfred A. Cohn (titles, screenplay), Frank Condon (story). **Cinematography:** Karl Struss. **Editing:** Glen Wheeler. **Cast:** Percy Marmont (John Smith), ZaSu Pitts (Mary Brown), Alice Davenport (Mrs. Rooney), Dorothy Dorr (Blondie), John T. Prince (uncredited). Charles R. Rogers Productions/Producers Distributing Corporation (PDC). **Release Date:** August 3, 1924.

Wine of Youth (1924). **Director/Producer:** King Vidor. **Writers:** Rachel Crothers (play "Mary the Third"), Carey Wilson (writer). **Cinematography:** John J. Mescall. **Art Direction:** Charles L. Cadwallader. **Assistant Director:** David Howard. **Cast:** Eleanor Boardman (Mary), James Morrison (Clinton), Johnnie Walker (William), ZaSu Pitts (Lucy) (scenes deleted), Niles Welch (Robert), Creighton Hale (Richard), Ben Lyon (Lynn), William Haines (Hal), William Collier Jr. (Max), Pauline Garon (Tish), Eulalie Jensen (Mother), E.J. Ratcliffe (Father), Gertrude Claire (Granny), Robert Agnew (Bobby), Lucille Hutton (Anne), Virginia Lee Corbin (Flapper), Gloria Heller [Anne Sheridan] (Flapper), Sidney De Grey (Doctor), Jean Arthur (Automobile Reveler, uncredited), Aggie Herring (the Cook, uncredited). Metro-Goldwyn Pictures Corporation. **Release Date:** September 15, 1924. 72 min.

The Fast Set (1924). **Director:** William C. de Mille. **Writers:** Clara Beranger (writer), Frederick Lonsdale (play "Spring Cleaning"). **Cinematography:** L. Guy Wilky. **Cast:** Betty Compson (Margaret Stone), Adolphe Menjou (Ernest Steel), Elliott Dexter (Richard), ZaSu Pitts (Mona), Dawn O'Day [Anne Shirley] (Little Margaret), Grace Carlyle (Jane Walton), Claire Adams (Fay Colleen), Rosalind Byrne (Connie Gallies), Edgar Norton (Archie Wells), Louis Natheaux (Billy Sommers), Eugenio de Liguoro (Walters), Fred Walton (Simpson), Christina Montt (uncredited). Famous Players–Lasky Corporation/Paramount Pictures. **Release Date:** October 20, 1924. 80 min. **Notes:** A. E. Matthews, Violet Heming, and Estelle Winwood starred in *Spring Cleaning* on Broadway (1923-24) for over 200 performances.

Secrets of the Night (1924). **Director:** Herbert Blaché. **Writers:** Guy Bolton, Max Marcin (play "The Nightcap"), Edward J. Montagne (adaptation/screenplay). **Cinematography:** Gilbert Warrenton. **Cast:** James Kirkwood (Robert Andrews), Madge Bellamy (Anne Maynard), Tom Ricketts (Jerry Hammond), Tom Guise (Colonel James Constance), Arthur Stuart Hull (Lester Knowles), Edward Cecil (Alfred Austin), Frederick Cole (Teddy Hammond), Rosemary Theby (Mrs. Lester Knowles), ZaSu Pitts (Celia Stebbins), Tom Wilson (Old Tom Jefferson White), Joseph Singleton (Charles), Bull Montana (the Killer), Tyrone Brereton (Anne's Brother), Otto Hoffman (the Coroner), Arthur Thalasso (Detective Reardon), Anton Vaverka (Joshua Brown). Universal Pictures (Universal Jewel). **Release Date:** November 12, 1924. 64 min. **Notes:** The Bolton-Marcin play *The Nightcap* ran for four months on Broadway in 1921 and starred Ronald Colman and Elisabeth Risdon. *The Nightcap* was the film's working title.

Greed (1924). **Director:** Erich von Stroheim. **Writers:** June Mathis (screen adaptation and dialogue), Joseph Farnham (titles), Frank Norris (novel *McTeague*). **Cinematography:** Wm. H. Daniels, Ben F. Reynolds. **Editing:** Jos. W. Farnham, Glenn Morgan (reconstruction), Frank E. Hull (uncredited), Rex Ingram (18-reel version, uncredited), June

Mathis (42-reel version, uncredited), Erich von Stroheim (42-reel version, uncredited), Grant Whytock (18-reel version, uncredited). **Art Direction:** Cedric Gibbons (credited, but reportedly not involved), Richard Day (uncredited), Erich von Stroheim (uncredited). **Production Supervisor:** Harry Rapf (uncredited). **Assistant Directors:** Louis Germonprez (uncredited), Edward Sowders (uncredited). **Settings:** Cedric Gibbons. **Consultant on Reconstruction:** Richard Koszarski. **Props:** Charles Rogers (uncredited), Frank Ybarra (uncredited). **Visual Effects:** Flame Effects: Sasha Leuterer (reconstruction). **Motion Control Effects:** Chad Mielke (reconstruction). **Assistant Camera:** Walter Bader (uncredited). **Camera Operator:** Paul Ivano (uncredited), Ernest B. Schoedsack (uncredited). **Still Photographer:** Warren Lynch (uncredited). **Assistant Editor:** Shimit Amin (reconstruction), Jarrett Fijal (reconstruction), Andrew Pierce (reconstruction), Jessica Kongthong (reconstruction), Marguerite Faust (uncredited). **Editorial Consultant:** Carol Littleton (reconstruction). **On-line Editor:** Russ Martin (reconstruction). **Cast:** ZaSu Pitts (Trina), Gibson Gowland (McTeague), Jean Hersholt (Marcus), Dale Fuller (Maria), Tempe Pigott (Mother McTeague), Sylvia Ashton ("Mommer" Sieppe), Chester Conklin ("Popper" Sieppe), Joan Standing (Selina), Jack Curtis (McTeague Sr., uncredited), William Barlow (the Minister, uncredited), James F. Fulton (Cribbens, uncredited), Lita Chevrier, Oscar Gottell, Otto Gottell (Sieppe Twins, uncredited), Frank Hayes (Charles W. Grannis, uncredited), Fanny Midgley (Miss Anastasia Baker, uncredited), Austen Jewell (August Sieppe, uncredited), Hughie Mack (Mr. Heise, uncredited), Erich von Stroheim (Balloon Vendor, uncredited), James Gibson (Deputy, uncredited), Jack McDonald (Placer County Sheriff, uncredited), William Mollenhauer (Palmist, uncredited), Erich von Ritzau (Dr. Painless Potter, uncredited), Edward Gaffney (uncredited), Cesare Gravina (Zwerkow, uncredited), Tiny Jones (Mrs. Heise, uncredited), Lon Poff (Man, uncredited), Reta Revela (Mrs. Ryer), J. Aldrich Libbey (Mr. Ryer), Florence Gibson (Hag), Bee Ho Gray (uncredited), Harold Henderson (uncredited), Hugh J. McCauley (the Photographer, uncredited), Max Tyron (Uncle Rudolph Oelbermann, uncredited), S.S. Simon (Joe Frenna, uncredited), James Wang (Chinese Cook, uncredited). Metro-Goldwyn Pictures Corporation. **Release Date:** December 26, 1924. 140 min./239 min. (1999 restored version).

The Great Divide (1925). **Director:** Reginald Barker. **Writers:** Benjamin Glazer (adaptation), Lenore J. Coffee (uncredited), Waldemar Young (writer), William Vaughn Moody (play), James J. Tynan (novel version of screenplay). **Cinematography:** Percy Hilburn. **Editing:** Robert Kern. **Art Direction:** Cedric Gibbons. **Costume Design:** Sophie Wachner. **Assistant Director:** Harry Schenck. **Cast:** Alice Terry (Ruth Jordan), Conway Tearle (Stephen Ghent), Wallace Beery (Dutch), Huntley Gordon (Philip Jordan), Allan Forrest (Dr. Winthrop Newbury), George Cooper (Shorty), ZaSu Pitts (Polly Jordan), William Orlamond (Lon). Metro-Goldwyn Pictures Corporation. **Release Date:** February 15, 1925. 80 min. **Notes:** This remake of *The Great Divide* (1915) was followed by *The Great Divide* (1929) and *Woman Hungry* (1931). The Broadway play premiered in 1907 and starred Henry Miller and Margaret Anglin. Laura Hope Crews originated the role on the stage that ZaSu played in the movie.

The Re-Creation of Brian Kent (1925). **Director:** Sam Wood. **Writers:** Mary Alice Scully, Arthur F. Statter (writers), Harold Bell Wright (novel). **Producer:** Sol Lesser. **Cinematography:** Glen MacWilliams. **Cast:**

Kenneth Harlan (Brian Kent), Helene Chadwick (Betty Joe), Mary Carr (Auntie Sue), ZaSu Pitts (Judy), Rosemary Theby (Mrs. Kent), T. Roy Barnes (Harry Green), Ralph Lewis (Homer Ward), Russell Simpson (Jap Taylor), DeWitt Jennings (Detective Ross), Russ Powell (Sheriff Knox). Sol Lesser Productions/Principal Distributing Corporation/States Rights Independent Exchanges. **Release Date:** February 15, 1925.

Old Shoes (1925). **Director/Story:** Frederick Stowers. **Cast:** Noah Beery (the Stepfather), Johnny Harron (the Boy), Viora Daniel, Ethel Grey Terry, ZaSu Pitts, Russell Simpson, Snitz Edwards. Peerless Pictures Corporation/Hollywood Pictures Corporation/States Rights Independent Exchanges. **Release Date:** March 1925. 70 min.

The Business of Love (1925). **Directors:** Irving Reis, Jess Robbins. **Cinematographer:** Irving Reis. **Cast:** Edward Everett Horton, Barbara Bedford, ZaSu Pitts, Tom Ricketts, Dorothy Wood, Carl Stockdale, Tom Murray, James Kelly, Stanley Taylor, Newton Hall. Astor Pictures Corporation/States Rights Independent Exchanges. **Release Date:** August 7, 1925.

A Woman's Faith (1925). **Director:** Edward Laemmle. **Writers:** Clarence Budington Kelland (novel *Miracle*), E.T. Lowe Jr. (adaptation), C.R. Wallace (writer). **Cinematographer:** John Stumar. **Cast:** Alma Rubens (Née Caron), Percy Marmont (Donovan Steele), Jean Hersholt (Cluny), ZaSu Pitts (Blanche), Hughie Mack (François), Cesare Gravina (Odilion Turcott), William H. Turner (Xavier Caron), André [George] Beranger (Leandre Turcott), Rosa Rosanova (Delima Turcott). Universal Pictures. **Release Date:** August 9, 1925. 70 min. **Notes:** This is also known as *The Clash*.

Pretty Ladies (1925). **Director:** Monta Bell. **Writers:** Joseph Farnham (titles), Alice D.G. Miller (writer). **Cinematography:** Ira H. Morgan. **Assistant Director:** Harold S. Bucquet. **Settings:** James Basevi, Cedric Gibbons. **Wardrobe:** Ethel P. Chaffin. **Cast:** ZaSu Pitts (Maggie Keenan), Tom Moore (Al Cassidy), Ann Pennington (Herself), Lilyan Tashman (Selma Larson), Bernard Randall (Aaron Savage), Helena D'Algy (Adrienne), Conrad Nagel (Dream Lover), Norma Shearer (Frances White), George K. Arthur (Roger Van Horn), Lucille Le Sueur [Joan Crawford] (Bobby, a Showgirl), Paul Ellis (Warren Hadley), Roy D'Arcy (Paul Thompson), Gwen Lee (Fay), Dorothy Seastrom (Diamond Tights), Lew Harvey (Will Rogers), Chad Huber (Frisco), Walter Shumway (Mr. Gallagher), Dan Crimmins (Mr. Shean), Jimmie Quinn (Eddie Cantor), Myrna Loy (uncredited), Bodil Rosing (uncredited). Metro-Goldwyn Pictures Corporation. **Release Date:** September 6, 1925.

Thunder Mountain (1925). **Director:** Victor Schertzinger. **Writers:** Pearl Franklin (play *Howdy, Folks!*), Elia W. Peattie (story "Thunder"), Eve Unsell (writer). **Cinematography:** Glen MacWilliams. **Property Master:** Joe Delfino. **Cast:** Madge Bellamy (Azalea), Leslie Fenton (Sam Martin), Alec B. Francis (Preacher), Paul Panzer (Morgan), Arthur Housman (Joe Givens), ZaSu Pitts (Mandy Coulter), Emily Fitzroy (Ma MacBirney), Dan Mason (Pa MacBirney), Otis Harlan (Jeff Coulter), Russell Simpson (Si Pace), Natalie Warfield (Mrs. Coulter). Fox Film Corporation. **Release Date:** October 11, 1925. 80 min. **Notes:** This was filmed on location in Santa Cruz, California.

Lazybones (1925). **Director:** Frank Borzage. **Writers:** Owen Davis (novel), Frances Marion (writer). **Executive Producer:** William Fox. **Cinematography:** Glen MacWilliams, George Schneiderman. **Cast:** Buck Jones (Lazybones), Madge Bellamy (Kit), Virginia Marshall (Kit as a Girl), Edythe Chapman (Mrs. Tuttle), Leslie Fenton (Dick Ritchie),

Jane Novak (Agnes Fanning), Emily Fitzroy (Mrs. Fanning), ZaSu Pitts (Ruth Fanning), William Bailey (Elmer Ballister). Fox Film Corporation. **Release Date:** November 6, 1925. 80 min.

Wages for Wives (1925). **Director:** Frank Borzage. **Writer:** Kenneth B. Clarke. **Cinematography:** Ernest G. Palm [Palmer]. **Assistant Director:** Bunny Dunn. **Cast:** Jacqueline Logan (Nell Bailey), Creighton Hale (Danny Kester), Earle Foxe (Hughie Logan), ZaSu Pitts (Luella Logan), Claude Gillingwater (Jim Bailey), David Butler (Chester Logan), Margaret Seddon (Annie Bailey), Margaret Livingston (Carol Bixby), Dan Mason (Mr. Tevis), Tom Ricketts (Judge McLean). Fox Film Corporation. **Release Date:** December 13, 1925. 70 min.

The Great Love (1925). **Director:** Marshall Neilan. **Writers:** Benjamin F. Glazer (writer), Marshall Neilan (story). **Cast:** Robert Agnew (Dr. Lawrence Tibbits), Viola Dana (Minette Bunker), Frank Currier (Mr. Bunker), ZaSu Pitts (Nancy), Chester Conklin (Perkins), Junior Coghlan [Frank Coghlan Jr.] (Patrick), Malcolm Waite (Tom Watson). Metro-Goldwyn-Mayer (MGM). **Release Date:** December 27, 1925.

Mannequin (1926). **Director/Producer:** James Cruze. **Writers:** Frances Agnew (writer), Fannie Hurst (story), Walter Woods (adaptation). **Cinematography:** Karl Brown. **Cast:** Alice Joyce (Selene Herrick), Warner Baxter (John Herrick), Dolores Costello (Joan Herrick), ZaSu Pitts (Annie Pogani), Walter Pidgeon (Martin Innesbrook), Freeman Wood (Terry Allen), Charlot Bird [Charlotte Bird] (Toto), Marcia Mae Jones. Famous Players–Lasky Corporation/Paramount Pictures. **Release Date:** January 11, 1926. 70 min.

What Happened to Jones (1926). **Director:** William A. Seiter. **Writers:** George Broadhurst (play), Melville W. Brown (screenplay/adaptation). **Cinematography:** Arthur Todd. **Editing:** John Rawlins. **Casting:** Fred A. Datig (uncredited). **Art Direction:** Leo E. Kuter. **Assistant Director:** Nate Watt. **Cast:** Reginald Denny (Tom Jones), Marian Nixon (Lucille Bigbee), Melbourne MacDowell (Mr. Bigbee), Frances Raymond (Mrs. Bigbee), Otis Harlan (Ebenezer Goodly), Emily Fitzroy (Mrs. Goodly), Margaret Quimby (Marjorie Goodly), Ben Hendricks Jr. (Richard), William Austin (Henry Fuller), Nina Romano (Minerva Starlight), ZaSu Pitts (Hilda), John Elliott (the Bishop), Edward Cecil (Smith), Broderick O'Farrell (Rector). **Release Date:** February 8, 1926. Universal Pictures (Universal Jewel). 70 min. **Notes:** ZaSu is billed as Zazu Pitts in the credits. The only surviving print of this film is housed at UCLA's Film and Television Archives. The play opened on Broadway in 1897 and starred George C. Boniface as Jones. The story was filmed before in 1915 and 1920.

Monte Carlo (1926). **Director:** Christy Cabanne. **Writers:** Joe Farnum (titles), Alice D.G. Miller (screenplay/adaptation), Carey Wilson (story). **Cinematography:** William H. Daniels. **Editing:** William LeVanway. **Art Direction:** Cedric Gibbons, Merrill Pye. **Costume Design:** André-ani, Kathleen Kay, Maude Marsh. **Cast:** Lew Cody (Tony Townsend), Gertrude Olmstead (Sally Roxford), Roy D'Arcy (Prince Boris), Karl Dane (the Doorman), ZaSu Pitts (Hope Durant), Trixie Friganza (Flossie Payne), Margaret Campbell (Grand Duchess Marie), André Lanoy (Ludvig), Max Barwyn (Sarleff), Barbara Shears (Princess Ilene), Harry Myers (Greves), Cesare Gravina (Count Davigny), Antonio D'Algy (Varo), Arthur Hoyt (Bancroft). **Release Date:** March 1, 1926. Metro-Goldwyn-Mayer (MGM).

Early to Wed (1926). **Director:** Frank Borzage. **Writer:** Kenneth B. Clarke. **Cinematography: Ernest G. Palmer. **Assistant Director:** Lew Borzage. **Cast:** Matt Moore (Tommy Carter), Kathryn Perry (Daphne Carter), Albert Gran (Cassius Hayden), Julia Swayne Gordon (Mrs. Hayden), Arthur Housman (Art Nevers), Rodney Hildebrand (Mike Dugan), ZaSu Pitts (Mrs. Dugan), Belva McKay (Mrs. Nevers), Ross McCutcheon (Bill Dugan), Harry A. Bailey (Pelton Jones). **Release Date:** April 25, 1926. Fox Film Corporation.

Sunny Side Up (1926). **Director:** Donald Crisp. **Writers:** Henry St. John Cooper (novel *Sunny Ducrow*), Beulah Marie Dix, Elmer Harris (adaptation). **Cinematography:** Peverell Marley. **Assistant Director:** Emile de Ruelle. **Cast:** Vera Reynolds (Sunny Ducrow), Edmund Burns (Stanley Dobrington), George K. Arthur (Bert Jackson), ZaSu Pitts (Evelyn), Ethel Clayton (Cissy Cason), Louis Natheaux (Stanley's Assistant), Sally Rand (Dancer), Jocelyn Lee (Showgirl), Majel Coleman (Showgirl). **Release Date:** August 2, 1926. DeMille Pictures Corporation/Producers Distributing Corporation (PDC). 66 min. **Notes:** This is not to be confused with the popular Charles Farrell–Janet Gaynor 1929 musical of the same name. Actor Donald Crisp directed over seventy movies between 1914 and 1930.

Risky Business (1926). **Director:** Alan Hale. **Writers:** Charles Brackett (story "Pearls Before Cecily"), Beulah Marie Dix (adaptation). **Cinematography:** James Diamond. **Editing:** Claude Berkeley. **Art Direction:** Max Parker. **Production Manager:** Gordon Cooper. **Assistant Director:** Harry Haskins. **Cast:** Vera Reynolds (Cecily Stoughton), Ethel Clayton (Mrs. Stoughton), Kenneth Thomson (Ted Pyncheon), Ward Crane (Coults-Browne), Louis Natheaux (Lawrence Wheaton), ZaSu Pitts (Agnes Wheaton), George Irving (Schubal Peabody), Louise Cabo (Rosalie). **Release Date:** October 4, 1926. DeMille Pictures Corporation/Producers Distributing Corporation (PDC). 86 min. **Notes:** This was actor Alan Hale's second to last directing job; he directed only eight movies, between 1915 and 1927.

Her Big Night (1926). **Director:** Melville W. Brown. **Writers:** Melville W. Brown (adaptation), Peggy Gaddis (story "Doubling for Lora"), Rex Taylor, Nita O'Neil (writers). **Cinematography:** Arthur Todd. **Cast:** Laura La Plante (Frances Norcross/Daphne Dix), Einar Hansen (Johnny Young), ZaSu Pitts (Gladys Smith), Tully Marshall (J.Q. Adams), Lee Moran (Tom Barrett), Mack Swain (Myers), John Roche (Allan Dix), William Austin (Harold Crosby), Nat Carr (Mr. Harmon), Cissy Fitzgerald (Mrs. Harmon). **Release Date:** December 5, 1926. Universal Pictures. 80 min.

Casey at the Bat (1927). **Director:** Monte Brice. **Writers:** Monte Brice, Reginald Morris (adaptation), Grant Clarke, Sam Hellman (titles), Hector Turnbull (story), Jules Furthman (writer), Ernest Lawrence Thayer (poem). **Producer:** Hector Turnbull. **Cinematography:** Barney McGill. **Cast:** Wallace Beery (Casey), Ford Sterling (O'Dowd), ZaSu Pitts (Camille), Sterling Holloway (Putnam), Spec O'Donnell (Spec), Iris Stuart (Trixie), Sidney Jarvis (McGraw), Lotus Thompson (Rosalind Byrne), Anne Sheridan (Floradora Girl), Doris Hill (Floradora Girl), Sally Blane (Floradora Girl). **Release Date:** March 8, 1927. Famous Players–Lasky Corporation/Paramount Pictures. 60 min. **Notes:** This classic story, subtitled "A Ballad of the Republic Sung in the Year 1888," first published in the *San Francisco Examiner* on June 3, 1888, was filmed at least three times previous — in 1899, 1913 and 1916. The latter starred De Wolf Hopper, who read the poem to acclaim in vaudeville. Starting in 1888, Hopper reportedly recited the poem over 10,000 times in his lifetime.

13 Washington Square (1928). **Director:** Melville W. Brown. **Writers:** Leroy Scott (novel *No. 13 Washington Square*), Harry O. Hoyt (screenplay/adaptation), Walter Anthony (titles). **Cinematography:** John Stumar. **Editing:** Ray Curtiss. **Cast:** Jean Hersholt ("Deacon" Pyecroft), Alice Joyce (Mrs. De Peyster), George Lewis (Jack De Peyster), ZaSu Pitts (Mathilde), Helen Foster (Mary Morgan), Helen Jerome Eddy (Olivetta), Julia Swayne Gordon (Mrs. Allistair), Jack McDonald (Mayfair), Jerry Gamble (Sparks). **Release Date:** January 1928. Universal Pictures. 60 min.

Wife Savers (1928). **Director:** Ralph Cedar. **Writers:** Tom J. Geraghty, Grover Jones (writers), George Marion Jr. (titles), Arthur Wimperis (play *Louie the 14th*). **Producer:** James Cruze. **Associate Producer:** B.P. Schulberg, **Cinematography:** Alfred Gilks, H. Kinley Martin. **Editing:** George Nichols Jr. **Cast:** Wallace Beery (Louis Hosenozzle), Raymond Hatton (Rodney Ramsbottom), ZaSu Pitts (Germaine), Sally Blane (Colette), Tom Kennedy (General Lavoris), Ford Sterling (Tavern Keeper), George Y. Harvey (the Major), August Tollaire (the Mayor). **Release Date:** January 7, 1928. Paramount Famous Lasky Corporation/Paramount Pictures. 60 min. **Notes:** *Louie the 14th*, produced by Florenz Ziegfeld, debuted on Broadway in 1925, running 319 performances. Featuring the music of Sigmund Romberg and Arthur Wimperis (who also wrote the book), it starred Leon Errol and Ethel Shutta.

Buck Privates (1928). **Director:** Melville W. Brown. **Writers:** Melville W. Brown (adaptation), John B. Clymer (writer), Albert DeMond (titles), Stuart N. Lake (story). **Cinematography:** John Stumar. **Editing:** Frank Atkinson, Ray Curtiss. **Cast:** Lya De Putti (Annie), Malcolm McGregor (John Smith), ZaSu Pitts (Hulda), James A. Marcus (Maj. Hartman), Eddie Gribbon (Sgt. Butts), Captain Ted Duncan (Capt. Marshall), Bud Jamison (Cupid Dodds), Les Bates (Mose Bloom). **Release Date:** June 3, 1928. Universal Pictures. 70 min.

The Wedding March (1928). **Director:** Erich von Stroheim. **Writers:** Harry Carr, Erich von Stroheim. **Producer:** Pat Powers. **Executive Producers:** Jesse L. Lasky, Adolph Zukor. **Music:** Louis De Francesco (uncredited), J.S. Zamecnik (uncredited). **Music Arranger:** John Leipold (uncredited). **Cinematography:** Ray Rennahan (Technicolor camera), Hal Mohr (uncredited), Ben F. Reynolds (uncredited), Buster Sorenson (uncredited). **Editing:** Frank E. Hull, Josef von Sternberg (uncredited), Erich von Stroheim (uncredited), Paul Weatherwax (uncredited). **Supervising Editor:** Julian Johnson. **Art Direction:** Richard Day, Erich von Stroheim (uncredited). **Costume Design:** Max Rée, Richard Day (uncredited), Erich von Stroheim (uncredited). **Assistant Directors:** Louis Germonprez, Edward Sowders (uncredited). **Photographer Associate:** Roy H. Klaffki. **Military Advisors:** Albert Conti, Donald Overall-Hatswell [D.R.O. Hatswell]. **Technical Advisors:** Archduke Leopold of Austria (uncredited), Wilhelm von Brincken (uncredited). **Cast:** Erich von Stroheim (Prince Nicki von Wildeliebe-Rauffenburg), Fay Wray (Mitzi Schrammell), Matthew Betz (Schani Eberle), ZaSu Pitts (Cecelia Schweisser), George Fawcett (Prince Ottokar von Wildeliebe Rauffenburg), Maude George (Princess Maria), George Nichols (Fortunat Schweisser), Dale Fuller (Katerina Schrammel), Hughie Mack (Schani's father), Cesare Gravina (Martin Schrammell), Sidney Bracey (Navratil), Anton Vaverka (Emperor Franz-Josef), Albert Conti, Claire Delmar, Peggy Eames, Ray Erlenborn, Carey Harrison, Danny Hoy, Hans Joby, Arthur Lubin, Madlyn Mougin, Harry Reinhardt, LaVerne Rooney, Don Ryan, Ferdinand Schumann-

Heink, Mme. Ernestine Schumann-Heink, Alec C. Snowden, Carolynne Snowden, Lucille Van Lent, Wilhelm von Brincken, Carl von Haartman, Lurie Weiss, Lulee Wilson (uncredited). **Release Date:** October 6, 1928. Paramount Famous Lasky Corporation/Paramount Pictures. 113 min. **Notes:** When shooting ran too long, Von Stroheim was forced to separate his material and make two films. The second film was called *The Honeymoon* (1928), at the time given only a limited release in Europe. *The Honeymoon* is considered a lost film.

Sins of the Fathers (1928). **Director:** Ludwig Berger. **Writers:** Norman Burnstine (story), Julian Johnson (titles), E. Lloyd Sheldon (writer). **Music:** Hugo Riesenfeld. **Cinematography:** Victor Milner. **Editing:** Frances Marsh. **Cast:** Emil Jannings (Wilhelm Spengler), Ruth Chatterton (Greta), Barry Norton (Tom Spengler), Jean Arthur (Mary Spengler), Jack Luden (Otto), ZaSu Pitts (Mother Spengler), Matthew Betz (Gus), Harry Cording (the Hijacker), Arthur Housman (the Count), Frank Reicher (the Eye Specialist), Douglas Haig (Tom as a Child), Dawn O'Day [Anne Shirley] (Mary as a Child), Milla Davenport, "Speed" Webb and His Orchestra. **Release Date:** December 29, 1928. Paramount Famous Lasky Corporation/Paramount Pictures. **Notes:** Only excerpts survive in the UCLA Film and Television Archives. This was Ruth Chatterton's only silent movie.

The Dummy (1929). **Director:** Robert Milton. **Writers:** Harriet Ford, Harvey J. O'Higgins (play), Herman J. Mankiewicz (writer), Joseph L. Mankiewicz (titles). **Music:** Max Bergunker (uncredited), Karl Hajos (uncredited), Oscar Potoker (uncredited). **Cinematography:** J. Roy Hunt. **Editing:** George Nichols Jr. **Assistant Director:** Morton Whitehill. **Supervisor:** Hector Turnbull. **Cast:** Ruth Chatterton (Agnes Meredith), Fredric March (Trumbull Meredith), John Cromwell (Walter Babbing), Fred Kohler (Joe Cooper), Mickey Bennett (Barney Cook), Vondell Darr (Peggy Meredith), Jack Oakie (Dopey Hart), ZaSu Pitts (Rose Gleason), Richard Tucker (Blackie Baker), Eugene Pallette (Madison), Mickey Daniels (Job Applicant, uncredited), Guy Oliver (Elevator Starter, uncredited). **Release Date:** March 9, 1929. Paramount Pictures. 60 min. **Notes:** The Harriet Ford-Harvey J. Higgins play ran on Broadway in 1914, with Ernest Truex in the lead. It was filmed before in 1917 with Jack Pickford.

The Squall (1929). **Director:** Alexander Korda. **Writers:** Jean Bart (play), Bradley King (screenplay/dialogue), Paul Perez (titles, uncredited). **Producers:** Alexander Korda, Ray Rockett. **Music:** Leo F. Forbstein. **Cinematography:** John F. Seitz. **Editing:** Edward Schroeder. **Art Direction:** Jack Okey, Anton Grot (uncredited). **Set Decoration:** Ray Moyer (uncredited). **Special Photography:** Alvin Knechtel. **Costume Design:** Max Rée. **Cast:** Richard Tucker (Josef Lajos), Alice Joyce (Maria Lajos), Loretta Young (Irma), Carroll Nye (Paul Lajos), ZaSu Pitts (Lena), Harry Cording (Peter), George Hackathorne (Niki), Marcia Harris (Aunt Anna), Knute Erickson (Uncle Dani), Myrna Loy (Nubi), Nicholas Soussanin (El Moro). **Release Date:** May 1929. First National Pictures/First National–Vitaphone Pictures/Warner Bros. Pictures. 105 min. (copyright length)/102 min. (Turner library print). **Notes:** *The Squall* played on Broadway from 1926 to 1927, running 444 performances. It starred Henry O'Neill, Dorothy Stickney, and Blanche Yurka.

Twin Beds (1929). **Director:** Alfred Santell. **Writers:** Salisbury Field, Margaret Mayo (play), F. McGrew Willis (screenplay/titles). **Cinematography:** Sol Polito. **Editing:** LeRoy Stone. **Cast:** Jack Mulhall (Danny

Brown), Patsy Ruth Miller (Elsie Dolan), Edythe Chapman (Ma Dolan), Knute Erickson (Pa Dolan), Jocelyn Lee (Mazie Dolan), Nita Martan (Bobby Dolan), ZaSu Pitts (Tillie), Armand Kaliz (Monty Solari), Gertrude Astor (Mrs. Solari), Carl Levinus (Jason Treejohn), Alice Lake (Mrs. Treejohn), Ben Hendricks Jr. (Pete Trapp), Eddie Gribbon (Red Trapp), Bert Roach (Edward J. Small). **Release Date:** July 14, 1929. First National Pictures/Warner Bros. Pictures. 70 min. **Notes:** Today the only known remaining material from this film are eight sound discs located in the UCLA Film and Television Archives. *Twin Beds* (based on the 1914 Broadway comedy) was filmed previously in 1920, with Carter DeHaven and Flora Parker DeHaven, and later in 1942 with George Brent and Joan Bennett.

The Argyle Case (1929). **Director:** Howard Bretherton. **Writers:** Harriet Ford, Harvey J. O'Higgins, William J. Burns (play), Harvey Thew (writer), De Leon Anthony (titles). **Cinematography:** James C. Van Trees. **Editing:** Thomas Pratt. **Cast:** Thomas Meighan (Alexander Kayton), H.B. Warner (Hurley), Lila Lee (Mary Morgan), John Darrow (Bruce Argyle), ZaSu Pitts (Mrs. Wyatt), Bert Roach (Joe), Wilbur Mack (Sam), Douglas Gerrard (Finley), Alona Marlowe (Kitty), James Quinn (Skidd), Gladys Brockwell (Mrs. Martin), Lew Harvey. **Release Date:** August 17, 1929. The Vitaphone Corporation/Warner Bros. Pictures. **Notes:** Based on a 1912-13 stage play, *The Argyle Case* was filmed once before, in 1917, with Robert Warwick and Frank McGlynn.

Oh, Yeah! (1929). **Director:** Tay Garnett. **Writers:** Tay Garnett (adaptation), A.W. Somerville (story "No Breaks"). **Music:** George Green, George Waggner. **Cinematography:** Arthur C. Miller. **Assistant Director:** Robert Fellows. **Sound:** Harold Stine, Earl A. Wolcott. **Dialogue Director:** James Gleason. **Cast:** Robert Armstrong (Dude), James Gleason (Dusty), Patricia Caron (Pinkie), ZaSu Pitts (the Elk), Budd Fine (Pop Eye), Frank Hagney (Hot Foot), Harry Tyler (Splinters), Paul Hurst (Superintendent). **Release Date:** October 19, 1929. Pathé Exchange. 74 min.

Paris (1929). **Director:** Clarence G. Badger. **Writers:** Martin Brown, E. Ray Goetz (musical play), Hope Loring (screenplay/titles). **Producer:** Robert North. **Music:** Edward Ward. **Cinematography:** Sol Polito. **Editing:** Edward Schroeder. **Dance Director:** Larry Ceballos. **Songs:** "An' Furthermore" (Harry Warren, Bud Green); "Wob-a-ly Walk" (Harry Warren, Bud Green); "Don't Look at Me That Way" (Cole Porter); "My Lover" (Eddie Ward, Al Bryan); "Crystal Girl" (Eddie Ward, Al Bryan); "Miss Wonderful" (Eddie Ward, Al Bryan); "I Wonder What Is Really on His Mind" (Eddie Ward, Al Bryan); "I'm a Little Negative" (Eddie Ward, Al Bryan); "Somebody Mighty Like You" (Eddie Ward, Al Bryan); "Among My Souvenirs" (Lawrence Wright, Edgar Leslie). **Cast:** Irène Bordoni (Vivienne Rolland), Jack Buchanan (Guy Pennell), Louise Closser Hale (Cora Sabbot), Jason Robards (Andrew Sabbot), ZaSu Pitts (Harriet), Margaret Fielding (Brenda Kaley). **Release Date:** November 7, 1929. First National Pictures. 97 min. **Notes:** Another lost film, all that survives of *Paris* are sound discs and sound tape reels in the UCLA Film and Television Archives. Bordoni also starred in the 1928-29 Broadway production, which had interpolated music by Cole Porter, including his classic "(Let's Do It) Let's Fall in Love."

The Locked Door (1929). **Director/Producer:** George Fitzmaurice. **Writers:** Earle Browne (additional dialogue), Channing Pollock (play *The Sign on the Door*), George Scarborough (dialogue), C. Gardner Sullivan (writer). **Cinematography:** Ray June. **Editing: Hal C. Kern. **Art Direction:** William Cameron Menzies. **Assistant Director:** Cullen Tate. **Assistant Camera:** Robert H. Planck. **Dialogue Director:** Earle Browne. **Cast:** Rod La Rocque (Frank Devereaux), Barbara Stanwyck (Ann Carter), William "Stage" Boyd (Lawrence Reagan), Betty Bronson (Helen Reagan), Harry Stubbs (the Waiter), Harry Mestayer (District Attorney), Mack Swain (Hotel Proprietor), ZaSu Pitts (Telephone Girl), George Bunny (the Valet), Purnell Pratt (Police Officer), Fred Warren (Photographer), Mary Ashcraft, Violet Bird, Earle Browne, Clarence Burton, Lita Chevret, Gilbert Clayton, Pauline Curley, Edgar Dearing, Edward Dillon, Kay English, Eleanor Fredericks, Paulette Goddard, Dorothy Gowan, Leona Leigh, Virginia McFadden, Fletcher Norton, Robert Schable, Charles Sullivan, Greta von Rue (uncredited bit parts). **Release Date:** November 16, 1929. George Fitzmaurice Productions/United Artists. 74 min. **Notes:** This was Barbara Stanwyck's first sound film. Incredibly, the story was filmed before as *The Sign on the Door* (1921), which had served as Norma Shearer's film debut. Lowell Sherman and Mary Ryan starred on Broadway in *The Sign on the Door* during 1919-20.

This Thing Called Love (1929). **Director:** Paul L. Stein. **Writers:** Edwin J. Burke (play), Horace Jackson (adaptation/screenplay). **Associate Producer:** Ralph Block. **Cinematography:** Norbert Brodine. **Editing:** Doane Harrison. **Art Direction:** Edward C. Jewell. **Costume Design:** Gwen Wakeling. **Assistant Director:** E.J. Babille. **Props:** Sydney M. Fogel. **Sound:** Charles O'Loughlin, Ben Winkler. **Cast:** Edmund Lowe (Robert Collings), Constance Bennett (Ann Marvin), Roscoe Karns (Harry Bertrand), ZaSu Pitts (Clara Bertrand), Carmelita Geraghty (Alvarez Guerra), John Roche (De Witt), Stuart Erwin (Fred), Ruth Taylor (Dolly), Wilson Benge (Dumary), Adele Watson (Secretary), Jean Harlow (Bit). **Release Date:** December 13, 1929. Pathé Exchange. 72 min. **Notes:** The 1928-29 Broadway comedy ran for 136 performances. It was filmed again in 1940, with Rosalind Russell and Melvyn Douglas.

No, No, Nanette (1930). **Director:** Clarence G. Badger. **Writers:** Otto A. Harbach, Frank Mandel (play), Howard Emmett Rogers (adaptation), Beatrice Van (dialogue). **Producer:** Ned Marin. **Music:** Cecil Copping (uncredited), Alois Reiser (uncredited). **Cinematography:** Sol Polito. **Editing:** Frank Mandel. **Recording Engineer:** Hal Bumbaugh. **Dance Numbers:** Larry Ceballos. **Cast:** Bernice Claire (Nanette), Alexander Gray (Tom Trainor), Lucien Littlefield (Jim Smith), Louise Fazenda (Sue Smith), Lilyan Tashman (Lucille), Bert Roach (Bill Early), ZaSu Pitts (Pauline), Mildred Harris (Betty), Henry Stockbridge (Brady), Jocelyn Lee (Flora). **Release Date:** February 16, 1930. First National Pictures. 98 min. (sound version). **Notes:** *No, No Nanette* was also released in a silent version. This classic musical comedy (which first opened on Broadway in 1925 with Louise Groody, Jack Barker and Charles Winninger) was adapted again for the screen in 1940 (also with ZaSu), and as a Doris Day–Gordon MacRae musical, *Tea for Two*, in 1950.

Honey (1930). **Director:** Wesley Ruggles. **Writers:** Alice Duer Miller (book *Come Out of the Kitchen*), A.E. Thomas (play *Come Out of the Kitchen*), Herman J. Mankiewicz (writer/titles). **Music:** Sam Coslow, W. Franke Harling, Richard Whiting. **Cinematography:** Henry W. Gerrard. **Sound:** Harry M. Lindgren. **Dance Director:** David Bennett. **Cast:** Nancy Carroll (Olivia Dangerfield), Stanley Smith (Burton Crane), Richard "Skeets" Gallagher (Charles Dangerfield), Lillian Roth (Cora Falkner), Harry Green (J. William Burnstein), Mitzi Green

(Doris), ZaSu Pitts (Mayme), Jobyna Howland (Mrs. Falkner), Charles Sellon (Randolph Weeks). **Release Date:** March 29, 1930. Paramount Famous Lasky Corporation/Paramount Pictures. 75 min. **Notes:** Filmed previously as *Come Out of the Kitchen* (1919), this story was later remade in England as *Come Out of the Pantry* (1935, with Jack Buchanan and Fay Wray) and *Spring in Park Lane* (1948, with Anna Neagle and Michael Wilding). A.E. Thomas's play *Come Out of the Kitchen* debuted on Broadway in 1916 and ran over 200 performances; it starred Ruth Chatterton, Bruce McRae, Robert Ames, William Boyd and Walter Connolly.

The Devil's Holiday (1930). **Director/Screenplay/Story:** Edmund Goulding. **Cinematography:** Harry Fischbeck, Enzo Riccioni. **Editing:** George Nichols Jr. **Recording Engineer:** Harry D. Mills. **Music Adaptors:** Howard Jackson (uncredited), John Leipold (uncredited). **Cast:** Nancy Carroll (Hallie Hobart), Phillips Holmes (David Stone), James Kirkwood (Mark Stone), Hobart Bosworth (Ezra Stone), Ned Sparks (Charlie Thorne), Morgan Farley (Monkey McConnell), Jed Prouty (Kent Carr), Paul Lukas (Dr. Reynolds), ZaSu Pitts (Ethel), Morton Downey (Freddie), Guy Oliver (Hammond), Jessie Pringle (Aunt Betty), Wade Boteler (House Detective), Laura Le Vernie (Madame Bernstein). **Release Date:** May 9, 1930. Paramount Publix Corporation/Paramount Pictures. 80 min.

Little Accident (1930). **Director:** William James Craft. **Writers:** Anthony Brown (dialogue), Floyd Dell (novel *An Unmarried Father*), Floyd Dell, Thomas Mitchell (play *The Little Accident*), Gladys Lehman, Gene Towne (screenplay). **Producer:** Carl Laemmle Jr. **Associate Producer:** Albert DeMond. **Cinematography:** Roy Overbaugh. **Editing:** Harry Lieb. **Art Direction:** Walter Koessler. **Costume Design:** Johanna Mathieson. **Recording Engineer:** C. Roy Hunter. **Supervising Editor:** Maurice Pivar. **Musical Director:** David Broekman. **Cast:** Douglas Fairbanks Jr. (Norman Overbeck), Anita Page (Isabel), Sally Blane (Isabel), ZaSu Pitts (Monica), Joan Marsh (Doris), Roscoe Karns (Gilbert), Slim Summerville (Hicks), Henry Armetta (Rudolpho Amendelara), Myrtle Stedman (Mrs. Overbeck), Albert Gran (Mr. Overbeck), Nora Cecil (Dr. Zernecke), Bertha Mann (Miss Hemingway), Gertrude Short (Miss Clark), Dot Farley (Mrs. Van Dine), Grace Cunard (uncredited), Walter Brennan (uncredited). **Release Date:** August 3, 1930. Universal Pictures. 82 min. **Notes:** Thomas Mitchell (who co-wrote the play) and Katherine Alexander starred in the popular 1928-29 Broadway play. Versions of the Dell-Mitchell play were filmed at least three other times: *Papa sans le savoir* (French, 1932), *Little Accident* (1939) and *Casanova Brown* (1944).

The Squealer (1930). **Director:** Harry J. Brown. **Writers:** Dorothy Howell (writer), Mark Linder (play), Casey Robinson (continuity), Jo Swerling (dialogue). **Producer:** Harry Cohn. **Cinematography:** Ted Tetzlaff. **Editing:** Leonard Wheeler. **Art Direction:** Edward C. Jewell. **Recording Engineer:** Edward Bernds. **Technical Director:** Edward Shulter. **Cast:** Jack Holt (Charles Hart), Dorothy Revier (Margaret Hart), Davey Lee (Bunny Hart), Matt Moore (John Sheridan), ZaSu Pitts (Bella), Robert Ellis (Valleti), Matthew Betz (Red Majors), Arthur Housman (Mitter Davis), Louis Natheaux (Ratface Edwards), Eddie Kane (Whisper), Eddie Sturgis (the Killer), Elmer Ballard (Pimply-Face). **Release Date:** August 20, 1930. Columbia Pictures. 67 min. **Notes:** The 1928 melodrama ran on Broadway for 64 performances, with Robert Bentley and Ruth Shepley.

All Quiet on the Western Front (1930). **Director:** Lewis Milestone. **Writers:** Erich

Maria Remarque (novel *Im Westen nichts Neues*), Maxwell Anderson (adaptation/dialogue), George Abbott (screenplay), Del Andrews (adaptation), C. Gardner Sullivan (supervising story chief), Walter Anthony (titles, uncredited). **Producer:** Carl Laemmle Jr. **Cinematography:** Arthur Edeson, Karl Freund (uncredited). **Editing:** Edgar Adams, Edward L. Cahn (uncredited), Milton Carruth (uncredited). **Art Direction:** Charles D. Hall, W.R. Schmitt. **Assistant Director:** Nate Watt. **Recording Supervisor:** C. Roy Hunter. **Sound Technician:** William Hedgcock (uncredited). **Special Photographic Effects:** Frank H. Booth (uncredited). **Special Effects:** Harry Lonsdale (uncredited). **Second Camera:** Tony Gaudio (uncredited). **Assistant Camera:** Cliff Shirpser (uncredited). **Supervising Editor:** Maurice Pivar. **Musical Director:** David Broekman (uncredited). **Advisor of Military History:** Hans von Morhart (uncredited). **Associate Director:** Nate Watt (uncredited). **Cast:** Louis Wolheim (Kat Katczinsky), Lewis Ayres (Paul Bäumer), John Wray (Himmelstoss), Arnold Lucy (Professor Kantorek), Ben Alexander (Franz Kemmerich), Scott Kolk (Leer), Owen Davis Jr. (Peter), Walter Browne Rogers (Behn), William Bakewell (Albert Kropp), Russell Gleason (Mueller), Richard Alexander (Westhus), Harold Goodwin (Detering), Slim Summerville (Tjaden), [G.] Pat Collins (Lieutenant Bertinck), Beryl Mercer (Mrs. Bäumer, Paul's Mother; sound version), Edmund Breese (Herr Meyer), ZaSu Pitts (Mrs. Baumer, silent version), Marion Clayton Anderson (Miss Anna Bäumer, uncredited), Poupée Andriot (French Girl, uncredited), Vince Barnett (Assistant Cook, uncredited), Daisy Belmore (Mrs. Kemmerick, uncredited), Glen Boles (Young Soldier, uncredited), Heinie Conklin (Joseph Hammacher, uncredited), Renée Damonde (French Girl, uncredited), Yola d'Avril (Suzanne, uncredited), Arthur Gardner (Student, uncredited), Raymond Griffith (Gérard Duval, uncredited), Ellen Hall (Young Girl, uncredited), William Irving (Ginger the Cook, uncredited), Frederick Kohner (uncredited), Tom London (Medic Orderly, uncredited), Bertha Mann (Sister Libertine, uncredited), Joan Marsh (Poster Girl, uncredited), Edwin Maxwell (Mr. Bäumer, uncredited), Maurice Murphy (Soldier, uncredited), Robert Parrish (bit part, uncredited), Bodil Rosing (Mother of Hospital Patient, uncredited), Wolfgang Staudte (uncredited), Jack Sutherland (uncredited), David Tyrell (Soldier, uncredited), Fred Zinnemann (uncredited), Lewis Milestone (hand double, Lew Ayres, uncredited). **Release Date:** August 24, 1930. Universal Pictures. 138 min (copyright length)/USA: 133 min (restored version: Library of Congress)/UK: 145 min (cut)/UK: 147 min (BBFC submission before censorship)/Germany: 136 min. **Notes:** ZaSu's cut scene was retained for the silent version of the film. *All Quiet on the Western Front* won Academy Awards for Best Picture and Best Director for Lewis Milestone.

Monte Carlo (1930). **Director/Producer:** Ernst Lubitsch. **Writers:** Hans Müller (play *The Blue Coast*), Booth Tarkington (novel *Monsieur Beaucaire*), Evelyn Greenleaf Sutherland (play *Monsieur Beaucaire*), Ernest Vajda (adaptation), Vincent Lawrence (additional dialogue). **Music:** W. Franke Harling, Richard Whiting, Karl Hajos (uncredited), Herman Hand (uncredited), Sigmund Krumgold (uncredited), John Leipold (uncredited). **Cinematography:** Victor Milner. **Editing:** Merrill G. White. **Costume Design:** Travis Banton (uncredited). **Recording Engineer:** Harry D. Mills (uncredited). **Camera Operator:** Lucien Ballard (uncredited). **Songs:** "Beyond the Blue Horizon" (Richard A. Whiting, W. Franke Harling, Leo Robin), performed by Jeanette MacDonald; "Give Me a Moment Please" (Richard A.

Whiting, W. Franke Harling, Leo Robin), performed by Jeanette MacDonald and Jack Buchanan; "Always in All Ways" (Richard A. Whiting, W. Franke Harling, Leo Robin), performed by Jeanette MacDonald and Jack Buchanan; "She'll Love Me and Like It" (Richard A. Whiting, W. Franke Harling, Leo Robin), performed by Jeanette MacDonald and Claud Allister; "Day of Days" (Richard A. Whiting, W. Franke Harling, Leo Robin), performed by Chorus; "Trimmin' the Women" (Richard A. Whiting, W. Franke Harling, Leo Robin), performed by Jack Buchanan, John Roche and Tyler Brooke; "Whatever It Is, It's Grand" (Richard A. Whiting, W. Franke Harling, Leo Robin), performed by Jeanette MacDonald and Jack Buchanan. **Cast:** Jack Buchanan (Count Rudolph Falliere, a.k.a. Rudy the Hairdresser), Jeanette MacDonald (Countess Helene Mara), Claud Allister (Prince Otto Von Seibenheim), ZaSu Pitts (Bertha), Tyler Brooke (Armand), John Roche (Paul), Lionel Belmore (Duke Gustave von Seibenheim), Albert Conti (Prince Otto's Companion/M.C), Helen Garden (Lady Mary in Stage Opera), Donald Novis (Monsieur Beaucaire in Stage Opera), Erik Bey (Lord Windorset), David Percy (Herald), Billy Bevan (Train Conductor, uncredited), Sidney Bracey (Hunchback at Casino, uncredited), John Carroll (Wedding Guest Officer, uncredited), Frances Dee (Receptionist, uncredited), Geraldine Dvorak (Extra in Casino, uncredited), Edgar Norton (uncredited), Rolfe Sedan (Hairdresser, uncredited). **Release Date:** August 27, 1930. Paramount Publix Corporation/Paramount Pictures. 90 min.

War Nurse (1930). **Director:** Edgar Selwyn. **Writers:** Becky Gardiner (continuity/dialogue), Joe Farnham (dialogue). **Cinematography:** Charles Roscher. **Editing:** William LeVanway. **Art Direction:** Cedric Gibbons. **Recording Director:** Douglas Shearer. **Wardrobe:** René Hubert. **Cast:** Robert Montgomery (Lt. Wally O'Brien), Anita Page (Joy Meadows), June Walker (Barbara "Babs" Whitney), Robert Ames (Lt. Robin "Robbie" Neil), ZaSu Pitts (Cushie), Marie Prevost (Rosalie Parker), Helen Jerome Eddy (Marian "Kansas"), Hedda Hopper (Mrs. Townsend), Edward Nugent (Lt. Frank Stevens), Martha Sleeper (Helen), Michael Vavitch (Doctor), James Bush (uncredited), Louis Mercier (Wounded French Soldier, uncredited), John Miljan (French Medical Officer, uncredited), Sandra Ravel (French Chanteuse, uncredited), Loretta Young (Nurse, uncredited). **Release Date:** November 22, 1930. Metro-Goldwyn-Mayer (MGM). 79 min. (Turner library print)/81 min. (copyright length). **Notes:** According to AFI, "*War Nurse* marked the first onscreen appearance of French actor Charles Boyer, who is seen briefly as a French surgeon. Although Boyer made the french-language version of *Big House* for MGM at around the same time as *War Nurse*, that film was not released in the United States."

River's End (1930). **Director:** Michael Curtiz. **Writers:** James Oliver Curwood (novel *The River's End*), Charles Kenyon (screenplay/dialogue). **Cinematography:** Robert Kurrle. **Editing:** Ralph Holt. **Costume Design:** Earl Luick. **Set Design:** Ben Carré (uncredited). **General Musical Director:** Erno Rapee. **Cast:** Charles Bickford (John Keith/Sgt. Connie Conniston), Evalyn Knapp (Mimi McDowell), J. Farrell MacDonald (Pat O'Toole), ZaSu Pitts (Louise), Walter McGrail (Sergeant Leslie Martin), David Torrence (Colonel McDowell), Junior Coghlan [Frank Coghlan Jr.] (Mickey O'Toole), Tom Santschi (Sergeant Sam Shotwell), Lionel Belmore (Mountie, uncredited), Willie Fung (Eskimo, uncredited), Frank Hagney (Mountie, uncredited), Tom London (uncredited), Cliff Saum (Mountie, uncredited). **Release Date:** November 1, 1930. Vitaphone Corporation/Warner Bros. Pictures. 75 min./74 min. (Turner library print). **Notes:** This story was filmed before in 1920 (with Lewis Stone) and remade by Warner Bros. in 1940 (with Dennis Morgan).

Sin Takes a Holiday (1930). **Director:** Paul L. Stein. **Writers:** Dorothy Cairns, Robert Milton (story), Horace Jackson (writer). **Producer:** E.B. Derr. **Music:** Francis Gromon (uncredited), Josiah Zuro (uncredited). **Cinematography:** John Mescall. **Editing:** Daniel Mandell. **Art Direction:** Carroll Clark. **Costume Design:** Gwen Wakeling. **Assistant Director:** E.J. Babille (uncredited). **Sound Engineer:** T.A. Carman, Charles O'Loughlin. **Still Photographer:** Emmett Schoenbaum (uncredited). **Musical Director:** Francis Gromon. **Cast:** Constance Bennett (Sylvia Brenner), Kenneth MacKenna (Gaylord Stanton), Basil Rathbone (Reginald "Reggie" Durant), Rita La Roy (Grace Lawrence), Louis John Bartels (Richards), John Roche (Sheridan), ZaSu Pitts (Anna "Annie"), Kendall Lee (Miss Munson), Murrel Finley (Ruth), Helen Johnson [Judith Wood] (Mrs. Graham), Fred Walton (Martin), Richard Carle (Minister, uncredited), Gino Corrado (Dressmaker, uncredited), George Davis (Butler at Villa, uncredited), Alphonse Martell (uncredited), Leo White (Photographer, uncredited). **Release Date:** November 10, 1930. Pathé Exchange. 81 min.

The Lottery Bride (1930). **Director:** Paul L. Stein. **Writers:** Horace Jackson, Howard Emmett Rogers (writers), Herbert Stothart (story "Bride 66"). **Producers:** Arthur Hammerstein, Joseph M. Schenck. **Cinematography:** Karl Freund, Ray June. **Editing:** Robert Kern. **Art Direction:** William Cameron Menzies. **Costume Design:** Alice O'Neill. **Production Manager:** Orville O. Dull. **Assistant Directors:** Lonnie D'Orsa, Walter Mayo. **Sound Technician:** Frank Maher. **Chief Sound Recordist:** J.T. Reed. **Editorial Advisor:** Hal C. Kern. **Music Arranger:** Hugo Riesenfeld. **Songs:** "Drinking Song" (Rudolf Friml, J. Keirn Brennan), performed by chorus; "Yubla" (Rudolf Friml, J. Keirn Brennan), performed by Jeanette MacDonald; "My Northern Light" (Rudolf Friml, J. Keirn Brennan), performed by John Garrick and Jeanette MacDonald; "Brother Love" (Rudolf Friml, J. Keirn Brennan), performed by Robert Chisholm, John Garrick and chorus; "High and Low" (Arthur Schwartz, Howard Dietz), performed by chorus; "Song of Napoli" (Rudolf Friml, J. Keirn Brennan), performed by Joseph Macaulay; "You're an Angel" (Rudolf Friml, J. Keirn Brennan), performed by Robert Chisholm and John Garrick; "I'll Follow the Trail" (Rudolf Friml, J. Keirn Brennan), performed by Robert Chisholm **Cast:** Jeanette MacDonald (Jenny Swanson), John Garrick (Chris Svenson), Joe E. Brown (Hoke Curtis), ZaSu Pitts (Hilda), Robert Chisholm (Olaf Svenson), Joseph Macaulay (Alberto), Harry Gribbon (Boris), Carroll Nye (Nels Swanson), Frank Brownlee (Guard, uncredited), Max Davidson (Marriage Broker, uncredited), Robert Homans (Miner, uncredited), Paul Hurst (Lottery Agent, uncredited). **Release Date:** November 28, 1930. Joseph M. Schenck Productions/United Artists. 80 min.

Passion Flower (1930). **Director:** William C. de Mille (uncredited). **Writers:** Kathleen Norris (novel), Martin Flavin (adaptation/dialogue), Laurence E. Johnson, Edith Fitzgerald (additional dialogue). **Producer:** William C. de Mille. **Cinematography:** Hal Rosson. **Editing:** Conrad A. Nervig. **Art Direction:** Cedric Gibbons. **Gowns:** Adrian. **Recording Director:** Douglas Shearer. **Recording Engineer:** James Brock (uncredited). **Cast:** Kay Francis (Dulce Morado), Kay Johnson (Katherine "Cassy" Pringle Wallace), Charles Bickford (Dan Wallace), Winter Hall (Leroy Pringle), Lewis Stone (Antonio "Tony"

Morado), ZaSu Pitts (Mrs. Harney), Dickie Moore (Tommy Wallace), Mary Carlisle (uncredited), Jay Eaton (uncredited), Ray Milland (uncredited), Herbert Prior (uncredited), C. Aubrey Smith (uncredited), Jack Trent (uncredited), Ellinor Vanderveer (uncredited). **Release Date:** December 6, 1930. Metro-Goldwyn-Mayer (MGM). 79 min.

Her Private Life (1930). **Director:** Alexander Korda. **Writers:** Zoe Akins (play *Declassee*), Forrest Halsey (screenplay/titles). **Producer:** Ned Marin. **Music:** Cecil Copping (uncredited), Alois Reiser (uncredited). **Cinematography:** John F. Seitz. **Editing:** Harold Young. **Costume Design:** Edward Stevenson. **Cast:** Billie Dove (Lady Helen Haden), Walter Pidgeon (Ned Thayer), Holmes Herbert (Rudolph Solomon), Montagu Love (Sir Bruce Haden), Thelma Todd (Mrs. Leslie), Roland Young (Charteris), Mary Forbes (Ladu Wildering), Brandon Hurst (Sir Emmett Wildering), ZaSu Pitts (Timmins). **Release Date:** December 15, 1930. First National Pictures. **Notes:** Under the play's original name, *Declassee*, this story was filmed in 1925 with Lloyd Hughes. *Declassee* ran on Broadway for 257 performances in 1919-20 and starred Ethel Barrymore.

Free Love (1930). **Director:** Hobart Henley. **Writers:** Winifred Dunn, Edwin Knopf (writers), Sidney Howard (play *Half Gods*). **Producer:** Carl Laemmle Jr. **Music:** Heinz Roemheld (uncredited). **Supervisor:** E.M. Asher. **Cast:** Conrad Nagel (Stephen Ferrier), Genevieve Tobin (Hope Ferrier), Monroe Owsley (Rush Begelow), Bertha Mann (Helena), Ilka Chase (Pauline), George Irving (Judge Sturgis), Reginald Pasch (Dr. Wolheim), Slim Summerville (Gas Inspector), ZaSu Pitts (Ada the Maid), Sidney Bracey (Butler), Bert Roach (uncredited). **Release Date:** December 1930. Universal Pictures. 70 min. **Notes:** The film's original title was to be *The Modern Wife*. Donn Cook and Mayo Methot starred in the Broadway 1929 production of *Half Gods*, which only lasted 17 performances.

Finn and Hattie (1931). **Directors:** Norman Z. McLeod, Norman Taurog. **Writers:** Joseph L. Mankiewicz (writer), Sam Mintz (story), Donald Ogden Stewart (novel *Mr. and Mrs. Haddock Abroad*). **Cinematography:** Devereaux Jennings. **Cast:** Leon Errol (Finley P. Haddock), Mitzi Green (Mildred), ZaSu Pitts (Mrs. Haddock), Jackie Searl (Sidney), Lilyan Tashman (the Princess), Mack Swain (Frenchman), Regis Toomey (Collins), Harry Beresford (New York Street Cleaner), Ethel Sutherland [Kenyon] (a Divorcee), Syd Saylor (the Brakeman), Louise Mackintosh (Aunt Letty), Eddie Dunn (Taxi Driver), Oscar Smith (Man), Pat Harmon (uncredited), Rolfe Sedan (uncredited). **Release Date:** February 28, 1931. Paramount Pictures. 78 min. **Notes:** The film's working title was *Finn and Hattie Abroad*.

The Bad Sister (1931). **Director:** Hobart Henley. **Writers:** Edwin H. Knopf (dialogue/screenplay), Tom Reed, Raymond L. Schrock (writers), Booth Tarkington (novel *The Flirt*). **Producer:** Carl Laemmle Jr. **Music:** David Broekman (uncredited). **Cinematography:** Karl Freund. **Editing:** Ted Kent. **Art Direction:** Walter R. Koessler. **Recording Supervisor:** C. Roy Hunter. **Supervising Editor:** Maurice Pivar. **Cast:** Conrad Nagel (Dr. Dick Lindley), Sidney Fox (Marianne Madison), Bette Davis (Laura Madison), ZaSu Pitts (Minnie), Slim Summerville (Sam), Charles Winninger (Mr. Madison), Emma Dunn (Mrs. Madison), Humphrey Bogart (Valentine Corliss), Bert Roach (Wade Trumbull), David Durand (Hedrick Madison), King Baggot (Policeman on Street, uncredited), Willie Best (uncredited), Helene Chadwick (Amy, uncredited), Dick Winslow (Paper Boy, uncredited), Charles Giblyn (uncredited), Cornelius Keefe (uncredited), Mary

Alden (uncredited), Sammy Blum (uncredited), Will Walling (uncredited), Grace Cunard (uncredited). **Release Date:** March 29, 1931. Universal Pictures. 68 min. **Notes:** This was Bette Davis' first film. Its original title was *Gambling Daughters*. Tarkington's novel was first filmed by Universal as *The Flirt* (1922), which was also directed by Hobart Henley.

Beyond Victory (1931). **Director:** John Robertson, Edward H. Griffith (uncredited). **Writers:** James Gleason, Horace Jackson (writers). **Producer:** E.B. Derr. **Music:** Arthur Alexander, Francis Gromon (uncredited). **Cinematography:** Norbert Brodine. **Editing:** Daniel Mandell. **Art Direction:** Carroll Clark. **Costume Design:** Gwen Wakeling. **Sound Engineer:** Harold Stine, Ben Winkler. **Musical Director:** Francis Gromon. **Prelude Effects:** William Dietz. **Cast:** Bill Boyd (Sgt. Bill Thatcher), James Gleason (Pvt. Jim "KP" Mobley), Lew Cody (Lew Cavanaugh), ZaSu Pitts (Mlle. Fritzi Mobley), Marion Shilling (Ina), Russell Gleason (Russell "Bud"), Lissi Arna (Katherina), Mary Carr (Bud's Mother), Fred Scott (Fred), Theodore von Eltz (Maj. Sparks), Frank Reicher (German Military Hospital Chief), Max Barwyn (German Doctor, uncredited), Wade Boteler (uncredited), Ed Brady (Sergeant, uncredited), E.H. Calvert (Commanding Officer, uncredited), Eddy Chandler (Lieutenant, uncredited), Charles Coleman (Sparrow, uncredited), Ethan Laidlaw (Soldier in Prelude, uncredited), Purnell Pratt (uncredited), Hedwiga Reicher (German Nurse, uncredited). **Release Date:** April 12, 1931. RKO Pathé Pictures. 70 min. **Notes:** Hedwiga Reicher was Frank Reicher's sister, and Russell Gleason was James Gleason's son. The AFI detailed that "Director Edward H. Griffith was brought in to shoot retakes. Modern sources also note that scenes featuring Helen Twelvetrees and June Collyer were edited out of the final film."

Seed (1931). **Director:** John M. Stahl. **Writers:** Gladys Lehman (writer), Charles G. Norris (story). **Producers:** Carl Laemmle Jr., John M. Stahl. **Music:** Heinz Roemheld (uncredited). **Cinematography:** Jackson Rose. **Editing:** Ted J. Kent, Arthur Tavares. **Orchestrator:** Adolph Fink (uncredited), Andor Pinte (uncredited), William Schiller (uncredited). **Stock Music:** J. Clifford (uncredited), Sam Perry (uncredited). **Cast:** John Boles (Bart Carter), Frances Dade (Nancy), Bette Davis (Margaret Carter), Raymond Hackett (Junior Carter), ZaSu Pitts (Jennie), Genevieve Tobin (Mildred), Richard Tucker (Bliss), Jack Willis (Dicky Carter), Lois Wilson (Peggy Carter), Dick Winslow (Johnny Carter), Don Cox (Dicky Carter as a Child), Terry Cox (Danny Carter as a Child), Dickie Moore (Johnny Carter as a Child), Helen Parrish (Margaret Carter as a Child), Kenneth Seiling (Junior Carter as a Child), Bill Willis (Danny Carter), Robert Gordon (Office Boy, uncredited). **Release Date:** May 14, 1931. Universal Pictures. 96 min.

Their Mad Moment (1931). **Directors:** Hamilton MacFadden (uncredited), Chandler Sprague (uncredited). **Writers:** Leon Gordon (writer), Eleanor Mercein (stories). **Music:** Richard Fall (uncredited). **Orchestrators:** Alfred Dalby (uncredited), Emil Gerstenberger (uncredited), Jack Virgil (uncredited). **Cast:** Warner Baxter (Esteban Cristera), Dorothy Mackaill (Emily Stanley), ZaSu Pitts (Miss Dibbs), Nance O'Neil (Grand Mere), Lawrence Grant (Sir Harry Congers), Leon Janney (Narcio), John St. Polis (Hotel Manager), Nella Walker (Suzanne Stanley), Mary Doran (Stancia), Wilson Benge (uncredited). **Release Date:** July 12, 1931. Fox Film Corporation. 55 min. **Notes:** The working titles for this film were *Basquerie* and *This Modern World*. Eleanor Mercein's stories originally appeared in *The Saturday Evening Post*, beginning with the story "Basquerie" in the July 3, 1926, issue, and ending with the story "Nostalgia" in the August 13, 1927, issue. 20th Century–Fox remade *Their Mad Moment* in 1941 as *The Perfect Snob*, directed by Ray McCarey, and starring Lynn Bari and Cornel Wilde.

A Woman of Experience (1931). **Director:** Harry Joe Brown. **Writers:** John Farrow (play *The Registered Woman*, dialogue and screenplay), Ralph F. Murphy (additional dialogue). **Producer:** Charles R. Rogers. **Cinematography:** Hal Mohr. **Editing:** Fred Allen. **Assistant Director:** Jay Marchant (uncredited). **Musical Director:** Arthur Lange. **Technical Advisor:** Captain Eugene Hager (uncredited). **Cast:** Helen Twelvetrees (Elsa Elsbergen), William Bakewell (Count Karl Runyi), Lew Cody (Captain Otto von Lichstein), H.B. Warner (Major Hugh Schmidt), ZaSu Pitts (Katie), C. Henry Gordon (Captain Muller), Nance O'Neil (Countess Runyi), George Fawcett (General), Franklin Pangborn (Hans, a Sailor), Edward Earle (Captain Kurt von Hausen), Ashley Buck (Heinrich), Bertha Mann (Red Cross Nurse), G. Pat Collins (Submarine Captain Franz), Harvey Clarke (Coachman), Lionel Belmore (Recruiting Speaker, uncredited), Max Davidson (Beer Garden Manager, uncredited), Alfred Hickman (Colonel, uncredited), William H. Tooker (Colonel, uncredited), Max Waizmann (Brunck, Otto's Servant, uncredited). **Release Date:** August 7, 1931. RKO Pathé Pictures. 74 min. **Notes:** *The Registered Woman* was the film's working title. There is no record of a play running on Broadway by John Farrow called *The Registered Woman*; it is possible that it remained unproduced.

The Big Gamble (1931). **Director:** Fred Niblo. **Writers:** Octavus Roy Cohen (story/novel *The Iron Chalice*), Walter De Leon, F. McGrew Willis (writers). **Producer:** Charles R. Rogers. **Associate Producer:** Harry Joe Brown. **Cinematography:** Hal Mohr. **Editing:** Joseph Kane. **Art Direction:** Carroll Clark. **Costume Design:** Gwen Wakeling. **Sound Engineers:** T.A. Carman, Charles O'Loughlin. **Musical Director:** Arthur Lange. **Cast:** Bill Boyd (Alan Beckwith), James Gleason (Fred "Squint" Dugan), Warner Oland (Andrew North), Dorothy Sebastian (Beverly Ames Beckwith), ZaSu Pitts (Nora Dugan), June MacCloy (Mae Robbins), William Collier Jr. (Johnnie Ames), Ralph Ince (Webb), Geneva Mitchell (Trixie), Sidney Bracey (Wedding Witness, uncredited), Eddy Chandler (Gangster Driver, uncredited), Charles K. Gerrard (uncredited), Edward McWade (Justice of the Peace, uncredited), Jack Richardson (uncredited), Phillips Smalley (uncredited), Fred Walton (Samuel, uncredited), Eric Wilton (Poker Player, uncredited). **Release Date:** September 27, 1931. RKO Pathé Pictures. 65 min. **Notes:** The film's working title was *The Iron Chalice*. The story was filmed previously in 1926 as *Red Dice*, directed by William K. Howard. Co-stars Bill "Hoppy" Boyd and Dorothy Sebastian were married (1930–36) in real life.

Penrod and Sam (1931). **Director:** William Beaudine. **Writers:** Booth Tarkington (story/novel), Waldemar Young (screenplay). **Music:** David Mendoza (uncredited). **Cinematography:** Roy Overbaugh. **Editing:** LeRoy Stone. **Art Direction:** John J. Hughes. **Costume Design:** Earl Luick. **Assistant Director:** Russell Saunders. **Cast:** Leon Janney (Penrod Schofield), Junior Coghlan [Frank Coghlan Jr.] (Sam Williams), Cameo the Dog (Duke Schofield, Penrod's Dog), Margaret Marquis (Marjorie "Margie" Jones), Billie Lord (George Hemingway "Georgie" Bassett), Nestor Aber [Michael Stuart] (Rodney Bitts), James Robinson (Herman Washington), Robert Dandrige (Verman Washington), Matt Moore (Henry Schofield),

Dorothy Peterson (Mrs. Mary Schofield), Helen Beaudine (Margaret Schofield), Johnny Arthur (Mr. Bassett), ZaSu Pitts (Mrs. Bassett), Charles Sellon (Mr. Bitts), Beaudine Anderson (Boy, uncredited), Wade Boteler (Mr. Williams, Sam's Dad; uncredited), Betty Jane Graham (Baby Amy Rensdale, uncredited), Gertrude Howard (Delia, uncredited), Gus Leonard (Violinist, uncredited), Sidney Miller (Maurice Levy, uncredited), Elizabeth Patterson (the Teacher, uncredited), Dorothy Vernon (Irate Mother at Birthday Party, uncredited). **Release Date:** October 3, 1931. First National Pictures/Warner Bros. Pictures. 71 min. **Notes:** Tarkington's *Penrod* was adapted for the screen at least three other times: *Penrod* (1922), *Penrod and Sam* (1923, also directed by William Beaudine), and *Penrod and Sam* (1937).

The Guardsman (1931). **Director:** Sidney Franklin. **Writers:** Ferenc Molnár (play *A testör*), Ernest Vajda (screenplay), Claudine West (continuity). **Producers:** Albert Lewin (uncredited), Irving Thalberg (uncredited). **Cinematography:** Norbert Brodine. **Editing:** Conrad A. Nervig. **Art Direction:** Cedric Gibbons. **Costume Design:** Adrian. **Assistant Director:** Harold S. Bucquet (uncredited). **Recording Director:** Douglas Shearer. **Supervisor:** Albert Lewin (uncredited). **Cast:** Alfred Lunt (the Actor), Lynn Fontanne (the Actress), Roland Young (Bernhardt the Critic), ZaSu Pitts (Liesl, the Maid), Maude Eburne (Mama), Herman Bing (a Creditor), Michael Mark (Valet, uncredited), Ann Dvorak (Fan, uncredited). **Release Date:** November 7, 1931. Metro-Goldwyn-Mayer (MGM). 82 min. **Notes:** Molnár's play opened in Budapest in 1911. In 1913, English versions were staged in London (*Playing with Fire*) and New York (*Where Ignorance Is Bliss*). However, it is acknowledged that the definitive English version, adapted by Philip Moeller, starred Alfred Lunt and Lynn Fontanne and opened in New York in 1924. There was a German film version released in 1925 called *Der Gardeoffizier*. *The Guardsman* was the Lunts' only starring film. They were both nominated for Academy Awards for their performances.

The Secret Witness (1931). **Director:** Thornton Freeland. **Writers:** Sam Spewack (novel *Murder in the Gilded Cage*/screenplay). **Cinematography:** Robert H. Planck. **Editing:** Louis Sackin. **Recording Engineer:** Corson Jowett. **Cast:** Una Merkel (Lois Martin), William Collier Jr. (Arthur Jones, a.k.a. Casey), ZaSu Pitts (Bella), Purnell Pratt (Captain McGowan), Ralf Harolde (Lewis Leroy), Clyde Cook (Larson), June Clyde (Tess Jones), Rita La Roy (Sylvia Folsom), Hooper Atchley (Herbert "Bert" Folsom), Paul Hurst (Brannigan), Nat Pendleton (Gunner), Greta Granstedt (Moll), Clarence Muse (Jeff), Billy Bletcher (voice), Mike Donlin (Mike), James Durkin (Detective, uncredited), Henry Hall (Police Commissioner Martin, uncredited), Maston Williams (Contact Detective, uncredited). **Release Date:** December 12, 1931. Columbia Pictures Corporation. 66 min. **Notes:** The working title of this film was *Terror by Night*.

The Unexpected Father (1932). **Director:** Thornton Freeland. **Writers:** Robert Keith, Max Lief, Dale Van Every (writers). **Producer:** Stanley Bergerman. **Music:** Sam Perry (uncredited). **Cinematography:** Jerome Ash. **Cast:** Slim Summerville (Jasper Jones), ZaSu Pitts (Polly Perkins), Cora Sue Collins (Judge), Alison Skipworth (Mrs. Hawkins), Dorothy Christy (Evelyn Smythe), Grayce Hampton (Mrs. Smythe), Claud Allister (Claude), Tyrell Davis (Reggie), Tom O'Brien (Policeman), Dick Cramer (Policeman). **Release Date:** January 3, 1932. Universal Pictures. 71 min. **Notes:** *Pudge* and *Papa Loves Mamma* were two of this film's working titles.

Broken Lullaby (1932). **Director:** Ernst Lubitsch. **Writers:** Reginald Berkeley, Samson Raphaelson, Ernest Vajda (writers), Maurice Rostand (play). **Music:** W. Franke Harling. **Cinematography:** Victor Milner. **Art Direction:** Hans Dreier. **Cast:** Lionel Barrymore (Dr. H. Holderlin), Nancy Carroll (Fraulein Elsa), Phillips Holmes (Paul Renaud), Louise Carter (Frau Holderlin), Tom Douglas (Walter Holderlin), Emma Dunn (Frau Muller), Lucien Littlefield (Herr Walter Schultz), Tully Marshall (Gravedigger), ZaSu Pitts (Anna), George Bickel (Herr Bresslauer), Lillian Elliott (Frau Bresslauer), Rodney McLennon (War Veteran), Joan Standing (Flower Shop Girl), Torben Meyer (Waiter at Inn), Marvin Stephens (Fritz), Reginald Pasch (Fritz's Father), Frank Sheridan (Priest), Ed Eberle (uncredited), Henry Fifer (uncredited), Anton Vaverka (uncredited), George Irving, George Davis, Julia Swayne Gordon. **Release Date:** January 24, 1932. Paramount Pictures. 76 min. **Notes:** The working titles for the film were *The Man I Killed* and *The Fifth Commandment*.

Steady Company (1932). **Director/Screenplay:** Edward I. Luddy. **Writers:** Earle Snell (story/dialogue). **Producer:** Carl Laemmle Jr. **Cinematography:** Charles J. Stumar. **Supervisor:** Henry Henigson. **Cast:** Norman Foster (Jim), June Clyde (Peggy), ZaSu Pitts (Dot), Henry Armetta (Tony), J. Farrell MacDonald (Hogan), Maurice Black (Blix), Morgan Wallace (Tuxedo Carter), Jack Perry (Pico Vacci), Morrie Cohan (Curly Blake), Willard Robertson (Pop Henley). **Release Date:** March 14, 1932. Universal Pictures. 65 min.

Shopworn (1932). **Director:** Nick Grinde. **Writers:** Sarah Y. Mason (original story), Sarah Y. Mason, Jo Swerling, Robert Riskin (screenplay). **Producer:** Harry Cohn. **Music:** Mischa Bakaleinikoff (uncredited), Irving Bibo (uncredited), Milan Roder (uncredited). **Cinematography:** Joseph Walker. **Editing:** Gene Havlick. **Assistant Director:** C. C. Coleman Jr. **Sound Recordist:** Glenn Rominger. **Cast:** Barbara Stanwyck (Kitty Lane), Regis Toomey (David Livingston), ZaSu Pitts (Aunt Dot), Lucien Littlefield (Fred), Clara Blandick (Mrs. Helen Livingston), Robert Alden (Toby), Oscar Apfel (Judge Forbes), Maude Turner Gordon (Mrs. Thorne), Albert Conti (Andre Renoir), James Durkin (District Attorney, scenes deleted), Sidney Bracey (Photographer, uncredited), Charles A. Browne (Cop, uncredited), Wallis Clark (Mr. Dean, uncredited), John Elliott (Judge, uncredited), Bess Flowers (Party Guest, uncredited), Selmer Jackson (Murray, uncredited), Louise Mackintosh (Party Guest, uncredited), Merrill McCormick (Construction Workman, uncredited), Broderick O'Farrell (Party Guest, uncredited), Hal Price (Detective Collins, uncredited), Joe Sawyer (Construction Camp Doctor, uncredited), Harry Semels (Construction Workman, uncredited), Harry Tenbrook (Construction Workman, uncredited). **Release Date:** March 25, 1932. Columbia Pictures Corporation. 72 min./66 min. (re-edited version).

Destry Rides Again (1932). **Director:** Ben Stoloff. **Writers:** Max Brand (novel), Isadore Bernstein (continuity), Robert Keith (dialogue), Richard Schayer (adaptation). **Producer:** Carl Laemmle Jr. **Associate Producer:** Stanley Bergerman. **Cinematography:** Dan Clark. **Editing:** Arthur Hilton. **Supervising Editor:** Maurice Pivar. **Cast:** Tom Mix (Tom Destry), Tony the Horse (Tony), Claudia Dell (Sally Dangerfield), ZaSu Pitts (Temperance Worker), Stanley Fields (Sheriff Jerry Wendell), Earle Foxe (Bren), Edward Peil Sr. (Frank Warren), Francis Ford (Judd Ogden), Frederick Howard (Edward Clifton), George Ernest (Willie), Edward LeSaint (Mr. Dangerfield), Andy Devine (Stage Passenger; scene deleted, uncredited), Ed Brady (Bartender, uncredited), Charles Brinley (Townsman, uncredited), Edmund Cobb (Townsman, uncredited), Charles K. French (Jury Foreman, uncredited), Harrison Greene (Bailiff, uncredited), Harry Harvey (Stage Passenger, uncredited), Allen Holbrook (Henchman, uncredited), John Ince (the Judge, uncredited), Tiny Jones (Townswoman, uncredited), Clyde Kinney (Clyde, uncredited), Chris-Pin Martin (Lopez, uncredited), Buck Moulton (Buck, uncredited), Harry Tenbrook (uncredited). **Release Date:** April 17, 1932. Universal Pictures. 61 min. **Notes:** Because of the classic status of the 1939 version of this story (starring James Stewart and Marlene Dietrich), this version was renamed *Justice Rides Again* for television. Location shooting took place at the Los Turas Ranch, Los Angeles, while the railroad train exteriors were shot in El Segundo, California. This was Tom Mix's first lead role in a talking picture. The story was remade again in 1954 as *Destry*, with Audie Murphy.

The Trial of Vivienne Ware (1932). **Director:** William K. Howard. **Writers:** Barry Conners, Philip Klein (writers), Kenneth M. Ellis (novel). **Music:** James F. Hanley. **Cinematography:** Ernest Palmer. **Editing:** Ralph Dietrich. **Art Direction:** Gordon Wiles. **Costume Design:** David Cox. **Incidental Music:** R.H. Bassett (uncredited), Hugo Friedhofer (uncredited). **Cast:** Joan Bennett (Vivienne Ware), Donald Cook (John Sutherland), Richard "Skeets" Gallagher (Graham McNally), ZaSu Pitts (Gladys Fairweather), Lilian Bond (Dolores Divine), Alan Dinehart (Prosecutor), Herbert Mundin (William Boggs), Howard Phillips (Minetti), William Pawley (Joseph Gilk), Noel Madison (Angelo Paroni), Jameson Thomas (Damon Fenwick), Ruth Selwyn (Mercedes Joy), Christian Rub (Axel Nordstrom), Maude Eburne (Mrs. Elizabeth Hardy), J. Maurice Sullivan [John M. Sullivan] (Judge Henderson), Sam Armstrong (Assistant Prosecuting Attorney, uncredited), Stanley Blystone (Cop, uncredited), Virginia True Boardman (Timid Juror, uncredited), Ward Bond (Johnson, uncredited), Wade Boteler (Cop, uncredited), Blanche Craig (Talkative Juror, uncredited), Edward Dillon (Mr. Hardy, uncredited), John Elliott (Police Captain, uncredited), Mildred Gaye (Dancer, uncredited), Mary Gordon (Matron, uncredited), Harriette Haddon (Dancer, uncredited), Chuck Hamilton (Court Officer, uncredited), Bert Hanlon (Juror, uncredited), Bo Peep Karlin (Dancer, uncredited), Fred Kelsey (Cop, uncredited), Joe King (Bailiff, uncredited), Margaret La Marr (Dancer, uncredited), Nora Lane (Evelyn Vandeler, uncredited), Mary Lansing (Dancer, uncredited), Fred Lee (Assistant Defense Attorney, uncredited), Tom London (Cop, uncredited), James T. Mack (Clerk of the Court, uncredited), Joe Mack (Court Usher, uncredited). Edwin Maxwell (Detective, uncredited), Harry McCoy (Cop, uncredited), Lucille Miller (Dancer, uncredited), Edmund Mortimer (Assistant Prosecuting Attorney, uncredited), Edward Mulligan (Court Usher, uncredited), Clarence Nordstrom (Cafe Singer, uncredited), Pat O'Malley (Broadcast Sergeant, uncredited), Bob Perry (Bailiff, uncredited), James Pierce (Cop, uncredited), Pat Somerset (Spectator, uncredited), Phil Tead (Mac, uncredited), Florence Turner (Juror, uncredited), William Worthington (Assistant Defense Attorney, uncredited), Marbeth Wright (Dancer, uncredited). **Release Date:** May 1, 1932. Fox Film Corporation. 56 min.

Strangers of the Evening (1932). **Director:** H. Bruce Humberstone. **Writers:** Tiffany Thayer (book *The Illustrious Corpse*), Stuart Anthony, Warren Duff (writers). **Producer:** Samuel Bischoff. **Music:** Val Burton. **Cinematography:** Arthur Edeson. **Editing:** Dave

Berg, Martin G. Cohn. **Set Decoration:** Ralph M. DeLacy. **Costume Design:** Elizabeth Coleman. **Property Master:** Edward G. Boyle. **Sound Recordist:** Corson Jowett. **Cast:** ZaSu Pitts (Sybil Smith), Lucien Littlefield (Frank "Snookie" Daniels, a.k.a. Richard Roe), Eugene Pallette (Detective Brubacher), Tully Marshall (Robert Daniels), Miriam Seeger (Ruth Daniels), Theodor Von Eltz (Dr. Raymond Everette), Warner Richmond (Dr. Joseph Chandler), Harold Waldridge (Tommy Freeman), Mahlon Hamilton (Charles E. Frisbee, Deputy District Attorney), Alan Roscoe (Sutherland), William Scott (2nd Passerby), Charles Williams (1st Passerby), James P. Burtis (Nolan), Francis Sayles (Roberts), Harry Bowen (Pete, uncredited), Ben Hall (Ed, uncredited), Edward LeSaint (Policeman, uncredited), Jack Pennick (Policeman, uncredited), Hal Price (Sgt. Collins, uncredited), Frank Rice (Policeman, uncredited), Harry Semels (Thug, uncredited). **Release Date:** May 15, 1932. Quadruple Film Corp./Tiffany Productions. 70 min. **Notes:** This marked the directorial debut of H. Bruce Humberstone. In 1942 the film was re-released as *The Hidden Corpse*.

Westward Passage (1932). **Director:** Robert Milton. **Writers:** Margaret Ayer Barnes (story), Bradley King (adaptation), Humphrey Pearson (dialogue). **Associate Producer:** Harry Joe Brown. **Executive Producer:** David O. Selznick. **Music:** Bernhard Kaun (uncredited), Harold Lewis (uncredited), Harry Tierney (uncredited). **Cinematography:** Lucien Andriot. **Editing:** Charles Craft. **Art Direction:** Carroll Clark. **Costume Design:** Josette De Lima (uncredited). **Sound Recordist:** E.A. Wolcott. **Costume Supervisor:** Margaret Pemberton. **Musical Director:** Max Steiner. **Cast:** Ann Harding (Olivia Van Tyne Allen Ottendorf), Laurence Olivier (Nicholas "Nick" Allen), ZaSu Pitts (Mrs. Truesdale), Irving Pichel (Harry Ottendorf), Juliette Compton (Henrietta), Emmett King (Mr. Henry P. Ottendorf), Florence Roberts (Mrs. Ottendorf), Ethel Griffies (Lady Caverly), Don Alvarado (Count Felipe DeLatorie), Bonita Granville (Little Olivia Allen, Age 9), Florence Lake (Elmer's Wife), Edgar Kennedy (Elmer), Herman Bing (Otto Hoopengarner), Irene Purcell (Baroness Diane von Stael), Joyce Compton (Lillie, uncredited), Nance O'Neil (Mrs. von Stael, uncredited), Julie Haydon (Bridesmaid, uncredited), Lee Phelps (Bartender, uncredited), Al Thompson (Chauffeur, uncredited), Lita Chevret (Woman at Party, uncredited). **Release Date:** May 27, 1932. RKO Pathé Pictures. 73 min.

Is My Face Red? (1932). **Director:** William A. Seiter. **Writers:** Ben Markson, Allen Rivkin (play), Ben Markson, Casey Robinson (screenplay). **Associate Producer:** Harry Joe Brown. **Executive Producer:** David O. Selznick. **Music:** Max Steiner. **Cinematography:** Leo Tover. **Art Direction:** Carroll Clark. **Musical Director:** Max Steiner. **Orchestrator:** Bernhard Kaun (uncredited). **Cast:** Helen Twelvetrees (Peggy Bannon), Ricardo Cortez (William Poster), Jill Esmond (Mildred Huntington), Robert Armstrong (Ed Maloney), Arline Judge (Bee), ZaSu Pitts (Telephone Operator), Clarence Muse (Horatio), Sidney Toler (Tony Mugatti), Fletcher Norton (Angelo Spinello), George Chandler (uncredited), Cecil Cunningham (uncredited), William B. Davidson (uncredited), Stuart Holmes (Radio Announcer, uncredited), Rochelle Hudson (uncredited), Anderson Lawler (uncredited), Dave O'Brien (uncredited), Richard Tucker (uncredited), James Donlan (uncredited), Lucy Beaumont (uncredited), Billy Engle (Barber, uncredited), Maude Turner Gordon (uncredited), Harry Stubbs (uncredited), Clarence Geldart (uncredited), Blanche Friderici (uncredited), William H. Tooker (uncredited), Nella

Walker (uncredited). **Release Date:** June 17, 1932. RKO Radio Pictures. 66 min. **Notes:** There is no record of a play running on Broadway by Ben Markson and Allen Rivkin called *Is My Face Red?*; it is possible that it remained unproduced.

Make Me a Star (1932). **Director:** William Beaudine. **Writers:** Harry Leon Wilson (novel *Merton of the Movies*), George S. Kaufman, Marc Connelly, Moss Hart (play *Merton of the Movies*), Sam Mintz, Walter De Leon, Arthur Kober (screenplay). **Producer:** B.P. Schulberg. **Music:** John Leipold (uncredited). **Cinematography:** Allan Siegler. **Editing:** Edward Dmytryk (uncredited), LeRoy Stone (uncredited). **Sound Department:** Earl S. Hayman (uncredited). **Assistant Camera:** George Bourne (uncredited). **Camera Operator:** Roy Eslick (uncredited). **Still Photographer:** Clifton Maupin (uncredited). **Cast:** Joan Blondell (Flips Montague), Stuart Erwin (Merton Gill), ZaSu Pitts (Mrs. Scudder), Ben Turpin (Ben the Crosseyed Man), Charles Sellon (Mr. Gashwiler), Florence Roberts (Mrs. Gashwiler), Helen Jerome Eddy (Tessie Kearns), Arthur Hoyt (Hardy Powell), [George] Dink Templeton (Buck Benson), Ruth Donnelly (the Countess), Sam Hardy (Jeff Baird), Oscar Apfel (Director Henshaw), Billy Bletcher (Actor, uncredited), A.S. "Pop" Byron (St. Peter, uncredited), Bud Jamison (Actor, uncredited), "Snub" Pollard (Actor, uncredited), Victor Potel (Actor, uncredited), Jim Mason (Extra, uncredited), Frank Mills (Chuck Collins, uncredited), Buddy Roosevelt (Cowboy, uncredited), Kent Taylor (Doorman, uncredited), Harry Tenbrook (Bus Driver, uncredited), Nick Thompson (Actor, uncredited), Bobby Vernon (Actor, uncredited), Polly Walters (Doris Randall, uncredited), Kathrin Clare Ward (Ma Patterson, uncredited), Gertrude Short (Girl, uncredited), Claudette Colbert (Herself, uncredited), Gary Cooper (Himself, uncredited), Tallulah Bankhead (Herself, uncredited), Jack Oakie (Himself, uncredited), Sylvia Sidney (Herself, uncredited), Fredric March (Himself, uncredited), Maurice Chevalier (Himself, uncredited), Charles Ruggles (Himself, uncredited), Clive Brook (Himself, uncredited), Phillips Holmes (Himself, uncredited), "Little Billy" Rhodes (Himself, uncredited). **Release Date:** July 1, 1932. Paramount Pictures/Paramount Publix Corporation. 86 min. **Notes:** The working titles of the film were *Gates of Hollywood* and *Half a Hero*. *Merton of the Movies* played successfully on Broadway in 1922-23 and starred Glenn Hunter. Harry Leon Wilson's novel was first filmed by Famous Players–Lasky in 1924 as *Merton of the Movies*, produced and directed by James Cruze, and starring Hunter and Viola Dana. It was filmed again in 1947 (as *Merton of the Movies*) by MGM as a vehicle for Red Skelton.

Roar of the Dragon (1932). **Director:** Wesley Ruggles. **Writers:** George Kibbe Turner (novel *A Passage to Hong Kong*), Merian C. Cooper, Jane Bigelow (story), Howard Estabrook (screenplay). **Executive Producer:** David O. Selznick. **Producer:** William LeBaron (uncredited). **Music:** Max Steiner (uncredited). **Cinematography:** Edward Cronjager. **Editing:** William Hamilton (uncredited). **Art Direction:** Carroll Clark. **Assistant Director:** Dewey Starkey (uncredited). **Sound Recordist:** John E. Tribby (uncredited). **Orchestrators:** Emil Gerstenberger (uncredited), Bernhard Kaun (uncredited). **Cast:** Richard Dix (Captain Chauncey Carson), Gwili Andre (Natascha), Edward Everett Horton (Busby), Arline Judge (Hortense "Bridgeport" O'Dare), ZaSu Pitts (Tourist), Dudley Digges (Mr. Johnson), C. Henry Gordon (Voronsky), William Orlamond (Dr. Pransnitz), Arthur Stone (Isaac Sholem), Toshi Mori (Butterfly), Will Stanton (Sailor Sam), Jimmy Wang (Hotel proprietor), Dave O'Brien (Submarine Crewman, uncredited), Peter Brocco (Wireless Operator, uncredited), Willie Fung (Chinese Sailor, uncredited), George Magrill (Sailor, uncredited), James P. Burtis (Mike, uncredited), Henry Guttman (Sailor, uncredited), Tetsu Komai (Bandit, uncredited), Michael Mark (Wounded Informant, uncredited). **Release Date:** July 8, 1932. RKO Radio Pictures. 69 min.

The Vanishing Frontier (1932). **Director:** Phil Rosen. **Writer:** Stuart Anthony (writer). **Producer:** Sam Jaffe. **Executive Producer:** Larry Darmour. **Cinematography:** James S. Brown Jr. **Cast:** Johnny Mack Brown (Kirby Tornell), Evalyn Knapp (Carol Winfield), ZaSu Pitts (Aunt Sylvia), Raymond Hatton (Hornet), Ben Alexander (Lucien Winfield), J. Farrell MacDonald (Waco), Wallace MacDonald (Captain Roger Kearney), George Irving (General Winfield), Joyzelle [Joyner] (Dolores), [Sam] Deacon McDaniels (Zeke), Soledad Jiménez (Mama Valdez, uncredited), Rebel (Horse, uncredited). **Release Date:** July 29, 1932. Larry Darmour Productions/Paramount Pictures. 65 min.

Blondie of the Follies (1932). **Director:** Edmund Goulding. **Writers:** Anita Loos (dialogue), Frances Marion (screenplay/story). **Producer:** Marion Davies. **Music:** William Axt. **Cinematography:** George Barnes. **Editing:** George Hively. **Art Direction:** Cedric Gibbons. **Costume Design:** Adrian. **Recording Director:** Douglas Shearer. **Cast:** Marion Davies (Blondie McClune), Robert Montgomery (Larry Belmont), Billie Dove (Lottie Callahan/Lurline Cavanaugh), Jimmy Durante (Jimmy), James Gleason (Pop McClune), ZaSu Pitts (Gertie), Sidney Toler (Pete), Douglass Dumbrille (Murchenson), Sarah Padden (Ma McClune), Louise Carter (Ma Callahan), Clyde Cook (Dancer), Billy Gilbert (Kinskey's Friend, uncredited), C. Montague Shaw (Specialist, uncredited), Charles Williams (Mr. Kinskey, uncredited), Wilbur Mack (Follies' Producer, uncredited), Bud Geary (Delivery Man, uncredited), John Davidson (Party Guest, uncredited), Oscar Apfel (Doctor, uncredited), Lee Phelps (Arthur, uncredited), Ronald R. Rondell (Man in Speakeasy, uncredited), Sherry Hall (Party Guest, uncredited), Harold Miller (uncredited), Dorothy Dixon (Acrobatic Dancer, uncredited), Harry Dixon (Acrobatic Dancer, uncredited), George Cooper (O'Brien, uncredited), Robert Strange (Specialist, uncredited), Bert Moorhouse (uncredited), Larry Steers (Party Guest, uncredited), Jay Eaton (Party Guest, uncredited), Edmund Mortimer (Party Guest, uncredited), Harry Wilson (Loading Dock Worker, uncredited), Edmund Goulding (Cameo, uncredited). **Release Date:** September 1, 1932. Cosmopolitan Productions/Metro-Goldwyn-Mayer (MGM). 91 min. **Notes:** *Good Time Girl* was the movie's working title.

The Crooked Circle (1932). **Director:** H. Bruce Humberstone. **Writers:** Ralph Spence (original screenplay), Tim Whelan (additional dialogue). **Producer:** William Sistrom. **Cinematography:** Robert B. Kurrle. **Editing:** Doane Harrison. **Art Direction:** Paul Roe Crawley. **Sound Engineer:** William Fox. **Musical Director:** Val Burton (uncredited). **Cast:** ZaSu Pitts (Nora Rafferty), James Gleason (Arthur Crimmer), Ben Lyon (Brand Osborne), Irene Purcell (Thelma Parker), C. Henry Gordon (Yoganda), Ray Hatton (Harmon), Roscoe Karns (Harry Carter), Berton Churchill (Col. Walters), Spencer Charters (Kinny), Robert Frazer (the Stranger), Ethel Clayton (Yvonne), Frank Reicher (Rankin), Christian Rub (Old Dan), Tom Kennedy (Mike), Paul Panzer (Cult Member, uncredited). **Release Date:** September 25, 1932. Sono Art-World Wide Pictures. 70 min.

Once in a Lifetime (1932). **Director:** Russell Mack. **Writers:** Moss Hart, George S. Kaufman (play), Seton I. Miller (adaptation). **Producer:** Carl Laemmle Jr. **Cinematography:** George Robinson. **Editing:** Robert Carlisle. **Stock Music:** David Broekman (uncredited). **Cast:** Jack Oakie (George Lewis), Sidney Fox (Susan Walker), Aline MacMahon (May Daniels), Russell Hopton (Jerome "Jerry" Hyland), Louise Fazenda (Helen Hobart), ZaSu Pitts (Miss Leyton), Gregory Ratoff (Herman Glogauer), Jobyna Howland (Mrs. Walker), Onslow Stevens (Lawrence Vail), Gregory Gaye (Rudolph Kammerling), Eddie Kane (Meterstein), Johnny Morris (Weiskopf), Frank LaRue (the Bishop), Margaret Lindsay (Dr. Lewis' Secretary), Walter Brennan (Lighting Technician, uncredited), Alan Ladd (Projectionist, uncredited), Mona Maris (Phyllis Fontaine, uncredited), Claudia Morgan (Miss Chasen, uncredited), Sam McDaniels (Porter, uncredited), Lew Kelly (Sign Painter, uncredited), Robert McWade (Mr. Walker, uncredited), Carol Tevis (Florabel Leigh, uncredited), Leyland Hodgson (Reporter, uncredited), Ralph Brooks (uncredited), Earl McCarthy (Bridegroom, uncredited). **Release Date:** October 2, 1932. Universal Pictures. 91 min. **Notes:** The Hart-Kaufman Broadway comedy (their first together) premiered on Broadway in 1930 and ran for over 300 performances. It starred Hugh O'Connell, Jean Dixon, Sally Phipps, and Spring Byington. BBC-TV, in association with WNET, produced a television adaptation of the play in 1988 starring Zoe Wanamaker, Niall Buggy and Kristoffer Tabori.

Madison Sq. Garden (1932). **Director:** Harry Joe Brown. **Writers:** Thomson Burtis (story), Allen Rivkin, P.J. Wolfson (writers). **Producer:** Charles R. Rogers. **Music:** Bernhard Kaun (uncredited). **Cinematography:** Henry Sharp. **Stunts:** Gil Perkins (uncredited). **Stock Music:** Karl Hajos (uncredited). **Technical Director:** Teddy Hayes. **Cast:** Jack Oakie (Eddie Burke), Thomas Meighan (Bill Carley), Marian Nixon (Bee), William Collier Sr. (Doc Williams), ZaSu Pitts (Florrie), Lew Cody (Rourke), William Boyd [William "Stage" Boyd] (Sloane), Warren Hymer (Brassie Randall), Robert Elliott (Honest John Miller), Joyce Compton (Joyce), Bert Gordon (Izzy), Noel Francis (Noel), Tom Sharkey [Sailor Sharkey] (Himself), Tommy Ryan (Himself), Stanislaus Zbyszko (Himself), Billy Papke (Himself), Mike Donlin (Himself), Tod Sloan (Himself), Damon Runyon (Himself), Grantland Rice (Himself), Jack Lait (Himself), Westbrook Pegler (Himself), Paul Gallico (Himself), Jack Johnson (Himself), Ed W. Smith (Himself), Oscar Apfel (Harrison, uncredited), Brooks Benedict (uncredited), Bruce Bennett (Wrestler, uncredited), Mushy Callahan (Kid McClune, uncredited), Dorothy Granger (uncredited), Fred Kelsey (House Detective, uncredited), William B. Davidson (uncredited), Greta Granstedt (Blonde, uncredited), Harry Stubbs (Ring Physician, uncredited), Tom Kennedy (Judge, uncredited), Budd Fine (Henchman, uncredited), Teddy Hayes (Himself, uncredited), G. Pat Collins (uncredited), Josephine Hill (uncredited), Lloyd Ingraham (Ring Announcer, uncredited), Geneva Mitchell (Girl, uncredited), Charles R. Moore (Bootblack, uncredited), James Donlan (Sports Reporter, uncredited), Arthur Hoyt (Desk Clerk, uncredited), Reed Howes (Reporter, uncredited), Gil Perkins (uncredited), Francis McDonald (Hood, uncredited), Jack Herrick (uncredited), Broderick O'Farrell (uncredited), Jack Kearns (Himself, uncredited), Al Freed (Judge, uncredited), John Kelly (uncredited), Harry Schultz (German Waiter, uncredited), Landers Stevens (uncredited), Wade Boteler (Det. Brody, uncredited), Mike Donovan (Cop, uncredited), Kit Guard (uncredited), Lou Magnolia (Himself, uncredited), Larry McGrath (Bellman, uncredited), Louis Natheaux (uncredited), Hal Price (uncredited), Cyril Ring (Reporter, uncredited), W.C. Robinson (uncredited), George Rosener (Crooked Fight Manager, uncredited), John Sheehan (Trainer, uncredited), Larry Steers (uncredited), Charles Sullivan (Trainer, uncredited), Charles Williams (Reporter, uncredited), Tammany Young (Reporter, uncredited). **Release Date:** November 4, 1932. Paramount Pictures. 74 min. **Notes:** Several scenes were filmed on location at Madison Square Garden in New York.

Back Street (1932). **Director:** John M. Stahl. **Writers:** Fannie Hurst (novel), Gladys Lehman, Gene Fowler (uncredited), Ben Hecht (uncredited), Lynn Starling (uncredited) (writers). **Producer:** Carl Laemmle Jr. **Associate Producer:** E.M. Asher (uncredited). **Music:** David Broekman (uncredited), James Dietrich (uncredited). **Cinematography:** Karl Freund (uncredited). **Art Direction:** Charles D. Hall (uncredited). **Costume Design:** Vera West (uncredited). **Makeup Artist:** Jack P. Pierce (uncredited). **Assistant Director:** Scott R. Beal (uncredited). **Sound Supervisor:** C. Roy Hunter (uncredited). **Musical Director:** David Broekman (uncredited). **Cast:** Irene Dunne (Ray Smith), John Boles (Walter Saxel), June Clyde (Freda Schmidt), George Meeker (Kurt Shendler), ZaSu Pitts (Mrs. Dole), Shirley Grey (Francine), Doris Lloyd (Saxel's Wife), William Bakewell (Richard Saxel), Arletta Duncan (Beth Saxel), Maude Turner Gordon (Mrs. Saxel Sr.), Walter Catlett (Bakeless), James Donlan (Profhero), Paul Weigel (Mr. Schmidt), Jane Darwell (Mrs. Schmidt), Robert McWade (Uncle Felix), Paul Fix (Hugo Hack), Russell Hopton (Reporter), Gene Morgan (Reporter), James Flavin (Reporter), Jim Farley (Conductor), Bob Burns (Streetcar Conductor), Rolfe Sedan (Croupier), Grace Hayle (Lady in Street), Jack Chefe (Onlooker), Gloria Stuart (uncredited), Betty Blythe (uncredited), Virginia Pearson (uncredited), Rose Dione (uncredited), Tom Karrigan (uncredited), Rosalie Roy (uncredited), Mahlon Hamilton (uncredited), Beulah Hutton (uncredited), Caryl Lincoln (uncredited). **Release Date:** December 30, 1932. Universal Pictures. 93 min. **Notes:** The Hurst novel was adapted twice more by Universal, both under the name *Back Street*: In 1941, directed by Robert Stevenson and starring Margaret Sullavan and Charles Boyer; and in 1961, directed by David Miller and starring Susan Hayward, John Gavin and Vera Miles.

They Just Had to Get Married (1932). **Director:** Edward Ludwig. **Writers:** Cyril Harcourt (play *A Pair of Silk Stockings*), Gladys Lehman, H.M. Walker, Preston Sturges (uncredited) (writers). **Music:** James Dietrich (uncredited). **Cinematography:** Edward Snyder. **Editing:** Ted J. Kent. **Makeup Artist:** Jack P. Pierce. **Assistant Director:** Edward Snyder. **Sound:** Gilbert Kurland. **Cast:** Slim Summerville (Sam Sutton), ZaSu Pitts (Molly), Roland Young (Hume), Verree Teasdale (Lola Montrose), C. Aubrey Smith (Hampton), Robert Greig (Radcliff), David Landau (Montrose), Elizabeth Patterson (Lizzie), Wallis Clark (Fairchilds), David Leo Tillotson (Wilmont), Vivien Oakland (Mrs. Fairchilds), William Burress (Bradford), Louise Mackintosh (Mrs. Bradford), Bertram Marburgh (Langley), Virginia Howell (Mrs. Langley), James Donlan (Clerk), Henry Armetta (Tony), Fifi D'Orsay (Marie), Cora Sue Collins (Rosalie), Guy Kibbee (uncredited). **Release Date:** January 5, 1933. Universal Pictures. 69 min. **Notes:** Kenneth Douglas and Caroline Bayley starred in the original 1914-15 Broadway production. Harcourt's play was previously filmed by Selznick as *A Pair of Silk Stockings* (1918), directed by

Walter Edwards and starring Constance Talmadge and Harrison Ford, and by Universal as *Silk Stockings* (1927), directed by Wesley Ruggles and starring Laura La Plante and John Harron.

Out All Night (1933). **Director:** Sam Taylor. **Writers:** William Anthony McGuire (writer), Tom Whelan (story). **Producer:** Carl Laemmle Jr. **Cinematography:** Jerome Ash. **Editing:** Bernard W. Burton. **Art Direction:** Thomas F. O'Neill. **Stock Music:** James F. Hanley (uncredited), Alfred Newman (uncredited). **Cast:** Slim Summerville (Ronald Colgate), ZaSu Pitts (Bonny), Laura Hope Crews (Mrs. Colgate), Shirley Grey (Kate), Alexander Carr (Rosemountain), Rollo Lloyd (David Arnold), Billy Barty (Child), Shirley Jane Temple (Child), Philip Purdy (Child), Gene Lewis (Tracy), Mae Busch (uncredited), Dorothy Bay (uncredited), Florence Enright (uncredited), Paul Hurst (uncredited). **Release Date:** April 8, 1933. Universal Pictures. 68 min. **Notes:** *Niagara Falls* was the film's working title.

Hello, Sister! (1933). **Directors:** Alan Crosland, Erich von Stroheim, Raoul Walsh, Alfred L. Werker. **Writers:** Dawn Powell (play *Walking Down Broadway*), Erich von Stroheim, Leonard Spigelgass (scenario), Geraldine Nomis (uncredited), Harry Ruskin (uncredited), Maurine Dallas Watkins (uncredited) (writers). **Producer:** Winfield R. Sheehan. **Associate Producer:** Sol M. Wurtzel. **Cinematography:** James Wong Howe. **Editing:** Frank E. Hull. **Costume Design:** Rita Kaufman. **Sound:** Alfred Bruzlin. **Wardrobe:** Sam Benson (uncredited). **Cast:** James Dunn (Jimmy), ZaSu Pitts (Millie), Boots Mallory (Peggy), Minna Gombell (Mona), Terrance Ray (Mac), Will Stanton

Out All Night (1933) sees a trembling ZaSu menaced by an Oriental "boogie man."

(Drunk), George Fawcett (Character), Howard Hickman (Character), Lloyd Hughes (Character), Astrid Allwyn (Girl), Wade Boteler (Fireman), James Flavin (Character), Claude King (Character), Henry Kolker (Bank President), Hattie McDaniel (Woman in Apartment House), Walter Walker (Man). **Release Date:** April 14, 1933. Fox Film Corporation. 62 min. **Notes:** Erich von Stroheim's last credited film as director, *Hello, Sister!* was taken away from him, and several directors were assigned to reshoot and rework his material. Originally titled *Walking Down Broadway*, it underwent many changes before being released more than a year later. Dawn Powell's play was unproduced.

Professional Sweetheart (1933). **Director:** William A. Seiter. **Writer:** Maurine Watkins (writer). **Executive Producer:** Merian C. Cooper. **Associate Producer:** H.N. Swanson. **Cinematography:** Edward Cronjager. **Editing:** James B. Morley. **Makeup Artist:** Mel Berns (uncredited). **Assistant Director:** Dewey Starkey (uncredited). **Art Department:** Carroll Clark, Van Nest Polglase. **Props:** Kenneth Holmes (uncredited). **Sound Recordist:** Clem Portman. **Camera Operator:** Robert De Grasse (uncredited). **Assistant Camera:** George E. Diskant (uncredited). **Chief Electrician:** Guy Gilman (uncredited). **Still Photographers:** Alexander Kahle (uncredited), John Miehle (uncredited). **Chief Grip:** Jim Kirley (uncredited). **Musical Director:** Roy Webb. **Cast:** Ginger Rogers (Glory Eden), Norman Foster (Jim Davey), ZaSu Pitts (Elmerada de Leon), Frank McHugh (Speed Dennis), Allen Jenkins (O'Connor), Gregory Ratoff (Samuel "Sam" Ipswich), Franklin Pangborn (Herbert Childress), Lucien Littlefield (Ed), Edgar Kennedy (Tim Kelsey), Frank Darien (Appleby), Sterling Holloway (Stu), Betty Furness (Blonde Reporter, uncredited), Theresa Harris (Vera, uncredited), Akim Tamiroff (Hotel Waiter, uncredited), June Brewster (Telephone Operator, uncredited), Mary MacLaren (Ipswich's Secretary, uncredited), Grace Hayle (Reporter, uncredited), Mike Lally (Studio Clerk, uncredited). **Release Date:** June 9, 1933. RKO Radio Pictures. 73 min. **Notes:** The working titles for this film were *Careless* and *Purity Girl*.

Her First Mate (1933). **Director:** William Wyler. **Writers:** Frank Craven, John Golden, Daniel Jarrett (play *Salt Water*), Clarence Marks, Earle Snell, H.M. Walker (screenplay). **Producer:** Carl Laemmle Jr. **Cinematography:** George Robinson. **Cast:** Slim Summerville (John Horner), ZaSu Pitts (Mary Horner), Una Merkel (Hattie), Warren Hymer (Percy), Berton Churchill (Davis), George F. Marion Sr. (Sam), Henry Armetta (Socrates), Jocelyn Lee, Herbert Clifton (Battleship Captain), Maurice Black (uncredited), Sheila Bromley (Passenger, uncredited), Sumner Getchell (uncredited), Pat Harmon (uncredited), Edward Hearn (Ferry Captain, uncredited), Marc Lawrence (Orderly, uncredited), Monte Montague (uncredited), Frank Moran (First Mate, uncredited), Lee Phelps (First Mate, uncredited), Frank Rice (Sailor, uncredited), Don Terry (Purser, uncredited), Clarence Wilson (Dr. Gray, uncredited), William Wyler (Man, uncredited). **Release Date:** September 1, 1933. Universal Pictures. 66 min. **Notes:** The comedy *Salt Water* ran on Broadway for four months (1929–30) and starred Frank Craven and Edythe Elliott.

Love, Honor and Oh, Baby! (1933). **Director:** Edward Buzzell. **Writers:** Edward Buzzell, Norman Krasna (uncredited) (writer), Howard Lindsay, Bertrand Robinson (play *Oh, Promise Me*). **Cinematography:** George Robinson. **Cast:** Slim Summerville (Mark Reed), ZaSu Pitts (Connie Clark), George Barbier (Jasper B. Ogden), Lucile Gleason (Flo Bowen), Verree Teasdale (Elsie

Carpenter), Donald Meek (Luther Bowen), Purnell Pratt (Marchall Durant), Adrienne Dore (Louise), Dorothy Granger (Mrs. Brown), Neely Edwards (Mr. Brown), Henry Kolker (the Judge). **Release Date:** October 1, 1933. Universal Pictures. 65 min. **Notes:** The working titles of this film were *Oh, Promise Me* and *Love, Honor, Oh, Baby!* Lee Tracy, Eleanore Bedford, Chester Clute and Donald Meek all appeared in the original Broadway version in 1930-31.

Meet the Baron (1933). **Director:** Walter Lang. **Writers:** Arthur Kober, Norman Krasna, Herman J. Mankiewicz, Allen Rivkin, William K. Wells, P.J. Wolfson (writers). **Producer:** David O. Selznick. **Music:** Jimmy McHugh. **Cinematography:** Allen G. Siegler. **Editing:** James E. Newcom. **Art Direction:** Howard Fisher, Franklin H. Webster, Edwin B. Willis. **Costume Design:** Dolly Tree. **Assistant Director:** Joe Boyle. **Recording Director:** Douglas Shearer. **Supervising Editor** (Musical Sequences): W. Donn Hayes. **Orchestra Director:** Oscar Radin. **Cast:** Jack Pearl (Julius/Baron Munchausen), Jimmy Durante (Joe McGoo), ZaSu Pitts (ZaSu), Ted Healy (Head Janitor), Edna May Oliver (Dean Primrose), Henry Kolker (the Real Baron Munchausen), William B. Davidson (General Broadcasting Representative), Moe Howard (Janitor), Larry Fine (Janitor), Curly Howard (Janitor), Ben Bard (Charley Montague), Sheila Bromley (uncredited), Don Brodie (Mayor's "Yes" Man, uncredited), Lynn Bari (College Girl, uncredited), Minerva Urecal (Downstairs Maid, uncredited), Willie Fung (Chinese Man, uncredited), Vera Lewis (Head Housekeeper, uncredited), Bruce Bennett (Passenger, uncredited), Mary Gordon (Washer Woman, uncredited), Eddie Quillan (Dock Extra, uncredited), Nora Cecil (Professor Winterbottom, uncredited), Chester Gan (Chinese Man, uncredited), Andrea Leeds (Girl on Phone, uncredited), Lionel Belmore (Explorer, uncredited), Marion Byron (uncredited), Robert Greig (uncredited), Claude King (Explorer, uncredited), Miriam Marlin (Chorine, uncredited), Greta Meyer (Aunt Sophie, uncredited) Margaret Nearing (Singer, uncredited), Frank O'Connor (Stable Boss, uncredited), Cyril Ring (Mayor's "Yes" Man, uncredited), Rolfe Sedan (uncredited), Helen Shipman (uncredited), Phil Tead (Bus Tour Guide, uncredited), Fred "Snowflake" Toones (Stable Groom, uncredited), Richard Tucker (Radio Station Boss, uncredited), Leo White (the Chef, uncredited). **Release Date:** October 20, 1933. Metro-Goldwyn-Mayer (MGM). 68 min. **Notes:** The working titles of this film were *The Big Liar* and *What a Liar!* In the onscreen credits, Jack Pearl is referred to as "the famous Baron Munchausen of the Air." Pearl played a popular German radio character, "Baron von Munchausen," which he had introduced in 1932 on the *Ziegfeld Follies of the Air* radio program. Later, the character appeared on *The Jack Pearl Show*, a weekly NBC show sponsored by Lucky Strike. Pearl's famous line was "Vas you dere, Sharlie?"

Aggie Appleby Maker of Men (1933). **Director:** Mark Sandrich. **Writers:** Joseph O. Kesselring (play), Humphrey Pearson, Edward Kaufman (screenplay). **Producer:** Pandro S. Berman. **Executive Producer:** Merian C. Cooper. **Music:** Roy Webb (uncredited). **Cinematography:** J. Roy Hunt. **Editing:** Basil Wrangell. **Art Direction:** Carroll Clark, Van Nest Polglase. **Assistant Director:** James Hartnett (uncredited). **Sound Recordist:** Bert S. Hodges. **Special Effects Supervisor:** Harry Redmond Sr. (uncredited). **Musical Director:** Max Steiner. **Orchestrator:** Bernhard Kaun (uncredited). **Cast:** Charles Farrell (Adoniram "Schlumpy" Schlump, a.k.a. Red Branahan), Wynne Gibson (Agnes "Aggie" Appleby), William Gargan (Red Branahan), ZaSu Pitts (Sybby "Sib"), Betty Furness (Evangeline), Blanche Friderici (Aunt Katherine), Jane Darwell (Mrs. Spence, uncredited), Edward Keane (Construction Boss, uncredited), Brooks Benedict (Hiring Clerk, uncredited), Walter Long (Red's Prison Cellmate, uncredited), Bud Geary (Prison Guard, uncredited), John Kelly (Butch, uncredited). **Release Date:** November 3, 1933. RKO Radio Pictures. 73 min. **Notes:** Sidney Lanfield was first set to direct, and Helen Mack was to play the lead role, but both were replaced just prior to shooting.

Mr. Skitch (1933). **Director:** James Cruze. **Writers:** Anne Cameron (story "Green Dice"), Sonya Levien, Ralph Spence (writers). **Music:** Peter Brunelli (uncredited), David Buttolph (uncredited), Louis De Francesco (uncredited). **Cinematography:** John F. Seitz. **Costume Design:** Rita Kaufman. **Art Department:** William Darling. **Sound:** W.D. Flick. **Musical Director:** Louis De Francesco. **Cast:** Will Rogers (Mr. Ira Skitch), Rochelle Hudson (Emily Skitch), ZaSu Pitts (Mrs. Maddie Skitch), Florence Desmond (Flo), Harry Green (Sam Cohen), Charles Starrett (Harvey Denby), Eugene Pallette (Cliff Merriweather), Cleora Robb (Winnie, uncredited), Glorea Robb (Minnie, uncredited), George Irving (uncredited), Charles Lane (Hotel Clerk, uncredited), Spencer Charters (Mr. Umpchay, uncredited), Charles Middleton (Joe, uncredited), Morgan Wallace (Jones, uncredited), Wally Albright (Little Ira, uncredited), Frank Melton (uncredited). **Release Date:** December 22, 1933. Fox Film Corporation. 70 min. **Notes:** The working titles of this film were *Green Dice* and *There's Always Tomorrow*. Some scenes were shot at the Grand Canyon in Arizona and at Yellowstone National Park in Wyoming. Florence Desmond does an impression of ZaSu in the film.

The Meanest Gal in Town (1934). **Director:** Russell Mack (uncredited). **Writers:** H.W. Hanemann, Russell Mack, Richard Schayer (writer), Arthur Horman (story). **Producer:** Russell Mack. **Executive Producer:** Merian C. Cooper. **Associate Producer:** H.N. Swanson. **Cinematography:** J. Roy Hunt. **Editing:** James B. Morley. **Art Direction:** Perry Ferguson, Van Nest Polglase. **Assistant Director:** Ray Lissner (uncredited). **Sound Recordist:** George D. Ellis. **Musical Director:** Max Steiner. **Stock Music:** Max Steiner (uncredited), Roy Webb (uncredited). **Cast:** ZaSu Pitts (Tillie Prescott), Pert Kelton (Lulu White), El Brendel (Chris Peterson), James Gleason (Duke Slater), Richard "Skeets" Gallagher (Jack Hayden), Edward McWade (Clark), John Carradine (Stranded Actor, uncredited), Arthur Hoyt (uncredited), Barney Furey (uncredited), Wallis Clark (Mr. Bowen, uncredited), Bud Geary (Loafer, uncredited), DeWitt Jennings (Police Chief, uncredited), Harry Holman (Mayor, uncredited), Vera Lewis (uncredited), Lew Kelly (uncredited), Ben Hendricks Jr. (Detective, uncredited), Dennis O'Keefe (uncredited), Frank Hagney (Angry Truck Driver, uncredited), John Hyams (George Spelvin, uncredited), Florence Roberts (uncredited), Kenner G. Kemp (Pool Hall Player, uncredited), John Marston (Clem Driscoll, uncredited), Robert McKenzie (Kingston Hotel Owner, uncredited), Harry Semels (uncredited), Ray Turner (Ivory, uncredited), Morgan Wallace (Sydney Sterling, uncredited), Jack Wise (Actor, uncredited). **Release Date:** January 12, 1934. RKO Radio Pictures. 62 min. **Notes:** The working title for this film was *Dummy's Vote*.

Two Alone (1934). **Director:** Elliott Nugent. **Writers:** Dan Totheroh (play *Wild Birds*), Josephine Lovett, Joseph Moncure March (writer). **Executive Producer:** Merian C. Cooper. **Associate Producer:** David Lewis.

Cinematography: Lucien Andriot. **Editing:** Arthur Roberts. **Art Direction:** Charles Kirk, Van Nest Polglase. **Assistant Director:** Charles Kerr (uncredited). **Sound Recordist:** John L. Cass. **Special Effects Supervisor:** Harry Redmond Sr. **Musical Director:** Max Steiner. **Stock Music:** Max Steiner (uncredited). **Cast:** Jean Parker (Mazie), Tom Brown (Adam), ZaSu Pitts (Esthey Roberts), Arthur Byron (Slag), Beulah Bondi (Mrs. Slag), Nydia Westman (Corie), Willard Robertson (George Marshall), Charley Grapewin (Sandy Roberts), Emerson Treacy (Milt Pollard), Paul Nicholson (the Sheriff), Jim Farley (uncredited), Edith Fellows (uncredited), Wade Boteler (uncredited), Zeffie Tilbury (uncredited). **Release Date:** January 26, 1934. RKO Radio Pictures. 75 min. **Notes:** The working titles for this film were *Wild Birds* and *Wild Bird*. The original leading lady, Dorothy Jordan, fell ill on location in Sonora, and her scenes were reshot with Jean Parker. The original Broadway production in 1925 ran only 44 performances and starred Mildred MacLeod, Donald Duff, and Florence Miller.

3 on a Honeymoon (1934). **Director:** James Tinling. **Writers:** Douglas Z. Doty, Edward T. Lowe Jr., Raymond Van Sickle, George Wright (writers), Ishbel Ross (novel *Promenade Deck*). **Producer:** John Stone. **Music:** Samuel Kaylin (uncredited). **Cinematography:** Arthur E. Arling, Joseph A. Valentine. **Editing:** Alex Troffey. **Costume Design:** Royer. **Wardrobe:** Sam Benson (uncredited). **Musical Director:** Samuel Kaylin. **Orchestrator:** William Spielter (uncredited). **Choreographer:** Dave Gould. **Cast:** Sally Eilers (Joan Foster), ZaSu Pitts (Alice Mudge), Henrietta Crosman ("Ma" Gillespie), Charles Starrett (Dick Charlton), Irene Hervey (Millicent Wells), Johnny Mack Brown (Chuck Wells), Russell Simpson (Ezra MacDuff), Cornelius Keefe (Phil Lang), Edward Earle (First Officer), Howard Lally (Third Officer), Wini Shaw (Singer), Ben Bard (Sanborn, uncredited), Frederick Burton (Ship's Captain, uncredited), Edward Gargan (Poker Player, uncredited), Hal Boyer (Guest, uncredited), Christina Montt (Fortune Teller, uncredited), Landers Stevens (Ship's Doctor, uncredited), Ernest Wood (Drunken Passenger, uncredited), George Davis (Guide, uncredited), Pat Moriarity (Assistant Engineer, uncredited), Morgan Wallace (Dunning, uncredited), Howard C. Hickman (Mr. Foster, uncredited), Joseph E. Bernard (Assistant Engineer, uncredited), Ruth Gillette (Mrs. Foster, uncredited), Maynard Holmes (Drunk, uncredited), Suzanne Kaaren (Flirt, uncredited), Caryl Lincoln (Guest, uncredited), Alphonse Martell (Headwaiter, uncredited), Eddie Phillips (Guest, uncredited), Gloria Roy (Passenger on Boat, uncredited), Countess Sonia (Specialty Dancer, uncredited). **Release Date:** March 23, 1934. Fox Film Corporation. 65 min. **Notes:** The working title for this film was *Promenade Deck*. Charles Starrett replaced Bruce Cabot as the male lead.

Sing and Like It (1934). **Director:** William A. Seiter. **Writers:** Aben Kandel (story "So You Won't Sing, Eh?"), Marion Dix, Laird Doyle (screenplay). **Executive Producer:** Merian C. Cooper. **Associate Producer:** Howard J. Green. **Cinematographer:** Nick Musuraca. **Editor:** George Crone. **Art Direction:** Al Herman, Van Nest Polglase. **Costume Design:** Walter Plunkett. **Assistant Director:** Edward Killy (uncredited). **Sound Recordist:** John L. Cass. **Musical Director:** Max Steiner. **Cast:** ZaSu Pitts (Annie Snodgrass), Pert Kelton (Ruby), Edward Everett Horton (Adam Frink), Nat Pendleton (T. Fenny Sylvester), Ned Sparks (Toots McGuire), Richard Carle (Mr. Abercrombie Hancock), John M. Qualen (Oswald), Matt McHugh (Junker), Stanley Fields (Butch), Joseph Sauers [Joe Sawyer] (Gunner),

William H. Griffith (Webster), Grace Hayle (Miss Fishbeck), Roy D'Arcy (Mr. Gregory), Arthur Hoyt, Frank Darien, George Davis, Paul Hurst, Oscar "Dutch" Hendrian, Sheldon Jett, Wilbur Mack, Francis McDonald, Bob Kortman, Jimmie Dundee, June Gittelson, Frank Mills, Jimmy O'Gatty, James C. Morton, Billy Gibson, George Lloyd, Frances Morris, Dewey Robinson, Clarence Stroud, Claude Stroud, Blue Washington, Jack Perry, Phil Tead (uncredited parts). **Release Date:** April 20, 1934. RKO Radio Pictures. 72 min. **Notes:** Throughout the film, the tone-deaf ZaSu sings Dave Dreyer and Roy Turk's "Your Mother." According to AFI, "In July 1934, the Catholic Church of Detroit placed *Sing and Like It* on its list of 'to be boycotted' films. Although no reason was given, it might have been because of the violence toward women."

Love Birds (1934). **Director:** William A. Seiter. **Writers:** Doris Anderson (writer), Clarence Marks, Dale Van Every (story), Henry Myers, Tom Reed, H.M. Walker (additional dialogue). **Producer:** Carl Laemmle Jr. **Associate Producer:** Dale Van Every. **Music:** Heinz Roemheld (uncredited). **Cinematography:** Norbert Brodine. **Editor:** Daniel Mandell. **Art Direction:** Charles D. Hall. **Makeup:** Jack P. Pierce. **Assistant Directors:** Ansel Friedberger (uncredited), Joseph A. McDonough (uncredited). **Sound Supervisor:** Gilbert Kurland (uncredited). **Dialogue Director:** Glenn Tryon (uncredited). **Cast:** Slim Summerville (Henry Whipple), ZaSu Pitts (Araminta Tootle), Mickey Rooney (Gladwyn Tootle), Frederick Burton (Barbwire), Emmett Vogan (Forbes), Dorothy Christy (Kitten), Maude Eburne (Mme. Bertha), Craig Reynolds (Bus Driver), Gertrude Short (Burlesque Girl), Clarence Wilson (Blewitt), Arthur Stone (Janitor), Ethel Mandell (Teacher), John T. Murray (Dentist). **Release Date:** May 4, 1934. Universal Pictures. 61 min. **Notes:** This film's working titles were *Two Clucks*, *Niagara* and *Niagara Falls*. *Niagara Falls* was also the alternate title for ZaSu's *Out All Night*, and the actual title for her 1941 Hal Roach "Streamline Feature."

Private Scandal (1934). **Director:** Ralph Murphy. **Writers:** Vera Caspary, Bruce Manning (story "In Conference"), Garrett Fort (writer). **Associate Producer:** Harry Joe Brown. **Producer:** Charles R. Rogers. **Executive Producer:** Emanuel Cohen (uncredited). **Cinematography:** Milton Krasner. **Art Direction:** David S. Garber. **Assistant Director:** Raoul Pagel. **Sound:** A.W. Singley. **Assistant Camera:** Irving Glassberg (uncredited). **Camera Operator:** Harry Hallenberger (uncredited). **Cast:** ZaSu Pitts (Miss Coates), Phillips Holmes (Cliff Barry), Mary Brian (Fran Somers), Ned Sparks (Inspector Riordan), Lew Cody (Benjamin J. Somers), June Brewster (Adele Smith), Harold Waldridge (Jerome), Jed Prouty (H.R. Robbins), Charles Sellon (Mr. Terwilliger), Rollo Lloyd (Insurance Agent Henry Lane), Olive Tell (Deborah Lane), Olin Howland (Ed, Coroner), Billy Franey (Macey, uncredited), James P. Burtis (Reporter, uncredited), David Callis (Photographer, uncredited), Shirley Chambers (Mrs. Belle Orrington, uncredited), George Guhl (Deputy Blaney, uncredited), Hale Hamilton (Jim Orrington, uncredited), Robert Homans (Clancy, uncredited), Fred Howard (Reporter, uncredited), Hans Joby (Jenkins, uncredited), James T. Mack (Photographer, uncredited), Greta Meyer (Wife — First Customer, uncredited), Charles Middleton (Mr. Baker, uncredited), John Qualen (Schultz, uncredited), Kane Richmond (Buddy, uncredited), Christian Rub (August — Second Customer, uncredited), Edward Thomas (Waiter, uncredited), Nick Thompson (Italian Counterman, uncredited), Charles Williams (Reporter, un-

Private Scandal (Paramount, 1934) co-starred ZaSu with Mary Brian and Phillips Holmes.

credited). **Release Date:** May 11, 1934. Paramount Pictures. 62 min. **Notes:** The source story, "In Conference," was unpublished.

Their Big Moment (1934). **Director:** James Cruze. **Writers:** Walter C. Hackett (play *Afterwards*), Arthur Caesar, Marion Dix (screenplay). **Executive Producer:** Pandro S. Berman. **Associate Producer:** Cliff Reid. **Cinematography:** Harold Wenstrom. **Editor:** William Hamilton. **Art Direction:** Van Nest Polglase. **Assistant Director:** Charles Kerr (uncredited). **Sound Recordist:** P.J. Faulkner Jr. **Camera Operator:** Joseph F. Biroc (uncredited). **Still Photographer:** Gaston Longet (uncredited). **Musical Director:** Max Steiner. **Cast:** ZaSu Pitts (Tillie Whim), Slim Summerville (Bill Ambrose), William Gaxton (the Great La Salle), Bruce Cabot (Lane Franklyn), Kay Johnson (Eve Farrington), Julie Haydon (Fay Harley), Ralph Morgan (Dr. Portman), Huntley Gordon (John Farrington), Tamara Geva (Lottie), Wallace MacDonald (Theater Manager, uncredited), Ed Brady (Stage Manager, uncredited), Frank Mills (Pilot, uncredited), Frank O'Connor (Detective, uncredited). **Release Date:** August 17, 1934. RKO Radio Pictures. 68 min. **Notes:** The working title for this film was *Afterwards*, the title of the original stage production.

Dames (1934). **Directors:** Ray Enright, Busby Berkeley. **Writers:** Robert Lord, Delmer Daves (story), Daves (screenplay). **Executive Producer:** Hal B. Wallis (uncredited). **Cinematography:** George Barnes, Sid Hickox, Sol Polito. **Editor:** Harold McLernon. **Art Direction:** Robert M. Haas, Willy Pogany. **Gowns:** Orry-Kelly. **Assistant Director:** Sherry Shourds (uncredited). **Props:** Gene Delaney (uncredited), Howard Oggle (uncredited). **Recording Engineer:** Stanley Jones (uncredited). **Chief Electricians:** Paul Burnett (uncredited), Frank Flanagan (uncredited), George Satterfield (uncredited). **Assistant Camera:** L. De Angelis (uncredited). **Still Photographer:** John Ellis (uncredited). **Camera Operators:** Al Green (uncredited), Warren Lynch (uncredited). **Chief Grips:** Dudie Maschmeyer (uncredited), Harold Noyes (uncredited). **Assistant Camera:** Jack Koffman (uncredited). **Cast:** Joan Blondell (Mabel Anderson), Dick Powell (James "Jimmy" Higgens), Ruby Keeler (Barbara Hemingway, a.k.a. Joan Grey), ZaSu Pitts (Matilda Ounce Hemingway), Guy Kibbee (Horace Peter Hemingway), Hugh Herbert (Ezra Ounce), Arthur Vinton (Bulger), Phil Regan (Johnny Harris), Arthur Aylesworth (Train Conductor), Johnny Arthur (Billings), Leila Bennett (Laura), Berton Churchill (Harold Ellsworthy Todd), Eddy Chandler (Guard, uncredited), Frank Darien (First Druggist, uncredited), Lester Dorr (Elevator Starter, uncredited), Sammy Fain (Buttercup Balmer, Songwriter, uncredited), Harry Holman (Third Druggist, uncredited), Sam Godfrey (Ounce's First Receptionist, uncredited), Dick French (Man on Ferry, uncredited), Eddie Kane (Harry, the Stage Manager; uncredited), Robert Emmett Keane (Man on Train, uncredited), Milton Kibbee (Reporter, uncredited), Larry McGrath (Sergeant at Jail, uncredited), Edmund Mortimer (Ounce's Second Receptionist, uncredited), Henry Roquemore (Board Member in Show, uncredited), Cliff Saum (Stagehand, uncredited), Lew Sherwood (Vocal Refrain, uncredited), Eddie Shubert (Eddie, Soda Jerk; uncredited), Phil Tead (Reporter, uncredited), Fred "Snowflake" Toones (Porter, uncredited), Leo White (Violin Player on Ferry, uncredited), Charles Williams (Dance Director, uncredited), Jack Wise (Second Druggist, uncredited), William Worthington (Board Member in Show, uncredited), Loretta Andrews, De Don Blunier, Diane Borget, Dolores Casey, Virginia Dabney, Mildred Dixon, Diane Douglas, Maxine Doyle, Ruth Eddings, Mary Egan, Gloria Faythe, Virginia Grey, Patricia Harper, Mary Lange, Lois Lindsay, Ethelreda Leopold, Nancy Lyon, Martha Merrill, Ruth Moody, Branche Macdonald, Jean Rogers, Victoria Vinton (Chorus Girls, uncredited). **Release Date:** September 1, 1934. Warner Bros. Pictures/Vitaphone Corporation. 91 min. **Notes:** Ruth Donnelly was considered for ZaSu's role of "Matilda."

Mrs. Wiggs of the Cabbage Patch (1934). **Director:** Norman Taurog. **Writers:** Alice Hegan Rice (novel), Anne Crawford Flexner (play), William Slavens McNutt, Jane Storm (writers). **Producer:** Douglas MacLean. **Music:** Val Burton (uncredited), John Leipold (uncredited). **Cinematography:** Charles Lang. **Art Direction:** Hans Dreier, Robert Odell. **Assistant Director:** Edward Montagne (uncredited). **Props:** Harry Caplan (uncredited). **Assistant Camera:** Cliff Shirpser (uncredited). **Cast:** Pauline Lord (Mrs. Elvira Wiggs), W.C. Fields (Mr. C. Ellsworth Stubbins), ZaSu Pitts (Miss Tabitha Hazy, Spinster), Evelyn Venable (Lucy Olcott), Kent Taylor (Bob Redding), Charles Middleton (Mr. Bagby), Donald Meek (Mr. Hiram Wiggs), Jimmy Butler (Bill Wiggs), George Breakston (Jimmy Wiggs), Edith Fellows (Australia Wiggs), Virginia Weidler (Europena Wiggs), Carmencita Johnson (Asia Wiggs), George Reed (Julius), Mildred Gover (Priscilla), Arthur Housman (Dick Harris), Walter Walker (Dr. Barton), Sam Flint (Railroad Agent Jenkins), James Robinson (Mose), Bentley Hewlett (Box Office Man), Eddie Tamblyn (Usher), Al Shaw (Co-

Married life was anything but blissful in *Mrs. Wiggs of the Cabbage Patch* once W.C. Fields sampled Miss Hazy's disappointing cooking.

median), Sam Lee (Comedian), Del Henderson (House Manager), George Pearce (Minister), Lillian Elliott (Mrs. Bagby), Earl Pingree (Brakeman), Ann Sheridan (Bit, uncredited). **Release Date:** October 28, 1934. Paramount Pictures. 80 min. **Notes:** Madge Carr Cook played Mrs. Wiggs in the original 1904-05 Broadway play. Helen Lowell played Miss Hazy in that production. Other films based on the story (and titled *Mrs. Wiggs of the Cabbage Patch*) are the 1919 production, directed by Hugh Ford and starring Marguerite Clark and Mary Carr, and the 1942 production, directed by Ralph Murphy and starring Fay Bainter and Hugh Herbert. World Film Corp. produced what seems to be the first adaptation, in 1914, starring Blanche Chapman, who played the part on stage.

The Gay Bride (1934). **Director:** Jack Conway. **Writers:** Charles Francis Coe (story "Repeal"), Bella Spewack, Sam Spewack (writers). **Producer:** John W. Considine Jr. **Music:** Jack Virgil, R.H. Bassett (uncredited). **Cinematography:** Ray June. **Editor:** Frank Sullivan. **Art Direction:** Cedric Gibbons. **Assistant Director:** Charles Dorian (uncredited). **Associate Art Directors:** Stan Rogers, Edwin B. Willis. **Recording Director:** Douglas Shearer. **Wardrobe:** Dolly Tree. **Cast:** Carole Lombard (Mary Magiz), Chester Morris (Jimmie "Office Boy" Burnham), ZaSu Pitts.(Mirabelle), Leo Carrillo (Mickey "The Greek" Mikapopoulis), Nat Pendleton (William T. "Shoots" Magiz), Sam Hardy (Daniel J. Dingle), Walter Walker (MacPherson), Eddie "Rochester" Anderson (Second Bootblack, uncredited), Gene Lockhart (Jim Smiley, uncredited), Irving Bacon (Weight Guesser, uncredited), Norman Ainsley (Waiter, uncredited), Art Jarrett (singer, uncredited), Jack Baxley (Bum, uncredited), Brooks Benedict (Wedding Guest, uncredited), Frank Darien (Mr. Bartlett, uncredited), Gordon De Main (Police Sergeant, uncredited), Clay Drew (Stage Doorman, uncredited), Herbert Evans (British Official, uncredited), Lew Harvey (Local Gangster, uncredited), Boothe Howard (Detroit Gangster, uncredited), Edward LeSaint (Justice of the Peace, uncredited), Wilbur Mack (Banker, uncredited), Fred Malatesta (French Officer, uncredited), Ray Mayer (Photographer, uncredited), Francis McDonald (Detroit Gangster, uncredited), Tom McGuire (Policeman, uncredited), Scott Moore (Bit Part, uncredited), Louis Natheaux (Conk, uncredited), Garry Owen (Reporter, uncredited), Lee Phelps (Guard, uncredited), Charles Sullivan (Taxi Driver, uncredited), Harry Tenbrook (Mechanic, uncredited), Fred "Snowflake" Toones (First Bootblack, uncredited), Joe Twerp (Laf Lafcadio, uncredited), Wilhelm von Brincken (German Official, uncredited), Bobby Watson (Auto Salesman, uncredited). **Release Date:** December 14, 1934. Metro-Goldwyn-Mayer (MGM). 80 min. **Notes:** The working title for this film was *Repeal*.

Ruggles of Red Gap (1935). **Director:** Leo McCarey. **Writers:** Harry Leon Wilson (novel), Humphrey Pearson (adaptation), Walter DeLeon, Harlan Thompson (screenplay). **Producer:** Arthur Hornblow Jr. **Cinematography:** Alfred Gilks. **Music:** Heinz Roemheld (uncredited). **Editor:** Edward Dmytryk (uncredited). **Art Direction:** Hans Dreier (uncredited), Robert Odell (uncredited). **Costume Design:** Travis Banton (uncredited). **Assistant Director:** F. Erickson (uncredited). **Sound:** Philip Wisdom (uncredited). **Cast:** Charles Laughton (Marmaduke Ruggles), Mary Boland (Effie Floud), Charlie Ruggles (Egbert Floud), ZaSu Pitts (Prunella Judson), Roland Young (George Vane Bassingwell), Leila Hyams (Nell Kenner), Maude Eburne ("Ma" Pettingill), Lucien Littlefield (Charles Belknap-Jackson), Leota Lorraine (Mrs. Charles Belknap-Jackson), James Burke (Jeff Tuttle), Del Henderson (Sam, Bartender), Clarence Wilson (Jake Henshaw), Ernie Adams (Dishwasher, uncredited), Augusta Anderson (Mrs. Wallaby, uncredited), Alyce Ardell (Lisette, uncredited), Harry Bernard (Harry, Bartender #2; uncredited), Harry Bowen (Photographer, uncredited), George Burton (Doc Squires, uncredited), Alex Chivra (Chef #1, uncredited), Heinie Conklin (Waiter at the Grill, uncredited), Jim Corey (Cowboy, uncredited), Carrie Daumery (Effie's Guest in Paris, uncredited), Sarah Edwards (Mrs. Myron Carey, uncredited), Charles Fallon (Max, uncredited), Brenda Fowler (Mrs. Judy Ballard, uncredited), Willie Fung (Willie, uncredited), Armand Kaliz (Clothing Salesman, uncredited), Jane Keckley (Cook, uncredited), Jane Kerr (Cook, uncredited), Lee Kohlmar (Jailer at Red Gap, uncredited), Isabel La Mal (Effie's Guest in Paris, uncredited), Edward LeSaint (Diner at the Grill, uncredited), Jack Norton (Barfly, uncredited), Patsy O'Byrne (Cook, uncredited), Frank O'Connor (Station Agent, uncredited), Albert Petit (Waiter at Carousel, uncredited), Victor Potel (Curly, uncredited), Frank Rice (Hank Adams, uncredited), Henry Roquemore (Fred, uncredited), Rolfe Sedan (Barber in Paris, uncredited), Genaro Spagnoli (Frank, Cab Driver; uncredited), Rafael Storm (Clothing Salesman, uncredited), Libby Taylor (Libby, uncredited), Jim Welch (Man in Saloon, uncredited), William Welsh (Eddie, uncredited). **Release Date:** March 8, 1935. Paramount Pictures. 90 min. **Notes:** *Ruggles of Red Gap* was nominated for an Academy Award for Best Picture of 1935.

Laughton was selected Best Actor of 1935 by the New York Film Critics Circle for his performance as Ruggles and his portrayal of Captain Bligh in *Mutiny on the Bounty*. *Ruggles of Red Gap* was one of *Film Daily*'s "Ten Best Pictures of 1935," and was listed in the 1935-36 *Motion Picture Almanac* as a March 1935 "Box Office Champion." Wilson's story was the source for a 1918 Essanay film, starring Taylor Holmes; a 1923 Famous Players–Lasky version, directed by James Cruze and starring Edward Everett Horton; and Paramount's *Fancy Pants* (1950), starring Bob Hope and Lucille Ball. *Ruggles of Red Gap* was also adapted as a musical comedy for a brief Broadway run in 1915-16, with music by Sigmund Romberg; Ralph Herz, Frederick Burton, Louise Closser Hale, and Jessie Ralph starred.

Spring Tonic (1935). **Director:** Clyde Bruckman. **Writers:** Frank Griffin (comedy sequences), H.W. Hanemann, Patterson McNutt (writers), Ben Hecht, Charles MacArthur (play), Howard Irving Young (adaptation). **Producer:** Robert Kane. **Cinematography:** L. William O'Connell. **Costume Design:** René Hubert. **Musical Director:** Arthur Lange. **Cast:** Lew Ayres (Caleb Enix), Claire Trevor (Betty Ingals), Walter Woolf King (José), Jack Haley (Sykes), ZaSu Pitts (Maggie), Tala Birell (Lola), Sig Ruman (Matt), Frank Mitchell (Griffen Nasher), Jack Durant (Camebridge Nasher), Herbert Mundin (Thompson), Henry Kolker (Mr. Enix), Laura Treadwell (Mrs. Enix), Douglas Wood (Mr. Ingalls), Helen Freeman (Mrs. Ingalls), Lynn Bari (Bridesmaid), Walter Brennan (uncredited), Eddy Chandler (uncredited), George Chandler (uncredited), Edgar Dearing (uncredited), Wilfred Hari (uncredited), Arthur Housman (uncredited), Lew Kelly (uncredited), Edgar Sherrod (uncredited). **Release Date:** June 27, 1935. Fox Film Corporation. 58 min. **Notes:** Alternate titles for this film were *Man-Eating Tiger* and *Hold That Tiger*. Harold Schuster shot additional scenes for the film.

She Gets Her Man (1935). **Director:** William Nigh. **Writers:** David Diamond, Aben Kandel (story), Aben Kandel (screenplay). **Producer:** David Diamond. **Music:** Karl Hajos, Arthur Morton. **Cinematography:** Norbert Brodine. **Editing:** Bernard W. Burton. **Musical Director:** C. Bakaleinikoff. **Cast:** ZaSu Pitts (Esmeralda), Hugh O'Connell (Windy), Helen Twelvetrees (Francine), Lucien Littlefield (Elmer), Edward Brophy (Flash), Warren Hymer (Spike), Bert Gordon (Goofy), Ward Bond (Chick), Frank Adams (Bumpkin, uncredited), Richard Alexander (Gangster, uncredited), Stanley Andrews (Kelly, uncredited), King Baggot (Businessman, uncredited), Constance Bergen (Gun Moll, uncredited), Raymond Brown (Barton, uncredited), John Carradine (Customer, uncredited), Russ Clark (Gangster, uncredited), George Cleveland (Drunk, uncredited), Nell Craig (Raid Leader, uncredited), Richard Cramer (Bookkeeper, uncredited), Helen Dickson (Raider, uncredited), Mike Donovan (Guard, uncredited), Lester Dorr (Photographer, uncredited), Virginia Grey (Club Woman, uncredited), Bernadene Hayes (Gun Moll, uncredited), Oscar "Dutch" Hendrian (Butch, uncredited), John Indrisano (Gangster, uncredited), Jack Kennedy (Police Captain, uncredited), Jane Kerr (Raider, uncredited), Isabel La Mal (Club Woman, uncredited), George Lloyd (Gangster, uncredited), Sam Lufkin (Gangster, uncredited), Evelyn Miller (Customer, uncredited), Monte Montague (Butler, uncredited), Ottola Nesmith (Club Woman, uncredited), Jack Norton (Drunk Reporter, uncredited), Georgia O'Dell (Spinster, uncredited), Anne O'Neal (Customer, uncredited), Blanche Payson (Raider, uncredited), Stanley Price (Reporter, uncredited), Archie

Robbins (Reporter, uncredited), Lew Seymour (Theater Manager, uncredited), Al St. John (Teller, uncredited), Charles Sullivan (Gangster, uncredited), Laura Treadwell (uncredited), Louis Vincenot (Chinese Merchant, uncredited), Sailor Vincent (uncredited), Emmett Vogan (Reporter, uncredited), Huey White (Gangster, uncredited). **Release Date:** August 5, 1935. Universal Pictures. 65 min.

Hot Tip (1935). **Directors:** James Gleason, Ray McCarey. **Writers:** Olive Cooper, Hugh Cummings, Louis Stevens. **Producer:** William Sistrom. **Cinematography:** Jack MacKenzie. **Costume Design:** Walter Plunkett. **Musical Director:** Alberto Colombo. **Cast:** ZaSu Pitts (Belle McGill), James Gleason (Jimmy McGill), Margaret Callahan (Jane McGill), Russell Gleason (Ben Johnson), Ray Mayer (Tyler), Willie Best (Apollo), J.M. Kerrigan (Matt), Arthur Stone (Harvey Hooper), Rollo Lloyd (Henry Crumm), Dell Henderson (Sheriff), Donald Kerr (Spider), Kitty McHugh (Queenie). **Release Date:** August 20, 1935. RKO Radio Pictures. 70 min. **Notes:** The working title for this film was *Leander Clicks*.

Going Highbrow (1935). **Director:** Robert Florey. **Writers:** Ralph Spence (story "Social Pirates"), Edward Kaufman, Sy Bartlett (screenplay), Ben Markson (additional dialogue). **Producer:** Samuel Bischoff (uncredited). **Music:** Louis Alter, John [Jack] Scholl. **Cinematography:** William Rees. **Editor:** Harold McLernon. **Art Direction:** Esdras Hartley. **Gowns:** Orry-Kelly. **Cast:** Guy Kibbee (Matt Upshaw), ZaSu Pitts (Mrs. Cora Upshaw), Edward Everett Horton (Augie Winterspoon), Ross Alexander (Harley Marsh), June Martel (Sandy Long), Gordon Westcott (Sam Long), Judy Canova (Annie), Nella Walker (Mrs. Forrester Marsh), Jack Norton (Sinclair), Arthur Treacher (Waiter), Joseph E. Bernard (Deck Steward) (uncredited), Paul de Rincon (Reporter, uncredited), Bill Elliott (Reporter, uncredited), Pauline Garon (Josephine, uncredited), Maude Turner Gordon (Mrs. Vandergrift, uncredited), Sherry Hall (Reporter, uncredited), Olaf Hytten (Watkins, uncredited), William Jeffrey (Cafe Proprietor, uncredited), Milton Kibbee (Reporter, uncredited), Paul Panzer (Diner, uncredited), Jack Richardson (Deck Steward, uncredited), Marshall Ruth (Room Steward, uncredited), Christiane Tourneur (French Actress, uncredited), Emmett Vogan (Reporter, uncredited), Leo White (Diner, uncredited), Tom Wilson (Diner, uncredited). **Release Date:** August 23, 1935. Warner Bros. Pictures. 67 min. **Notes:** The film's working titles were *Crashing Society* and *Social Pirates*. *Daily Variety* noted that both Joan Blondell and Aline MacMahon were considered for ZaSu's role.

The Affair of Susan (1935). **Director:** Kurt Neumann. **Writers:** Mann Page (story), Clarence Marks, Andrew Bennison, H.M. Walker (writer). **Associate Producer:** David Diamond. **Executive Producer:** Fred S. Meyer (uncredited). **Music:** Franz Waxman, David Klatzkin (uncredited), Jack Yellen (uncredited). **Cinematography:** Norbert Brodine. **Editing:** Philip Cahn. **Art Direction:** Thomas F. O'Neill. **Assistant Director:** Phil Karlson (uncredited). **Sound Supervisor:** Gilbert Kurland. **Musical Director:** C. Bakaleinikoff (uncredited). **Cast:** ZaSu Pitts (Susan Todd), Hugh O'Connell (Dudley Stone), Walter Catlett (Gilbert), Tom Dugan (Jeff Barnes), Inez Courtney (Mrs. Barnes), James Burke (Hogan), Nan Grey (Miss Skelly), Irene Franklin (Miss Perkins), William Pawley (Policeman), Wally Albright (uncredited), Irving Bacon (Spieler, uncredited), Jack Baxley (Spieler, uncredited), Constance Bergen (Girl, uncredited), Mae Busch (Mrs. Hogan, uncredited), Ralph Byrd (Mechanic, uncredited), Willy Castello (uncredited), Jack Cheatham (Policeman, uncredited), Phyllis Crane (Girl, uncredited), Jack Daley (Spieler, uncredited), Al Ferguson (Mechanic, uncredited), Allan Fox (Mechanic, uncredited), Bert Gordon (Hot Dog Man, uncredited), Dorothy Granger (Girl, uncredited), Harrison Greene (Bath House Attendant, uncredited), Charles Hammer (Mechanic, uncredited), Earle Hodgins (Spieler, uncredited), Hyram A. Hoover (Mechanic, uncredited), Lois January (Girl, uncredited), Suzanne Kaaren (Girl on Beach, uncredited), Lew Kelly (Concessionaire, uncredited), Jack Kennedy (Police Sergeant, uncredited), Julie Kingdon (Girl, uncredited), John King (Boy in Fun House, uncredited), Dixie Martin (Girl, uncredited), Monte Montague (Bus Driver, uncredited), Gene Morgan (Bath House Attendant, uncredited), Jack Mower (Mechanic, uncredited), Buster Phelps (Son, uncredited), Peter Potter (Boy at Coal Mine, uncredited), Buddy Roosevelt (Taxi Driver, uncredited), Teru Shimada (Spieler, uncredited), Gertrude Short (Girl, uncredited), Anya Taranda (Girl, uncredited), Phil Tead (Spieler, uncredited), Carol Tevis (Girl, uncredited), Anders Van Haden (Spieler, uncredited), Pat West (Bath House Attendant, uncredited), Otto Yamaoka (Spieler, uncredited). **Release Date:** September 1, 1935. Universal Pictures. 62 min. **Notes:** *Alone Together* was the film's working title.

13 Hours by Air (1936). **Director:** Mitchell Leisen. **Writers:** Frank Mitchell Dazey, Bogart Rogers (story "Wild Wings"), Kenyon Nicholson (writer), Bogart Rogers (screenplay). **Producer:** E. Lloyd Sheldon. **Cinematography:** Theodor Sparkuhl. **Editing:** Doane Harrison. **Art Direction:** Hans Dreier, John B. Goodman. **Set Decoration:** A.E. Freudeman. **Sound:** Louis Mesenkop, M.M. Paggi. **Special Camera Effects:** Farciot Edouart, Gordon Jennings. **Cast:** Fred MacMurray (Jack Gordon), Joan Bennett (Felice Rollins), ZaSu Pitts (Miss Harkins), Alan Baxter (Curtis Palmer), Fred Keating (Gregore Stephani), Brian Donlevy (Dr. Evarts), John Howard (Freddie Scott), Adrienne Marden (Ann McKenna), Ruth Donnelly (Vi Johnson), Benny Bartlett (Waldemar Pitt III), Grace Bradley (Trixie La Brey), Dean Jagger (Hap Waller), Jack Mulhall (Horace Lander), Granville Bates (Pop Andrews), Arthur Singley (Pete Stevens), Clyde Dilson (Fat Richhauser), Mildred Stone (Ruth Bradford), Bud Flannagan [Dennis O'Keefe] (Baker), Henry Arthur (Assistant Clerk, uncredited), John Juettner (Co-Pilot, uncredited), Marie Prevost (Waitress, uncredited), Ed Schaefer (Harry, uncredited), Gertrude Short (Waitress, uncredited), Bruce Warren (Tex Doyle, uncredited). **Release Date:** April 30, 1936. Paramount Pictures. 77 min. **Notes:** First called *Twenty Hours by Air*, the title was changed when aviators Jimmy Doolittle, Wiley Post, and Roscoe Turner flew various 13-hour cross-country flights, thus making the title meaningless and outdated. Some scenes were filmed on location at Alhambra Airport, California, in Cleveland, Ohio, and Beaver Dam, Wisconsin, the latter being star Fred MacMurray's hometown.

Mad Holiday (1936). **Director:** George B. Seitz. **Writers:** Florence Ryerson, Edgar Allan Woolf (writer), Joseph Santley (story "Murder in a Chinese Theatre"). **Producer:** Harry Rapf. **Music:** William Axt. **Cinematography:** Joseph Ruttenberg. **Editing:** George Boemler. **Art Direction:** Cedric Gibbons. **Costume Design:** Dolly Tree. **Assistant Director:** Dolph Zimmer. **Associate Art Directors:** Stan Rogers, Edwin B. Willis. **Recording Director:** Douglas Shearer. **Cast:** Edmund Lowe (Philip Trent), Elissa Landi (Peter Dean), ZaSu Pitts (Mrs. Fay Kinney), Ted Healy (Mert Morgan), Edmund Gwenn

(Williams), Edgar Kennedy (Donovan), Soo Yong (Li Tai), Walter Kingsford (Ben Kelvin), Herbert Rawlinson (Captain Bromley), Raymond Hatton (Cokey Joe Ferris), Rafaela Ottiano (Ning), Harlan Briggs (Mr. Kinney), Gustav von Seyffertitz (Hendrick Van Mier), King Baggot (Director, uncredited), Chester Gan (Vendor, uncredited), Richard Hakins (uncredited), Sherry Hall (Radio Operator, uncredited), Russell Hicks (Chief Gibbs, uncredited), Richard Loo (Li Yat, uncredited), Wilbur Mack (Mayor Howell, uncredited), Adrian Rosley (Official Guide, uncredited), Charles Trowbridge (Doctor, uncredited). **Release Date:** November 13, 1936. Metro-Goldwyn-Mayer (MGM). 71 min. **Notes:** Early titles for this film were *The Cock-Eyed Cruise* and *The White Dragon*.

The Plot Thickens (1936). **Director:** Ben Holmes. **Writers:** Stuart Palmer (story), Jack Townley, Clarence Upson Young (writer). **Associate Producer:** William Sistrom. **Executive Producer:** Samuel J. Briskin (uncredited). **Cinematography:** Nick Musuraca. **Editing:** John Lockert. **Art Direction:** Van Nest Polglase. **Set Decoration:** Darrell Silvera. **Gowns:** Edward Stevenson. **Associate Art Director:** Feild Gray. **Sound Recordist:** George D. Ellis. **Cast:** James Gleason (Oscar Piper), ZaSu Pitts (Hildegarde Withers), Owen Davis Jr. (Robert "Bob" Wilkins), Louise Latimer (Alice Stevens), Arthur Aylesworth (Kendall), Paul Fix (Joe), Richard Tucker (John Carter), Barbara Barondess (Marie), James Donlan (Jim), Agnes Anderson (Dagmar), Oscar Apfel (H. G. Robbins), Alyce Ardell (Josephine, uncredited), John T. Bambury (Midget, uncredited), Billy Dooley (Gas Station Attendant, uncredited), Frank Fanning (Detective Fanning, uncredited), Mary Gordon (Woman, uncredited), Reed Howes (Museum Guard, uncredited), John Indrisano (Man in Line, uncredited), Lew Kelly (Cassidy, uncredited), John Miltern (Mr. Gordon, uncredited), Tom Quinn (First Hatless Suspect, uncredited), Bodil Rosing (Theresa, uncredited), George Sorel (Man, uncredited). **Release Date:** December 11, 1936. RKO Radio Pictures. 69 min. **Notes:** *The Riddle of the Dangling Pearl* was the film's working title. This was the fifth in the series of Hildegarde Withers RKO mysteries, the others being *Penguin Pool Murder* (1932), *Murder on the Blackboard* (1934), *Murder on a Honeymoon* (1935), and *Murder on a Bridle Path* (1936). ZaSu took over the role from Edna May Oliver (three films) and Helen Broderick (one), and would play the character once more (wrapping up the series) in *Forty Naughty Girls* (1937). Others to play the role were Agnes Moorehead (in a 1950s TV pilot, *Amazing Miss Withers*, with Paul Kelly) and Eve Arden (in the 1972 television movie *A Very Missing Person*, with James Gregory).

Sing Me a Love Song (1936). **Director:** Ray Enright. **Writers:** Sig Herzig, Jerry Wald (writer), Harry Sauber (story), Pat C. Flick (additional dialogue, uncredited). **Producer:** Samuel Bischoff (uncredited). **Executive Producers:** Hal B. Wallis, Jack L. Warner (uncredited). **Cinematography:** Arthur Todd. **Editing:** Thomas Pratt. **Gowns:** Milo Anderson. **Assistant Director:** Lee Katz (uncredited). **Musical Director:** Leo F. Forbstein. **Dialogue Director:** Gene Lewis. **Cast:** James Melton (Jerry Haines), Patricia Ellis (Jean Martin), Hugh Herbert (Siegfried Hammerschlag), ZaSu Pitts (Gwen Logan), Allen Jenkins ("Chris" Cross), Nat Pendleton (Rocky), William Arnold (Waiter, uncredited), Herbert Ashley (Policeman, uncredited), Granville Bates (Mr. Goodrich, uncredited), Walter Catlett (Mr. Sprague, uncredited), Hobart Cavanaugh (Mr. Barton, uncredited), Glen Cavender (Elevator Starter, uncredited), Carrie Daumery (Customer, uncredited), Don Downen (Elevator Operator, uncredited), Ralph Dunn (Store

Cashier, uncredited), Betty Farrington (Customer, uncredited), Eddie Graham (Store Employee, uncredited), George Guhl (Policeman, uncredited), Charles Halton (Mr. Willard, uncredited), Gordon Hart (Caldwell, uncredited), Harry Hollingsworth (Detective, uncredited), Stuart Holmes (Browsing Customer, uncredited), Dennis Moore (Blakeley, uncredited), Lyle Moraine (Bellboy, uncredited), John T. Murray (Radio Salesman, uncredited), Robert Emmett O'Connor (Detective, uncredited), Paul Panzer (Floorwalker Jones, uncredited), Linda Perry (Miss Joyce, uncredited), Charles Richman (Mr. Malcolm, uncredited), Tom Ricketts (Siegfried's Pool Opponent, uncredited), Adrian Rosley (Waiter, uncredited), Cliff Saum (Policeman, uncredited), George Sorel (Headwaiter, uncredited), Larry Steers (Night Club Patron, uncredited), Emmett Vogan (Floorwalker, uncredited), Charles Williams (Man, uncredited), Jack Wise (Store Employee, uncredited). **Release Date:** January 9, 1937. Warner Bros.–First National Pictures/Cosmopolitan Productions. 75 min. **Notes:** Ann Sheridan's and Georgia Caine's scenes have been deleted from reissue prints. The film's working titles were *Come Up Smiling* and *Let's Pretend*. Hugh Herbert is featured in a *triple* role — as two brothers and their own father. Marie Wilson was original assigned the part ZaSu eventually played; the producers ultimately determined that Wilson was too young for the role.

Wanted! (1937). **Director/Producer:** George King. **Writers:** H.F. Maltby (writer), Brock Williams (play). **Cinematography:** Jack Parker. **Assistant Director:** E.M. Smedley-Aston (uncredited). **Musical Director:** Colin Wark. **Cast:** ZaSu Pitts (Winnie Oatfield), Claude Dampier (Henry Oatfield), Mark Daly (Mr. Smithers), Norma Varden (Mrs. Smithers), Finlay Currie (Uncle Mart), Kathleen Harrison (Belinda), Billy Holland (Harry the Hick), Stella Bonheur (Baby Face), Billy Bray (Sparrow Hawkins), Arthur Goullet (Bonelli), Alfred Wellesley (Lord Hotbury), Mabel Twemlow (Lady Hotbury), D.J. Williams (Captain McTurk), Bryan Herbert (Police Constable Gribble). UK. George King Productions/Sound City Films. 69 min.

Merry Comes to Town (1937). **Director/Producer:** George King. **Writers:** Evadne Price (story), Brock Williams (writer). **Cinematography:** Hone Glendinning. **Art Direction:** Jack Hallward. **Assistant Director:** M. Smedley-Aston (uncredited). **Cast:** ZaSu Pitts, Guy Newall (Prof. John Stafford), Betty Ann Davies (Marjorie Stafford), Stella Arbenina (Mme. Saroni), Bernard Clifton (Dennis Stafford), Margaret Watson (Grandmother Stafford), Basil Langton (Noel Slater), Muriel George (Cook), Tom Helmore (Peter Bell), Cecil Mannering (Horace Bell), George Sims (Sales Manager), W.T. Ellwanger (Mr. Ramp), Arthur Finn (Mr. Walheimer), Sybil Grove (Zoe), Dorothy Bush, Hermione Gingold (Ida Witherspoon), Mabel Twemlow (Mrs. C. Wriggle), Jack Hellier, Janet Fitzpatrick (Woman, uncredited), Margaret Yarde (uncredited). UK. Embassy Pictures (Associated) Ltd./Sound City Films. 79 min.

Forty Naughty Girls (1937). **Director:** Edward F. Cline. **Writers:** Stuart Palmer (novel *The Riddle of the Forty Naughty Girls*), John Grey (screenplay). **Producer:** William Sistrom. **Executive Producer:** Samuel J. Briskin (uncredited). **Music:** Roy Webb (uncredited). **Cinematography:** Russell Metty. **Editing:** John Lockert. **Art Direction:** Van Nest Polglase. **Costume Design:** Renié. **Assistant Director:** Ruby Rosenberg (uncredited). **Associate Art Director:** Feild M. Gray. **Sound Recordist:** Earl A. Wolcott. **Musical Director:** Roy Webb. **Cast:** James Gleason (Inspector Oscar Piper), ZaSu Pitts (Hildegarde Withers), Marjorie Lord (June Preston),

George Shelley (Bert), Joan Woodbury (Rita Marlowe), Frank M. Thomas (Jeff "Pop" Plummer), Tom Kennedy (Detective Casey), Alan Edwards (Ricky Rickman), Alden Chase (Tommy Washburn), Eddie Marr (Edward C. "Windy" Bennett), Ada Leonard (Lil), Barbara Pepper (Alice), Eddie Borden (Stage Board Man, uncredited), Lynton Brent (Ticket Taker, uncredited), William Corson (Man, uncredited), Bud Jamison (Theater Doorman, uncredited), Donald Kerr (Boy, uncredited), Edward LeSaint (Coroner, uncredited), Robert McKenzie (Max, uncredited), Frank O'Connor (Stage Manager, uncredited), Elizabeth Russell (Woman, uncredited). **Release Date:** September 24, 1937. RKO Radio Pictures. 63 min. **Notes:** This was ZaSu's second film as Hildegarde Withers, school teacher-turned-detective. *The Riddle of the Forty Naughty Girls,* the source novel's title, was the film's working title. Edward Cline replaced Ben Holmes as director. See also *The Plot Thickens* (1936).

52nd Street (1937). **Director:** Harold Young. **Writers:** Grover Jones, Sid Silvers. **Producer:** Walter Wanger. **Music:** Alfred Newman (uncredited), David Raksin (uncredited). **Cinematography:** George Schneiderman. **Editing:** William Reynolds. **Costume Design:** Helen Taylor. **Musical Director:** Alfred Newman. **Cast:** Ian Hunter (Rufus Rondell), Dorothy Peterson (Adela Rondell), ZaSu Pitts (Letitia Rondell), Pat Paterson (Margaret Rondell), Leo Carrillo (Fiorello Zamarelli), Kenny Baker (Benjamin "Benny" Zamarelli), Marla Shelton (Evelyn Macy Rondell), Ella Logan (Betty), Virginia Verrill (Pat Patterson's singing double, uncredited), Collette Lyons (Minnie), Al Shean (Klauber), Sid Silvers (Sid), Jack White (Jack), Jack Adair (Porky), George Tapps (Dancer), Jerry Colonna (Specialty Vocalist), Roman Bohnen (James), Wade Boteler (Butler), Pat Harrington Sr., Al Norman (Dancer), Maurice Rocco, Ralph Brooks (uncredited), Jack Kenny (uncredited), Mary MacLaren (uncredited), Frank Mills (Party Guest, uncredited), Edmund Mortimer (uncredited), Frank O'Connor (Policeman, uncredited), Cyril Ring (uncredited), Dorothy Saulter (uncredited), Jim Thorpe (Street Thug, uncredited), Delmar Watson (Young Benjamin, uncredited). **Release Date:** November 19, 1937. Walter Wanger Productions/United Artists. 80 min. **Notes:** The blocks of New York City's 52nd Street, between Fifth Avenue and Seventh Avenue, were renowned in the 1930s until the '60s for the wealth of jazz clubs featuring such musical artists as Billie Holiday, Fats Waller, Dizzy Gillespie, Charlie Parker, Miles Davis, Louis Prima, Art Tatum, Thelonious Monk, and many others.

The Lady's from Kentucky (1939). **Director:** Alexander Hall. **Writers:** Malcolm Stuart Boylan (writer), Rowland Brown (story). **Producer:** Jeff Lazarus. **Music:** John Leipold, Leo Shuken. **Cinematography:** Theodor Sparkuhl. **Editing:** Harvey Johnston. **Cast:** George Raft (Marty Black), Ellen Drew (Penelope "Penny" Hollis), Hugh Herbert (Mousey Johnson), ZaSu Pitts (Dulcey Lee), Louise Beavers (Aunt Tina), Lew Payton (Sixty), Forrester Harvey (Nonny Watkins), Edward Pawley (Spike Cronin), Gilbert Emery (Pinckney Rodell), Jimmy Bristow (Brewster), Stanley Andrews (Doctor), George Anderson (Joe Lane), Robert Milasch (Big Longshoreman, uncredited), Mike Arnold (Cantankerous, uncredited), Hooper Atchley (Surgeon, uncredited), Irving Bacon (Information Clerk, uncredited), Bill Cartledge (Jones, uncredited), Nell Craig (Nurse, uncredited), Hal K. Dawson (Announcer, uncredited), Paula DeCardo (Bit, uncredited), Fern Emmett (Nurse, uncredited), James Flavin (Bit, uncredited), Gus Glassmire (Judge, uncredited), Roger Gray (Waiter, uncredited), Tom Hanlon (Announcer, uncredited), Carol Holloway (Nurse, uncredited), Eugene Jackson (Winfield, uncredited), George Melford (Veterinarian, uncredited), John Merton (Gambler, uncredited), Helaine Moler (Bit, uncredited), Frank Moran (Customer, uncredited), Paul Newlan (Gambler, uncredited), Mickey O'Boyle (Boy, uncredited), Bob Perry (Dealer, uncredited), Jack Raymond (Customer, uncredited), Virginia Sale (Cashier, uncredited), Robert R. Stephenson (Gambler, uncredited), Carl Stockdale (Veterinarian, uncredited), Harry Tenbrook (Longshoreman, uncredited), Charles Trowbridge (Charles Butler, uncredited), George Turner (Longshoreman, uncredited), Archie Twitchell (Radio Announcer, uncredited), Harry Tyler (Carter, uncredited), Frankie Van (Taxi Driver, uncredited), Gloria Williams (Nurse, uncredited), Charles C. Wilson (Bit, uncredited). **Release Date:** April 28, 1939. Paramount Pictures. 67 min. **Notes:** *The Gambler and the Lady* was the film's working title.

Naughty but Nice (1939). **Director:** Ray Enright. **Writers:** Richard Macaulay, Jerry Wald (screenplay). **Associate Producer:** Samuel Bischoff (uncredited), Hal B. Wallis (uncredited). **Music:** Harry Warren. **Cinematography:** Arthur L. Todd. **Editing:** Thomas Richards. **Art Direction:** Max Parker. **Gowns:** Howard Shoup. **Assistant Director:** Jesse Hibbs (uncredited). **Sound:** [Charles] David Forrest, Francis J. Scheid. **Musical Director:** Leo F. Forbstein. **Music Arranger:** Ray Heindorf. **Dialogue Director:** Hugh Cummings. **Cast:** Ann Sheridan (Zelda Manion), Dick Powell (Professor Donald "Don" Hardwick), Gale Page (Linda McKay), Helen Broderick (Aunt Martha Hogan), Ronald Reagan (Ed "Eddie" Clark), Allen Jenkins (Joe Dirk), ZaSu Pitts (Aunt Penelope Hardwick), Maxie Rosenbloom (Killer), Jerry Colonna (Allie Gray), Luis Alberni (Stanislaus Pysinski), Vera Lewis (Aunt Annabella Hardwick), Elizabeth Dunne (Aunt Henrietta Hardwick), Bill Davidson (Samuel Hudson), Granville Bates (Judge Kenneth B. Walters), Halliwell Hobbes (Dean Burton), John Ridgely (Harry, uncredited), Hobart Cavanaugh (Piano Tuner, uncredited), Sidney Bracey (Professor, uncredited), Daisy Bufford (Daisy, uncredited), Nat Carr (Extra, uncredited), Maurice Cass (Mr. Maurice, uncredited), Elise Cavanna (Pansey, uncredited), Bert Hanlon (Arranger Johnny Collins, uncredited), Grady Sutton (Mr. Mankton, uncredited), Glen Cavender (Extra, uncredited), Sol Gorss (Taxi Driver, uncredited), William Gould (Bailiff, uncredited), Peter Lind Hayes (Bandleader, uncredited), David Newell (Attorney, uncredited), Stuart Holmes (Capt. Gregory Waddington-Smith, uncredited), Eddie Graham (Attorney, uncredited), Selmer Jackson (Attorney, uncredited), Harrison Greene (Bartender, uncredited), Jerry Mandy (Waiter, uncredited), Frank Mayo (Frank, uncredited), John Harron (Freddie, uncredited), Al Herman (Waiter, uncredited), Al Lloyd (Radio Listener, uncredited), Edward McWade (Professor Trill, uncredited), Jack Mower (Professor, uncredited), William Newell (Arranger, uncredited), Wedgwood Nowell (Professor, uncredited), Garry Owen (Bartender, uncredited), Herbert Rawlinson (Hardwick's Attorney, uncredited), Sally Sage (Miss Danning, uncredited), Cliff Saum (Radio Announcer, uncredited), Bobby Sherwood (Announcer, uncredited), Larry Steers (Extra, uncredited), Leo White (Extra, uncredited), Ernest Wood (First Headwaiter, uncredited). **Release Date:** July 1, 1939. Warner Bros. Pictures. 89 min. **Notes:** The working title for this picture was *The Professor Steps Out*.

Mickey the Kid (1939). **Director:** Arthur Lubin. **Writers:** Gordon Kahn, Doris Malloy. **Producer:** Herman Schlom. **Music:** Cy

Feuer, William Lava (uncredited). **Cinematography:** Jack A. Marta. **Editing:** Murray Seldeen. **Costume Design:** Adele Palmer. **Cast:** Bruce Cabot (Jim Larch, a.k.a. Jim Adams), Ralph Byrd (Dr. Ben Cameron), ZaSu Pitts (Lilly Handy), Tommy Ryan (Mickey Larch, a.k.a. Mickey Adams), Jessie Ralph (Veronica M. Hudson), June Storey (Sheila Roberts), Bennie Bartlett (Joe Fisher), J. Farrell MacDonald (Sheriff J.J. Willoughby), John Qualen (Mailman), Robert Elliott (FBI Agent Farrow), Scotty Beckett (Bobby), James Flavin (Sanders), Archie Twitchell (Shelby), Dorothy Adams (Student's Mother, uncredited), Kenne Duncan (Henchman, uncredited), Dwight Frye (Henchman Bruno, uncredited), Helen Mack (Telephone Operator, uncredited), Cy Kendall (Waldo, uncredited), Frank Sully (Curly, uncredited), Al Hill (Henchman, uncredited). **Release Date:** July 3, 1939. Republic Pictures. 68 min. **Notes:** The working title for this film was *Stand Up and Sing*.

Nurse Edith Cavell (1939). **Director:** Herbert Wilcox. **Writers:** Reginald Berkeley (story "Dawn"), Michael Hogan (writer). **Producer:** Herbert Wilcox. **Associate Producer:** Merrill G. White. **Music:** Anthony Collins. **Cinematography:** Joseph H. August, Freddie Young. **Editing:** Elmo Williams. **Art Direction:** Lawrence P. Williams. **Gowns:** Edward Stevenson. **Special Effects:** Vernon L. Walker. **Cast:** Anna Neagle (Nurse Edith Cavell), Edna May Oliver (Countess de Mavon), George Sanders (Capt. Heinrichs), May Robson (Mme. Rappard), ZaSu Pitts (Mme. Moulin), H.B. Warner (Hugh Gibson), Sophie Stewart (Sister Williams), Mary Howard (Nurse O'Brien), Robert Coote (Bungey), Martin Kosleck (Pierre), Gui Ignon (Cobbler), Lionel Royce (Gen. von Ehrhardt), James Butler (Jean Rappard), Rex Downing (François Rappard), Henry Brandon (Lt. Schultz), Louis V. Arco (Pvt. Rammler, uncredited), Egon Brecher (Dr. Gunther, uncredited), Adrienne D'Ambricourt (uncredited), Richard Deane (Lt. Wilson, uncredited), Joe De Stefani (Manager, uncredited), Ernst Deutsch (Dr. Schroeder, uncredited), William Edmunds (Albert, uncredited), Gilbert Emery (Brand Whitlock, uncredited), Jack Gargan (German Soldier, uncredited), Eugene Gericke (Young German Soldier, uncredited), Halliwell Hobbes (British Chaplain, uncredited), Willy Kaufman (Baron von Weser, uncredited), Fritz Leiber (Sadi Kirschen, uncredited), Torben Meyer (Bit, uncredited), Lucien Prival (Lt. Schmidt, uncredited), Frank Reicher (Baron von Bissing, uncredited), Bert Roach (George Moulin, uncredited), Bodil Rosing (Charlotte, uncredited), Robert R. Stephenson (German Officer, uncredited), Henry Victor (Jaubec, uncredited), Wilhelm von Brincken (German Firing Squad Officer, uncredited), Gustav von Seyffertitz (President of Trial Court, uncredited). **Release Date:** September 1, 1939. Imperadio Pictures Ltd./RKO Radio Pictures. 108 min. **Notes:** *Nurse Edith Cavell* was based on a true story of a heroic World War I British nurse (born in 1865) shot by a German firing squad in 1915 in Brussels. For this, the first of several RKO releases, British writer/producer Herbert Wilcox imported his wife, actress Anna Neagle, to Hollywood to film with an American cast and crew. Anthony Collins was nominated for an Academy Award in the Music (Original Score) category.

Eternally Yours (1939). **Director/Producer:** Tay Garnett. **Writers:** Gene Towne, Graham Baker. **Executive Producer:** Walter Wanger (uncredited). **Music:** Werner Janssen. **Director of Photography:** Merritt Gerstad. **Editing:** Otho Lovering, Dorothy Spencer. **Art Direction:** Alexander Golitzen. **Costume Design:** Travis Banton. **Assistant Director:** Charles Kerr. **Interior Decoration:** Julia

Heron. **Associate Art Director:** Richard Irvine. **Sound:** Fred Lau. **Special Photographic Effects:** Ray Binger. **Aerial Director of Photography:** Paul Mantz (uncredited). **Gowns** (for Loretta Young): Irene. **Musical Director:** Werner Janssen. **Cast:** Loretta Young (Anita), David Niven (Tony), Hugh Herbert (Benton), Billie Burke (Aunt Abby), C. Aubrey Smith (Gramps), Raymond Walburn (Mr. Bingham), ZaSu Pitts (Mrs. Bingham), Broderick Crawford (Don), Virginia Field (Lola De Vere), Eve Arden (Gloria), Ralph Graves (Mr. Morrisey), Lionel Pape (Mr. Howard), Fred Keating (Master of Ceremonies), Richard Allen (Detective, uncredited), Granville Bates (Ship Captain, uncredited), May Beatty (Dowager, uncredited), Hillary Brooke (Blonde on Stage, uncredited), George Cathrey (Officer, uncredited), Pat Davis (British Pilot, uncredited), Mary Field (Peabody's Housekeeper, uncredited), Bess Flowers (Extra, uncredited), Tay Garnett (Pilot, uncredited), Jack Green (Detective, uncredited), Larry Harris (Boy Boxer, uncredited), Al Hill (Heckler, uncredited), Leyland Hodgson (Captain Vickers, uncredited), Arthur Stuart Hull (Extra, uncredited), Dickie Jackson (Boy Boxer, uncredited), Walter James (Police Official, uncredited), Frank Jaquet (Doctor, uncredited), Paul Le Paul (Butler, uncredited), Ralph McCullough (Ship's Officer, uncredited), Doreen McKay (Girl at Shower, uncredited), Dennie Moore (Waitress, uncredited), Edmund Mortimer (Extra, uncredited), Ralph Norwood (Waiter, uncredited), William H. O'Brien (Nightclub Waiter, uncredited), Broderick O'Farrell (Ship's officer, uncredited), Franklin Parker (Croupier, uncredited), Claude Payton (Scotland Yard Man, uncredited), Jack Perrin (Ship's Officer, uncredited), John Rice (Scotland Yard Man, uncredited), Walter Sande (Ralph, uncredited), Edwin Stanley (Reno Lawyer Jones, uncredited), Larry Steers (Extra, uncredited), Eleanor Stewart (Girl at Shower, uncredited), Patricia Stillman (Girl at Shower, uncredited), Luana Walters (Girl at Shower, uncredited), Billy Wayne (Stage Manager, uncredited), Evelyn Woodbury (Girl at Shower, uncredited), Douglas Wood (Phillips, uncredited). **Release Date:** October 7, 1939. Walter Wanger Productions/United Artists. 95 min. **Notes:** The working title for this film was *Whose Wife*. Werner Janssen was nominated for an Academy Award in the Music (Original Score) category.

It All Came True (1940). **Director:** Lewis Seiler. **Writers:** Louis Bromfield (story "Better Than Life"), Michael Fessier, Lawrence Kimble (screenplay). **Producer:** Mark Hellinger. **Executive Producers:** Jack L. Warner, Hal B. Wallis (uncredited). **Music:** Howard Jackson (uncredited), Heinz Roemheld (uncredited). **Cinematography:** Ernie Haller. **Editing:** Thomas Richards. **Art Direction:** Max Parker. **Gowns:** Howard Shoup. **Makeup Artist:** Perc Westmore. **Assistant Director:** Russell Saunders (uncredited). **Sound:** Dolph Thomas. **Special Effects:** Edwin B. DuPar (uncredited), Byron Haskin (uncredited). **Musical Director:** Leo F. Forbstein. **Music Arranger:** Ray Heindorf, Frank Perkins. **Dialogue Director:** Robert Foulk. **Director of Dance Numbers:** Dave Gould. **Animal Trainer:** William MacAllister Weatherwax (uncredited). **Cast:** Ann Sheridan (Sarah Jane Ryan, a.k.a. Sal), Jeffrey Lynn (Tommy Taylor), Humphrey Bogart (Grasselli, a.k.a. Chips Maguire), ZaSu Pitts (Miss Flint), Una O'Connor (Maggie Ryan), Jessie Busley (Mrs. Nora Taylor), John Litel (Mr. "Doc" Roberts), Grant Mitchell (Mr. Rene Salmon), Felix Bressart (the Great Boldini), Charles Judels (Henri Pepi de Bordeaux), Brandon Tynan (Mr. Van Diver), Howard Hickman (Mr. Prendergast), Herbert Vigran (Monks), Tommy Reilly (Performer), the Elderbloom Chorus (Group

Performers), Bender and Daum (Performing Duo), White and Stanley (Performing Duo), the Lady Killer's Quartet (Singing Quartet), Aldrich Bowker (Father McDuffy, uncredited), Eddy Chandler (Danny, uncredited), Frank Fanning (Detective, uncredited), James Flavin (Doorman, uncredited), Bess Flowers (Lady in Audience, uncredited), Edward Gargan (Police Desk Sergeant, uncredited), Chuck Hamilton (Policeman, uncredited), Max Hoffman Jr. (Doorman, uncredited), Jack Mower (Policeman, uncredited), Lee Phelps (Police Officer Pegasee, uncredited), Dale Van Sickel (Extra, uncredited), Claude Wisberg (Special Delivery Boy, uncredited). **Release Date:** April 6, 1940. First National Pictures/Warner Bros. Pictures. 97 min.

No, No, Nanette (1940). **Director:** Herbert Wilcox. **Writers:** Frank Mandel, Otto A. Harbach, Vincent Youmans, Emil Nyitray (play), Ken Englund (screenplay). **Producer:** Herbert Wilcox. **Associate Producer:** Merrill G. White. **Director of Photography:** Russell Metty. **Editing:** Elmo Williams. **Art Direction:** L.P. Williams. **Set Decoration:** Darrell Silvera. **Gowns:** Edward Stevenson. **Assistant Director:** Kenneth Holmes, Lloyd Richards. **Sound Recordist:** Richard Van Hessen. **Special Effects:** Vernon L. Walker. **Musical Director:** Anthony Collins. **Choreographer:** Aida Broadbent. **Songs:** "I Want to Be Happy" (Vincent Youmans, Otto Harbach, Irving Caesar); "Tea for Two" (Vincent Youmans, Otto Harbach, Irving Caesar); "No, No Nanette" (Vincent Youmans, Otto Harbach, Irving Caesar); "Where Has My Hubby Gone" (Vincent Youmans, Otto Harbach, Irving Caesar); and "Take a Little One Step" (Vincent Youmans, Otto Harbach, Irving Caesar). **Cast:** Anna Neagle (Nanette), Richard Carlson (Tom Gillespie), Victor Mature (William Trainor), Roland Young (Mr. "Happy" Jimmy Smith), Helen Broderick (Mrs. Susan Smith), ZaSu Pitts (Pauline), Eve Arden (Kitty), Billy Gilbert (Styles), Tamara (Sonya), Stuart Robertson (Stillwater Jr./Stillwater Sr.), Dorothea Kent (Betty), Aubrey Mather (Remington), Mary Gordon (Gertrude), Russell Hicks ("Hutch" Hutchinson), Margaret Armstrong (Dowager, uncredited), Muriel Barr (Show Girl, uncredited), Brooks Benedict (Birthday Party Guest, uncredited), Joan Blair (Woman, uncredited), Maurice Cass (Art Critic, uncredited), Dora Clement (Woman, uncredited), Mary Currier (Woman, uncredited), John Dilson (Desk Clerk, uncredited), Lester Dorr (Travel Agent, uncredited), Jean Fenwick (Woman, uncredited), Bess Flowers (Birthday Party Guest, uncredited), Chris Franke (Hansom Driver, uncredited), Dick French (Congratulator, uncredited), Marion Graham (Show Girl, uncredited), Paul Irving (Art Critic, uncredited), Ethelreda Leopold (uncredited), Keye Luke (Sung, uncredited), Torben Meyer (Furtlemertle, uncredited), Harold Miller (Man in Elevator, uncredited), Frank Mills (Taxi Driver, uncredited), George Noisom (Messenger Boy, uncredited), Sally Payne (Maid, uncredited), Frank Puglia (Art Critic, uncredited), Tom Quinn (Congratulator, uncredited), Joey Ray (Desk Clerk, uncredited), Cyril Ring (Desk Clerk, uncredited), Ronald R. Rondell (Man, uncredited), Benny Rubin (Max, uncredited), Julius Tannen (Disturbed Airline Passenger, uncredited), Rosella Towne (Stewardess, uncredited), Minerva Urecal (Woman in Airport, uncredited), Victor Wong (John, uncredited), Georgiana Young (Show Girl, uncredited). **Release Date:** December 20, 1940. Suffolk Productions/RKO Radio Pictures. 96 min. **Notes:** ZaSu also appeared in the 1930 film version of *No, No, Nanette*.

Uncle Joe (1941). **Directors:** Howard M. Railsback, Raymond E. Swartley. **Writers:** G.M. Rohrbach (story), Al Weeks (screenplay). **Cinematography:** Harry Neumann.

Composer: Marvin Hatley. **Cast:** Slim Summerville (Uncle Joe), ZaSu Pitts (Aunt Julia), Gale Storm (Clare), William B. Davidson (J. K. Day), Dorothy Peterson (Margaret Day), Dick Hogan (Bill), Frank Coghlan Jr. (Dick), Jimmy Butler (Bob), Maynard Holmes (Skinny), Brenda Henderson (Ann), John Holland (Paul Darcey), Marvin Hatley (Bandleader). **Release Date:** 1941. Wilding Picture Productions/John Deere. 51 min.

Broadway Limited (1941). **Director:** Gordon Douglas. **Writer:** Rian James (story "The Baby Vanishes"). **Producer:** Hal Roach. **Music:** Charles Previn. **Cinematography:** Henry Sharp. **Editing:** Bert Jordan. **Art Direction:** Nicolai Remisoff. **Set Decoration:** W.L. Stevens. **Gowns:** Coyla Davis. **Assistant Director:** Harve Foster. **Second Unit Director:** Hal Roach Jr. **Sound:** William Randall. **Special Effects:** Roy Seawright, Frank Young. **Musical Director:** Marvin Hatley. **Cast:** Victor McLaglen (Maurice "Mike" Monohan), Marjorie Woodworth (April Tremaine, formerly Mary Potter), Dennis O'Keefe (Dr. Harvey North), Patsy Kelly (Patsy Riley), ZaSu Pitts (Myra Prottle), Leonid Kinskey (Ivan Makail Ivanski), George E. Stone (Lefty), Gay Ellen Dakin (the Baby), Charles Wilson (Detective), John Sheehan (Train Conductor), Edgar Edwards (State Trooper), Eric Alden (State Trooper), Sam McDaniels (Train Porter), Eddie Acuff (Engineer's Assistant, uncredited), Richard Alexander (Would-Be Kidnapper, uncredited), George Chandler (Photographer, uncredited), Jack Gargan (Man, uncredited), Bud Geary (Train Fireman, uncredited), Gibson Gowland (Cafe Customer, uncredited), Al Hill (Henchman, uncredited), Edward Keane (Man, uncredited), George Lloyd (Train Engineer, uncredited), J. Farrell MacDonald (RR Line Supt. Mulcahey, uncredited), Tommy Mack (Cafe Customer, uncredited), William Newell (Train Fireman, uncredited), Frank Orth (Lew, uncredited), Jack Rice (Reporter, uncredited), Will Stanton (Cafe Customer, uncredited), Charles Sullivan (Tough, uncredited), Jim Toney (Cafe Customer, uncredited), Duke York (Relief Train Engineer, uncredited). **Release Date:** June 13, 1941. Hal Roach Studios/United Artists. 75 min.

Niagara Falls (1941). **Director:** Gordon Douglas. **Writers:** Eugene Conrad, Paul Girard Smith, Hal Yates (writer). **Producer:** Fred Guiol (uncredited). **Executive Producer:** Hal Roach (uncredited). **Cinematography:** Robert Pittack. **Editing:** Bert Jordan. **Art Direction:** Charles D. Hall. **Set Decoration:** W.L. Stevens. **Costume Design:** Irene Saltern. **Assistant Director:** Eddie Montagne. **Sound:** William Randall. **Special Effects:** Roy Seawright. **Musical Director:** Edward Ward. **Cast:** Marjorie Woodworth (Margie Blake), Tom Brown (Tom Wilson), ZaSu Pitts (Emmy Sawyer), Slim Summerville (Sam Sawyer), Chester Clute (Hotel Manager Potter), Edgar Dearing (Motorcycle Cop), Ed Gargan (Chuck), Gladys Blake (Trixie), Leon Belasco (Head Waiter), Rand Brooks (Honeymooner), Margaret Roach (Honeymooner), Jack Rice (Hotel Desk Clerk), Carlyle Blackwell Jr. (Hotel Guest, uncredited), John Davidson (Hotel Clerk, uncredited), Marjorie Deanne (Hotel Guest, uncredited), Joseph Depew (Elevator Boy, uncredited), Dudley Dickerson (Hotel Janitor, uncredited), Jack Egan (Hotel Guest, uncredited), Frank Faylen (Man, uncredited), Bud Geary (Man, uncredited), Charlie Hall (Bellhop, uncredited), Eddie Hall (Bellboy, uncredited), Robert Kent (Hotel Guest, uncredited), Gwen Kenyon (Hotel Guest, uncredited), Ethelreda Leopold (Hotel Guest, uncredited), Lois Lindsay (Hotel Guest, uncredited), Patsy Mace (Hotel Guest, uncredited), Tommy Mack (Peanut Vendor, uncredited), Gertrude Messinger (Telephone

Operator, uncredited), Irving Mitchell (Mr. Clark, uncredited), Barry Norton (Hotel Guest, uncredited), Dave Willock (Bellboy, uncredited). **Release Date:** October 17, 1941. Hal Roach Studios/United Artists. 43 min. **Notes:** This was one of Hal Roach's "Streamlined Features."

Miss Polly (1941). **Director:** Fred Guiol. **Writers:** Eugene Conrad, Edward E. Seabrook (screenplay). **Producer:** Hal Roach. **Music:** Edward Ward. **Cinematography:** Robert Pittack. **Editing:** Richard Currier. **Cast:** ZaSu Pitts (Miss Pandora Polly), Slim Summerville (Slim Wilkins), Kathleen Howard (Mrs. Minerva Snodgrass), Brenda Forbes (Patsy), Elyse Knox (Barbara Snodgrass), Dick Clayton (Eddie), Dink Trout (Postman Wilbur Boggs), William Newell (New Postman Hubert), Ferris Taylor (Mayor Walsh), Fern Emmett (Mrs. Frisbee), Vera Lewis (Elvira Pennywinkle), Sara Edwards (Angie Turner), Virginia Sale (Orsina Wiggins), Walter Baldwin (Lem Wiggins), Mickey Daniels (Elmer), George Pembroke (Town Constable), Syd Saylor (Drug Store Owner), Buster Brodie (Bald-Headed Man, uncredited), George Chandler (Townsman, uncredited), Rube Dalroy (Townsman, uncredited), Jim Farley (Jim Pennywinkle, uncredited). Eddie Hall (Speeder, uncredited), Noel Neill (School Girl, uncredited), Margaret Roach (School Girl, uncredited), Elizabeth Russell (Woman, uncredited), Walter Soderling (Pop Parsons, uncredited), Carl Stockdale (Pop Parsons, uncredited), Bill Wolfe (Henry Wiggins, uncredited). **Release Date:** November 14, 1941. Hal Roach Studios/United Artists. 45 min. **Notes:** This was another of Hal Roach's "Streamlined Features."

Mexican Spitfire's Baby (1941). **Director:** Leslie Goodwins. **Writers:** Jerome Cady, Charles E. Roberts (writer). **Producer:** Cliff Reid. **Cinematography:** Jack MacKenzie. **Editing:** Theron Warth. **Art Direction:** Van Nest Polglase. **Costume Design:** Renié. **Associate Art Director:** Carroll Clark. **Sound:** Corson Jowett. **Musical Director:** C. Bakaleinikoff. **Cast:** Lupe Velez (Carmelita Lindsay), Leon Errol (Uncle Matt Lindsay/Lord Basil Epping), Charles "Buddy" Rogers (Dennis Lindsay), ZaSu Pitts (Miss Emily Pepper), Elisabeth Risdon (Aunt Della), Fritz Feld (Lt. Pierre Gaston de la Blanc), Marion Martin (Fifi), Lloyd Corrigan (Chumley), Lydia Bilbrook (Lady Ada Epping), Jack Arnold [Vinton Haworth] (Hotel Clerk), Jack Grey (Reporter), Jane Patten (Stenographer), Jane Woodworth (Cashier), Charles Bates (uncredited), Jack Briggs (Orchestra Leader, uncredited), Jack Gardner (Photographer, uncredited), James Harrison (Reporter, uncredited), Tom Kennedy (Sheriff Judson, uncredited), Donald Kerr (John, uncredited), Buddy Messinger (Reporter, uncredited), Ted O'Shea (Manager, uncredited), Dick Rush (Cop, uncredited), Chester Tallman (Photographer, uncredited), Max Wagner (Bartender, uncredited). **Release Date:** November 28, 1941. RKO Radio Pictures. 69 min. **Notes:** The working title of this film was *Lord Epping Sees a Ghost*. This was the fourth entry in RKO's Mexican Spitfire series starring Lupe Velez, the others being *The Girl from Mexico* (1939), *Mexican Spitfire* (1940), *Mexican Spitfire Out West* (1940), *Mexican Spitfire at Sea* (1942), *Mexican Spitfire Sees a Ghost* (1942), *Mexican Spitfire's Elephant* (1942), and *Mexican Spitfire's Blessed Event* (1943).

Weekend for Three (1941). **Director:** Irving Reis. **Writers:** Budd Schulberg (story), Dorothy Parker, Alan Campbell (screenplay). **Producer:** Tay Garnett. **Music:** Roy Webb. **Cinematography:** Russell Metty. **Editing:** Desmond Marquette. **Art Direction:** Van Nest Polglase. **Gowns:** Edward Stevenson. **Assistant Director:** William Dorfman. **Associate **Art Director:** Albert D'Agostino. **Sound Recordist:** Richard Van Hessen. **Musical Director:** C. Bakaleinikoff. **Cast:** Dennis O'Keefe (Jim Craig), Jane Wyatt (Ellen Craig), Phillip Reed (Randy Bloodworth), Edward Everett Horton (Fred Stonebraker), ZaSu Pitts (Anna), Franklin Pangborn (Number Seven, Old Field Inn Waiter), Marion Martin (Mrs. Gloria Weatherby), Hans Conried (Old Field Inn Desk Clerk), Mady Lawrence (Miss Bailey), Brooks Benedict (Extra, uncredited), Jack Gargan (Extra, uncredited), Russell Wade (Extra, uncredited), Marie Windsor (Extra, uncredited). **Release Date:** December 12, 1941. RKO Radio Pictures. 65 min.

Mexican Spitfire at Sea (1942). **Director:** Leslie Goodwins. **Writers:** Jerry Cady, Charles E. Roberts (writer). **Producer:** Cliff Reid. **Cinematography:** Jack MacKenzie. **Editing:** Theron Warth. **Art Direction:** Albert S. D'Agostino, Walter E. Keller. **Costume Design:** Edward Stevenson. **Sound Recordist:** Earl A. Wolcott. **Musical Director:** C. Bakaleinikoff. **Cast:** Lupe Velez (Carmelita Lindsay), Leon Errol (Uncle Matt Lindsay/Lord Basil Epping), Charles "Buddy" Rogers (Dennis Lindsay), ZaSu Pitts (Miss Pepper), Elisabeth Risdon (Aunt Della Lindsay), Florence Bates (Mrs. Baldwin), Marion Martin (Fifi Russell), Lydia Bilbrook (Lady Ada Epping), Eddie Dunn (Mr. George Skinner), Harry Holman (Mr. Joshua Baldwin), Marten Lamont (Purser), Mary Field (Agnes, uncredited), John Maguire (First Officer Reynolds, uncredited), Richard Martin (Steward, uncredited), Lew Davis (Ship's Waiter, uncredited), Warren Jackson (Shipboard Reporter, uncredited), Wayne McCoy (Steward, uncredited), Ferris Taylor (Captain Nelson, uncredited), Julie Warren (Maid at Party, uncredited). **Release Date:** March 13, 1942. RKO Radio Pictures. 72 min. **Notes:** This marked ZaSu's second appearance in the series. See also *Mexican Spitfire's Baby* (1941).

The Bashful Bachelor (1942). **Director:** Malcolm St. Clair. **Writers:** Chester Lauck, Norris Goff (story), Chandler Sprague (screenplay). **Producer:** Jack William Votion. **Director of Photography:** Paul Ivano. **Editing:** W. Duncan Mansfield. **Art Direction:** Bernard Herzbrun. **Production Manager:** Ben Hersh. **Assistant Director:** Charles Kerr. **Set Dresser:** Earl Wooden. **Sound Recordist:** Ferrel Redd. **Musical Director:** Lud Gluskin. **Cast:** Chester Lauck (Lum Edwards), Norris Goff (Abner Peabody), ZaSu Pitts (Geraldine), Grady Sutton (Cedric Wiehunt), Oscar O'Shea (Squire Skimp), Louise Currie (Marjorie), Constance Purdy (Widder Abernathy), Irving Bacon (Sheriff/Fire Chief), Earle Hodgins (Joseph Abernathy), Benny Rubin (Pitch Man), Fred Burns (Man on Telephone, uncredited), Horace B. Carpenter (Search Party Member, uncredited), Jim Farley (Trainer of Brown Bess, uncredited), Otto Hoffman (Judge Akins, uncredited), Harry Holman (Knute, uncredited), Tiny Jones (Woman at Carnival, uncredited), Frank Mills (Bill, uncredited), Ralph Sanford (Butch, uncredited), James Westerfield (Carnival Pitchman, uncredited). **Release Date:** March 19, 1942. Voco Productions Inc./RKO Radio Pictures. 78 min. **Notes:** Chester Lauck and Norris Goff's *Lum and Abner* started on radio in 1932 and was very popular with audiences for its folksy, rural humor. Before going off the air in 1954, RKO starred the duo in a series of comedies: *Dreaming Out Loud* (1940), *The Bashful Bachelor* (1942), *So This Is Washington* (1943), *Two Weeks to Live* (1943), *Goin' to Town* (1944), and *Partners in Time* (1946). *Lum and Abner Abroad* (1956), released by Howco Productions, was a hodgepodge of three pilots meant for TV edited together to make a feature. ZaSu also appeared on radio with the duo as a regular in the '40s.

So's Your Aunt Emma (1942). **Director:** Jean Yarbrough. **Writers:** Harry Hervey

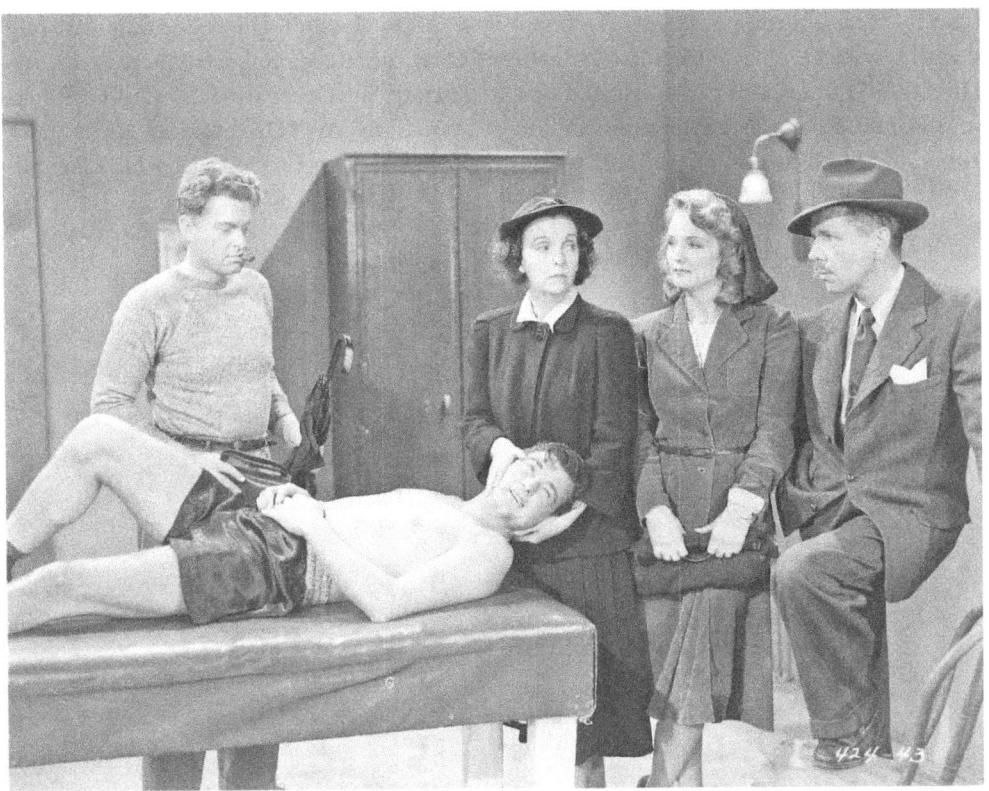

So's Your Aunt Emma (aka *Meet the Mob*, 1942) was a low-budget crime comedy. From left, George Aldredge, Bud McTaggert, ZaSu Pitts, Elizabeth Russell and Roger Pryor.

(story "Aunt Emma Paints the Town"), George Bricker, Edmond Kelso (writer). **Producer:** Lindsley Parsons. **Associate Producer:** Barney Sarecky. **Cinematography:** Mack Stengler. **Editing:** Jack Ogilvie. **Production Manager:** William Strohback [Strohbach]. **Sound Director:** Glen Glenn. **Musical Director:** Edward Kay. **Song:** "I Can't Get You Out of My Mind" (Harry Tobias, Edward Kay). **Technical Director:** Dave Milton. **Cast:** ZaSu Pitts (Aunt Emma Bates), Roger Pryor (Terry Connors), Warren Hymer (Joe Gormley), Douglas Fowley (Gus Hammond), Gwen Kenyon (Maris), Elizabeth Russell (Zelda Lafontaine), Tristram Coffin (Flower Henderson), [Malcolm] Bud McTaggart (Mickey O'Banion), Stan Blystone (Det. Lt. Miller), Dick Elliott (Evans), Eleanor Counts (Gracie), Jack Mulhall (Reporter Burns), Jack Chefe (Waiter, uncredited), Lew Davis (Cigar Counterman, uncredited), George DeNormand (the Referee, uncredited), Lester Dorr (Herman "Duke" Miles, uncredited), George Eldredge (Jake, uncredited), Donald Kerr (the Sailor, uncredited), Wilbur Mack (Copy Boy, uncredited), Irving Mitchell (Rex Crenshaw, uncredited), Wheeler Oakman (Blackie Hale, uncredited), Gene O'Donnell (Steve, uncredited). **Release Date:** April 17, 1942. Monogram Pictures Corporation. 62 min. **Notes:** The working title for the film was *Aunt Emma Paints the Town*. The feature is also known as *Meet the Mob*.

Tish (1942). **Director:** S. Sylvan Simon. **Writers:** Mary Roberts Rinehart (stories), Annalee Whitmore Jacoby, Tom Seller (adaptation), Harry Ruskin (screenplay). **Producer:** Orville O. Dull. **Music:** David Snell. **Director of Photography:** Paul Vogel. **Editing:** Robert J. Kern. **Art Direction:** Cedric Gibbons. **Set Decoration:** Edwin B. Willis. **Costume Design:** Howard Shoup. **Assistant Director:** Alfred Raboch (uncredited). **Associate Set Decorator:** Edward G. Boyle. **Associate Art Director:** Eddie Imazu, William Ferrari (uncredited). **Recording Di-

Tish (MGM, 1942) details the misadventures of a trio of spinsters who attempt to raise an infant. Marjorie Main (center) is surrounded by Aline MacMahon (left), Lee Bowman, and ZaSu Pitts.

rector: Douglas Shearer. **Cast:** Marjorie Main (Miss Letitia "Tish" Carberry), ZaSu Pitts (Aggie Pilkington), Aline MacMahon (Lizzie Wilkins), Susan Peters (Cora Edwards Bowzer), Lee Bowman (Charles Sands), Guy Kibbee (Judge Horace Bowser), Virginia Grey (Katherine "Kit" Bowser Sands), Richard Quine (Theodore "Ted" Bowser), Sam Ash (Man on Street, uncredited), King Baggot (Man on Street, uncredited), Nora Cecil (Spinster, uncredited), St. Luke's Episcopal Church Choristers (Singers at Wedding, uncredited), Ruby Dandridge (Violet, uncredited), William Farnum (John, uncredited), Howard C. Hickman (Mr. Fielding Kelbridge, uncredited), Gertrude Hoffman (Spinster, uncredited), George Humbert (Tony, uncredited), Jennie Mac (Spinster, uncredited), George Noisom (Special Delivery Boy, uncredited), Robert Emmett O'Connor (Game Warden, uncredited), George Ovey (Boardinghouse Man, uncredited), Paul Scardon (Toronto Postal Clerk, uncredited), Al Shean (Reverend Ostermaier, uncredited), Kathryn Sheldon (Spinster, uncredited), Byron Shores (Dr. McRegan, uncredited), Gerald Oliver Smith (Parkins, uncredited), Arthur Space (Court Clerk, uncredited), Alice Ward (Nurse, uncredited), Robert Wayne (Man, uncredited), Rudy Wissler (Newsboy, uncredited). **Release Date:** 1942. Metro-Goldwyn-Mayer (MGM). 84 min. **Notes:** Mary Roberts Rinehart first wrote the novel *Tish* in 1916. Subsequent tales featuring "Tish" were published as novels and short stories in *The Saturday Evening Post* in the '30s. MGM first had *Tish* in mind as a vehicle for Marie Dressler before she died in 1934.

Let's Face It (1943). **Director:** Sidney Lanfield. **Writers:** Dorothy Fields, Herbert Fields (play *Let's Face It*), Russell G. Medcraft, Norma Mitchell (play *Cradle Snatchers*), Harry Tugend (writer). **Associate Producer:** Fred Kohlmar. **Cinematography:** Lionel Lindon. **Editing:** Paul Weatherwax. **Art Direction:** Hans Dreier, [A.] Earl Hedrick. **Set Decoration:** Raymond Moyer. **Assistant Director:** Lonnie D'Orsa. **Sound:** Hugo Grenzbach, Don Johnson. **Musical Director:** Robert Emmett Dolan. **Cast:** Bob Hope (Jerry Walker), Betty Hutton (Winnie Porter), ZaSu Pitts (Cornelia Figeson), Phyllis Povah (Nancy Collister), Dave Willock (Barney Hilliard), Eve Arden (Maggie Watson), Cully Richards (Frankie Burns), Marjorie Weaver (Jean Blanchard), Dona Drake (Muriel), Raymond Walburn (Julian Watson), Andrew Tombes (Judge Henry Pigeon), Arthur Loft (George Collister), Joe Sawyer (Sergeant Wiggins), Grace Hayle (Mrs. Wigglesworth), Evelyn Dockson (Mrs. Taylor), Morris Ankrum (Man, uncredited), Lena Belle (Lena, uncredited), Helena Brinton (Helena, uncredited), Barbara Brooks (Barbara, uncredited), Joyce Compton (Wiggin's Girl, uncredited), William B. Davidson (Man in Boat, uncredited), Yvonne De Carlo (Chorus Girl, uncredited), Eddie Dew (Sergeant, uncredited), Eddie Dunn (Cop, uncredited), Brooke Evans (Milkmaid, uncredited), Julie Gibson (Chorus Girl, uncredited), Eddie Hall (Philip, uncredited), Jayne Hazard (Chorus Girl, uncredited), Jerry James (Man, uncredited), Ellen Johnson (Ellen, uncredited), Debbra Keith (Betty, uncredited), Donald Kerr (Specialty Dancer, uncredited), Kay Linaker (Canteen Hostess, uncredited), George Meader (Justice of the Peace, uncredited), Andria Moreland (Milkmaid, uncredited), Frederic Nay (Walsh, uncredited), Noel Neill (Chorus Girl, uncredited), Emory Parnell (Colonel, uncredited), Barbara Pepper (Daisy, uncredited), Eleanore Prentiss (Woman, uncredited), Hal Rand (Man, uncredited), Allen Ray (Man, uncredited), Robin Raymond (Mimi, uncredited), Cyril Ring (Head Waiter, uncredited), Lionel Royce (Submarine Commander, uncredited), Phyllis Ruth (Lulu, uncredited),

Florence Shirley (Woman, uncredited), Elinor Troy (Elinor, uncredited), Marie Windsor (Chorus Girl, uncredited). **Release Date:** August 5, 1943. Paramount Pictures. 76 min. **Notes:** The source play, *Cradle Snatchers*, debuted on Broadway in 1925. In its cast were Mary Boland, Raymond Hackett, Edna May Oliver and Humphrey Bogart. The musical *Let's Face It!*, starring Danny Kaye and Eve Arden, ran on Broadway from 1941 to 1943. Other films based on Medcraft and Mitchell's play are Fox's *The Cradle Snatchers* (1927), directed by Howard Hawks, and starring Louise Fazenda and J. Farrell MacDonald; and Fox's 1929 film *Why Leave Home?*, starring Sue Carol and Nick Stuart.

Breakfast in Hollywood (1946). **Director:** Harold Schuster. **Writer:** Earl W. Baldwin. **Producer:** Robert S. Golden. **Cinematography:** Russell Metty. **Editing:** Bernard W. Burton. **Production Design:** William Flannery. **Production Manager:** Harold Lewis. **Assistant Director:** Harold Godsoe. **Sound:** Max Hutchinson. **Musical Director:** Nat Finston. **Dialogue Director:** Dixie McCoy. **Songs:** "A Hat for Hedda Hopper" (Spike Jones, John Elliot), performed by Spike Jones and His City Slickers (vocal: Del Porter); "The Glow Worm" (Paul Linke, Lilla Cayley Robinson), performed by Spike Jones and His City Slickers; "It's Better to Be Yourself" (Nat "King" Cole, Bob Levinson, Howard Leeds), performed by the King Cole Trio; "Solid Potato Salad," performed by the King Cole Trio; "If I Had a Wishing Ring" (Louis Alter, Marla Shelton), performed by Andy Russell; "Magic Is the Moonlight," performed by Andy Russell; "Amour, Amour, Amour," performed by Andy Russell. **Cast:** Tom Breneman (Himself), Bonita Granville (Dorothy Larson), Beulah Bondi (Mrs. Annie Reed), Edward Ryan (Ken Smith), Raymond Walburn (Richard Cartwright), Billie Burke (Mrs. Frances Cartwright), ZaSu Pitts (Elvira Spriggens), Hedda Hopper (Herself), Andy Russell (Himself), Spike Jones (Himself), Nat "King" Cole (Himself), Herman Bing (Herman, uncredited), Ida Breneman (Herself, uncredited), Lillian Bronson (Miss Hammer, uncredited), James Conaty (Audience Table Extra, uncredited), Alice Cooper (Herself, Gary Cooper's Mother; uncredited), Lester Dorr (Waiter, uncredited), Robert Dudley (Man, uncredited), Dick Elliott (Man in Bus Depot, uncredited), Mary Field (Miss Field, uncredited), Byron Foulger (Mr. Henderson, uncredited), Red Ingle (City Slicker Vocalist, uncredited), Thomas E. Jackson (Bartender, uncredited), Lois January (Gloria Stapleton, uncredited), Anna Le Sueur (Herself, Joan Crawford's Mother; uncredited), Howard Negley (Bus Driver, uncredited), William Newell (Cop, uncredited), Sarah Padden (Mrs. Marie Edgedaw, uncredited), Lee Phelps (Cop, uncredited) Del Porter (City Slicker Vocalist, uncredited), Syd Saylor (Mechanic, uncredited), Minerva Urecal (Miss Mullins, uncredited), Billy Wayne (Bus Depot Guard, uncredited), Matt Willis (Cop, uncredited). **Release Date:** February 26, 1946. Golden Pictures/United Artists. 90 min. **Notes:** The film's working title was *Tom Breneman's Breakfast in Hollywood*. The picture was inspired by the very popular thirty-minute radio program, *Breakfast in Hollywood*, hosted by Tom Breneman from 1941 until his untimely death in 1948.

The Perfect Marriage (1947). **Director:** Lewis Allen. **Writers:** Samson Raphaelson (play), Leonard Spigelgass (writer). **Producer:** Hal B. Wallis. **Music:** Friedrich Hollaender. **Cinematography:** Russell Metty. **Editing:** Ellsworth Hoagland. **Art Direction:** Lionel Banks. **Set Decoration:** Sam Comer, Grace Gregory. **Costume Design:** Edith Head. **Makeup Supervisor:** Wally Westmore. **Assistant Director:** Chico Alonso. **Sound:** Harry Lindgren, Joel Moss. **Orches-**

trator: Charles Bradshaw (uncredited), Sidney Cutner (uncredited), George Parrish (uncredited), Leo Shuken (uncredited). **Cast:** Loretta Young (Maggie Williams), David Niven (Dale Williams), Eddie Albert (Gil Cummins), Charles Ruggles (Dale Williams Sr.), Virginia Field (Gloria), Rita Johnson (Mabel Manning), ZaSu Pitts (Rosa), Nina Griffith (Cookie Williams), Nana Bryant (Corinne Williams), Jerome Cowan (Addison Manning), Luella Gear (Dolly Haggerty), Howard Freeman (Peter Haggerty), Walter Baldwin (Horse Ring Attendant, uncredited), Jack Chefe (uncredited), Carol Coombs (Lola, uncredited), Catherine Craig (Julie Camberwell, uncredited), Boyd Davis (Doctor, uncredited), Ann Doran (Secretary, uncredited), Jimmie Dundee (uncredited), Frank Ferguson (Gentleman, uncredited), Joseph J. Greene (uncredited), Lyle Latell Bulaski (uncredited), John Maxwell (uncredited), Howard M. Mitchell (uncredited), Georges Renavent (Waiter Captain, uncredited), Albin Robeling (Waiter, uncredited), Nick Stewart (uncredited), Libby Taylor (uncredited), John Vosper (Jack Camberwell, uncredited). **Release Date:** January 24, 1947. Paramount Pictures. 88 min. **Notes:** Miriam Hopkins and Victor Jory starred on Broadway in *The Perfect Marriage* for 92 performances in 1944-45.

Life with Father (1947). **Director:** Michael Curtiz. **Writers:** Clarence Day (memoir), Howard Lindsay, Russel Crouse (play), Donald Ogden Stewart (writer). **Producer:** Robert Buckner. **Executive Producer:** Jack L. Warner. **Music:** Max Steiner. **Cinematography:** [J.] Peverell Marley, William V. Skall. **Editing:** George Amy. **Art Direction:** Robert [M.] Haas. **Set Decoration:** [George] James Hopkins. **Makeup Artist:** Perc Westmore. **Assistant Director:** Robert Vreeland (uncredited). **Sound:** C.A. Riggs. **Special Effects:** Ray Foster. **Special Effects Director:** William [C.] McGann. **Wardrobe:** Milo Anderson. **Associate Color Director** (Technicolor): Monroe W. Burbank. **Montage:** James Leicester. **Orchestrator:** Murray Cutter. **Musical Director:** Leo F. Forbstein. **Dialogue Director:** Herschel Daugherty. **Technical Advisor:** Mrs. Clarence Day. **Cast:** William Powell (Clarence Day Sr.), Irene Dunne (Vinnie Day), Elizabeth Taylor (Mary Skinner), Edmund Gwenn (the Rev. Dr. Lloyd), ZaSu Pitts (Cora Cartwright), Jimmy Lydon (Clarence Day Jr.), Emma Dunn (Margaret), Moroni Olsen (Dr. Humphries), Elisabeth Risdon (Mrs. Whitehead), Derek Scott (Harlan Day), Johnny Calkins (Whitney Day), Martin Milner (John Day), Heather Wilde (Annie), Monte Blue (the Policeman), Mary Field (Nora), Queenie Leonard (Maggie), Frank Elliott (Dr. Somers), Jean Andren (Mother of Twin Boys, uncredited), Russell Arms (Operator, uncredited), John Beck (Perkins, uncredited),

Life with Father (1947) was a lavish Technicolor film version of the long-running stage hit. ZaSu was featured as wealthy Cousin Cora.

Joseph E. Bernard (Cashier, uncredited), Clara Blandick (Miss Wiggins, uncredited), Loie Bridge (Corsetierre, uncredited), David Cavendish (Churchgoer, uncredited), Arlene Dahl (Girl, uncredited), Jean Del Val (François, uncredited), Nancy Evans (Delia, uncredited), Creighton Hale (Father of Twin Boys, uncredited), Hallene Hill (Churchgoer, uncredited), Douglas Kennedy (Mr. Morley, uncredited), Faith Kruger (Hilda, uncredited), Elaine Lange (Ellen, uncredited), Jack Martin (Chef, uncredited), Philo McCullough (Milk Man, uncredited), George Meader (Salesman, uncredited), James Metcalf (Customer, uncredited), Michael and Ralph Mineo (Twin Boys, uncredited), Clara Reid (Cleaning Woman, uncredited), Lucille Shamburger (Nursemaid, uncredited), Henry Sylvester (Churchgoer, uncredited), Laura Treadwell (Churchgoer, uncredited), Gertrude Valerie (Churchgoer, uncredited), Philip Van Zandt (Clerk, uncredited). **Release Date:** September 13, 1947. Warner Bros. Pictures. Color. 118 min. **Notes:** Clarence Day Jr.'s books were originally published as a series of essays in *Harpers*, *The New York Evening Post*, and *The New Yorker*. Howard Lindsay and Russel Crouse's play ran on Broadway from 1939 to 1947, amassing over 3,000 performances. Ruth Hammond first played Cora in the original production. Both Samuel Goldwyn (in 1940) and Mary Pickford (in 1944) tried to obtain the property before Warner Bros. secured the screen rights in late 1944. As for casting, Howard Lindsay and Dorothy Stickney, stars of the Broadway production, tested for the lead roles; Rosalind Russell, Bette Davis, Rosemary DeCamp and Mary Pickford tested for the Mother role; and Fredric March and Ronald Colman were thought of for Father. Cora Witherspoon tested for ZaSu's eventual part of Cora. Unfortunately, according to production reports, director Michael Curtiz did not like ZaSu Pitts' performance to such an extent that he attempted to replace her mid-film; but, as no acceptable substitute could be found, she continued in the role. The film earned Academy Award nominations for Powell (Best Actor), Robert Haas (Art Direction), George James Hopkins (Set Decoration), Peverell Marley and William V. Skall (Best Color Cinematography), and Max Steiner (Best Musical Score).

Francis (1950). **Director:** Arthur Lubin. **Writers:** David Stern (novel/screenplay). **Producer:** Robert Arthur. **Music:** Frank Skinner, Walter Scharf (uncredited). **Cinematography:** Irving Glassberg. **Editing:** Milton Carruth. **Art Direction:** Bernard Herzbrun, Richard H. Riedel. **Set Decoration:** A. Roland Fields, Russell A. Gausman. **Costume Design:** Rosemary Odell. **Makeup Artist:** Ann Locker, Bud Westmore. **Hair Stylist:** Joan St. Oegger. **Production Manager:** Edward Dodds. **Assistant Director:** John Sherwood. **Sound:** Leslie I. Carey, Corson Jowett. **Special Effects:** David S. Horsley. **Still Photographer:** Glen Adams. **Grip:** Everett Brown. **Gaffer:** Norton Kurland. **Camera Operator:** Dick Towers. **Script Supervisor:** Adele Cannon. **Dialogue Director:** Joan Hathaway. **Animal Trainer:** Lester Hilton. **Technical Advisor:** Major M.H. Lencer. **Cast:** Donald O'Connor (Peter Stirling), Patricia Medina (Maureen Gelder), ZaSu Pitts (Nurse Valerie Humpert), Ray Collins (Col. Hooker), John McIntyre [McIntire] (Gen. Stevens), Eduard Franz (Col. Plepper), Howland Chamberlain (Maj. Nadel), James Todd (Col. Saunders), Robert Warwick (Col. Carmichael), Frank Faylen (Sgt. Chillingbacker), Anthony [Tony] Curtis (Capt. Jones), Mikel Conrad (Maj. Garber), Loren Tindall (Maj. Richards), Charles Meredith (Banker Munroe), Fred Aldrich (Soldier Patient in Psychiatric Ward, uncredited), Robert Anderson (Capt. Grant, uncredited), Robert Blunt (Second Ambulance

Man, uncredited), Laura K. Brooks (Visitor, uncredited), Roger Cole (Correspondent, uncredited), Robert Conte (Photographer, uncredited), Helen Dickson (Bank Customer, uncredited), Richard Farmer (Marine Corps. Captain, uncredited), Al Ferguson (Capt. Dean, at Dance; uncredited), Harold Fong (Japanese Soldier, uncredited), Jack Gargan (Bank Employee, uncredited), Tim Graham (Lt. Bremm, uncredited), Sam Harris (Officer, uncredited), Harry Harvey (Correspondent, uncredited), Jim Hayward (Capt. Norman, uncredited), Judd Holdren (First Ambulance Man, uncredited), Ted Jordan (General's Aide, uncredited), Marvin Kaplan (First Medical Corps Lieutenant, uncredited), Joseph Kim (Japanese Lt. Taki, uncredited), John Laird (Switchboard Operator, uncredited), James Linn (Correspondent, uncredited), Mickey McCardle (Captain Anderson, at Dance; uncredited), Fraser McMinn (Second Medical Corps. Lieutenant, uncredited), Roger Moore (Marine Corps. Major, uncredited), Howard Negley (Correspondent, uncredited), Peter Prouse (Correspondent, uncredited), Jon Riffel (Switchboard Operator, uncredited), Jack Shutta (Sgt. Miller, uncredited), Larry Steers (Officer, uncredited), Chill Wills (Voice of Francis the Talking Mule, uncredited), Duke York (Sgt. Poor, G2; uncredited). **Release Date:** February 1950. Universal International Pictures (UI). 91 min. **Notes:** Francis won the first-ever PATSY award as 1951's Performing Animal Top Star of the Year. Universal would make seven *Francis* movies: *Francis* (1950), *Francis Goes to the Races* (1951), *Francis Goes to West Point* (1952), *Francis Covers the Big Town* (1953), *Francis Joins the WACS* (1954), *Francis in the Navy* (1955), and *Francis in the Haunted House* (1956). Six starred Donald O'Connor, with Chill Wills providing the mule's voice and Arthur Lubin directing. The series' final film, *Francis in the Haunted House*, starred Mickey Rooney, while Paul Frees voiced Francis and Charles Lamont directed. Arthur Lubin later created a similar television series, *Mister Ed* (1961–66). ZaSu would reprise her role in *Francis Joins the WACS*.

Denver and Rio Grande (1952). **Director:** Byron Haskin. **Writer:** Frank Gruber. **Producer:** Nat Holt. **Associate Producer:** Harry Templeton. **Music:** Paul Sawtell. **Cinematography:** Ray Rennahan. **Editing:** Stanley E. Johnson. **Art Direction:** Franz Bachelin, Hal Pereira. **Set Decoration:** Sam Comer, Bertram C. Granger. **Costume Design:** Edith Head. **Makeup Artist:** Wally Westmore. **Construction Coordinator:** Gene Lauritzen. **Stunts:** Jimmie Dundee (uncredited), George Magrill (uncredited), Leo J. McMahon (uncredited), Jack Montgomery (uncredited), Bob Morgan (uncredited), Harvey Parry (uncredited). **Process Photographer:** Farciot Edouart. **Color Consultant:** Robert Brower. **Cast:** Edmond O'Brien (Jim Vesser), Sterling Hayden (McCabe), Dean Jagger (Gen. William J. Palmer), Laura Elliott [Kasey Rogers] (Linda Nelson, alias Linda Prescott), Lyle Bettger (Johnny Buff), J. Carrol Naish (Gil Harkness), ZaSu Pitts (Jane Dwyer), Tom Powers (Sloan), Robert Barrat (Charlie Haskins), Paul Fix (Engineer Moynihan), Don Haggerty (Bob Nelson), James Burke (Sheriff Ed Johnson), Jack Daly (Tolliver, uncredited), Lester Dorr (Dealer, uncredited), Jimmie Dundee (Train Engineer, uncredited), George Magrill (Railroad Worker, uncredited), Forrest Taylor (Mac, uncredited). **Release Date:** May 16, 1952. Paramount Pictures. 89 min.

Francis Joins the WACS (1954). **Director:** Arthur Lubin. **Writers:** Herbert Baker (story), Devery Freeman, James B. Allardice (writer), Dorothy Reid [Davenport] (additional dialogue). **Producer:** Ted Richmond. **Music:** Irving Gertz (uncredited). **Cinematography:** Irving Glassberg. **Editing:** Ted

J. Kent, Russell F. Schoengarth. **Art Direction:** Robert Clatworthy, Alexander Golitzen. **Set Decoration:** Oliver Emert, Russell A. Gausman. **Hair Stylist:** Joan St. Oegger. **Makeup Artist:** Bud Westmore. **Assistant Director:** John Sherwood. **Sound:** Glenn E. Anderson, Leslie I. Carey. **Special Photography:** David S. Horsley. **Music Supervisor:** Joseph Gershenson. **Technical Advisor:** Lane Carlson. **Song:** "Song of the Women's Army Corps" (Camilla Mays Frank). **Cast:** Donald O'Connor (Peter Stirling), Julia [Julie] Adams (Capt. Jane Parker), Chill Wills (Gen. Benjamin Kaye/voice of Francis), Mamie Van Doren (Cpl. Bunky Hilstrom), Lynn Bari (Maj. Louise Simpson), ZaSu Pitts (Lt. Valerie Humpert), Joan Shawlee (Sgt. Kipp), Allison Hayes (Lt. Dickson), Mara Corday (Kate), Karen Kadler (Marge), Elsie Holmes (Bessie), Anthony Radecki (General's Aide), Olan Soule (Capt. Creavy), Patti McKay (Lt. Burke), Richard Deems (Jeep Driver, uncredited), Joel Allen (Military Policeman, uncredited), Dan Barton (Corporal MacDonald, uncredited), Bobette Bentley (WAC MP, uncredited), Henry Blair (Tommy, uncredited), Lyle Bond (Announcer, uncredited), Robert Bray (MP Sgt. Kreuger, uncredited), Rye Butler (Leader, uncredited), John Close (Military Policeman, uncredited), James Coffey (Patrol Leader, uncredited), Kathleen Dennis (Bit, uncredited), Frances Farwell (Husky WAC, uncredited), Anthony Garcen (Patrol Leader, uncredited), Phil Garris (Soldier, uncredited), Richard Grant (Patrol Leader, uncredited), Robert Haines (Bit, uncredited), Michael Hall (George, uncredited), Ed Haskett (Bit, uncredited), Bonnie Henjum (Bit, uncredited), James Hyland (Newspaper Man, uncredited), Mitchell Kowall (Patrol Leader, uncredited), Paul Kruger (Bit, uncredited), Harold Lockwood (Bit, uncredited), Herbert Lytton (Army Photo Developer, uncredited), Muriel Mansell (WAC MP, uncredited), Danna McGraw (WAC Sergeant, uncredited), Tyler McVey (Referee, uncredited), Carl O'Bryan (Bit, uncredited), Voltaire Perkins (Jack, uncredited), John Phillips (Fred, uncredited), William Phipps (Jeep Driver #1, uncredited), Jeanne Shores (WAC Corporal, uncredited), Barbara Smith (Bit, uncredited), Jeanne Tatum (Sergeant, uncredited), Rusty Wescoatt (Brakeman, uncredited), Stuart Wilson (Captain, uncredited), Sam Woody (Blue Soldier, uncredited), Lynn Wright (Bit, uncredited). **Release Date:** July 30, 1954. Universal International Pictures (UI). 95 min. **Notes:** Some scenes were shot on location at the Fort Ord Army base outside Monterey, California. This is ZaSu's second (and last) appearance in the series. See also *Francis* (1950).

This Could Be the Night (1957). **Director:** Robert Wise. **Writers:** Cordelia Baird Gross (short stories), Isobel Lennart (writer). **Producer:** Joe Pasternak. **Director of Photography:** Russell Harlan. **Editing:** George Boemler. **Art Direction:** Paul Groesse, William A. Horning. **Set Decoration:** Robert R. Benton, Edwin B. Willis. **Hair Stylist:** Sydney Guilaroff. **Makeup Artist:** William Tuttle. **Assistant Director:** Ridgeway Callow. **Recording Supervisor:** Dr. Wesley C. Miller. **Special Effects:** Lee LeBlanc. **Music Coordinator:** Irving Aaronson. **Musical Numbers Staging:** Jack Baker. **Orchestrator:** Skip Martin, Billy May, Don Simpson, Robert Van Eps. **Music Supervisor:** George Stoll. **Vocal Supervisor:** Robert Tucker. **Songs:** "I'm Gonna Live Till I Die" (Mann Curtis, Walter Kent, Al Hoffman), performed by Julie Wilson, with Ray Anthony and his Orchestra; "This Could Be the Night" (Nicholas Brodszky, Sammy Cahn), performed by Julie Wilson, with Ray Anthony and his Orchestra; "Trumpet Boogie" (Ray Anthony and George Williams), performed by Ray Anthony and His Orchestra; "I Got It Bad and That Ain't Good" (Duke Ellington and Paul Francis Webster), performed by Julie Wilson; "Hustlin' Newsgal" (George Stoll), performed by Neile Adams; "Sadie Green (the Vamp of New Orleans)" (Gilbert Wells, Johnny Dunn), performed by Julie Wilson; "Taking a Chance on Love" (Vernon Duke, John La Touche, Ted Fetter), performed by Julie Wilson; "I've Got You Under My Skin" (Cole Porter), performed by Ray Anthony and His Orchestra; "Just You, Just Me" (Jesse Greer, Raymond Klages), performed by Ray Anthony and His Orchestra; "Mambo Cambo" (Pete Rugolo), performed by Ray Anthony and His Orchestra; "Blue Moon" (Richard Rodgers, Lorenz Hart), performed by Ray Anthony and His Orchestra; "Club Tonic Blues" (Marvin Wright, Jack Baker, Jackie Mills), performed by Ray Anthony and His Orchestra; "Bunny Hop" (Leonard Auletti); "Dream Dancing" (Donald J. Simpson). **Cast:** Jean Simmons (Anne Leeds), Paul Douglas (Rocco), Anthony Franciosa (Tony Armotti), Julie Wilson (Ivy Corlane), Neile Adams (Patsy St. Clair), Joan Blondell (Crystal St. Clair), J. Carrol Naish (Leon), Rafael Campos (Hussein Mohammed), ZaSu Pitts (Mrs. Katie Shea), Tom Helmore (Stowe Devlin), Murvyn Vye (Waxie London), Vaughn Taylor (Ziggy Dawit), Frank Ferguson (Mr. Shea), William Ogden Joyce (Bruce Cameron), James Todd (Mr. Hallerby), Ray Anthony (Himself), Chuck Berry (Cameo, uncredited), June Blair (Chorus Girl, uncredited), Richard Collier (Homer, uncredited), Walter Davis Jr. (Himself, uncredited), Bruno Della Santina (Waiter, uncredited), Matty Fain (Nightclub Guest, uncredited), Bess Flowers (Nightclub Extra, uncredited), Tim Graham (Official, uncredited), John Harding (Eduardo, uncredited), Percy Helton (Charlie, uncredited), Harry Hines (Nightclub Guest, uncredited), Edna Holland (Teacher, uncredited), Sid Kane (Waiter, uncredited), Len Lesser (Piano Tuner, uncredited), Nora Marlowe (Mrs. Gretchma, uncredited), Gregg Martell (Nightclub Guest, uncredited), Bill McLean (Male Cooking Contestant, uncredited), Sid Melton (Taxi Driver, uncredited), Ernesto Molinari (Waiter, uncredited), Gloria Pall (New Girl, uncredited), Paul Petersen (Joey, uncredited), Andrew Robinson (Himself, Archie Savage Trio; uncredited), Archie Savage (Himself, Archie Savage Trio; uncredited), Lew Smith (Waiter, uncredited), Billy Stoll (Boy, uncredited), Leonard Strong (Mr. Bernbaum, uncredited), Nita Talbot (Chorus Girl, uncredited), Betty Uitti (Sexy Girl, uncredited), Charles Wagenheim (Mike, uncredited), Ray Walker (Master of Ceremonies at Cooking Contest, uncredited). **Release Date:** May 14, 1957. Metro-Goldwyn-Mayer (MGM). 104 min. **Notes:** The working title for the film was *Protection Is a Tough Racket*, the name of the original source material, a magazine story written by Cordelia Baird Gross. The screen rights were originally purchased by Paramount Pictures in 1954. By the next year it was purchased by MGM, with James Cagney in mind for the lead. Cagney balked and was replaced by Paul Douglas. *This Could Be the Night* marked Anthony Franciosa's first released film as an actor; his two other 1957 films were the classics *A Face in the Crowd* and *A Hatful of Rain*. Portions of *This Could Be the Night* were shot on location in New York City.

Teen-Age Millionaire (1961). **Director:** Lawrence Doheny. **Writers:** Lawrence F. Doheny, Harry Spalding (writer). **Producer:** Howard B. Kreitsek. **Cinematography:** Gordon Avil, Arthur J. Ornitz. **Editing:** Jack Ruggiero. **Art Direction:** Rolland M. Brooks, Howard Hollander, Paul Sylbert. **Set Decoration:** Harry Gordon. **Songs:** "Teenage Millionaire" (Billy May, H.B. Cross & Bill Loose), performed by Jimmy Clanton; "Possibility" (Jimmy Clanton), performed by Jimmy Clanton; "Smokie, Part 2" (Bill Black), performed by Bill Black's Combo; "The Way I Am" (Peter Udell, Gary Geld), performed by Jackie Wilson; "Somebody Nobody Wants" (Sylvia Dee, George Goehring), performed by Dion; "Show Me" (Berry Gordy Jr.), performed by Marv Johnson; "Hello Mr. Dream" (Bobby Bare), performed by Vicki Spencer; "The Jet" (Kal Mann), performed by Chubby Checker; "Back to School Blues" (Bobby Bare, Louise Bell), performed by Jack Larson; "Green Light" (Jimmy Clanton), performed by Jimmy Clanton; "Kissin' Game" (Jerry Vance, Terry Philips), performed by Dion; "I Wait" (Vicki Spencer), performed by Vicki Spencer; "Let's Twist Again" (Kal Mann, Dave Appell), performed by Chubby Checker; "Oh Mary" (Berry Gordy Jr.), performed by Marv Johnson; "Yogi" (Bill Black), performed by Bill Black's Combo; "Twistin' U.S.A." (Kal Mann), recording by Chubby Checker; "Dance the Mess Around" (Kal Mann, Dave Appell), recording by Chubby Checker; "Lonely Life" (Al Kasha, Alan Thomas), performed by Jackie Wilson; "Green Light/Finale" (Jimmy Clanton), performed by Jimmy Clanton. **Cast:** Jimmy Clanton (Bobby Chalmers), Rocky Graziano (Rocky), ZaSu Pitts (Aunt Theodora), Diane Jergens (Bambi), Joan Tabor (Adrienne), Sid Gould (Sheldon Vale), Maurice Gosfield (Ernie), Eileen O'Neill (Desidieria), Chubby Checker (Himself), Bill Black's Combo (Themselves), Dion [DiMucci] (Himself), Marv Johnson (Himself), Jack Larson (Himself), Vicki Spencer (Herself), Jackie Wilson (Himself). **Release Date:** August 1961. Clifton Productions/Ludlow Productions/United Artists. 84 min.

The Thrill of It All (1963). **Director:** Norman Jewison. **Writers:** Larry Gelbart, Carl Reiner (story), Carl Reiner (screenplay). **Producer:** Ross Hunter, Martin Melcher. **Music:** Frank De Vol. **Cinematography:** Russell Metty. **Editing:** Milton Carruth. **Art Direction:** Robert Boyle, Alexander Golitzen. **Set Decoration:** Howard Bristol. **Gowns:** Jean Louis. **Hair Stylist:** Larry Germain. **Makeup Artist:** Bud Westmore. **Unit Production Manager:** Norman Deming. **Executive in Charge of Production:** Edward Muhl. **Assistant Director:** Phil Bowles. **Property Master:** Peter Satori (uncredited). **Sound:** William G. Russell, Waldon O. Watson. **Music Supervisor:** Joseph Gershenson. **Dialogue Coach:** Norman Stuart. **Cast:** Doris Day (Beverly Boyer), James Garner (Dr. Gerald Boyer), Arlene Francis (Mrs. Fraleigh), Edward Andrews (Gardiner Fraleigh), Reginald Owen (Old Tom Fraleigh), ZaSu Pitts (Olivia), Elliott Reid (Mike Palmer), Alice Pearce (Irving's Wife), Kym Karath (Maggie Boyer), Brian Nash (Andy Boyer), Lucy Landau (Mrs. Goethe), Paul Hartman (Dr. Taylor), Hayden Rorke (Billings), Alex Gerry (Stokely), Robert Gallagher (Van Camp), Anne Newman (Miss Thompson), Burt Mustin (the Fraleigh Butler), Hedley Mattingly (Sidney), Robert Strauss (Chief Truck Driver), Maurice Gosfield (Truck Driver), William Bramley (Angry Driver), Pamela Curran (Spot Checker), Herbie Faye (Irving), Lenny Kent (Cabbie), John Alderman (Mr. Caputo), Len Weinrib (Truck driver), Richard Alden (Onlooker, uncredited), Lillian Culver (Autograph Seeker, uncredited), John Daheim (Mounted Policeman, uncredited), King Donovan (uncredited), Ross Elliott (uncredited), Bess Flowers (Party Guest, uncredited), Gertrude Flynn (Autograph Seeker, uncredited), Jacques Foti (Maitre d', uncredited), Paul Frees (Voice of TV Announcer, uncredited), Tim Graham (Guard, uncredited), Hallene Hill (Busybody, uncredited), Kenner G. Kemp (Man, uncredited), Bernie Kopell (Commercial Director, uncredited), Dorothy Neumann (Spinster, uncredited), Carl Reiner (German Officer/Cad/Cowboy, uncredited), Cosmo Sardo (Man in Elevator, uncredited). **Release Date:** July 17, 1963. Ross Hunter Pro-

In 1962 ZaSu returned to the sound stages at Universal, where she had appeared in many comedy shorts. The occasion was the filming of *The Thrill of It All*, starring Doris Day and James Garner. ZaSu's role was that of the fretful housekeeper Olivia. Here she is greeted by young producer Ross Hunter.

ductions Inc./Universal International Pictures (UI). 108 min.

It's a Mad Mad Mad Mad World (1963). **Director/Producer:** Stanley Kramer. **Writers:** William Rose, Tania Rose (story/screenplay). **Music:** Ernest Gold. **Director of Photography:** Ernest Laszlo. **Editing:** Gene Fowler Jr., Robert C. Jones, Frederic Knudtson. **Production Design:** Rudolph Sternad. **Art Direction:** Gordon Gurnee. **Set Decoration:** Joseph Kish. **Costume Design:** Bill

Thomas. **Makeup Artist:** George Lane, Lynn Reynolds, Steven Clensos (uncredited), Rolf Miller (uncredited). **Hair Stylist:** Connie Nichols. **Production Manager:** Clem Beauchamp, Adrian Woolery (animation, uncredited). **Assistant Directors:** George Batcheller, Bert Chervin, Charles Scott. **Second Unit Director:** Carey Loftin (uncredited). **Property Master:** Art Cole. **Sound Editor:** Walter Elliott. **Sound Re-Recordist:** Roy Granville, Clem Portman, Vinton Vernon. **Sound Engineer:** John [K.] Kean. **Sound Supervisor:** Gordon Sawyer (uncredited). **Boom Operator:** Glenn E. Anderson (uncredited). **Assistant Foley Artist:** Richard Portman (uncredited). **Special Effects:** Danny Lee, Chuck Gaspar (uncredited). **Photographic Effects:** Linwood G. Dunn, James B. Gordon. **Process Photography:** Farciot Edouart. **Miniatures:** Marcel Delgado (uncredited). **Miniature Maker:** Jim Danforth (uncredited). **Visual Effects:** Willis H. O'Brien (uncredited). **Stunt Supervisor:** Carey Loftin. **Stunts:** Max Balchowsky (uncredited), Paul Baxley (uncredited), May Boss (uncredited), Richard E. Butler (uncredited), Tap Canutt (uncredited), Bill Couch (uncredited), Chuck Couch (uncredited), Philip Crawford (uncredited), Dick Crockett (uncredited), John Daheim (uncredited), Carol Daniels (uncredited), George DeNormand (uncredited), Gary Epper (uncredited), Stephanie Epper (uncredited), Fred Gabourie (uncredited), Dick Geary (uncredited), Sol Gorss (uncredited), Chuck Hayward (uncredited), Bob Herron (uncredited), Robert F. Hoy (uncredited), John Hudkins (uncredited), Loren Janes (uncredited), Walt La Rue (uncredited), Carey Loftin (uncredited), Paul Mantz (uncredited), Harvey Parry (uncredited), Regis Parton (uncredited), Gil Perkins (uncredited), Jack Perkins (uncredited), Janos Prohaska (uncredited), George Robotham (uncredited), Wally Rose (uncredited), Carl Saxe (uncredited), Fred Scheiwiller (uncredited), Bill Shannon (uncredited), Alex Sharp (uncredited), Paul Stader (uncredited), Tom Steele (uncredited), Frank Tallman (uncredited), Helen Thurston (uncredited), Buddy Van Horn (uncredited), Dale Van Sickel (uncredited), Jesse Wayne (uncredited), Marvin Willens (uncredited). **Chief Gaffer:** Joe Edesa. **Assistant Camera:** Richard Johnson. **Company Grip:** Morris Rosen. **Assistant Company Grip:** Martin Kashuk. **Camera Operator:** Charles [F.] Wheeler. **Second Unit Camera Operator:** James King (uncredited). **Animators:** Bob Carlson (uncredited), Hugh Childs (uncredited), Tab Collar (uncredited), Jim Danforth (uncredited), Art Goodman (uncredited), Bernard Gruver (uncredited), Oscar Hansson (uncredited), Ruth Kissane (uncredited), Bror Lansing (uncredited), Ed Levitt (uncredited), Mary Mathews (uncredited), Bill Melendez (uncredited), Carl Pederson (uncredited), Beverly Robbins (uncredited), Charles Smith (uncredited), Danny Smith (uncredited), Frank Smith (uncredited), Irene Wyman (uncredited). **Costume Supervisor:** Joe King. **Music Editor:** Art Dunham. **Music Coordinator:** Robert Helfer (uncredited). **Orchestrator:** Albert Woodbury (uncredited). **Title Design:** Saul Bass. **Cast:** Spencer Tracy (Capt. C. G. Culpepper), Milton Berle (J. Russell Finch), Sid Caesar (Melville Crump, DDS), Buddy Hackett (Benjy Benjamin), Ethel Merman (Mrs. Marcus), Mickey Rooney (Ding "Dingy" Bell), Dick Shawn (Sylvester Marcus), Phil Silvers (Otto Meyer), Terry-Thomas (Lt. Col. J. Algernon Hawthorne), Jonathan Winters (Lennie Pike), Edie Adams (Monica Crump), Dorothy Provine (Emeline Marcus-Finch), Eddie "Rochester" Anderson (Second Cab Driver), Jim Backus (Tyler Fitzgerald), Ben Blue (Biplane Pilot), Joe E. Brown (Union Official), Alan Carney (Police Sergeant), Chick Chandler (Detective), Barrie Chase (Sylvester's Girlfriend), Lloyd Corrigan (the Mayor), William Demarest (Police Chief Aloysius), Andy Devine (Sheriff of Crockett County), Selma Diamond (voice of Ginger Culpepper), Peter Falk (Third Cab Driver), Norman Fell (Detective), Paul Ford (Col. Wilberforce), Stan Freberg (Deputy Sheriff), Louise Glenn (voice of Billie Sue Culpepper), Leo Gorcey (First Cab Driver), Sterling Holloway (Fire Chief), Edward Everett Horton (Mr. Dinckler), Marvin Kaplan (Irwin), Buster Keaton (Jimmy the Crook), Don Knotts (Nervous Motorist), Charles Lane (Airport Manager), Mike Mazurki (Miner), Charles McGraw (Lt. Matthews), Cliff Norton (Reporter), ZaSu Pitts (Gertie), Carl Reiner (Tower Controller), Madlyn Rhue (Secretary Schwartz), Roy Roberts (Policeman), Arnold Stang (Ray), Nick Stewart (Migrant Truck Driver), Moe Howard, Larry Fine, Joe DeRita (Firemen), Sammee Tong (Chinese Laundryman), Jesse White (Radio Tower Operator), Jimmy Durante (Smiler Grogan), Jack Benny (Man in Car in Desert, uncredited), Paul Birch (Policeman, uncredited), John Clarke (Helicopter Pilot, uncredited), Stanley Clements (Detective, uncredited), Howard Da Silva (Airport Officer, uncredited), Minta Durfee (Bit, uncredited), Roy Engel (Patrolman/Police Radio Voice Unit F-14, uncredited), James Flavin (Patrolman, uncredited), Nicholas Georgiade (Detective, uncredited), Stacy Harris (Police Radio Voice Unit F-7, uncredited), Don C. Harvey (Policeman, uncredited), Allen Jenkins (Police Officer, uncredited), Robert Karnes (Police Officer Simmy, uncredited), Tom Kennedy (Traffic Cop, uncredited), Harry Lauter (Police Dispatcher, uncredited), Ben Lessy (George, uncredited), Bobo Lewis (Pilot's Wife, uncredited), Jerry Lewis (Man Who Runs Over Hat, uncredited), Bob Mazurki (Eddie, uncredited), Barbara Pepper (Bit, uncredited), Eddie Ryder (Air Traffic Control Tower Staffer, uncredited), Charles Sherlock (Extra, uncredited), Eddie Smith (Extra, uncredited), Doodles Weaver (Hardware Store Clerk, uncredited). **Release Date:** November 7, 1963. Casey Productions/United Artists. 182 min. (laserdisc version; extended re-edit) × 174 min. (restored video version) × 154 min. (edited version) × 192 min. (original version). **Notes:** This film was originally presented in Cinerama. Location shooting took place at Santa Rosita Beach State Park, California, and on various highways from Colorado to San Diego.

Television Credits

The Chevrolet Tele-Theatre ("The Flattering Word," 11/22/48) — **Director:** Gordon Duff. **Writer:** Alexander Pushkin. **Cast:** ZaSu Pitts, John Carradine.

The Philco Television Playhouse ("Ramshackle Inn," 1/2/49) — **Writer:** George Batson. **Cast:** Bert Lytell (host), ZaSu Pitts, Joe Downing. This was a television version of the Broadway show featuring ZaSu, which opened on January 5, 1944.

Texaco Star Theater (11/7/50) — **Cast:** Milton Berle, ZaSu Pitts, Jane Froman, Hugh Herbert.

What's My Line? (Episode #107, 6/15/52)

The Name's the Same (12/10/52) — **Cast:** ZaSu Pitts (herself, contestant), Joan Alexander. Quiz show.

The Spike Jones Show ("Charity Bazaar," 4/3/54) — **Cast:** Spike Jones, Helen Grayco, Sir Frederick Gas [Earl Bennett] (Fortune Teller), Peter James (Knife Thrower), Freddy Morgan (Space Boy), George Rock (Half Man-Half Woman), Billy Barty, ZaSu Pitts (Herself), Dick Shanahan, Jad Paul, LaVerne Pearson (Laughing Lady), Roger Donley, Bernie Jones, Bill Hamilton, Ray Heath, Bill DePew.

General Electric Theater ("Pardon My Aunt," 4/4/54) — **Producer:** Joseph Sistrom.

Director: Jean Yarbrough. **Writer:** Robert Riley Crutcher. **Cinematography:** Stuart Thompson. **Cast:** Richard Carlson (Archie Hawkins), Claudia Barrett (Elaine Parker), ZaSu Pitts (Aunt Laura), Bill Phillips (George Hanson), James Flavin, Charles Cane, Jack Lomas, Merrily Gay Reynolds, Ronald Reagan (Host).

Kraft Television Theatre ("The Happy Touch," 8/4/54) — **Writers:** Kathleen Lindsay and Robert H. Lindsay. **Story:** Ed Beloin and Henry Garson. **Cast:** Ed Herlihy (Announcer), ZaSu Pitts (Ellie), Margaret Hamilton, Doro Merande, Chet Stratton.

The Best of Broadway ("The Man Who Came to Dinner," 10/13/54) — **Producer:** Martin Manulis. **Director:** David Alexander. **Writer** (adaptation): Ronald Alexander. **Writers** (play): Moss Hart & George S. Kaufman. **Music:** David Broekman. **Cast:** Monty Woolley (Sheridan Whiteside), Merle Oberon (Maggie Cutler), Joan Bennett (Lorraine Sheldon), Bert Lahr (Banjo), Buster Keaton (Dr. Bradley), William Prince (Bert Jefferson), ZaSu Pitts (Miss Preen), Howard St. John (Mr. Stanley), Catherine Doucet (Harriet Stanley), Sylvia Field (Mrs. Stanley), Reginald Gardiner (Beverly Carlton), Margaret Hamilton (Sarah), Frank Tweddell (John). **Notes:** The Moss Hart/George S. Kaufman play opened on Broadway on October 16, 1939, starring Monty Woolley, Edith Atwater, David Burns, Carol Goodner, Lorraine Sheldon, John Hoysradt, and Mary Wickes as Miss Preen. The Warner Bros. film version of 1941 starred Woolley, Ann Sheridan, Bette Davis, Billie Burke, Reginald Gardiner, Jimmy Durante, and, again as Miss Preen, Mary Wickes.

Screen Directors Playhouse ("The Silent Partner," 12/21/55) — **Executive Director:** Sidney S. Van Keuren. **Director:** George Marshall. **Writers:** Barbara Hammer & George Marshall. **Director of Photography:** Ed Dupar. **Cast:** Buster Keaton (Kelsey Dutton), ZaSu Pitts (Selma), Evelyn Ankers (Miss Loving), Joe E. Brown (Arthur Vail), Jack Kruschen (Ernie), Jack Elam (Shanks), Percy Helton (Barney), Joseph Corey (Arnold), Lyle Latell (Ernie's Friend), Charles Horvath (Barber), Bob Hope (Himself), "Snub" Pollard.

The 20th Century-Fox Hour ("Mr. Belvedere," 4/18/56) — **Director:** James V. Kern. **Writers:** Peggy Chantler Dick and John L. Greene. **Story:** Gwen Davenport. **Cast:** Reginald Gardiner (Mr. Lynn Belvedere), Eddie Bracken (Harry King), Margaret Hayes (Tracey King), Joyce Holden (Edna), ZaSu Pitts (Miss Appleton), Don Beddoe (Mr. Taylor), Eleanor Audley (Mrs. Hammond), Howard Wendell (Mr. Hammond), Ray Ferrell (Bobby King), Todd Ferrell (Mark King), Kim Tyler (Peter King), Robert Foulk (MacPherson). **Notes:** This show was renamed in syndication "The Genius" on *TV Hour of Stars*. The character of Mr. Belvedere was first seen on screen in the Fox film *Sitting Pretty* (1948), with Clifton Webb, Maureen O'Hara and Robert Young. This production is based on that film's screenplay. Lynn Belvedere to Miss Appleton: "It is poetic justice for the stool pigeon to be roasted."

The Jackie Gleason Show (9/29/56) — **Writer:** Joe Bigelow. **Cast:** William Boyd (Hopalong Cassidy), Art Carney, Edward G. Robinson, Charles Laughton, Peter Lorre, ZaSu Pitts, Rudy Vallee, Audrey Meadows, the June Taylor Dancers.

Private Secretary ("Not Quite Paradise," 2/3/57) — **Producer:** Jack Chertok. **Associate Producer:** Arthur Hoffe. **Production Executive:** Harry Poppe. **Director:** Oscar Rudolph. **Story & Teleplay:** Leonard Gershe. **Story:** Ned Marin. **Cinematography:** Robert Pittack. **Editing:** Axel Hubert Sr. **Art Direction:** Howard Campbell. **Set Decoration: William Stevens. **Costume Design:** Eloise Jensson. **Makeup:** Gene Hibbs. **Hair Stylist:** Gertrude Wheeler. **Assistant Director:** Lester D. Guthrie. **Property Master:** Clem Widrig. **Sound Recordist:** Robert Post. **Electrical Department:** Edward Petzoldt. **Editorial Supervisor:** Ben Marmon. **Cast:** Ann Sothern (Susan Camille MacNamara), Don Porter (Peter Sands), Ann Tyrrell (Vi Praskins), ZaSu Pitts (Aunt Martha), Hope Summers (Della Loganbury).

Kodak Presents: Disneyland '59 (1959) — **Cast:** Walt Disney (Host), Joanna Miller (Herself), Annette Funicello (Herself), Roberta Shore (Herself), June Haver (Herself), Roy Williams (Himself), Christopher Miller (Himself), Tim Considine (Himself), Tricia Nixon (Herself), Julie Nixon (Herself), David Nelson (Himself), Pat Nixon (Herself), Julia Meade (Herself), Harriet Nelson (Herself), Hedda Hopper (Herself), Richard Nixon (Himself), Ricky Nelson (Himself), Art Linkletter (Himself), Tom Tryon (Himself), John Russell (Himself), Clint Eastwood (Himself), Rex Allen (Himself), Bobby Diamond (Himself), Guy Williams (Himself), Gene Sheldon (Himself), Henry Calvin (Himself), Lawrence Welk (Himself), Chill Wills (Himself), Don DeFore (Himself), Sammee Tong (Himself), Roy Disney (Himself), Jon Provost (Himself), ZaSu Pitts (Herself), Edgar Bergen (Himself), Jock Mahoney (Himself), Wally Boag (Himself), George Putnam (Himself), Meredith Willson (Himself), Charles C. Kirkpatrick (Himself), Stuart Nelson (Himself), Mildred Nelson (Herself), Nels P. Nelson (Himself), Kirk Nelson (Himself), Karl Nelson (Himself), Robert Loggia (Himself), Jeffrey Hunter (Himself), Ozzie Nelson (Himself), Dennis Hopper (Himself), Marvin Miller (Himself).

The Dennis O'Keefe Show ("Dimples," 4/12/60) — **Cast:** Dennis O'Keefe (Hal Towne), Ricky Kelman (Randy Towne), Hope Emerson (Amelia "Sarge" Sargent), Eloise Hardt (Karen Hadley), Eddie Ryder (Eliot), Lester Matthews (Sylvester Barnes), Merry Martin (Susan Kimbal), ZaSu Pitts (Loretta Kimbal), Tom Nolan (Irving Gallop), Anthony De Mario (Tony the Matre'd), Cynthia Lourdes (Blonde on Phone).

Hot Off the Wire (a.k.a. *The Jim Backus Show*) ("Dear Minnie") — **Cast:** Jim Backus (John Michael "Mike" O'Toole), Nita Talbot (Dora), Bobs Watson (Sidney), ZaSu Pitts (Minnie Morgan), Hanley Stafford (Chester).

Guestward Ho! ("Lonesome's Gal," 5/11/61) — **Cast:** Mark Miller (Bill Hooton), Joanne Dru (Babs Hooton), J. Carrol Naish (Hawkeye), Flip Mark (Brook Hooton), Earle Hodgins (Lonesome), Jolene Brand (Pink Cloud), A.C. Montenaro (Rocky), ZaSu Pitts (Erna Lou).

Perry Mason ("The Case of the Absent Artist," 3/17/62) — **Associate Producer:** Jackson Gillis. **Director:** Arthur Marks. **Writer:** Robert C. Dennis. **Cinematography:** Robert G. Hager. **Film Editing:** John D. Faure. **Art Direction:** Lewis Creber. **Cast:** Raymond Burr (Perry Mason), Barbara Hale (Della Street), William Hopper (Paul Drake), William Talman (Hamilton Burger), Wesley Lau (Lt. Andy Anderson), Victor Buono (Alexander Glovatski), ZaSu Pitts (Daphne Whilom), Richard Erdman (Charles "Monty" Montrose), Arline Sax [Arlene Martel] (Fiona Cregan), Mark Roberts (Otto Gervaert/Gabe Phillips), Wynn Pearce (Pete Manders), Barney Phillips (Newburgh), Pamela Curran (Leslie Lawrence), Lane Bradford (Arnold Buck), Jay Barney (Harry Clark), Bill Zuckert (Judge), Wes Bishop (Agnew), Carl Don (Myer), Marshall Kent (Man), Mabel Rea (Girl), Ann Staunton (Woman), Patrick Waltz (Court Clerk).

Burke's Law ("Who Killed Holly Howard?," 9/20/63) — **Director:** Hy Averback. **Writers:** Albert Beich, William H. Wright. **Cast:** Gene Barry (Capt. Amos Burke), Gary Conway (Det. Tim Tilson), Regis Toomey (Det. Les Hart), Leon Lontoc (Henry), Elizabeth Allen (Sophia), William Bendix (Fred Hopke), Bruce Cabot (Thomas Mathewson), Rod Cameron (Harry Joe Murdock), Fred Clark ("Mac" McNulty), Jay C. Flippen (Bill, Desk Sergeant), Sir Cedric Hardwicke (John Busch), Stephen McNally (Ed Nickerson), Suzy Parker (Bridget Jenkins), ZaSu Pitts (Mrs. Bowie), Will Rogers Jr. (Vaughn Moore), Barry Kelley (Lt. Joe Nolan), Michael Fox (Police Officer), Buddy Lewis (Construction Worker), Kathy Kersh (Candy).

Oh, Susanna!/The Gale Storm Show **Episode Guide—Regular Cast:** Gale Storm (Susanna Pomeroy), ZaSu Pitts (Elvira Nugent), Roy Roberts (Capt. Simon P. Huxley), James Fairfax (Cedric, the Steward), Joe Cranston (Anderson), Ray Montgomery (Dr. Jones).

Oh, Susanna!/Gale Storm Season 1

1. "Italian Movie Actress" (9/29/56) — Guest cast: Jimmy Lydon.
2. "The Chimpanzee" (10/6/56) — Guest cast: J. Pat O'Malley, Lucy Lancaster, Dan Barton, Eleanor Audley, Eddie Parks.
3. "Passenger Incognito" (10/13/56) — Guest cast: Nancy Kulp, Paul Bryar, Maurice Marsac, Paul Maxey, Max Showalter.
4. "Bonnie Lassie" (10/20/56) — Guest cast: Irene Corlett, Francis DeSales, Eric Wilton, Frank Wilcox, Lumsden Hare.
5. "Too Many Maharanis" (10/27/56) — Guest cast: Narda Onyx, Isabel Randolph.
6. "Nicked in Naples" (11/10/56) — Guest cast: Penny Stanton, Jay Novello.
7. "The Immigrants" (11/17/56) — Guest cast: Jimmy Lydon, Jeri Lou James, Harold Dyrenforth, Kaaren Verne, Peter Votrian.
8. "Susanna Strikes Back" (11/24/56) — Guest cast: Jimmy Lydon, Paula Winslowe, Richard Collier, Robert Cornthwaite, Jean Bartel, Dick Elliott.
9. "Hold That Tiger" (12/1/56) — Guest cast: Robert Kennedy, Reginald Singh, Raymond Bailey, Robert Clarke, Rex Evans.
10. "The Witch Doctor" (12/8/56) — Guest cast: Barbara Slade, William Swan, Susan Andrews, Tod Andrews, Chuck Connors.
11. "A Night in Monte Carlo" (12/15/56) — Guest cast: Eric Feldary, Stephen DeKassy, Arthur Brunner, Franco Corsaro, Peggy Knudsen, John Archer.
12. "Capri" (12/22/56) — Guest cast: Tony Romano, Vincent Padula, Alberto Villa, Paul Picerni.
13. "The Magician" (12/29/56) — Guest cast: Frank Kreig, James Gavin, Lowell Gilmore, Lillian Culver, Alan Reed.
14. "Girls! Girls! Girls!" (1/5/57) — Guest cast: Joi Lansing, Patrick McVey, Lisa Davis, Joan Lora, Shirley Russell.
15. "Desirable Alien" (1/12/57) — Guest cast: Glenn Langan, Douglass Dumbrille.
16. "Foreign Intrigue" (1/19/57)
17. "Goodbye Kiss" (1/26/57)
18. "Super Snoop" (2/2/57) — Guest cast: Mira McKinney, Reginald Sheffield, William Pullen, Ted Bliss, Charles Schroeder.
19. "Checkmate" (2/9/57) — Guest cast: David Stollery, Morey Amsterdam.
20. "Swiss Miss" (2/16/57) — Guest cast: John Banner, Ernest Sarracino, Marjorie Bennett, Jimmy Karath, Sven Hugo Borg.
21. "The Blarney Stone" (2/23/57) — Guest cast: Woodrow Chambers, Sarah Selby, James Flavin, Hazel Sherbett, Grace Albertson.
22. "Volcano" (3/2/57) — Guest cast: Jimmy Lydon, Robert Warwick, Lani McIntire, Falpava Misilagi.
23. "Indian Giver" (a.k.a. "The Indian Givers") (3/9/57) — Guest cast: John Hoyt,

Richard Garland, Douglass Dumbrille, Helen Mayon, Jonathan Hole, Lester Miller.

24. "Susanna, the Chaperone" (3/16/57)—Guest cast: Joan Swift.

25. "Gypping the Gypsies" (3/23/57)—Guest cast: Anthony Dexter, Peter Cole, Lou Krugman, Joan Lora, Irene James.

26. "Maid in Sweden" (3/30/57)—Guest cast: Isabelle Dwan, Whit Bissell, John Yates Jr., Chuck James, Guy Way.

27. "Trouble in Trinidad" (4/6/57)—Guest cast: Jimmy Lydon, Don Beddoe, Claud Allister, Ted de Corsia, Peter Mamakos, Chet Stratton.

28. "Model Apartment" (4/13/57)—Guest cast: Peter Adams, Peter Damon, Carol Kelly, Johnny Silver, Charle Arvit.

29. "Singapore Fling" (4/20/57)—Guest cast: Paul Daibou, Sandra Stone, Christian Drake, Charles Irwin, Keye Luke, Warren Lee, Paul Daibou, Sandra Stone.

30. "The Parisian Touch" (4/27/57)—Guest cast: Dick Elliott, Elvia Allman, Gil Frye, Ramsay Hill, Georgette Duval, Vincent Padula.

31. "Action in Acapulco" (5/4/57)—Guest cast: William Pullen, Harry Atrion, Henry Kulky, Leonard Bremen, Don Diamond.

32. "Wedding in Majorca" (5/18/57)—Guest cast: Anthony DeMarco, Manuel Paris, Nancy Halley, Jean Carson, Oliver Cuff.

33. "Sing, Susanna, Sing" (5/25/57)—Guest cast: Craig Stevens, Lillian Bronson, Peter Coe, Don Diamond, Norman Livetti.

34. "Stop, Thief" (6/1/57)—Guest cast: Brad Dexter, Mario Siletti, Sammy White, Don Orlando.

35. "'Alp, 'Alp" (6/8/57)—Guest cast: Richard Webb, Grant Withers, Irene Seidner, Edythe Case.

36. "A Hit in Tahiti" (6/15/57)—Guest cast: Lila Lee, Steve Dunne.

OH, SUSANNA!/GALE STORM SEASON 2

37. "Pat on the Back" (9/14/57)—Guest cast: Pat Boone, Leonard Carey, Paul Hahn.

38. "Susanna Plays Cupid" (9/21/57)—Guest cast: Jim Backus, Eleanor Audley, Robert Carson.

39. "Pirate Treasure" (9/28/57)—Guest cast: Mark Dana, Madge Blake.

40. "Susanna Strikes Oil" (10/5/57)—Guest cast: Rudolph Anders, Robin Moore, Michael St. Angel, Dan Seymour.

41. "It's Only Money" (10/12/57)—Guest cast: John Russell, Dennis Moore, Paul Hahn.

42. "Honolulu Native" (a.k.a. "Honolulu Honeymoon") (10/19/57)—Guest cast: Linda Leighton, Patrick Waltz, Dan Jenkins.

43. "Susanna's Baby" (10/26/57)—Guest cast: Joyce Taylor, Coulter Irwin, Susanna Bonnell, Arline Anderson.

44. "A Lass in Alaska" (11/2/57)—Guest cast: William Bishop, Irving Bacon, Queenie Leonard.

45. "The Phantom Valice" (11/9/57)—Guest cast: Jimmy Lydon, Robert Blackwell, Percy Helton, Joe Cranston, Peter Bonnell, Paul Bonnell.

46. "For Money or Love" (11/16/57)—Guest cast: Floyd Simmons, Diane Brewster, Pierre Watkin, Robert Regas.

47. "Aladdin's Lamp" (11/23/57)—Guest cast: Richard Avonde, Nacho Galindo, John Harmon, Rodolfo Hoyos Jr.

48. "The Kid from Korea" (11/30/57)—Guest cast: Warren Hsieh.

49. "Mardi Gras" (12/7/57)—Guest cast: Mike Connors, Neil Hamilton, Phil Arnold, Dorothy Neumann, Lillian Culver.

50. "Dutch Treatment" (12/14/57)—Guest cast: Marjorie Bennett, Charles Lane.

51. "Susanna Goes Native" (12/21/57)—Guest cast: King Donovan, Liam Sullivan.

52. "Friday the Thirteenth" (12/28/57)—Guest cast: Cheerio Meredith, Junius Matthews.

53. "The Ouija Board" (1/4/58)—Guest cast: Mark Dana, Colin Campbell, Arthur Gould-Porter.
54. "Angela the Angel" (1/11/58)—Guest cast: Queenie Leonard, Evelyn Rudie.
55. "Lovey-Dovey" (1/18/58)—Guest cast: Russell Arms, Vera Vague [Barbara Jo Allen], Judi Meredith.
56. "The Case of the Chinese Puzzle" (1/25/58)—Guest cast: Douglas Fowley, Keye Luke, Ray Walker, Lisa Lu, Gai Lee.
57. "Royal Welcome" (2/1/58)—Guest cast: Don Kennedy, Beryl Machin, Molly Roden.
58. "Susanna Takes a Husband" (2/8/58)—Guest cast: Margaret Hamilton, Kitty Larsen, William Roerick, Maurice Marsac, Wilbur Mack.
59. "Taking Ways" (2/15/58)—Guest cast: Nestor Paiva, Robert Riordan, June Vincent.
60. "Ride 'Em Cowgirl" (2/22/58)—Guest cast: Ken Clark, Edward Colmans, Lois Corbett.
61. "Bye Bye Banshee" (3/1/58)
62. "A Beautiful Friendship" (3/8/58)—Guest cast: Addison Richards.
63. "Ghosts Aboard" (3/15/58)—Guest cast: Ralph Dumke, Ruth Lee.
64. "How to Catch a Man" (3/22/58)—Guest cast: Tom Helmore, Betty Lynn.
65. "Our Dear Captain" (3/29/58)—Guest cast: Robert Burton, Kay Haydn, Don Kennedy, Molly Roden, Ralph Smiley.
66. "Susanna and the Pirates" (4/5/58)—Guest cast: Don Durant.
67. "Happily Unmarried" (4/12/58)—Guest cast: Burt Mustin, Mary Young.
68. "Bamboozled in Bombay" (4/26/58)—Guest cast: Paul Picerni, Jack Kruschen, Diana Crawford, Charity Grace.
69. "Not So Innocents Abroad" (5/3/58)—Guest cast: Edd Byrnes, Kem Dibbs, Yvonne Lime, John Indrisano, Ruth Perrott.
70. "A Date with a Wolf" (5/10/58)
71. "Beat the Band" (5/31/58)—Guest cast: Steven Geray, Kay E. Kuter, O.Z. Whitehead, Sam Wolfe.

OH, SUSANNA!/GALE STORM SEASON 3

72. "Diamonds Are a Girl's Best Friend" (9/6/58)—Guest cast: John Agar, Dub Taylor.
73. "Happy Birthday, Captain" (9/13/58)—Guest cast: Eugene Borden, Robert Emmett Keane.
74. "The Truth Machine" (9/20/58)—Guest cast: Charles Herbert, Rolfe Sedan.
75. "Hayride Ahoy" (9/27/58)—Guest cast: Edgar Buchanan, George Cisar, Carlos Romero.
76. "Painted in Paris" (10/4/58)
77. "The Sweepstakes Ticket" (10/4/58)
78. "Secret Assignment" (10/18/58)—Guest cast: Richard Davies, John Holland, Raymond Greenleaf, Morgan Jones, Eleanor Lucky.
79. "Heaven Scent" (10/18/58)—Guest cast: Jacques Bergerac.
80. "Love and Kisses" (10/18/58)—Guest cast: Herbert Lytton, Andra Martin, Martin Freed, Michael Ross.
81. "You Gotta Have Charm" (11/8/58)—Guest cast: Jack Mulhall, Paula Winslowe, Carol Morris, Warren Frost, Sandra Wirth.
82. "The Case of the Music Box Thief" (11/15/58)
83. "Susanna the Matchmaker" (11/22/58)—Guest cast: Claire Carleton, Maria Palmer, Rita Lynn.
84. "Adventure in Alaska" (12/6/58)—Guest cast: Nancy Millard.
85. "Robot from Inner Space" (12/13/58)—Guest cast: Robby the Robot.
86. "Don't Give Up the Ship" (12/20/58)—Guest cast: Keith Andes, Jimmy Lydon, Frances Mercer, Tom Palmer.
87. "Make Mine Music" (12/27/58)—Guest cast: Salvatore Baccaloni.

88. "How to Make Enemies" (1/3/59)—Guest cast: Robert Anderson.

89. "One Captain Too Many" (1/10/59)—Guest cast: Charles Lane.

90. "On the Dot" (1/17/59)—Guest cast: Billy Vaughn.

91. "The Honeymoon Suite" (1/24/59)—Guest cast: Doug McClure.

92. "It's Murder My Dear" (1/31/59)—Guest cast: Frank Cady, Geraldine Hall, Boris Karloff, Frank Kreig.

93. "The Battle of Bull Run" (2/7/59)—Guest cast: Elena Verdugo, Don Orlando, Scott Elliott, Gil Frye.

94. "Jailmates" (2/28/59)—Guest cast: Lorne Greene, Ashley Cowan, Vera Denham, Nancy Millard.

95. "An Old Chinese Custom" (3/7/59)—Guest cast: James Hong, Nico Minardos.

96. "Dutch Treat" (3/14/59)—Guest cast: John Bleifer.

97. "Alias Susanna Valentine" (3/21/59)—Guest cast: Paul Bryar, Lillian Culver, Harry Jackson, D'Ette La Rue.

98. "Clip That Coupon" (3/28/59)—Guest cast: Robert Anderson, Jonathan Hole, Mike Keene, Nancy Millard, Stephen Roberts.

99. "Who Stole That Melody?" (4/4/59)—Guest cast: Buddy Bregman, Jerome Cowan, Joe Cranston.

100. "Susanna, the Babysitter" (4/11/59)—Guest cast: Norma Varden, Susan Reilly LeHane, Stephen Hammer, Nancy DeCarl, Gregory Irvin.

OH, SUSANNA!/GALE STORM SEASON 4

101. "One, Two, Ski!" (10/1/59)—Guest cast: Gene Nelson, Anna-Lisa, Bob Hopkins, Cosmo Sardo.

102. "The Card Shark" (10/8/59)—Guest cast: William Frawley, Lillian Bronson, Ben Welden, Helen Kleeb, Fred Kruger.

103. "The Million Dollar Mutt" (10/15/59)—Guest cast: Don Diamond, Frank Albertson.

104. "Come Back Little Beatnik" (10/22/59)—Guest cast: Jerry Colonna, Richard Deacon, Joseph Conley.

105. "Calling Scotland Yard" (10/29/59)—Guest cast: Edward Ashley, Alan Caillou, Stanley Fraser, Milton Frome, Lillian Kemble-Cooper, Hilda Plowright, John Van Dreelen.

106. "Happy Horoscope" (11/5/59)—Guest cast: Allyn Joslyn.

107. "Nugey, Come Home" (11/12/59)—Guest cast: Mabel Rea, Robert Beecher.

108. "The Swedish Steward" (11/19/59)—Guest cast: John Qualen.

109. "Goodbye Doctor" (11/26/59)—Guest cast: Marjorie Bennett, Rolfe Sedan.

110. "Family Reunion" (12/3/59)—Guest cast: Hope Summers.

111. "Wedding at Sea" (12/10/59)—Guest cast: Ron Hagerthy.

112. "Spanish Souvenir" (12/17/59)—Guest cast: Howard McNear, Henry Corden.

113. "Captain Daddy" (12/24/59)—Guest cast: Frank Killmond, Ruth Perrott, David Addis, Chris Essay.

114. "Susanna's True Confession" (12/31/59)—Guest cast: Robert Q. Lewis.

115. "African Drums" (1/7/60)—Guest cast: Robert Griffin.

116. "No Tears for the Captain" (1/14/60)—Guest cast: Liam Sullivan.

117. "Love by Yiminy" (1/21/60)—Guest cast: John Qualen.

118. "A Trip for Auntie" (1/28/60)

119. "Birthday for Gino" (2/4/60)—Guest cast: Bart Bradley, Tom Andre, Alan Roberts.

120. "S.O.S. Dad" (2/11/60)—Guest cast: Andre Phillips, Luis Van Rooten.

121. "Mother Steps Out" (2/18/60)—Guest cast: Eleanor Audley, Willis Bouchey.

122. "Captain Courageous" (2/25/60)—Guest cast: Nancy Kulp.

123. "One Coin in the Fountain" (3/3/

60) — Guest cast: Arlen Stuart, Sid Melton, Natividad Vacío, Rodolfo Hoyos Jr., Nestor Paiva, Salvador Baguez.
124. "Made in Hong Kong" (3/10/60) — Guest cast: Philip Ahn.
125. "It's Magic" (3/17/60) — Guest cast: Alan Mowbray, Lillian Culver, Sid Melton.
126. "Show Biz" (3/24/60) — Guest cast: Jack Albertson, Mel Prestidge.

Radio Credits

— — February 27, 1932. KNX. This was a broadcast to promote her shorts with Thelma Todd. It was heard on the West Coast only.

Hollywood on the Air. June 5, 1933. NBC. Buck Jones, Russ Colombo, Allen Jenkins, Franklin Pangborn, Ginger Rogers, Gregory Ratoff, Harry Jackson and His Orchestra, Lucien Littlefield, Norman Foster, ZaSu Pitts.

The Lux Radio Theatre. October 28, 1935. CBS. "Dulcy." Sponsored by: Lux. George S. Kaufman (author), Harold Vermilyea, James Marr, Leslie Adams, Clifford Walker, ZaSu Pitts, Gene Lockhart, Donald Foster, Douglas Garrick (host), Marc Connelly (author), Mary Mason, Mary Newton, Stuart Fox, Ben Grauer (announcer), Anthony Stanford (director), Robert Armbruster (music director), George Wells (adaptor), Betty Hanna (commercial spokesman).

Hall of Fame. June 16, 1936. With Edward Everett Horton, ZaSu Pitts.

The Kraft Music Hall. May 27, 1937. Red net. Bing Crosby, Bob Burns, Gail Patrick, Jimmy Dorsey and His Orchestra, Rudolf Gonz, the Paul Taylor Choristers, ZaSu Pitts.

The Chase and Sanborn Hour. July 4, 1937. Red net. ZaSu Pitts, Dorothy Lamour, W. C. Fields, Edgar Bergen, Don Ameche (host), Don Briggs (announcer), Robert Armbruster and His Orchestra, Hoagy Carmichael, Margaret Brayton, ZaSu Pitts.

The Baker's Broadcast. November 7, 1937. Blue net. Bud Hiestand (announcer), Feg Murray (host), Harriet Hilliard, Ozzie Nelson and His Orchestra, Ralph Bellamy (narrator), ZaSu Pitts.

The Rudy Vallee Hour. August 18, 1938. Red net. Rudy Vallee, The Connecticut Yankees, ZaSu Pitts, Tom Howard, George Shelton, Walter Hampden, Graham McNamee (announcer).

The Quaker Party. October 1, 1938. NBC net. Bea Wain, Dan Seymour, Larry Clinton and His Orchestra, Tommy Riggs, ZaSu Pitts.

Fibber McGee and Molly. October 4, 1938. NBC. ZaSu Pitts.

The Lifebuoy Show. November 29, 1938. CBS net. Al Jolson, Martha Raye, Tiny Ruffner (announcer), Lud Gluskin and His Orchestra, Harry Einstein, ZaSu Pitts.

Fibber McGee and Company. February 7, 1939. NBC net. Bill Thompson, Billy Mills and His Orchestra, Harlow Wilcox, Harold Peary, Isabel Randolph, Jim Jordan, Walter Tetley, ZaSu Pitts.

Fibber McGee and Company. February 21, 1939. NBC net. Bill Thompson, Billy Mills and His Orchestra, Harlow Wilcox, Harold Peary, Isabel Randolph, Jim Jordan, Verna Felton, Walter Tetley, ZaSu Pitts.

Fibber McGee and Company. March 7, 1939. NBC net. Bill Thompson, Billy Mills and His Orchestra, Harlow Wilcox, Isabel Randolph, Jim Jordan, Mel Blanc, ZaSu Pitts.

Fibber McGee and Company. March 21, 1939. NBC net. Bill Thompson, Billy Mills and His Orchestra, Harlow Wilcox, Harold Peary, Jim Jordan, Mel Blanc, ZaSu Pitts.

Fibber McGee and Company. April 11, 1939.

NBC net. Bill Thompson, Billy Mills and His Orchestra, Harlow Wilcox, Harold Peary, Isabel Randolph, Jim Jordan, Mel Blanc, ZaSu Pitts.

Tuesday Night Party. April 25, 1939. Dick Powell, Martha Raye, ZaSu Pitts.

The Lux Radio Theatre. July 10, 1939. CBS net. "Ruggles of Red Gap." Charles Laughton, ZaSu Pitts, Charles Ruggles, Cecil B. DeMille, Louis Silvers (music director), Melville Ruick (announcer), Walter DeLeon (screenwriter), Harlan Thompson (screenwriter), Humphrey Pearson (screenwriter), Harry Leon Wilson (author), Herbert Peacock (intermission guest: famous butler), Eric Snowden, Lelah Tyler, Hal K. Dawson, Verna Felton, Stanley Farrar, Earle Ross, Joseph Du Val (double), Mary Cecil (double), Frank Nelson (double, program opening announcer), Margaret Brayton (double), Myron Gary (double), Georgia Simmons, Marie Hammond, Frank Marton, Ross Forrester (double), Marilyn Stuart (commercial spokesman), Florence Baker (commercial spokesman), Jane Lauren (commercial spokesman: double), Justina Wayne (commercial spokesman: double), Frank Woodruff (director), George Wells (adaptor), Charlie Forsyth (sound effects).

The Gulf Screen Guild Theatre. October 8, 1939. CBS net. "Revue." Bob Hope, Connie Boswell, Gary Cooper (narrator), Roger Pryor (host), ZaSu Pitts, Oscar Bradley and His Orchestra, John Conte (announcer).

Sunshine Inn. November 3, 1939. ZaSu Pitts.

Big Sister. February 12, 1940. CBS. ZaSu begins her run as Aunt Mamie Wayne from New York City.

The Kate Smith Show. February 18, 1944. ZaSu presents the sketch "Derricks on in a Hill."

The Lum and Abner Show. March 27, 1949. CBS net. Chester Lauck, Andy Devine, ZaSu Pitts, Norris Goff, Edna Best, Opie Cates and His Orchestra, Wendell Niles (announcer).

The Lum and Abner Show. April 24, 1949. CBS net. Andy Devine, Chester Lauck, Edna Best, Norris Goff, Opie Cates, Wendell Niles (announcer), ZaSu Pitts.

The Lum and Abner Show. June 5, 1949. CBS net. Andy Devine, Chester Lauck, Norris Goff, Opie Cates, Wendell Niles (announcer), ZaSu Pitts.

The Lum and Abner Show. November 2, 1949. CBS net. Andy Devine, Chester Lauck, Norris Goff, Opie Cates (music), ZaSu Pitts, Betty Boyle (writer), Jay Summers (writer), Larry Berns (director), Wendell Niles (announcer).

The Lum and Abner Show. November 16, 1949. CBS net. Andy Devine, Betty Boyle, Chester Lauck, Dink Trout, Jay Thomas (writer), Larry Bird (director), Norris Goff, Opie Cates, Paul Masterson (announcer), Tennessee Ernie Ford, ZaSu Pitts.

The Lum and Abner Show. November 23, 1949. CBS net. Andy Devine, Chester Lauck, Dink Trout, Norris Goff, Opie Cates, ZaSu Pitts.

The Lum and Abner Show. January 4, 1950. CBS net. Andy Devine, Chester Lauck, Norris Goff, Opie Cates, ZaSu Pitts.

The Lum and Abner Show. March 8, 1950. CBS net. Andy Devine, Betty Boyle, Chester Lauck, Jay Thomas (writer), Larry Bird (director), Norris Goff, Opie Cates, Wendell Niles (announcer), ZaSu Pitts.

The Lum and Abner Show. April 5, 1950. CBS net. Andy Devine, Betty Boyle, Chester Lauck, Cliff Arquette, Ken Niles (announcer), Larry Berns (producer, director), Norris Goff, Opie Cates and His Orchestra, Roz Rogers (writer), Willard Waterman, ZaSu Pitts.

The Lum and Abner Show. April 12, 1950. CBS net. Andy Devine, Chester Lauck, Cliff Arquette, Jim Backus, Norris Goff, Opie Cates, ZaSu Pitts.

The Lum and Abner Show. April 19, 1950. CBS net. Betty Boyle, Chester Lauck, Cliff Arquette, Ken Niles (announcer), Norris Goff, Opie Cates and His Orchestra, Roz Rogers (writer), Willard Waterman, ZaSu Pitts.

The Lum and Abner Show. April 26, 1950. CBS net. Betty Boyle, Chester Lauck, Cliff Arquette, Herb Vigran, Isabel Randolph, Ken Niles (announcer), Larry Berns (producer, director), Norris Goff, Opie Cates and His Orchestra, Roz Rogers (writer), ZaSu Pitts.

Stage Appearances

September 1930: ZaSu took part in a presentation of the Dominoes charitable organization variety program, playing lead in a playlet "Scarlet." Also participating were Nancy Carroll and Thelma Todd.

Summer 1938: ZaSu performed an act on the national Vaudeville circuit, assisted by Cliff Hall.

1942: ZaSu joined other celebrities in a benefit performance of Noel Coward's *Tonight at 8:30* for British War Relief.

1942: Stock tour, *Her First Murder*.

1943: Midwest stock tour, *The Bat*, with Jane Darwell.

December 1943: Pre-opening tryout, *Ramshackle Inn*, at Norfolk, Virginia.

January 5, 1944: Broadway debut, *Ramshackle Inn*.

Summer 1946: Stock tour, *Cordelia*.

Summer 1947: Stock tour, *The Late Christopher Bean*.

Summer 1948: Stock tour, *The Late Christopher Bean*.

Summer 1952: East Coast stock tour, *Ramshackle Inn*.

January 20, 1953: Broadway opening, *The Bat*, with Lucile Watson.

Summer 1953: Stock tour, *The Bat*.

1956: Pasadena Playhouse production of *The Solid Gold Cadillac*.

1957: Pasadena Playhouse production of *The Curious Miss Carraway*.

1960: Pasadena Playhouse production of *The Curious Savage*.

1962: Pasadena Playhouse production of *Everybody Loves Opal*.

BIBLIOGRAPHY

Books

AFI: *American Film Institute Catalog of Motion Pictures Produced in the United States Feature Films, 1911–1930.* Berkeley: University of California Press.

AFI: *American Film Institute Catalog of Motion Pictures Produced in the United States Feature Films, 1931–40.* Berkeley: University of California Press.

AFI: *American Film Institute Catalog of Motion Pictures Produced in the United States Feature Films 1941–1950.* Berkeley: University of California Press.

Bakewell, William. *Hollywood Be Thy Name: Random Recollections of a Movie Veteran from Silents to Talkies to TV.* Metuchen, NJ: Scarecrow Press, 1991.

Black, Shirley Temple. *Child Star: An Autobiography.* New York: McGraw-Hill, 1988.

Braff, Richard E. *The Universal Silents.* Jefferson, NC: McFarland, 1995.

Brownlow, Kevin. *The Parade's Gone By.* New York: Alfred Knopf, 1968.

Champlin, Charles, and Linda Klinger. *Legends of the Silent Screen: A Collection of U.S. Postage Stamps.* Washington, DC: United States Postal Service, 1994.

Dowd, Nancy. *King Vidor.* Metuchen, NJ: Scarecrow Press, 1988.

Drew, William. *At the Center of the Frame.* Lanham, MD: Vestal Press, 1999.

Hamann, G.D. *ZaSu Pitts in the '30s.* PA: Filming Today Press, 2001.

Higham, Charles, and Joel Greenberg. *The Celluloid Muse: Hollywood Directors Speak.* New York: Signet, 1972.

Keylin, Arleen, and Suri Fleischer. *Hollywood Album: Obits from the New York Times.* New York: Arno, 1977.

LeBow, Guy. *Are We on the Air? The Hilarious, Scandalous Confessions of a TV Pioneer.* New York: C.P.I. Books, 1992.

Lenning, Arthur. *Stroheim.* Lexington, KY: University Press of Kentucky, 2000.

Maltin, Leonard. *The Great Movie Shorts.* New York: Crown, 1992.

Martin, Mary. *My Heart Belongs.* New York: Warner Books, 1976.

Mordden, Ethan. *Movie Star: A Look at the Women Who Made Hollywood.* New York: St. Martin's Press, 1983.

Oakie, Jack. *Jack Oakie's Double Takes.* San Francisco, CA: Strawberry Hill Press, 1980.

Pitts, Michael R. *Famous Movie Detectives.* Metuchen, NJ: Scarecrow Press, 1991.

Pitts, ZaSu. *Candy Hits: The Famous Star's Own Candy Recipes.* New York: Duell, Sloan & Pearce, 1963.

Quinlan, David. *Illustrated Encyclopedia of Movie Characters.* New York: Harmony, 1985.

Sale, Virginia. *American Monologues.* New York: Samuel French, 1952.

Spears, Jack. *Hollywood: The Golden Era.* New York: Castle, 1971.

Springer, John, and Jack Hamilton. *They Had Faces Then.* Secaucus, NJ: Citadel, 1974.

Taylor, Deems. *A Pictorial History of the Movies.* New York: Simon & Schuster, 1943.

Vidor, King. *A Tree Is a Tree.* New York: Harcourt Brace, 1953.

Von Stroheim, Erich. *Greed: A Film.* New York: Simon & Schuster, 1972.

Magazines

American Home Magazine, June 1944. "A Cooking Fool Is ZaSu Pitts," Maybelle Manning.

Classic Images, December 2006. "Hands and Heart: The Life and Career of ZaSu Pitts," Charles Stumpf.

Colliers, June 1936. "Mr. Woodall's Wife," Kyle Crichton.

Films in Review, June/July 1980. "ZaSu Pitts," DeWitt Bodeen.
Films of the Golden Age
House and Garden
Liberty
LIFE
LOOK
Motion Picture
New Movie Magazine
Newsweek
Parsons Art & Humanities Council, 1998. "ZaSu Pitts in Parson, Kansas," Randy Roberts.
Photoplay
Radio Mirror
Radio Stars
Saturday Evening Post
Stage Magazine
Time
TV/Radio Mirror
Variety

Newspapers

Boston Globe
Chicago Sunday Tribune
Chicago Tribune
Daily Variety
Film Daily
Hollywood Citizen News
Illustrated Daily News
Los Angeles Evening Herald
Los Angeles Examiner
Los Angeles Post Record
Milwaukee Journal
Motion Picture Herald
Parson Daily Eclipse
Parsons Weekly Sun
Sandusky Star Journal
Santa Cruz Sentinel

INDEX

Aaronson, Irving 174
Abbe, Charles 119
Abbott, George 92, 130
Aber, Nestor 135
"Action in Acapulco" 183
Acuff, Eddie 164
Adair, Jack 159
Adams, Claire 120
Adams, Dorothy 161
Adams, Edgar 130
Adams, Edie 178
Adams, Ernie 153
Adams, Frank 154
Adams, Glen 172
Adams, Jimmie 119
Adams, Julia [Julie] 93, 174
Adams, Leslie 186
Adams, Neile 175
Adams, Peter 183
Addis, David 185
Adrian, Gibbons 132, 136, 141
"Adventure in Alaska" 184
Adventure in Baltimore 71
The Affair of Susan 68, 155
"African Drums" 185
Afterwards 150
Agar, John 71, 184
Aggie Appleby Maker of Men 60, 146
Agnew, Frances 123
Agnew, Robert 120, 123
Ahn, Philip 186
Ainsley, Norman 153
Ainsworth, Phil 17
Aitken, Spottiswoode 114, 119
Akins, Zoe 133
"Aladdin's Lamp" 183
Alberni, Luis 160
Albert, Eddie 171
Albertson, Frank 185
Albertson, Grace 182
Albertson, Jack 186
Albertson, Mabel 102
Albright, Wally 147, 155
The Alcoa Hour 39
Alden, Eric 164
Alden, Mary 133, 134
Alden, Richard 176
Alden, Robert 137
Alderman, John 176
Aldrich, Fred 172
Alexander, Arthur 134
Alexander, Ben 50, 130, 141
Alexander, David 180

Alexander, Ernie 112
Alexander, Frank 110, 113
Alexander, Joan 179
Alexander, Katherine 129
Alexander, Maurine 85
Alexander, Richard 130, 154, 164
Alexander, Ronald 180
Alexander, Ross 67, 155
"Alias Susanna Valentine" 185
All Quiet on the Western Front 41, 42, 129, 130
Allardice, James B. 173
Allen, Alfred 115, 116
Allen, Barbara Jo 184
Allen, Elizabeth 182
Allen, Fred 135
Allen, Joel 174
Allen, Lewis 170
Allen, Rex 181
Allen, Richard 162
Allister, Claud 48, 111, 131, 136, 183
Allman, Elvia 183
Allwyn, Astrid 145
Alone Together 156
Alonso, Chico 170
"'Alp, 'Alp" 183
Alter, Louis 155
Alum and Eve 51, 112
Alvarado, Don 139
"Always in All Ways" 131
Always Together 101
Amazing Miss Withers 157
Ameche, Don 186
The American Home 72
American Magazine 71
Ames, Robert 129, 131
Amin, Shimit 121
"Among My Souvenirs" 127
"Amour, Amour, Amour" 170
Amsterdam, Morey 182
Amy, George 171
"An' Furthermore" 127
Anders, Rudolph 183
Anderson, Agnes 157
Anderson, Arline 183
Anderson, Augusta 153
Anderson, Beaudine 136
Anderson, Dame Judith 108
Anderson, Dave 110
Anderson, Doris 149
Anderson, Eddie "Rochester" 152, 178

Anderson, George 159
Anderson, Glenn E. 174, 178
Anderson, Marion Clayton 130
Anderson, Maxwell 130
Anderson, Milo 157, 171
Anderson, Robert 172, 185
Andes, Keith 184
Andre, Gwili 50, 140
Andre, Tom 185
André-ani 123
Andren, Jean 171
Andrews, Del 130
Andrews, Edward 176
Andrews, Loretta 151
Andrews, Stanley 154, 159
Andrews, Susan 182
Andrews, Tod 182
Andriot, Lucien 139, 148
Andriot, Poupée 130
"Angela the Angel" 184
Anglin, Margaret 121
Ankers, Evelyn 180
Ankrum, Morris 169
Anna-Lisa 185
Anthony, De Leon 127
Anthony, Ray 174, 175
Anthony, Stuart 138, 141
Anthony, Walter 125, 130
Apfel, Oscar 137, 140, 141, 142, 157
Appell, Dave 176
Appling, Bert 110
Arabian Love 17
Arbenina, Stella 158
Archduke Leopold of Austria 125
Archer, John 182
Arco, Louis V. 161
Ardell, Alyce 153, 157
Arden, Eve 80, 84, 157, 162, 163, 169, 170
Are We on the Air? The Hilarious, Scandalous Confessions of a TV Pioneer (book) 108
The Argyle Case 40, 127
Arling, Arthur E. 148
Armbruster, Robert 186
Armetta, Henry 43, 129, 137, 143, 145
Arms, Russell 171, 184
Armstrong, Margaret 163
Armstrong, Robert 40, 50, 127, 139
Armstrong, Sam 138

Index

Army Girl 39
Arna, Lissi 134
Arnold, Jack 165
Arnold, Mike 159
Arnold, Phil 183
Arnold, William 157
Arquette, Cliff 187, 188
Arthur, George K. 31, 122, 124
Arthur, Henry 156
Arthur, Jean 38, 120, 126
Arthur, Johnny 136, 151
Arthur, Robert 172
Arvit, Charle 183
As the Sun Went Down 11, 115
Ash, Jerome 136, 144
Ash, Sam 169
Ashcraft, Mary 128
Asher, E.M. 133, 143
Ashley, Edward 185
Ashley, Herbert 157
Ashton, Sylvia 116, 117, 118, 121
Asleep in the Feet 56, 112
Astor, Gertrude 127
Astor, Mary 74
Atchley, Hooper 136, 159
Atkinson, Brooks 87, 102
Atkinson, Frank 125
Atrion, Harry 183
Atwater, Edith 180
Audley, Eleanor 180, 182, 183, 185
August, Joseph H. 161
Auletti, Leonard 175
"Aunt Emma Paints the Town" 167
Aunt Emma Paints the Town 167
Austin, Albert 110
Austin, Frank 111
Austin, William 123, 124
Averback, Hy 182
Avil, Gordon 175
Avonde, Richard 183
Axt, William 141, 156
Aylesworth, Arthur 151, 157
Ayres, Agnes 118
Ayres, Lewis 41, 67, 68, 130, 154

Babille, E.J. 128, 132
"The Baby Vanishes" 164
Baccaloni, Salvatore 184
Bachelin, Franz 173
Back Street 52, 53, 143
"Back to School Blues" 176
Backus, Jim 178, 181, 183, 188
Bacon, Irving 153, 155, 159, 166, 183
The Bad Sister 44, 133
Bader, Walter 121
Badger, Clarence G. 127, 128
Baggot, King 133, 154, 157, 169
Baguez, Salvador 186
Bailey, Harry A. 124
Bailey, Raymond 182
Bailey, William 123
Bainbridge, W.H. 116
Bainter, Fay 152
Bakaleinikoff, C. 154, 155, 165, 166
Bakaleinikoff, Mischa 137
Baker, Allen 119

Baker, Eddie 9, 109
Baker, Florence 187
Baker, George D. 115
Baker, Graham 161
Baker, Herbert 173
Baker, Jack 174, 175
Baker, Kenny 76, 159
Baker, Nellie Bly 119
The Baker's Broadcast 186
Bakewell, William 41, 45, 130, 135, 143
Balchowsky, Max 178
Baldridge, Bert 118
Baldwin, Earl W. 170
Baldwin, Ruth Ann 9, 113
Baldwin, Walter 165, 171
Ball, Lucille 154
Ballard, Elmer 129
Ballard, Lucien 130
Ballyhoo 67
"Bamboozled in Bombay" 184
Bambury, John T. 157
Bankhead, Tallulah 48, 140
Banks, Lionel 170
Bann, Richard W. 48
Banner, John 182
Banton, Travis 130, 153, 161
Bara, Theda 95, 106
Barbier, George 58, 145
Bard, Ben 146, 148
Bare, Bobby 176
The Bargain of the Century 56, 113
Bari, Lynn 135, 146, 154, 174
Barker, Reginald 121
Barlow, William 121
Barnes, George 141, 150
Barnes, Margaret Ayer 139
Barnes, T. Roy 14, 117, 122
Barnett, Vince 130
Barney, Jay 181
"Baron von Munchausen" 146
Barondess, Barbara 157
Barr, Muriel 163
Barrat, Robert 173
Barrett, Claudia 95, 180
Barry, Gene 182
Barry, Wesley 14, 113, 114
Barrymore, Ethel 133
Barrymore, Lionel 18, 48, 118, 137
Bart, Jean 126
Bartel, Jean 182
Bartels, Louis John 132
Bartlett, Benny [Bennie] 70, 156, 161
Bartlett, Sy 155
Barton, Dan 174, 182
Barty, Billy 144, 179
Barwyn, Max 123, 134
Basevi, James 122
The Bashful Bachelor 82, 83, 166
Basquerie 134
"Basquerie" 135
Bass, Saul 178
Bassett, R.H. 138, 152
The Bat (play) 84, 94, 188
Batcheller, George 178
Bates, Charles 165
Bates, Florence 166

Bates, Granville 156, 157, 160, 162
Bates, Les 125
Bateson, James 76
Batson, George 85, 87, 95, 179
"The Battle of Bull Run" 185
The Battling Bellboy 9, 109
Bauchens, Anne 119
Baxley, Jack 153, 155
Baxley, Paul 178
Baxter, Alan 156
Baxter, Warner 30, 46, 123, 134
Bay, Dorothy 144
Bayley, Caroline 143
Beal, Scott R. 143
"Beat the Band" 184
Beatty, May 162
Beauchamp, Clem 178
Beaudine, Helen 136
Beaudine, William [W.W.] 9, 109, 110, 135, 140
Beaumont, Lucy 139
"A Beautiful Friendship" 184
Beauty and the Bus 57
Beavers, Louise 159
Beck, John 171
Beckett, Scotty 161
Beddoe, Don 180, 183
Bedford, Barbara 122
Bedford, Eleanore 146
Beecher, Robert 185
Beery, Noah 14, 28, 117, 122
Beery, Wallace 14, 28, 33, 34, 66, 91, 117, 121, 124, 125
Beggars of Life 106
Behind the Map 9, 109
Beich, Albert 182
Belasco, Leon 164
Bell, Louise 176
Bell, Monta 28, 122
Bellamy, Madge 20, 29, 30, 120, 122
Bellamy, Ralph 186
Belle, Lena 169
Belmore, Daisy 130
Belmore, Lionel 131, 135, 146
Beloin, Ed 180
Belvedere, Lynn 180
Bendix, William 182
Benedict, Brooks 142, 147, 153, 163, 166
Benge, Wilson 128, 134
Ben-Hur 25
Bennett, Alma 119
Bennett, Bruce 142, 146
Bennett, Constance 41, 43, 70, 128, 132
Bennett, David 128
Bennett, Earl 179
Bennett, Joan 49, 70, 96, 127, 138, 156, 180
Bennett, Leila 151
Bennett, Marjorie 182, 183, 185
Bennett, Mickey 126
Bennett, Richard 18, 117
Bennison, Andrew 155
Benny, Jack 179
Benson, Sam 144, 148
Bentley, Bobette 174

Bentley, Robert 129
Benton, Robert R. 174
Beranger, André [George] 122
Beranger, Clara 120
Beresford, Harry 133
Berg, Dave 138, 139
Bergen, Constance 154, 155
Bergen, Edgar 181, 186
Berger, Ludwig 126
Bergerac, Jacques 184
Bergerman, Stanley 136, 137
Bergman, Henry 110
Bergunker, Max 126
Berkeley, Busby 63, 150
Berkeley, Claude 124
Berkeley, Reginald 137, 161
Berle, Milton 93, 113, 178, 179
Berman, Pandro S. 146, 150
Bern, Paul 18, 19
Bernard, Harry 112, 113, 153
Bernard, Joseph E. 148, 155, 172
Bernds, Edward 129
Berns, Larry 187, 188
Berns, Mel 145
Bernstein, Isadore 137
Berrell, George W. 116
Berry, Chuck 175
Berry, Admiral Robert 105
Best, Edna 187
Best, Willie 133, 155
The Best of Broadway 96, 180
The Best of the Post 90
"Better Than Life" 162
Better Times 13, 116
Bettger, Lyle 173
Betz, Matthew 36, 43, 125, 126, 129
Bevan, Billy 131
Bey, Erik 131
"Beyond the Blue Horizon" 130
Beyond Victory 44, 134
Bibo, Irving 137
Bickel, George 137
Bickford, Charles 43, 44, 131, 132
Biddle, Craig, Jr. 118
The Big Gamble 46, 135
The Big House 91, 131
The Big Liar 146
Big Sister 82, 187
Bigelow, Jane 140
Bigelow, Joe 180
Bilbrook, Lydia 165, 166
Bing, Herman 46, 136, 139, 170
Binger, Ray 119, 162
Birch, Paul 179
Bird, Charlot [Charlotte] 123
Bird, Larry 187
Bird, Violet 128
Birell, Tala 154
Biroc, Joseph F. 150
The Birth of a Nation 21
"Birthday for Gino" 185
Bischoff, Samuel 138, 155, 157, 160
Bishop, Wes 181
Bishop, William 183
Bissell, Whit 183
Bitzer, G.W. 115
Blaché, Herbert 120

Black, Bill 175, 176
Black, Maurice 110, 137, 145
Blackwell, Carlyle, Jr. 164
Blackwell, Robert 183
Blair, Henry 174
Blair, Joan 163
Blair, June 175
Blake, Gladys 164
Blake, Loretta 114
Blake, Madge 183
Blanc, Mel 186, 187
Blanchard, Dudley 113
Blandick, Clara 49, 137, 172
Blane, Sally 34, 43, 124, 125, 129
"The Blarney Stone" 182
Blees, William 85
Bleifer, John 185
Bletcher, Billy 112, 113, 136, 140
Blind Husbands 21
Blinn, Holbrook 21
Bliss, Ted 182
Block, Ralph 128
Blondell, Joan 50, 100, 140, 151, 155, 175
Blondie of the Follies 50, 141
Blue, Ben 178
Blue, Monte 30, 171
The Blue Coast 130
"Blue Moon" 175
Blum, Sammy 134
Blunier, De Don 151
Blunt, Robert 172
Blystone, Stanley 138, 167
Blythe, Betty 143
Boag, Wally 181
Boardman, Eleanor 118, 120
Boardman, Virginia True 138
Bob Hampton of Placer 14
The Body Punch 19
Boemler, George 156, 174
Bogart, Humphrey 44, 80, 133, 162, 170
Bohnen, Roman 159
Boland, Mary 67, 153, 170
The Bold and the Beautiful 101
Boles, Glen 130
Boles, John 44, 53, 134, 143
Bolton, Guy 120
Bond, Lilian 138
Bond, Lyle 174
Bond, Ward 138, 154
Bondi, Beulah 61, 88, 148, 170
Bonheur, Stella 158
Boniface, George C. 123
Boniface, Symona 111
Bonnell, Paul 183
Bonnell, Peter 183
Bonnell, Susanna 183
Bonner, Marjorie 119
"Bonnie Lassie" 182
Boone, Pat 183
Booth, Frank H. 130
Borden, Eddie 159
Borden, Eugene 184
Bordoni, Irène 40, 127
Borg, Sven Hugo 182
Borget, Diane 151
"The Borrowed Duchess" 115

Borzage, Frank 30, 31, 122, 123
Borzage, Lew 124
Boss, May 178
Boswell, Connie 187
Bosworth, Hobart 129
Boteler, Wade 129, 134, 136, 138, 142, 145, 148, 159
Bouchey, Willis 185
Bourne, George 140
Bow, Clara 56, 106
Bowen, Harry 139, 153
Bowker, Aldrich 163
Bowles, Phil 176
Bowman, Lee 83, 169
Boyd, Bill "Hoppy" 44, 46, 134, 135
Boyd, William "Stage" 40, 51, 119, 128, 129, 142, 180
Boyer, Charles 131, 143
Boyer, Hal 148
Boylan, Malcolm Stuart 159
Boyle, Betty 187, 188
Boyle, Edward G. 139, 168
Boyle, Joe 146
Boyle, Robert 176
Bracey, Sidney 117, 125, 131, 133, 135, 137, 160
Bracken, Eddie 180
Brackett, Charles 31, 124
Bradford, James C. 119
Bradford, Lane 181
Bradley, Bart 185
Bradley, Grace 156
Bradley, Oscar 187
Bradshaw, Charles 171
Brady, Ed 134, 137, 150
Brainerd, Eleanor Hoyt 114
Bramley, William 176
Brand, Jolene 181
Brand, Max 137
Brandon, Henry 161
Braughall, Jack 117
Bray, Billy 158
Bray, Robert 174
Brayton, Margaret 186, 187
Breakfast in Hollywood 88, 170
Breakston, George 151
Brecher, Egon 161
Breese, Edmund 130
Bregman, Buddy 185
Bremen, Leonard 183
Breneman, Ida 170
Breneman, Tom 88, 170
Brennan, Walter 129, 142, 154
Brent, George 127
Brent, Lynton 159
Brereton, Tyrone 120
Bressart, Felix 162
Bretherton, Howard 127
Brewster, Diane 183
Brewster, June 145, 149
Brian, Mary 63, 149
Brice, Fanny 30, 79
Brice, Monte 124
Bricker, George 167
"Bride 66" 132
Bridge, Loie 172

Briggs, Don 186
Briggs, Harlan 157
Briggs, Jack 165
Bright Skies 13, 117
Brinley, Charles 138
Brinton, Helena 169
Briskin, Samuel J. 157, 158
Bristol, Howard 176
Bristow, Jimmy 159
Broadbent, Aida 163
Broadhurst, George 123
Broadway Limited 80–81, 106, 164
Broadway to Hollywood 39
Brocco, Peter 141
Brock, James 132
Brockwell, Gladys 127
Broderick, Helen 74, 79, 80, 157, 160, 163
Brodie, Buster 165
Brodie, Don 146
Brodine, Norbert 128, 134, 136, 149, 154, 155
Brodszky, Nicholas 174
Broekman, David 129, 130, 133, 142, 143, 180
Broken Lullaby 48, 137
Bromfield, Louis 162
Bromley, Sheila 145, 146
Bronson, Betty 128
Bronson, Lillian 170, 183, 185
Brook, Clive 140
Brooke, Hillary 162
Brooke, Tyler 131
Brooks, Barbara 169
Brooks, Laura K. 173
Brooks, Louise 106
Brooks, Ralph 142, 159
Brooks, Rand 164
Brooks, Rolland M. 175
Brooks, Sammy 110
Brophy, Edward 154
"Brother Love" 132
Brower, Robert 117, 173
Brown, Anthony 129
Brown, Everett 172
Brown, Gilmor 97
Brown, Harry J. 129
Brown, Harry Joe 46, 51, 135, 139, 142, 149
Brown, James S., Jr. 141
Brown, Joe E. 43, 87, 96, 132, 178, 180
Brown, Johnny Mack 50, 141, 148
Brown, Karl 115, 117, 123
Brown, Martin 127
Brown, Melville W. 110, 123, 124, 125
Brown, Raymond 154
Brown, Rowland 159
Brown, Tom 61, 81, 148, 164
Brown, W. Graham 115
Brown, W.H. [William H.] 117
Browne, Charles A. 137
Browne, Earle 127, 128
Brownlee, Frank 132
Bruce, Kate 115
Bruckman, Clyde 154
Brunelli, Peter 147

Brunner, Arthur 182
Brunton, William 116
Bruzlin, Alfred 144
Bryant, Nana 171
Bryar, Paul 182, 185
Buchanan, Edgar 184
Buchanan, Jack 40, 127, 131
Buck, Ashley 135
Buck Privates 34, 125
Buckland, Wilfred 114
Buckner, Robert 171
Bucquet, Harold S. 122, 136
Buell, Jed 77
Bufford, Daisy 160
Buggy, Niall 142
Bulaski, Lyle Latell 171
Bumbaugh, Hal 128
Bunny, George 128
"Bunny Hop" 175
Buono, Victor 181
Burbank, Monroe W. 171
Burgess, William 115
Burke, Billie 80, 87, 88, 162, 170, 180
Burke, Edwin J. 54, 128
Burke, James 153, 155, 173
Burke, Joseph 119
Burke's Law (television series) 104, 182
Burnett, Frances Hodgson 114
Burnett, Paul 151
Burnham, Frances 116
The Burning Trail 19
Burns, Bob 143, 186
Burns, Bobby 111, 112
Burns, David 180
Burns, Edmund 31, 124
Burns, Fred 166
Burns, William J. 127
Burnstine, Norman 126
Burr, Raymond 181
Burress, William 143
Burtis, James P. 56, 112, 113, 139, 141, 149
Burtis, Thomson 142
Burton, Bernard W. 144, 154, 170
Burton, Clarence 118, 128
Burton, Frederick 148, 149, 154
Burton, George 153
Burton, Robert 184
Burton, Val 138, 141, 151
Busch, Mae 144, 155
Bush, Dorothy 158
Bush, James 131
The Business of Love 29, 122
Busley, Jessie 162
Butler, David 13, 115, 116, 118, 123
Butler, Fred J. 118
Butler, James 161
Butler, Jimmy 151, 164
Butler, Richard E. 178
Butler, Rye 174
Butterworth, Ernest 115
Buttolph, David 147
Buzzell, Edward 145
By Request 89
"Bye Bye Banshee" 184
Byington, Spring 142

Byrd, Ralph 80, 155, 161
Byrne, Rosalind 120
Byrnes, Edd 184
Byron, A.S. "Pop" 140
Byron, Arthur 61, 148
Byron, George 110
Byron, Marion 146

Cabanne, Christy 31, 123
Cabo, Louise 124
Cabot, Bruce 64, 80, 148, 150, 161, 182
Cadwallader, Charles L. 120
Cady, Frank 185
Cady, Jerome 165
Cady, Jerry 166
Caesar, Arthur 150
Caesar, Sid 178
Cagney, James 175
Cahn, Edward L. 130
Cahn, Philip 155
Cahn, Sammy 174
Caillou, Alan 185
Caine, Georgia 158
Cairns, Dorothy 132
Calkins, Johnny 171
Callahan, Margaret 85, 155
Callahan, Mushy 142
"Calling Scotland Yard" 185
Callis, David 149
Callow, Ridgeway 174
Calloway, Cab 52
Calvert, E.H. 134
Calvin, Henry 181
Cameron, Anne 147
Cameron, Rod 182
Campbell, Alan 165
Campbell, Colin 184
Campbell, Eric 9
Campbell, Evelyn 118
Campbell, Howard 180
Campbell, Margaret 123
Campeau, Frank 114
Campos, Rafael 175
Candy Hits by ZaSu Pitts 32, 33
Cane, Charles 180
Canning the Cannibal King 9, 109
Cannon, Adele 172
Canova, Judy 67, 155
Cantor, Eddie 30
Canutt, Tap 178
Caplan, Harry 151
Capra, Frank 78, 102
"Capri" 182
"Captain Courageous" 185
"Captain Daddy" 185
"The Card Shark" 185
Careless 145
Carey, Leonard 183
Carey, Leslie I. 172, 174
Carillo, Leo 76
Carle, Richard 132, 148
Carleton, Claire 184
Carlisle, Mary 133
Carlisle, Robert 142
Carlson, Bob 178
Carlson, Lane 174
Carlson, Richard 80, 95, 163, 180

Carlyle, Grace 120
Carman, T.A. 132, 135
Carmichael, Hoagy 186
Carney, Alan 178
Carney, Art 180
Carol, Sue 170
Caron, Patricia 127
Carpenter, Horace B. 166
Carr, Alexander 144
Carr, Harry 125
Carr, Mary 28, 122, 134, 152
Carr, Nat 124, 160
Carradine, John 147, 154, 179
Carré, Ben 131
Carrillo, Leo 67, 152, 159
Carroll, John 131
Carroll, Nancy 41, 42, 43, 48, 128, 129, 137, 188
Carruth, Milton 130, 172, 176
"Carry Me Back to the Lone Prairie" (song) 75
Carson, Jean 183
Carson, Robert 183
Carter, Louise 137, 141
Cartledge, Bill 159
Casanova Brown 129
Case, Edythe 183
"The Case of the Absent Artist" 181
"The Case of the Chinese Puzzle" 184
"The Case of the Music Box Thief" 184
Casey, Dolores 151
Casey at the Bat 33, 34, 124
Caspary, Vera 149
Cass, John L. 148
Cass, Maurice 160, 163
Castello, Willy 155
Catch as Catch Can 46, 106, 110
Cates, Opie 187, 188
Catholic Motion Picture Guild 30
Cathrey, George 162
Catlett, Walter 68, 75, 143, 155, 157
Cavanaugh, Hobart 157, 160
Cavanna, Elise 160
Cavender, Glen 157, 160
Cavendish, David 172
Ceballos, Larry 127, 128
Cecil, Edward 120, 123
Cecil, Mary 187
Cecil, Nora 112, 129, 146, 169
Cedar, Ralph 125
Cedric 136, 141
Chadwick, Helene 28, 122, 133
Chaffin, Ethel P. 122
Chain Lightning 19
Challenger, Percy 117
Chamberlain, Howland 172
Chambers, Shirley 149
Chambers, Woodrow 182
The Champ 91
Chandler, Chick 178
Chandler, Eddy 134, 135, 151, 154, 163
Chandler, George 139, 154, 164, 165

Chaney, Lon 11, 105, 115
Changing Husbands 20, 119
Channing, Carol 92
Chaplin, Charles 9, 106, 110
Chaplin, Minnie 110
Chaplin, Syd 110
Chapman, Blanche 152
Chapman, Edythe 14, 30, 114, 117, 122, 127
"Charity Bazaar" (television sketch) 95, 179
Charters, Spencer 141, 147
Chase, Alden 159
Chase, Barrie 178
Chase, Charley 45, 56, 113
Chase, Ilka 133
The Chase and Sanborn Hour 186
Chatterton, Ruth 39, 126, 129
Chautard, Emile 14, 117
Cheatham, Jack 156
Checker, Chubby 176
"Checkmate" 182
Chefe, Jack 143, 167, 171
Chertok, Jack 180
Chervin, Bert 178
Chester, Charva 94
Chevalier, Maurice 140
Chevret, Lita 128, 139
Chevrier, Lita 121
The Chevrolet Tele-Theatre 92, 179
Childs, Hugh 178
Child of Divorce 90
Child Star 56
"The Chimpanzee" 182
Chisholm, Robert 132
Chivra, Alex 153
The Chorus Girl's Romance 14, 17
Christy, Dorothy 136, 149
Churchill, Berton 141, 145, 151
Cinémathèque 27
Cisar, George 184
Claire, Bernice 41, 128
Claire, Gertrude 119, 120
Clanton, Jimmy 175, 176
Clark, Carroll 132, 134, 135, 139, 140, 145, 146, 165
Clark, Dan 137
Clark, Dr. H.H. 4
Clark, Fred 182
Clark, Ken 184
Clark, Marguerite 152
Clark, Russ 154
Clark, Wallis 137, 143, 147
Clarke, Grant 124
Clarke, Harvey 135
Clarke, John 179
Clarke, Kenneth B. 123
Clarke, Robert 182
The Clash 122
Clatworthy, Robert 174
Clayton, Dick 81, 165
Clayton, Ethel 31, 116, 117, 124, 141
Clayton, Gilbert 128
Clement, Dora 163
Clements, Stanley 179
Clensos, Steven 178
Cleveland, George 154
Clifford, J. 134

Clifford, Jack 113
Clifton, Bernard 158
Clifton, Herbert 145
Cline, Edward 158, 159
Clinton, Larry 186
"Clip That Coupon" 185
Clipped Wings 54
Close, John 174
"Club Tonic Blues" 175
Clute, Chester 146, 164
Clyde, June 49, 136, 137, 143
Clymer, John B. 125
Cobb, Edmund 138
The Cock-Eyed Cruise 157
Cody, Lew 31, 44, 45, 51, 63, 116, 123, 134, 135, 142, 149
Coe, Charles Francis 152
Coe, Peter 183
Coffee, Lenore J. 121
Coffey, James 174
Coffin, Tristram 83, 84, 167
Coghlan, Junior [Frank Jr.] 46, 123, 131, 135, 164
Cohan, Morrie 137
Cohen, Emanuel 149
Cohen, Octavus Roy 135
Cohn, Alfred A. 120
Cohn, Harry 129, 137
Cohn, Martin G. 139
Colberg, Rev. James P. 104
Colbert, Claudette 74, 79, 140
Cole, Art 178
Cole, Frederick 120
Cole, Nat "King" 88, 170
Cole, Peter 183
Cole, Roger 173
Cole, Slim 110
Coleman, C.C., Jr. 137
Coleman, Charles 134
Coleman, Elizabeth 139
Coleman, Majel 124
Collar, Tab 178
Collier, Richard 175, 182
Collier, William, Jr. 120, 135, 136
Collier, William, Sr. 51, 142
Collins, Anthony 161, 163
Collins, Cora Sue 48, 56, 136, 143
Collins, [G.] Pat 130, 135, 142
Collins, Monte 112, 120
Collins, Phil 107
Collins, Ray 172
Collyer, June 134
Colman, Ronald 18, 120, 172
Colmans, Edward 184
Colombo, Alberto 155
Colombo, Russ 186
Colonna, Jerry 76, 79, 159, 160, 185
"Come Back Little Beatnik" 185
Come Out of the Kitchen 128, 129
Come Out of the Pantry 129
Come Up Smiling 158
Comer, Sam 170, 173
Compson, Betty 9, 20, 120
Compton, Joyce 139, 142, 169
Compton, Juliette 139
Conaty, James 170
Condon, Frank 120

Conklin, Chester 15, 118, 121, 123
Conklin, Heinie 130, 153
Conklin, William 119
Conley, Joseph 185
Connelly, Edward 119
Connelly, Marc 140, 186
Conners, Barry 138
Connolly, Walter 129
Connors, Chuck 182
Connors, Mike 183
Conrad, Eugene 164, 165
Conrad, Mikel 172
Conried, Hans 166
Considine, John W., Jr. 152
Considine, Tim 181
Conte, John 187
Conte, Robert 173
Conti, Albert 125, 131, 137
Converse, Lawrence 17
Conway, Gary 182
Conway, Jack 152
Cook, Clyde 136, 141
Cook, Donald 49, 138
Cook, Donn 133
Cook, John 109
Cook, Madge Carr 152
Cook, William Wallace 113
Cooke, Baldwin 110
Cooke, Johnnie 109
Coombs, Carol 171
Cooper, Alice 170
Cooper, Edna Mae 116
Cooper, Gary 66, 70, 102, 104, 140, 187
Cooper, George 121, 141
Cooper, Gordon 124
Cooper, Henry St. John 31, 124
Cooper, Jackie 3087,
Cooper, Merian C. 140, 145, 146, 147, 148
Cooper, Miriam 118
Cooper, Olive 155
Coote, Robert 161
Copping, Cecil 128, 133
Corbett, Lois 184
Corbin, Virginia Lee 120
Corday, Mara 174
Cordelia (play) 87–88, 188
Corden, Henry 185
Cording, Harry 40, 126
Corey, Jim 153
Corey, Joseph 180
Corlett, Irene 182
Cornthwaite, Robert 182
Corrado, Gino 132
Corrigan, Lloyd 165, 178
Corsaro, Franco 182
Corson, William 159
Cortez, Ricardo 50, 139
Coslow, Sam 128
Costello, Dolores 30, 123
Couch, Bill 178
Couch, Chuck 178
"Country Love" 117
Counts, Eleanor 167
Courtney, Inez 155
Cowan, Ashley 185
Cowan, Jerome 171, 185

Cowan, Sada 119
Coward, Noël 83
Cowl, Jane 87
Cox, David 138
Cox, Don 134
Cox, Terry 134
The Cradle of Souls 115
The Cradle Snatchers 170
Cradle Snatchers 84, 169, 170
Craft, Charles 139
Craft, William James 129
Craig, Blanche 138
Craig, Catherine 171
Craig, Nell 154, 159
Cramer, Richard 136, 154
Crane, Phyllis 156
Crane, Ward 124
Crane, William H. 118
Cranston, Joe 182, 183, 185
Crashing Society 155
Craven, Frank 145
Crawford, Broderick 80, 162
Crawford, Diana 184
Crawford, Joan 28, 30, 66, 74, 122
Crawford, Philip 178
Crawley, Paul Roe 141
Creber, Lewis 181
Crews, Laura Hope 56, 121, 144
Crichton, Kyle 7
Crimmins, Dan 122
Crisp, Donald 31, 124
Crockett, Dick 178
Cromer, Harold "Stumpy" 93
Cromwell, John 126
Crone, George 148
Cronjager, Edward 140, 145
The Crooked Circle 51, 141
Crosby, Bing 66, 186
Crosland, Alan 144
Crosman, Henrietta 148
Cross, H.B. 175
Crothers, Rachel 120
Crouse, Russel 171, 172
Crowell, Josephine 113
Croy, Homer 119
Crutcher, Robert Riley 180
Cruze, James 14, 16, 30, 117, 123, 125, 140, 147, 150, 154
"Crystal Girl" 127
Cuff, Oliver 183
Cukor, George 79
Culver, Lillian 176, 182, 183, 185, 186
Culver, Mary 118
Cummings, Hugh 155, 160
Cummings, Irving 116
Cunard, Grace 129, 134
Cunningham, Cecil 139
Cunningham, Jack 109
The Curious Miss Carraway (play) 100, 101, 188
The Curious Savage (play) 102, 188
Curley, Pauline 128
Curran, Pamela 176, 181
Currie, Finlay 158
Currie, Louise 166
Currier, Frank 123
Currier, Mary 163

Currier, Richard 110, 111, 112, 165
Curtis, Allen 110
Curtis, Anthony [Tony] 172
Curtis, Jack 121
Curtis, Mann 174
Curtiss, Ray 125
Curtiz, Michael 43, 131, 171, 172
Curwood, James Oliver 43, 131
Cutner, Sidney 171
Cutter, Murray 171

Dabney, Virginia 151
Dade, Frances 44, 134
D'Agostino, Albert 166
Daheim, John 176, 178
Dahl, Arlene 172
Daibou, Paul 183
Daily Variety 155
Dakin, Gay Ellen 164
D'Albrook, Sidney 118
Dalby, Alfred 134
Daley, Jack 156
D'Algy, Antonio 123
D'Algy, Helena 122
Dalroy, Rube 165
Daly, Jack 173
Daly, Mark 158
D'Ambricourt, Adrienne 111, 161
Dames 63, 105, 150
Damon, Peter 183
Damonde, Renée 130
Dampier, Claude 158
Dana, Mark 183, 184
Dana, Viola 14, 123, 140
"Dance the Mess Around" 176
Dandridge, Ruby 169
Dandrige, Robert 135
Dane, Karl 123
Danforth, Jim 178
A Dangerous Woman! (play) 88
Daniel, Viora 122
Daniels, Carol 178
Daniels, Mickey 110, 126, 165
Daniels, William H. 120, 123
D'Arcy, Roy 122, 123, 149
Darien, Frank 145, 149, 151, 153
Darling, William 147
Darmour, Larry 141
Darr, Vondell 126
Darrow, John 127
"D'Artagnan of Kansas" 114
Darwell, Jane 60, 84, 143, 147, 188
Da Silva, Howard 179
"A Date with a Wolf" 184
Datig, Fred A. 123
Daugherty, Herschel 171
A Daughter of Luxury 14, 117
Daughters of Today 20, 119
Daumery, Carrie 111, 153, 157
Davenport, Alice 120
Davenport, Gwen 180
Davenport, Harry 118
Davenport, Milla 117, 126
Daves 150
Daves, Delmer 150
Davidson, Bill 160
Davidson, John 141, 164
Davidson, Max 132, 135

Davidson, William B. 139, 142, 146, 164, 169
Davies, Betty Ann 158
Davies, Marion 50, 51, 141
Davies, Richard 184
Davis, Bette 44, 133, 134, 172, 180
Davis, Boyd 171
Davis, Coyla 164
Davis, Edith 87
Davis, George 132, 137, 148, 149
Davis, Lew 166, 167
Davis, Lisa 182
Davis, Miles 159
Davis, Nancy 87
Davis, Owen 122
Davis, Owen, Jr. 130, 157
Davis, Pat 162
Davis, Tyrell 136
Davis, Walter, Jr. 175
D'Avril, Yola 130
Daw, Marjorie 14, 113, 114, 117
"Dawn" 161
Dawson, Hal K. 159, 187
Day, Clarence 171
Day, Mrs. Clarence 171
Day, Clarence, Jr. 172
Day, Doris 104, 128, 176
Day, Richard 121, 125
"Day of Days" 131
Dazey, Frank 118, 156
Deacon, Richard 185
Deane, Richard 161
De Angelis, L. 151
Deanne, Marjorie 164
"Dear Minnie" 181
Dearing, Edgar 128, 154, 164
DeCamp, Rosemary 172
DeCardo, Paula 159
DeCarl, Nancy 185
De Carlo, Yvonne 169
Declassee 133
de Corsia, Ted 183
Dee, Frances 131
Dee, Sylvia 176
Deely, Ben 17
Deems, Richard 174
DeFore, Don 181
De Francesco, Louis 125, 147
De Grasse, Robert 145
De Grey, Sidney 120
DeHaven, Carter 127
DeHaven, Flora Parker 127
DeKassy, Stephen 182
Del Val, Jean 172
DeLacy, Ralph M. 139
Delaney, Gene 151
Delavanti, Edward 117
DeLeon [De Leon], Walter 135, 140, 153, 187
Delfino, Joe 122
Delgado, Marcel 178
de Liguoro, Eugenio 120
De Lima, Josette 139
Dell, Claudia 137
Dell, Floyd 129
Delmar, Claire 125
De Main, Gordon 153
DeMarco, Anthony 183

Demarest, William 178
De Mario, Anthony 181
DeMille, Cecil B. 20, 90, 119, 187
de Mille, William C. 20, 120, 132
Deming, Norman 176
DeMond, Albert 125, 129
Dempster, Carol 115
Denham, Vera 185
Dennis, Kathleen 174
Dennis, Robert C. 181
Denny, Reginald 30, 123
The Dennis O'Keefe Show 181
DeNormand, George 167, 178
Denver and Rio Grande 8, 94, 173
DePew, Bill 179
Depew, Hap 112, 113
Depew, Joseph 164
De Putti, Lya 34, 125
de Rincon, Paul 155
DeRita, Joe 179
Derr, E.B. 132, 134
"Derricks on in a Hill" 187
de Ruelle, Emile 124
DeSales, Francis 182
A Desert Dilemma 9, 109
"Desirable Alien" 182
Deslys, Kay 113
Desmond, Florence 147
Desperate Trails 17
De Stefani, Joe 161
Destry 49, 138
Destry Rides Again 49, 137
Deutsch, Ernst 161
De Valentina, Rudolpho 115
De Vaull, William 116, 118
Deverich, Nat G. 114
The Devil's Holiday 42, 129
Devine, Andy 92, 137, 179, 187, 188
De Vol, Frank 176
Dew, Eddie 169
Dexter, Anthony 183
Dexter, Brad 183
Dexter, Elliott 120
Diamond, Bobby 181
Diamond, David 154, 155
Diamond, Don 183, 185
Diamond, James 124
Diamond, Selma 179
"Diamonds Are a Girl's Best Friend" (song) 92, 184
Dibbs, Kem 184
Dick, Peggy Chantler 180
Dickerson, Dudley 164
Dickson, Charles 114
Dickson, Helen 154, 173
Dietrich, James 143
Dietrich, Marlene 49, 56, 70
Dietrich, Ralph 138
Dietz, William 134
Digges, Dudley 140
Dillon, Edward 110, 128, 138
Dilson, Clyde 156
Dilson, John 163
"Dimples" 181
[DiMucci], Dion 176
Dinehart, Alan 138
Dinner at Eight 39

Dinty 14
Dione, Rose 143
"Discipline of Ginevra" 115
Diskant, George E. 145
Disney, Roy 181
Disney, Walt 181
Dix, Beulah Marie 31, 116, 117, 124
Dix, Marion 148, 150
Dix, Richard 14, 50, 140
Dixon, Dorothy 141
Dixon, Harry 141
Dixon, Jean 142
Dixon, Mildred 151
Dmytryk, Edward 140, 153
Dockson, Evelyn 169
Dodds, Edward 172
Dodge, Anna 116
A Dog of the Regiment 30
A Dog's Life 9, 110
Doheny, Lawrence F. 175
Dolan, Robert Emmett 169
Don, Carl 181
Donlan, James 139, 142, 143, 157
Donlevy, Brian 70, 156
Donley, Roger 179
Donlin, Mike 51, 136, 142
Donnelly, Ruth 50, 140, 151, 156
Donovan, King 176, 183
Donovan, Mike 142, 154
"Don't Give Up the Ship" 184
"Don't Look at Me That Way" 127
Dooley, Billy 157
Doolittle, Jimmy 156
Doran, Ann 171
Doran, Mary 134
Dore, Adrienne 146
Dorfman, William 165
Doria, Vera 115
Dorian, Charles 152
Dorr, Dorothy 120
Dorr, Lester 151, 154, 163, 167, 170, 173
D'Orsa, Lonnie 132, 169
D'Orsay, Fifi 143
Dorsey, Jimmy 186
Doty, Douglas Z. 148
"Doubling for Lora" 124
Doucet, Catherine 180
Dougherty, Virgil "Jack" 18, 19
Douglas, Diane 151
Douglas, Gordon 111, 164
Douglas, Kenneth 143
Douglas, Melvyn 128
Douglas, Paul 100, 175
Douglas, Tom 137
Dove, Billie 14, 40, 50, 117, 133, 141
Dowling, Joseph 118
Downen, Don 157
Downey, Morton 129
Downing, Joe 85, 179
Downing, Rex 161
Doyle, Laird 148
Doyle, Maxine 151
Drake, Christian 183
Drake, Dona 169
Draper, Ruth 115
"Dream Dancing" 175

INDEX

Dreaming Out Loud 166
Dreier, Hans 137, 151, 153, 156, 169
Dressler, Marie 48, 66, 169
Drew, Clay 153
Drew, Donna 113
Drew, Ellen 78, 159
Dreyer, Dave 149
"Drinking Song" 132
Dru, Joanne 181
Dudley, Robert 170
Duff, Donald 148
Duff, Gordon 179
Duff, Warren 138
Dugan, Cal 116
Dugan, Tom 155
Duke, Vernon 175
"Dulcy" 68, 186
Dull, Orville O. 132, 168
Dumbrille, Douglass 51, 141, 182, 183
Dumke, Ralph 184
The Dummy 2, 39, 126
Dummy's Vote 147
Dunbar, Helen 116, 119
Duncan, Arletta 143
Duncan, Bud 110
Duncan, Kenne 161
Duncan, Captain Ted 125
Dundee, Jimmie 149, 171, 173
Dunham, Art 178
Dunn, Bunny 123
Dunn, Eddie 111, 112, 133, 166, 169
Dunn, Emma 44, 133, 137, 171
Dunn, James 54, 144
Dunn, Johnny 175
Dunn, Linwood G. 178
Dunn, Ralph 157
Dunn, Winifred 133
Dunne, Elizabeth 160
Dunne, Irene 52, 53, 90, 143, 171
Dunne, Steve 183
Dunstedter, Eddie 96
Dupar, Ed 180
DuPar, Edwin B. 162
Durand, David 133
Durant, Don 184
Durant, Jack 154
Durante, Jimmy 51, 60, 141, 146, 179, 180
Durfee, Minta 179
Durkin, James 136, 137
"Dutch Treat" 185
"Dutch Treatment" 183
Duval, Georgette 183
Du Val, Joseph 187
Du Vaull, William 116
Dvorak, Ann 136
Dvorak, Geraldine 131
Dwan, Allan 114
Dwan, Isabelle 183
Dye, John 105
Dyer, William 113, 118
Dyrenforth, Harold 182

Eames, Peggy 125
Earle, Edward 135, 148
Early to Wed 31, 123
Eastwood, Clint 93, 181
Eaton, Jay 133, 141
Eberle, Ed 137
Eburne, Maude 46, 66, 67, 136, 138, 149, 153
Eddings, Ruth 151
Eddy, Helen Jerome 113, 125, 131, 140
Edesa, Joe 178
Edeson, Arthur 130, 138
Edeson, Robert 119
Edginton, May 119
Edmunds, William 161
Edouart, Farciot 156, 173, 178
Edwards, Alan 159
Edwards, Edgar 164
Edwards, Neely 146
Edwards, Sara 165
Edwards, Sarah 153
Edwards, Snitz 118, 122
Edwards, Ted 110
Edwards, Walter 114, 115, 144
Egan, Jack 164
Egan, Mary 151
Eilers, Sally 62, 148
Einstein, Harry 186
Elam, Jack 180
Eldredge, George 167
Elkas, Edward 119
Ellington, Duke 174, 175
Elliott, Bill 110, 155
Elliott, Dick 167, 170, 182, 183
Elliott, Edythe 145
Elliott, Frank 119, 171
Elliott, John 123, 137, 138
Elliott, Laura 173
Elliott, Lillian 137, 152
Elliott, Robert 142, 161
Elliott, Ross 176
Elliott, Scott 185
Elliott, Walter 178
Ellis, George D. 147, 157
Ellis, John 151
Ellis, Kenneth M. 138
Ellis, Patricia 74, 157
Ellis, Paul 122
Ellis, Robert 129
Ellwanger, W.T. 158
Emerson, Hope 181
Emert, Oliver 174
Emery, Gilbert 159, 161
Emmett, Fern 159, 165
Engel, Roy 179
Engle, Billy 139
English, Kay 128
Englund, Ken 163
Enright, Florence 144
Enright, Ray 63, 150, 157, 160
Epper, Gary 178
Epper, Stephanie 178
Erdman, Richard 181
Erickson, F. 153
Erickson, Knute 126, 127
Erlenborn, Ray 125
Ernest, George 137
Errol, Leon 44, 82, 125, 133, 165, 166
Erwin, Stuart 50, 128, 140

Eslick, Roy 140
Esmelton, Fred 118
Esmond, Jill 50, 139
Essay, Chris 185
Estabrook, Howard 140
The Eternal City 18
Eternally Yours 80, 88, 161
Evans, Brooke 169
Evans, Herbert 153
Evans, Madge 39, 48
Evans, Nancy 172
Evans, Rex 182
Everybody Loves Opal (play) 103–104, 188
Eyman, Scott 25

A Face in the Crowd 175
Fain, Matty 175
Fain, Sammy 151
Fairbanks, Douglas 9, 114
Fairbanks, Douglas, Jr. 42, 129
Faire, Virginia Brown 19
Fairfax, James 182
The Falcon's Adventure 90
Falk, Peter 179
Fall, Richard 134
Fallon, Charles 153
"Family Reunion" 185
Fanchon the Cricket 7
Fancy Pants 154
Fanning, Frank 157, 163
Fargo, Dorothy 5, 6, 10, 12–13, 29, 33, 71, 90, 103, 104
Farley, Dot 15, 118, 129
Farley, Jim 115, 143, 148, 165, 166
Farley, Morgan 129
Farmer, Richard 173
Farnham, Joseph 26, 120, 122, 131
Farnum, Joe 123
Farnum, William 169
Farrar, Stanley 187
Farrell, Charles 31, 60, 124, 146
Farrington, Betty 158
Farrow, John 46, 135
Farwell, Frances 174
The Fast Set 20, 120
Faulkner, P.J., Jr. 150
Faure, John D. 181
Faust, Marguerite 121
Fawcett, George 11, 115, 119, 125, 135, 145
Fay, Hugh 116
Faye, Herbie 176
Faye, Julia 119
Faylen, Frank 164, 172
Faythe, Gloria 151
Fazenda, Louise 15, 51, 95, 118, 128, 142, 170
Feld, Fritz 165
Feldary, Eric 182
Feldman, Gladys 119
Fell, Norman 179
Fellows, Edith 148, 151
Fellows, Robert 127
Felton, Verna 186, 187
Fenton, Leslie 29, 30, 122
Fenwick, Jean 163
Ferguson, Al 156, 173

Ferguson, Casson 114
Ferguson, Frank 171, 175
Ferguson, Perry 147
Ferrari, William 168
Ferrell, Ray 180
Ferrell, Todd 180
Fessier, Michael 162
Fette, Lillian 55
Fetter, Ted 175
Feuer, Cy 160, 161
Fibber McGee and Company 186
Fibber McGee and Molly 77, 186
Field, Mary 162, 166, 170, 171
Field, Salisbury 126
Field, Sylvia 96, 180
Field, Virginia 80, 162, 171
Fielding, Margaret 127
Fields, A. Roland 172
Fields, Dorothy 169
Fields, Herbert 169
Fields, Ron 107
Fields, Stanley 137, 148
Fields, W.C. 65, 105, 107, 151, 186
Fifer, Henry 137
The Fifth Commandment 137
52nd Street 76, 159
Fijal, Jarrett 121
Fillmore, Russell 87
Film Daily 154
Fine, Budd 127, 142
Fine, Larry 146, 179
Finian's Rainbow 76
Fink, Adolph 134
Finley, Murrel 132
Finn, Arthur 158
Finn and Hattie 44, 133
Finn and Hattie Abroad 133
Finston, Nat 170
Fischbeck, Harry 129
Fisher, Howard 146
Fitzgerald, Cissy 113, 124
Fitzgerald, Edith 132
Fitzgerald, F. Scott 14
Fitzmaurice, George 127
Fitzpatrick, Janet 158
Fitzroy, Emily 30, 122, 123
Fitzroy, Louis 110
Fix, Paul 143, 157, 173
Flame of Youth 17
Flanagan, Frank 151
Flannagan, Bud 156
Flannery, William 170
"The Flattering Word" (play) 92, 179
Flavin, James 143, 145, 159, 161, 163, 179, 180, 182
Flavin, Martin 132
Fleischer, Max 52
Fleming, Una 115
Fleming, Victor 114
Flexner, Anne Crawford 151
Flick, Pat C. 157
Flick, W.D. 147
Flint, Sam 151
Flippen, Jay C. 182
The Flirt 133, 134
Florey, Robert 155

Flowers, Bess 137, 162, 163, 175, 176
Flying Colors 57
Flynn, Gertrude 176
Fogel, Sydney M. 128
Follies on Horseback 77
Fong, Harold 173
Fontanne, Lynn 46, 136
Foolish Wives 21
Footner, Hulbert 117
"For Money or Love" 183
For the Defense 14, 117
Forbes, Brenda 81, 165
Forbes, Mary 133
Forbstein, Leo F. 126, 157, 160, 162, 171
Force, Charles 110
Ford, Francis 137
Ford, Glenn 102
Ford, Harriet 126, 127
Ford, Harrison 11, 114, 115, 144
Ford, Hugh 152
Ford, John 17, 71
Ford, Paul 179
Ford, Tennessee Ernie 187
"Foreign Intrigue" 182
Forman, Tom 118
Forrest, Allan 121
Forrest, [Charles] David 160
Forrester, Elizabeth 111
Forrester, Ross 187
Forsyth, Charlie 187
Fort, Garrett 149
Fort Apache 71
Fortson, Henry 117
Forty 157
Forty Naughty Girls 76, 158
'49–'17 113
Foster, Donald 186
Foster, Harve 164
Foster, Helen 125
Foster, Norman 49, 58, 137, 145, 186
Foster, Ray 171
Foti, Jacques 176
Foulger, Byron 170
Foulk, Robert 162, 180
Fountain, Leatrice Gilbert 19
Fowler, Almeda 112
Fowler, Brenda 153
Fowler, Gene 143
Fowler, Gene, Jr. 177
Fowley, Douglas 83, 167, 184
Fox, Allan 156
Fox, Earle 30
Fox, Michael 182
Fox, Sidney 44, 51, 133, 142
Fox, Stuart 186
Fox, William 122, 141
Foxe, Earle 123, 137
Franciosa, Anthony 100, 175
Francis 92–93, 172, 173, 174
Francis, Alec B. 29, 118, 122
Francis, Arlene 176
Francis, Kay 44, 132
Francis, Noel 142
Francis Covers the Big Town 173
Francis Goes to the Races 173

Francis Goes to West Point 173
Francis in the Haunted House 173
Francis in the Navy 173
Francis Joins the WACS 93, 106, 173
Francisco, Betty 118
Franey, William [Billy] 15, 9, 109, 110, 119, 149
Frank, Bernice 118
Franke, Chris 163
Franklin, Irene 155
Franklin, Pearl 29, 122
Franklin, Sidney 136
Franz, Eduard 172
Fraser, Stanley 185
Frawley, William 185
Frazer, Robert 141
Freberg, Stan 179
Fredericks, Eleanor 128
Free Love 44, 133
Freed, Al 142
Freed, Martin 184
Freeland, Thornton 136
Freeman, Devery 173
Freeman, Helen 154
Freeman, Howard 171
Frees, Paul 173, 176
French, Charles K. 138
French, Dick 151, 163
Freudeman, A.E. 156
Freund, Karl 130, 132, 133, 143
"Friday the Thirteenth" 183
Friderici, Blanche 139, 147
Friedberger, Ansel 149
Friedhofer, Hugo 138
Fries, Otto 111, 112
Friganza, Trixie 30, 123
Froman, Jane 179
Frome, Milton 185
Frost, Warren 184
Frye, Dwight 161
Frye, Gil 183, 185
Fuller, Dale 25, 118, 121, 125
Fulton, James F. 121
Fulton, Maude 43
Fung, Willie 131, 141, 146, 153
Funicello, Annette 181
Furey, Barney 147
Furness, Betty 60, 145, 147
Furthman, Jules 124

Gable, Clark 39, 66, 67, 74, 75
Gabourie, Fred 178
Gaddis, Peggy 124
Gadsden, Jacqueline 119
Gaffney, Edward 121
Galindo, Nacho 183
Gallagher, Richard "Skeets" 49, 61, 128, 138, 147
Gallagher, Robert 176
Gallery, Ann 87, 94
Gallery, Don 18, 19, 55, 71, 74, 75, 100–102
Gallery, Tom 13, 14, 15, 17, 30, 39, 70, 108, 117, 118
Gallico, Paul 142
Gamble, Jerry 125
The Gambler and the Lady 160

Index

Gambling Daughters 134
Gan, Chester 146, 157
Garber, David S. 149
Garbo, Greta 18, 56, 61, 66, 74
Garcen, Anthony 174
Garden, Helen 131
Der Gardeoffizier 136
Gardiner, Becky 131
Gardiner, Reginald 96, 180
Gardner, Arthur 130
Gardner, Ed 89
Gardner, Jack 117, 165
Gargan, Edward 148, 163, 164
Gargan, Jack 161, 164, 166, 173
Gargan, William 60, 146, 147
Garland, Richard 183
Garland, Robert 87
Garner, James 104, 176
Garnett, Tay 40, 127, 161, 162, 165
Garon, Pauline 120, 155
Garrick, Douglas 186
Garrick, John 43, 132
Garris, Phil 174
Garson, Henry 180
Garvin, Anita 112
Gary, Myron 187
Gas, Sir Frederick 179
Gasnier, Louis J. 118
Gaspar, Chuck 178
Gates of Hollywood 140
Gaudio, Tony 130
Gausman, Russell A. 172, 174
Gavin, James 182
Gavin, John 49, 143
Gaxton, William 64, 150
The Gay Bride 66, 152
Gaye, Gregory 142
Gaye, Mildred 138
Gaynor, Janet 31, 66, 124
The Gazebo 102
Gear, Luella 171
Geary, Bud 141, 147, 164
Geary, Dick 178
Gelbart, Larry 176
Geld, Gary 176
Geldart, Clarence 139
Gemora, Charles 111
General Electric Theater 95, 179
"The Genius" 180
Gentlemen Prefer Blondes 92
George, Maude 125
George, Muriel 158
George White's Scandals 106
Georgiade, Nicholas 179
Geraghty, Carmelita 128
Geraghty, Tom J. 125
Gerard, Carl 117
Geray, Steven 184
Gerdes [Gordes], Emma 114, 115
Gericke, Eugene 161
Germain, Larry 176
Germonprez, Louis 121, 125
Gerrard, Charles K. 135
Gerrard, Douglas 127
Gerrard, Henry W. 128
Gerry, Alex 176
Gershe, Leonard 180
Gershenson, Joseph 174, 176

Gerstad, Merritt 161
Gerstenberger, Emil 134, 140
Gertz, Irving 173
Getchell, Sumner 145
Geva, Tamara 150
"Ghosts Aboard" 184
Gianaclis, Nicholas 90
Gibbons, Cedric 121, 122, 123, 131, 132, 152, 156, 168
Giblyn, Charles 133
Gibson, Billy 149
Gibson, Florence 121
Gibson, James 121
Gibson, Julie 169
Gibson, Tom 109, 110
Gibson, Wynne 60, 146
Gilbert, Billy 45, 110, 111, 112, 113, 141, 163
Gilbert, John 19, 39, 106
Gilks, Alfred 125, 153
Gillespie, Dizzy 159
Gillette, Ruth 148
Gillingwater, Claude 118, 123
Gillis, Jackson 181
Gilman, Guy 145
Gilmore, Lowell 182
Gingold, Hermione 76, 158
Girard, Joseph 9, 113
A Girl in Every Port 106
The Girl from Mexico 165
The Girl from Montmartre 18
The Girl Who Came Back 14, 118
"Girls! Girls! Girls!" 182
Gish, Lillian 11, 22, 97, 115
Gittelson, June 149
"Give Me a Moment Please" 130
Glass, Gaston 118
Glassberg, Irving 149, 172, 173
Glassmire, Gus 159
Glazer, Benjamin 121, 123
Gleason, James 40, 43, 44, 46, 51, 61, 68, 74, 76, 127, 134, 135, 141, 147, 155, 157, 158
Gleason, Lucile 145
Gleason, Russell 130, 134, 155
Glendinning, Hone 158
Glenn, Glen 167
Glenn, Louise 179
Glennon, Bert 119
"The Glow Worm" 170
Gluskin, Lud 166, 186
Goddard, Paulette 112, 128
Godfrey, Sam 151
Godsoe, Harold 170
Goehring, George 176
Goetz, E. Ray 127
Goff, Norris 82, 83, 166, 187, 188
Goin' to Town 67, 166
Going Highbrow 67, 69, 155
Gold, Ernest 177
Golden, John 145
Golden, Robert S. 170
The Goldfish 20, 119
Goldwyn, Samuel 172
Golitzen, Alexander 161, 174, 176
Gombell, Minna 144
Gonder, William 117
Gone with the Wind 78

Gonz, Rudolf 186
Good Night, Paul 11, 114
Good Time Girl 141
"Goodbye Doctor" 185
"Goodbye Kiss" 182
Goodman, Art 178
Goodman, John B. 156
Goodner, Carol 180
Goodwin, Harold 115, 130
Goodwins, Leslie 165, 166
Gorcey, Leo 179
Gordes, Emma 113
Gordon, Bert 142, 154, 156
Gordon, C. Henry 135, 140, 141
Gordon, Dorothy 118
Gordon, Harry 175
Gordon, Huntley 121, 150
Gordon, James B. 178
Gordon, Julia Swayne 124, 125, 137
Gordon, Leon 134
Gordon, Mary 138, 146, 157, 163
Gordon, Maude Turner 137, 139, 143, 155
Gordon, Robert 134
Gordy, Berry, Jr. 176
Gorss, Sol 160, 178
Gosfield, Maurice 176
Gottell, Oscar 121
Gottell, Otto 121
Gould, Dave 148, 162
Gould, Sid 176
Gould, William 160
Gould-Porter, Arthur 184
Goulding, Edmund 42, 129, 141
Goullet, Arthur 158
Gover, Mildred 151
Gowan, Dorothy 128
Gowland, Gibson 21, 121, 164
Grace, Charity 184
Graham, Betty Jane 136
Graham, Eddie 158, 160
Graham, Marion 163
Graham, Tim 173, 175, 176
Gran, Albert 124, 129
The Grand Dame 57
Grand Larceny 14
La Grande Illusion 54
Granger, Bertram C. 173
Granger, Dorothy 110, 142, 146, 156
Granstedt, Greta 136, 142
Grant, Lawrence 14, 134
Grant, Richard 174
Granville, Bonita 88, 139, 170
Granville, Fred 115
Granville, Roy 178
The Grapes of Wrath 84
Grapewin, Charley 61, 148
Grassby, Bertram 117
Grauer, Ben 186
Graves, Ralph 20, 119, 162
Gravina, Cesare 121, 122, 123, 125
Gray, Alexander 41, 128
Gray, Bee Ho 121
Gray, Feild 157, 158
Gray, Roger 159
Grayco, Helen 179

Graziano, Rocky 176
The Great Divide 28, 121
The Great Love 30, 123
The Greatest Thing in Life 10–11, 115
Greed 1, 2, 21, 22–28, 105, 107, 120
Green, Al 151
Green, George 127
Green, Harry 128, 147
Green, Howard J. 148
Green, Jack 162
Green, Mitzi 128, 133
"Green Dice" 147
Green Dice 147
"Green Light" 176
Greene, Harrison 138, 156, 160
Greene, James 111, 112, 113
Greene, John L. 180
Greene, Joseph J. 171
Greene, Lorne 185
Greenleaf, Raymond 184
Greenwood, Charlotte 87
Greenwood, Winifred 116
Greer, Jesse 175
Gregory, Grace 170
Greig, Robert 143, 146
Grenzbach, Hugo 169
Grey, Jack 165
Grey, John 158
Grey, Nan 155
Grey, Shirley 143, 144
Grey, Virginia 104, 151, 154, 169
Gribbon, Eddie 125, 127
Gribbon, Harry 132
Griffies, Ethel 139
Griffin, Frank 154
Griffin, Robert 185
Griffith, D.W. 10, 115
Griffith, Edward H. 134
Griffith, Julia 112
Griffith, Katherine 114
Griffith, Nina 171
Griffith, Raymond 119, 130
Griffith, William H. 149
Grinde, Nick 49, 137
Groesse, Paul 174
Gromon, Francis 132, 134
Gross, Cordelia Baird 174, 175
Grot, Anton 126
Grove, Sybil 158
Gruber, Frank 173
Gruver, Bernard 178
Guard, Kit 111, 142
The Guardsman 46, 136
Guestward Ho! (television series) 102, 181
Guhl, George 149, 158
Guilaroff, Sydney 174
Guiol, Fred 164, 165
Guise, Tom 120
The Gulf Screen Guild Theatre 187
Gurnee, Gordon 177
Guthrie, Lester D. 181
Guttman, Henry 141
Gwenn, Edmund 74, 156, 171
"Gypping the Gypsies" 183

Haas, Robert M. 151, 171, 172
Hackathorne, George 116, 126
Hackett, Buddy 178
Hackett, Raymond 134, 170
Hackett, Walter C. 150
Hackman, Gene 100
Haddon, Harriette 138
Haefeli, Charles 110
Hager, Captain Eugene 135
Hager, Robert G. 181
Hagerthy, Ron 185
Haggerty, Don 173
Hagney, Frank 127, 131, 147
Hahn, Paul 183
Haig, Douglas 126
Haines, Robert 174
Haines, William 118, 120
Hajos, Karl 126, 130, 142, 154
Hakins, Richard 157
Hale, Alan 31, 124
Hale, Barbara 181
Hale, Creighton 15, 30, 118, 120, 123, 172
Hale, Louise Closser 117, 127, 154
Haley, Jack 67, 68, 154
Half a Hero 140
Half Gods 133
Hall, Alexander 159
Hall, Ben 139
Hall, Charles D. 110, 130, 143, 149, 164
Hall, Charlie 110, 111, 112, 113
Hall, Cliff 76, 188
Hall, Eddie 164, 165, 169
Hall, Ellen 130
Hall, Geraldine 185
Hall, Henry 136
Hall, Michael 174
Hall, Newton 122
Hall, Sherry 141, 155, 157
Hall, Winter 132
Hall of Fame 186
Hallenberger, Harry 149
Haller, Ernie 162
Halley, Nancy 183
Hallward, Jack 158
Halperin, Victor Hugo 118
Halsey, Forrest 133
Halton, Charles 158
Hamilton, Bill 179
Hamilton, Chuck 138, 163
Hamilton, Cosmo 116
Hamilton, Hale 149
Hamilton, Mahlon 139, 143
Hamilton, Margaret 96, 180, 184
Hamilton, Neil 183
Hamilton, William 140, 150
Hammer, Barbara 180
Hammer, Charles 156
Hammer, Stephen 185
Hammerstein, Arthur 132
Hammond, Marie 187
Hammond, Ruth 172
Hampden, Walter 186
Hampton, Grayce 136
Hamrick, Burwell 114
Hand, Herman 130
Hanemann, H.W. 147, 154

Hanley, James F. 138, 144
Hanlon, Bert 138, 160
Hanlon, Tom 160
Hanna, Betty 186
Hansen, Einar 124
Hansson, Oscar 178
"Happily Unmarried" 184
"Happy Birthday, Captain" 184
"Happy Horoscope" 185
"The Happy Touch" (television sketch) 180
Harbach, Otto A. 128, 163
Harcourt, Cyril 115, 143
Harding, Ann 50, 139
Harding, John 175
Hardt, Eloise 181
Hardwicke, Sir Cedric 182
Hardy, Oliver 48, 56, 111
Hardy, Sam 140, 152
Hare, Lumsden 182
Hari, Wilfred 154
Harlan, Kenneth 28, 118, 122
Harlan, Otis 122, 123
Harlan, Russell 174
Harling, W. Franke 128, 130, 131, 137
Harlow, Jean 18, 67, 128
Harmon, John 183
Harmon, Pat 133, 145
Harolde, Ralf 136
Harper, Patricia 151
Harriet and the Piper 17
Harrington, Pat, Sr. 159
Harris, Elmer 124
Harris, Harry B. 119
Harris, Larry 162
Harris, Marcia 126
Harris, Mildred 128
Harris, Sam 173
Harris, Stacy 179
Harris, Theresa 145
Harrison, Carey 125
Harrison, Doane 128, 141, 156
Harrison, James 165
Harrison, Kathleen 158
Harron, John 144, 160
Harron, Johnny 28, 122
Harron, Robert 115
Hart, Gordon 158
Hart, Lallah 116
Hart, Lorenz 175
Hart, Moss 140, 142, 180
Hartley, Esdras 155
Hartman, Paul 176
Hartnett, James 146
Harvey, Don C. 179
Harvey, Forrester 159
Harvey, George Y. 125
Harvey, Harry 138, 173
Harvey, Lew 122, 127, 153
Harvey, Mabelle 114
Haskett, Ed 174
Haskin, Byron 8, 22, 94, 162, 173
Haskins, Harry 124
"A Hat for Hedda Hopper" 170
Hatch, Riley 119
A Hatful of Rain 175
Hathaway, Joan 172

Hatley, Marvin 113, 164
Hatswell, D.R.O. 125
Hatton, Raymond 34, 50, 118, 119, 125, 141, 157
Haunted Island 19
Haver, June 181
Haver, Phyllis 113
Havey, Maie B. 114
Havlick, Gene 137
Hawks, Howard 114, 170
Haworth, Vinton 165
Hayden, Sterling 94, 173
Haydn, Kay 184
Haydon, Julie 64, 139, 150
Hayes, Allison 174
Hayes, Bernadene 154
Hayes, Frank 116, 121
Hayes, Margaret 180
Hayes, Peter Lind 160
Hayes, Teddy 142
Hayes, W. Donn 146
Hayle, Grace 143, 145, 149, 169
Hayman, Earl S. 140
"Hayride Ahoy" 184
Hayward, Chuck 178
Hayward, Jim 173
Hayward, Susan 143
Hazard, Jayne 169
He Had 'Em Buffaloed 9, 109
Head, Edith 88, 170, 173
Healy, Ted 146, 156
Hearn, Edward 119, 145
Heart of Twenty 14, 117
Heath, Ray 179
"Heaven Scent" 184
Hecht, Ben 143, 154
Hedgcock, William 130
Hedrick, [A.] Earl 169
Heidi 39
Heindorf, Ray 160, 162
Helfer, Robert 178
Hell Below 39
Heller, Gloria 120
Hellier, Jack 158
Hellinger, Mark 162
Hellman, Sam 124
"Hello Mr. Dream" 176
Hello, Sister! 54, 144, 145
Helmore, Tom 158, 175, 184
Helton, Percy 175, 180, 183
Heming, Violet 120
Hemingway, Ernest 17
Henderson, Brenda 164
Henderson, Del [Dell] 152, 153, 155
Henderson, Harold 121
Hendrian, Oscar "Dutch" 149, 154
Hendricks, Ben, Jr. 123, 127, 147
Henigson, Henry 137
Henjum, Bonnie 174
Henley, Hobart 133, 134
Henry, Gale 9, 15, 110, 118
Her Big Night 31, 124
Her First Mate 58, 145
Her First Murder (play) 83, 188
Her Private Life 40, 133
Herbert, Bryan 158
Herbert, Charles 184

Herbert, H.J. 119
Herbert, Holmes 40, 133
Herbert, Hugh 64, 75, 78, 80, 93, 151, 152, 157, 158, 159, 162, 179
Herbert, Jack 115
Here Comes the Clowns 39
Herlihy, Ed 180
Herman, Al 148, 160
Hernandez, Anna 116
Heron, Julia 161, 162
Herrick, Jack 142
Herring, Aggie 120
Herron, Bob 178
Hersh, Ben 166
Hersholt, Jean 20, 22, 29, 34, 35, 113, 119, 121, 122, 125
Hervey, Harry 166
Hervey, Irene 148
Herz, Ralph 154
Herzbrun, Bernard 166, 172
Herzig, Sig 157
Hewlett, Bentley 151
Hibbs, Gene 181
Hibbs, Jesse 160
Hickman, Alfred 135
Hickman, Charles 118
Hickman, Howard 145, 148, 162, 169
Hickox, Sid 150
Hicks, Russell 157, 163
The Hidden Corpse 139
Hiers, Walter 117
Hiestand, Bud 186
Higgin, Howard 119
Higgins, Harvey J. 126
"High and Low" 132
Highway of Life 39
Hilburn, Percy 121
Hildebrand, Rodney 124
Hill, Al 161, 162, 164
Hill, Doris 124
Hill, Hallene 172, 176
Hill, Jack 111
Hill, Josephine 142
Hill, Ramsay 183
Hilliard, Harriet 186
Hilton, Arthur 137
Hilton, Lester 172
Hines, Harry 175
Hines, Margie 52
Hirschfeld, Al 106
His Fatal Beauty 9, 109
His, Hers and Theirs 43
"A Hit in Tahiti" 183
Hively, George 141
Hoadley, C.B. 109, 110
Hoagland, Ellsworth 170
Hobbes, Halliwell 160, 161
Hodges, Bert S. 146
Hodgins, Earle 156, 166, 181
Hodgson, Leyland 142, 162
Hoffe, Arthur 180
Hoffman, Al 174
Hoffman, Gertrude 169
Hoffman, Max, Jr. 163
Hoffman, Otto 120, 166
Hoffman, Renaud 120
Hogan, Dick 164

Hogan, Michael 161
Holbrook, Allen 138
Hold That Tiger 154
"Hold That Tiger" 182
Holden, Joyce 180
Holderness, Fay 113, 116
Holdren, Judd 173
Hole, Jonathan 183, 185
Holiday, Billie 159
Hollaender, Friedrich 170
Holland, Billy 158
Holland, Edna 175
Holland, John 164, 184
Hollander, Howard 175
Hollingsworth, Alfred 116
Hollingsworth, Harry 158
Holloway, Carol 160
Holloway, Sterling 34, 113, 124, 145, 179
Hollywood 15
Hollywood on the Air 186
Holman, Harry 147, 151, 166
Holmes, Ben 157, 159
Holmes, Elsie 174
Holmes, Kenneth 145, 163
Holmes, Maynard 148, 164
Holmes, Phillips 48, 63, 129, 137, 140, 149
Holmes, Stuart 46, 111, 118, 139, 158, 160
Holmes, Taylor 154
Holt, Jack 43, 129
Holt, Nat 173
Holt, Ralph 131
Holubar, Allen 115
Homans, Robert 132, 149
Home Struck 30
Home Stuff 14
Home Wanted 39
Honey 41, 128
The Honeymoon 35, 37, 126
"The Honeymoon Suite" 185
Hong, James 185
"Honolulu Honeymoon" 183
"Honolulu Native" 183
Hoover, Hyram A. 156
Hope, Bob 84, 154, 169, 180, 187
Hopkins, Bob 185
Hopkins, [George] James 171, 172
Hopkins, Miriam 171
Hopper, Dennis 181
Hopper, De Wolf 124
Hopper, E. Mason 115
Hopper, Hedda 48, 131, 170, 181
Hopper, William 181
Hopton, Russell 142, 143
Horman, Arthur 147
Hornblow, Arthur, Jr. 153
Horne, James W. 111
Horning, William A. 174
Horsley, David S. 172, 174
Horton, Edi 33
Horton, Edward Everett 29, 50, 67, 77, 81, 87, 92, 122, 140, 148, 154, 155, 166, 179, 186
Horvath, Charles 180
Hot Off the Wire 181
Hot Tip 68, 155

Housman, Arthur 29, 122, 124, 126, 129, 151, 154
How Could You, Jean? 11, 114
"How to Catch a Man" 184
"How to Make Enemies" 185
Howard, Boothe 153
Howard, Curly 146
Howard, David 120
Howard, Fred 137, 149
Howard, Gertrude 136
Howard, John 156
Howard, Kathleen 81, 165
Howard, Mary 161
Howard, Moe 146, 179
Howard, Sidney 133
Howard, Tom 186
Howard, William K. 135, 138
Howdy, Folks! 29, 122
Howe, James Wong 144
Howell, Dorothy 129
Howell, Virginia 143
Howes, Reed 110, 142, 157
Howland, Jobyna 129, 142
Howland, Louis 116
Howland, Olin 149
Hoy, Danny 125
Hoy, Robert F. 178
Hoyos, Rodolfo, Jr. 183, 186
Hoysradt, John 180
Hoyt, Arthur 14, 117, 123, 140, 142, 147, 149
Hoyt, Harry O. 125
Hoyt, John 182
Hsieh, Warren 183
Hubbard, Lucien 119
Huber, Chad 122
Hubert, Axel, Sr. 180
Hubert, René 131, 154
Hudkins, John 178
Hudson, Rochelle 60, 139, 147
Hughes, J.J. 117
Hughes, John J. 135
Hughes, Lloyd 133, 145
Hull, Arthur Stuart 120, 162
Hull, Frank E. 120, 125, 144
Humberstone, H. Bruce 138, 139, 141
Humbert, George 169
Humphrey, Hal 88
Hunt, J. Roy 126, 146, 147
Hunter, C. Roy 129, 130, 143
Hunter, Glenn 119, 140
Hunter, Ian 159
Hunter, Jeffrey 181
Hunter, Ross 176
Huntley, Fred 115
Hurst, Brandon 133
Hurst, Fannie 53, 123, 143
Hurst, Paul 127, 132, 136, 144, 149
"Hustlin' Newsgal" 175
Hutchinson, Josephine 114
Hutchinson, Max 170
Hutton, Betty 84, 169
Hutton, Beulah 143
Hutton, Lucille 120
Hyams, John 147
Hyams, Leila 30, 153
Hyer, Martha 93

Hyland, James 174
Hymer, Warren 83, 142, 145, 154, 167
Hytten, Olaf 155

"I Can't Get You Out of My Mind" 167
"I Got It Bad and That Ain't Good" 174
I Know My Love 94
"I Wait" 176
"I Want to Be Happy" 163
"I Wonder What Is Really on His Mind" 127
"If I Had a Wishing Ring" 170
Ignon, Gui 161
"I'll Follow the Trail" 132
The Illustrious Corpse 50, 138
Im Westen nichts Neues 130
"I'm a Little Negative" 127
"I'm Gonna Live Till I Die" 174
"An Imaginary Personal Appearance Act for ZaSu Pitts" (monologue) 95
Imazu, Eddie 168
"The Immigrants" 182
"The Imposter" 118
The Imposter 118
"In Conference" 149, 150
Ince, John 138
Ince, Ralph 135
"Indian Giver" 182
"The Indian Givers" 183
Indrisano, John 154, 157, 184
Ingle, Red 170
Ingraham, Lloyd 142
Ingram, Jack 26
Ingram, Rex 120
Irene 162
Iribe, Paul 119
The Iron Chalice 135
Irvin, Gregory 185
Irvine, Richard 162
Irving, George 124, 133, 137, 141, 147
Irving, Paul 163
Irving, William 130
Irwin, Charles 183
Irwin, Coulter 183
Is Matrimony a Failure? 14, 117
Is My Face Red? 50, 139, 140
The Island of Lost Heels 113
It All Came True 80, 106, 162
"Italian Movie Actress" 182
It's a Mad Mad Mad Mad World 104, 105, 177
"It's Better to Be Yourself" 170
"It's Magic" 186
"It's Murder My Dear" 185
"It's Only Money" 183
Ivano, Paul 121, 166
I've Got to Sing a Torch Song (Merrie Melody Cartoon) 61
"I've Got You Under My Skin" 175
Ivers, Julia Crawford 114, 115

The Jack Pearl Show 146
The Jackie Gleason Show 180
Jackson, Cornwall 105

Jackson, Dickie 162
Jackson, Eugene 160
Jackson, Harry 185, 186
Jackson, Horace 44, 128, 132, 134
Jackson, Howard 129, 162
Jackson, Peaches 115
Jackson, Selmer 137, 160
Jackson, Thomas E. 170
Jackson, Warren 166
Jacoby, Annalee Whitmore 167
Jaffe, Sam 141
Jagger, Dean 94, 156, 173
"Jailmates" 185
James, Chuck 183
James, Irene 183
James, Jeri Lou 182
James, Jerry 169
James, Peter 179
James, Rian 164
James, Walter 162
Jamieson [Jamison], Bud 110, 111, 112, 125, 140, 159
Janes, Loren 178
Janie 101
Janie Gets Married 101
Janney, Leon 46, 134, 135
Jannings, Emil 38, 126
Janssen, David 93
Janssen, Werner 161, 162
January, Lois 156, 170
Jaquet, Frank 162
Jarrett, Art 153
Jarrett, Daniel 145
Jarvis, Sydney [Sidney] 111, 113, 124
Jason, Sybil 114
The Jazz Singer 39
Jefferson, Thomas 116
Jeffrey, Paul 117
Jeffrey, William 155
Jeffries, Herb 78
Jeffries, James 30
Jenkins, Allen 57, 75, 79, 145, 157, 160, 179, 186
Jenkins, Burke 117
Jenkins, Dan 183
Jennings, Devereaux 133
Jennings, DeWitt 122, 147
Jennings, Gordon 156
Jensen, Eulalie 120
Jensson, Eloise 181
Jergens, Diane 176
"The Jet" 176
Jett, Sheldon 149
Jewell, Austen 121
Jewell, Edward C. 128, 129
Jewison, Norman 176
The Jim Backus Show 181
Jiménez, Soledad 141
Jobson, Edward 118
Joby, Hans 125, 149
Johnson, Carmencita 151
Johnson, Don 169
Johnson, Ellen 169
Johnson, Emory 115
Johnson, Helen 132
Johnson, Jack 51, 142
Johnson [Johnston; Johnstone], Julanne [Julianne] 116, 118

Johnson, Julian 125, 126
Johnson, Kay 44, 132, 150
Johnson, Laurence E. 132
Johnson, Marv 176
Johnson, Richard 178
Johnson, Rita 171
Johnson, Stanley E. 173
Johnston, Agnes Christine 118
Johnston, Harvey 159
Jolson, Al 39, 77, 186
Joker Comedies 9
Jones, Bernie 179
Jones, Buck 29, 122, 186
Jones, Grover 125, 159
Jones, Jennie 13
Jones, Marcia Mae 123
Jones, Morgan 184
Jones, Park 110
Jones, Robert C. 177
Jones, Spike 170, 179
Jones, Stanley 151
Jones, Tiny 121, 138, 166
Jordan, Bert 164
Jordan, Dorothy 148
Jordan, Jim 186, 187
Jordan, Ted 173
Jory, Victor 171
Joslyn, Allyn 185
Jowett, Corson 136, 139, 165, 172
Joy, Gloria 115
Joy, Leatrice 19, 20, 119
Joyce, Alice 30, 31, 34, 35, 123, 125, 126
Joyce, William Ogden 175
[Joyner], Joyzelle 141
Judels, Charles 46, 111, 162
Judge, Arline 139, 140
Juettner, John 156
June, Ray 127, 132, 152
"Just You, Just Me" 175
Justice Rides Again 49, 138

Kaaren, Suzanne 148, 156
Kadler, Karen 174
Kahle, Alexander 145
Kahn, Gordon 160
Kaliz, Armand 127, 153
Kandel, Aben 148, 154
Kane, Eddie 129, 142, 151
Kane, Joseph 135
Kane, Robert 154
Kane, Sid 175
Kaplan, Marvin 173, 179
Karath, Jimmy 182
Karath, Kym 176
Karlin, Bo Peep 138
Karloff, Boris 97, 185
Karlson, Phil 155
Karnes, Robert 179
Karns, Roscoe 41, 43, 51, 116, 128, 129, 141
Karrigan, Tom 143
Karson, Lee 97
Kasha, Al 176
Kashuk, Martin 178
The Kate Smith Show 187
Katz, Lee 157
Kaufman, Edward 146, 155

Kaufman, George S. 140, 142, 180, 186
Kaufman, Rita 144, 147
Kaufman, Willy 161
Kaun, Bernhard 139, 140, 142, 146
Kay, Edward 167
Kay, Kathleen 123
Kaye, Danny 170
Kaylin, Samuel 148
Kean, John [K.] 178
Keane, Edward 147, 164
Keane, Robert Emmett 151, 184
Kearns, Jack 142
Keating, Fred 156, 162
Keaton, Buster 96, 106, 179, 180
Keckley, Jane 153
Keefe, Cornelius 133, 148
Keeler, Ruby 63, 80, 151
Keene, Mike 185
Keener, Hazel 118
Keith, Debbra 169
Keith, Robert 136, 137
Kelland, Clarence Budington 122
Keller, Walter E. 166
Kelley, Barry 182
Kelley, James T. 110
Kelly, Carol 183
Kelly, James 122
Kelly, John 142, 147
Kelly, Lew 142, 147, 154, 156, 157
Kelly, Patsy 57, 80, 81, 104, 106, 164
Kelman, Ricky 181
Kelsey, Fred 115, 138, 142
Kelso, Edmond 167
Kelso, Mayme [Maym] 113, 116, 117
Kelton, Pert 61, 62, 147, 148
Kemble-Cooper, Lillian 185
Kemp, Kenner G. 147, 176
Kendall, Cy 161
Kendall, Don 184
Kennedy, Douglas 172
Kennedy, Edgar 50, 57, 74, 139, 145, 157
Kennedy, Edith 117
Kennedy, Jack 154, 156
Kennedy, Robert 182
Kennedy, Tom 30, 125, 141, 142, 159, 165, 179
Kenny, Jack 159
Kent, Dorothea 163
Kent, Lenny 176
Kent, Marshall 181
Kent, Robert 164
Kent, Ted J. 133, 134, 143, 173, 174
Kent, Walter 174
Kenton, Erle C. 118
Kenyon, Charles 131
Kenyon, Gwen 164, 167
Kern, Hal C. 128, 132
Kern, James V. 180
Kern, Robert 121, 132, 168
Kerr, Charles 148, 150, 161, 166
Kerr, Donald 155, 159, 165, 167, 169
Kerr, Jane 153, 154

Kerrigan, J.M. 155
Kerry, Norman 11, 114, 115
Kersh, Kathy 182
Kesselring, Joseph O. 146
Keystone Kops 106
Kibbee, Guy 64, 67, 69, 83, 89, 143, 151, 155, 169
Kibbee, Milton 151, 155
"The Kid from Korea" 183
Killmond, Frank 185
Killy, Edward 148
Kim, Joseph 173
Kimble, Lawrence 162
King, Bradley 126, 139
King, Claude 145, 146
King, Emmett 139
King, George 76, 158
King, James 178
King, Joe 138, 178
King, John 156
King, Walter Woolf 154
Kingdon, Julie 156
Kingsford, Walter 157
Kingsley, Sidney 39
Kinney, Clyde 138
Kinskey, Leonid 81, 164
Kirk, Charles 148
Kirkham, Kathleen 114
Kirkland, Hardee 117
Kirkpatrick, Charles C. 181
Kirkwood, James 14, 20, 120, 129
Kirley, Jim 145
Kish, Joseph 177
Kissane, Ruth 178
"Kissin' Game" 176
Klaffki, Roy H. 125
Klages, Raymond 175
Klatzkin, David 155
Kleeb, Helen 185
Klein, Philip 138
Knapp, Evalyn 50, 131, 141
Knechtel, Alvin 126
Knopf, Edwin 133
Knotts, Don 179
Knowland, Senator Joseph 100
Knox, Elyse 81, 165
Knudsen, Peggy 182
Knudtson, Frederic 177
Kober, Arthur 140, 146
Kodak Presents: Disneyland '59 181
Koessler, Walter 129, 133
Koffman, Jack 151
Kohler, Fred 126
Kohlmar, Fred 169
Kohlmar, Lee 153
Kohner, Frederick 130
Kolk, Scott 130
Kolker, Henry 117, 145, 146, 154
Komai, Tetsu 141
Kongthong, Jessica 121
Kopell, Bernie 176
Korda, Alexander 40, 126, 133
Kornman, Mary 110, 113
Kortman, Bob 149
Kosleck, Martin 161
Kosloff, Theodore 119
Koszarski, Richard 121
Kowall, Mitchell 174

The Kraft Music Hall 186
Kraft Television Theatre 95, 180
Kramer, Stanley 104, 177
Krasna, Norman 145, 146
Krasner, Milton 149
Kreig, Frank 182, 185
Kreitsek, Howard B. 175
Kruger, Faith 172
Kruger, Fred 185
Kruger, Paul 174
Krugman, Lou 183
Krumgold, Sigmund 130
Kruschen, Jack 180, 184
Kulky, Henry 183
Kulp, Nancy 182, 185
Kurland, Gilbert 143, 149, 155
Kurland, Norton 172
Kurrle, Robert 131, 141
Kuter, Kay E. 184
Kuter, Leo E. 123

Ladd, Alan 142
The Lady's from Kentucky 78, 95, 159
A Lady's Name 11, 115
Laemmle, Carl, Jr. 129, 130, 133, 134, 137, 142, 143, 144, 145, 149
Laemmle, Edward 122
Lahr, Bert 96, 180
Laidlaw, Ethan 134
Laird, John 173
Lait, Jack 142
Lake, Alice 127
Lake, Florence 50, 139
Lake, Stuart N. 125
Lally, Howard 148
Lally, Mike 145
La Mal, Isabel 153, 154
La Marr, Barbara 16–19, 118
La Marr, Margaret 138
Lamont, Charles 173
Lamont, Marten 166
Lamour, Dorothy 186
Lancaster, Lucy 182
Lanchester, Elsa 97
The Land of Jazz 17
Landau, David 143
Landau, Lucy 176
Landi, Elissa 74, 156
Landis, Cullen 117
Lane, Allan 111
Lane, Charles 147, 179, 183, 185
Lane, George 178
Lane, Nora 138
Lanfield, Sidney 147, 169
Lang, Charles 151
Lang, Walter 146
Langan, Glenn 182
Langdon, Harry 78
Lange, Arthur 135, 154
Lange, Elaine 172
Lange, Mary 151
Langford, Frances 88
Langton, Basil 158
Lanoy, André 123
Lansing, Bror 178
Lansing, Joi 182
Lansing, Mary 138

La Plante, Laura 31, 124, 144
La Rocque, Rod 20, 40, 119, 128
La Roy, Rita 132, 136
Larsen, Kitty 184
Larson, Dr. Edwin 61
Larson, Jack 176
La Rue, D'Ette 185
La Rue, Fontaine 119
LaRue, Frank 142
La Rue, Walt 178
Lasky, Jesse L. 95, 125
"A Lass in Alaska" 183
Laszlo, Ernest 177
The Late Christopher Bean (play) 89, 90, 92, 188
Latell, Lyle 180
Latimer, Louise 157
La Touche, John 175
Lau, Fred 162
Lau, Wesley 181
Lauck, Chester 82, 83, 166, 187, 188
Laughton, Charles 66, 67, 97, 153, 154, 180, 187
Laurel, Stan 12, 48, 56, 58, 60, 111
Lauren, Jane 187
Laurie, Piper 93
Lauritzen, Gene 173
Lauter, Harry 179
Lava, William 161
Lavelle, Kay 112
La Verne, Lucille 119
Law, Burton 109
Lawler, Anderson 139
Lawrence, Mady 166
Lawrence, Marc 145
Lawrence, Vincent 130
Lawrence, William E. 114
Lawshe, Ed 117
Lazarus, Jeff 159
Lazybones 2, 29–30, 122
Leander Clicks 155
LeBaron, William 140
LeBlanc, Lee 174
LeBow, Guy 108
Lee, Danny 178
Lee, Davey 129
Lee, Fred 138
Lee, Gai 184
Lee, Gwen 122
Lee, Jocelyn 124, 127, 128, 145
Lee, Kendall 132
Lee, Lila 14, 117, 127, 183
Lee, Ruth 184
Lee, Sam 152
Lee, Warren 183
Leeds, Andrea 146
Leezer, John W. 117
Legend of Hollywood 20, 120
LeHane, Susan Reilly 185
Lehman, Gladys 129, 134, 143
Leiber, Fritz 161
Leicester, James 171
Leigh, Leona 128
Leighton, Lillian 115, 116, 117
Leighton, Linda 183
Leipold, John 125, 129, 130, 140, 151, 159

Leisen, Mitchell 70, 156
Lencer, Major M.H. 172
Lennart, Isobel 174
Lennig, Arthur 21, 22, 35, 53
Leonard, Ada 159
Leonard, Gus 136
Leonard, Queenie 171, 183, 184
Leopold, Ethelreda 151, 163, 164
Le Paul, Paul 162
LeSaint, Edward 137, 139, 153, 159
Leslie, Joan 101
Lesser, Len 175
Lesser, Sol 121
Lessy, Ben 179
Lester, Kate 119
Lestina, Adolph 115
Le Sueur, Anna 170
Le Sueur, Lucille 122
"(Let's Do It) Let's Fall in Love" 127
Let's Do Things 45, 110
Let's Face It (film) 84, 169, 170
Let's Face It! (musical) 170
"Let's Not Talk About Love" (song) 84
Let's Pretend 158
"Let's Twist Again" 176
Leuterer, Sasha 121
Levant, Oscar 89
LeVanway, William 123, 131
Le Vernie, Laura 129
Levien, Sonya 147
Levinus, Carl 127
Levitt, Ed 178
Lewin, Albert 136
Lewis, Bobo 179
Lewis, Buddy 182
Lewis, David 147
Lewis, Gene 144, 157
Lewis, George 115, 125
Lewis, Harold 139, 170
Lewis, Jerry 179
Lewis, Ralph 118, 122
Lewis, Robert Q. 185
Lewis, Vera 116, 146, 147, 160, 165
Libbey, J. Aldrich 121
Lieb, Harry 129
Lief, Max 136
Life with Father 76, 90, 91, 106, 171
The Lifebuoy Show 186
Lightfoot, Morey 111
Lime, Yvonne 184
The Limited Mail 30
Linaker, Kay 169
Lincoln, Caryl 143, 148
Lincoln, Elmo 115
Lind, Billie 117
Linder, Mark 129
Lindgren, Harry 128, 170
Lindon, Lionel 169
Lindsay, Howard 145, 171, 172
Lindsay, Kathleen 180
Lindsay, Lois 151, 164
Lindsay, Margaret 142
Lindsay, Robert H. 180
Linkletter, Art 181
Linn, James 173

Linow, Ivan 110
Lion of Hollywood 25–26
Lissner, Ray 147
Litel, John 162
Little Accident 42, 129
The Little Grey Mouse 17
Little Lord Fauntleroy 114
The Little Match Girl 39
The Little Princess 10, 105, 114
Littlefield, Lucien 48, 50, 57, 68, 118, 128, 137, 139, 145, 153, 154, 186
Littleton, Carol 121
Livetti, Norman 183
Livingston, Margaret 123
Lloyd, Al 160
Lloyd, Art 110, 111, 112, 113
Lloyd, Doris 143
Lloyd, George 149, 154, 164
Lloyd, Harold 13, 106
Lloyd, Rollo 144, 149, 155
The Locked Door 40, 127
Locker, Ann 172
Lockert, John 157, 158
Lockhart, Gene 152, 153, 186
Lockwood, Harold 174
Loder, John 48, 92, 111
Loew, Marcus 25, 26
Loft, Arthur 169
Loftin, Carey 178
Logan, Ella 76, 159
Logan, Jacqueline 30, 123
Loggia, Robert 181
Lomas, Jack 180
Lombard, Carole 66, 152
London, Tom 130, 131, 138
"Lonely Life" 176
"Lonesome's Gal" (television episode) 102, 181
Long, Walter 147
Longet, Gaston 150
Lonsdale, Frederick 20, 120
Lonsdale, Harry 130
Lontoc, Leon 182
Loo, Richard 157
Loos, Anita 51, 92, 141
Loose, Bill 175
Lora, Joan 182, 183
Lord, Billie 46, 135
Lord, Marjorie 158
Lord, Pauline 64, 65, 89, 151
Lord, Robert 150
Lord Epping Sees a Ghost 165
Loring, Hope 115, 127
Lorraine, Harry 118
Lorraine, Leota 153
Lorre, Peter 180
The Lottery Bride 43, 132
Louie the 14th 125
Louis, Jean 176
Lourdes, Cynthia 181
Love, Montagu 40, 133
Love 74
"Love and Kisses" 184
Love Birds 63, 149
"Love by Yiminy" 185
Love, Honor and Oh, Baby! 58, 145

Love, Honor, Oh, Baby! 146
Lovering, Otho 161
Lovett, Josephine 147
"Lovey-Dovey" 184
Lowe, Edmund 41, 74, 128, 156
Lowe, Edward T., Jr. 122, 148
Lowell, Helen 65, 152
Loy, Myrna 28, 40, 122, 126
Lu, Lisa 184
Lubin, Arthur 125, 160, 172, 173
Lubitsch, Ernst 43, 48, 130, 137
Lucas, Wilfred 111
Lucky, Eleanor 184
Lucy, Arnold 130
Luddy, Edward I. 137
Luden, Jack 126
Ludwig, Edward 143
Lufkin, Sam 112, 154
Luick, Earl 131, 135
Lukas, Paul 129
Luke, Keye 163, 183, 184
Lum and Abner (radio) 82, 92, 166
Lum and Abner Abroad 166
The Lum and Abner Show 187, 188
Lundin, Walter 111
Lunt, Alfred 46, 136
Lux Presents Hollywood 68
The Lux Radio Theatre 186, 187
Lydon, Jimmy 90, 171, 182, 183, 184
Lyle, F.R., Jr. 114
Lynch, Warren 121, 151
Lynn, Betty 184
Lynn, Jeffrey 80, 162
Lynn, Rita 184
Lyon, Ben 51, 120, 141
Lyon, Nancy 151
Lyons, Collette 159
Lytell, Bert 18, 179
Lytell, Jack 16
Lytell, Wilfred 119
Lytton, Herbert 174, 184

Mac, Jennie 169
MacArthur, Charles 154
Macaulay, Joseph 132
Macaulay, Richard 160
MacCloy, June 135
Macdonald, Branche 151
MacDonald, Buddy 48, 111
MacDonald, J. Farrell 80, 131, 137, 141, 161, 164, 170
MacDonald, Jeanette 43, 130, 131, 132
MacDonald, Wallace 141, 150
MacDowell, Melbourne 123
Mace, Patsy 164
MacFadden, Hamilton 134
MacFarlane, John 14, 117
Machin, Beryl 184
Mack, Bobbie 9, 109, 110
Mack, Fred 116
Mack, Helen 147, 161
Mack, Hughie 116, 121, 122, 125
Mack, James T. 138, 149
Mack, Joe 138
Mack, Russell 142, 147
Mack, Tommy 164

Mack, Wilbur 127, 141, 149, 153, 157, 167, 184
Mackaill, Dorothy 46, 134
MacKenna, Kenneth 132
MacKenzie, Jack 155, 165, 166
Mackintosh, Louise 133, 137, 143
MacLaren, Mary 145, 159
MacLean, Douglas 151
MacLeod, Mildred 148
MacMahon, Aline 51, 83, 142, 155, 169
MacMurray, Fred 70, 156
Macpherson, Jeanie 119
MacRae, Gordon 128
MacWilliams, Glen 121, 122
Mad Holiday 74, 156
"Made in Hong Kong" 186
Madison, Noel 138
Madison Sq. Garden 51, 142
"Magic Is the Moonlight" 170
"The Magician" 182
Magnolia, Lou 143
Magrill, George 141, 173
Maguire, John 166
Maher, Frank 132
Mahoney, Jock 181
Mahoney, Wilkies 76
"Maid in Sweden" 183
Maids a la Mode 56, 112
Mailes, Charles Hill 115
Main, Marjorie 83, 169
Make Me a Star 50, 140
"Make Mine Music" 184
Malatesta, Fred 115, 118, 153
Mallory, Boots 54, 144
Malloy, Doris 160
Maltby, H.F. 158
Mamakos, Peter 183
"Mambo Cambo" 175
Man-Eating Tiger 154
The Man from Funeral Range 17
The Man I Killed 137
"The Man Who Came to Dinner" (television sketch) 96, 180
Mandel, Frank 128, 163
Mandell, Daniel 132, 134, 149
Mandell, Ethel 149
Mandy, Jerry 110, 160
Mankiewicz, Herman J. 126, 128, 146
Mankiewicz, Joseph L. 44, 126, 133
Mann, Alice 119
Mann, Bertha 129, 130, 133, 135
Mann, Hank 15, 118
Mann, Kal 176
Mannequin 2, 30, 31, 123
Mannering, Cecil 158
Manning, Aileen 117
Manning, Bruce 149
Mansell, Muriel 174
Mansfield, W. Duncan 166
Mantz, Paul 162, 178
Manulis, Martin 180
Marburgh, Bertram 143
March, Fredric 39, 126, 140, 172
March, Joseph Moncure 147
Marchant, Jay 135

Marcin, Max 120
Marcus, James A. 125
Marcus, Morton 107
Marden, Adrienne 156
"Mardi Gras" 183
Marier, Captain Victor 115
Marin, Ned 128, 133, 180
Marinoff, Fania 21
Marion, Frances 9, 10, 11, 51, 91–92, 95, 113, 114, 122, 141
Marion, George, Jr. 125
Marion, George F., Sr. 145
Maris, Mona 142
Mark, Flip 181
Mark, Michael 136, 141
Marks, Arthur 181
Marks, Clarence 145, 149, 155
Markson, Ben 139, 140, 155
Marley, Peverell 124, 171, 172
Marlin, Miriam 146
Marlowe, Alona 127
Marlowe, Nora 175
Marmon, Ben 181
Marmont, Percy 20, 29, 120, 122
Marquette, Desmond 165
Marquis, Margaret 135
Marr, Eddie 159
Marr, James 186
Marsac, Maurice 182, 184
Marsh, Frances 126
Marsh, Joan 114, 115, 129, 130
Marsh, Maude 123
Marshall, George 45, 96, 102, 111, 112, 180
Marshall, Roy H. 116
Marshall, Tully 14, 114, 117, 124, 137, 139
Marshall, Virginia 122
Marshall, William 118
Marstini, Rosita 114
Marston, John 147
Marta, Jack A. 161
Martan, Nita 127
Martel, Arlene 181
Martel, June 67, 155
Martell, Alphonse 132, 148
Martell, Gregg 175
Martin, Andra 184
Martin, Chris-Pin 138
Martin, Dixie 156
Martin, H. Kinley 125
Martin, Jack 172
Martin, John 5
Martin, Marion 82, 165, 166
Martin, Mary 91
Martin, Merry 181
Martin, Richard 166
Martin, Russ 121
Martin, Skip 174
Martindel, Edward 118
Martinelli, Arthur 117
Marton, Frank 187
Mary of the Woods 15
"Mary the Third" 120
Maschmeyer, Dudie 151
Mason, Dan 117, 122, 123
Mason, Jim 140
Mason, Mary 186

Mason, Sarah Y. 14, 49, 117, 137
Masterson, Paul 187
Mather, Aubrey 163
Mathews, Mary 178
Mathieson, Johanna 129
Mathis, June 25, 118, 120, 121
Matthews, A.E. 120
Matthews, Junius 183
Matthews, Lester 181
Mattingly, Hedley 176
Mattox, Martha 118
Mature, Victor 80, 163
Maupin, Clifton 140
Maxey, Paul 182
Maxwell, Edwin 130, 138
Maxwell, John 171
May, Billy 96, 174, 175
May, Doris 15, 118
Mayer, Louis B. 17, 25–26, 27
Mayer, Ray 153, 155
Mayne, Eric 119
Mayo, Frank 160
Mayo, Margaret 126
Mayo, Walter 132
Mayon, Helen 183
Mazurki, Bob 179
Mazurki, Mike 179
McAvoy, May 119
McBan, Mickey 118
McCall, E.M. 109
McCardle, Mickey 173
McCarey, Leo 677, 153
McCarey, Ray 68, 135, 155
McCarthy, Earl 142
McCarthy, M.J. 110
McCauley, Hugh J. 121
McClure, Doug 185
McCormac, Muriel 118
McCormick, Merrill 137
McCoy, Dixie 170
McCoy, Harry 138
McCoy, Wayne 166
McCullough, Philo 119, 172
McCullough, Ralph 162
McCutcheon, Ross 124
McDaniel, George 114
McDaniel, Hattie 145
McDaniels, [Sam] Deacon 141, 142, 164
McDermott, John 117, 118
McDonald, Francis 142, 149, 153
McDonald, Jack 113, 116, 121, 125
McDonough, Joseph A. 149
McDowell, Nelson 112
McFadden, Virginia 128
McFarland, George "Spanky" 56, 113
McGann, William [C.] 171
McGill, Barney 124
McGiver, John 102
McGlynn, Frank 127
McGrail, Walter 131
McGrath, Larry 143, 151
McGraw, Charles 179
McGraw, Danna 174
McGregor, Malcolm 34, 125
McGuire, Tom 153
McGuire, William Anthony 144

McHugh, Frank 57, 145
McHugh, Jimmy 146
McHugh, Kitty 155
McHugh, Matt 148
McIntire, Lani 182
McIntyre [McIntire], John 172
McKay, Belva 124
McKay, Doreen 162
McKay, Patti 174
McKenzie, Robert 147, 159
McKinney, Mira 182
McLaglen, Victor 81, 164
McLean, Bill 175
McLennon, Rodney 137
McLeod, Norman Z. 133
McLernon, Harold 150, 151, 155
McMahon, Leo J. 173
McManus, Louis 112, 113
McMinn, Fraser 173
McNally, Stephen 182
McNamee, Graham 186
McNear, Howard 185
McNutt, Patterson 154
McNutt, William Slavens 151
McRae, Bruce 129
McTaggart, [Malcolm] Bud 167
McTeague 1, 21, 121
McVey, L.S. 110
McVey, Patrick 182
McVey, Tyler 174
McWade, Edward 135, 147, 160
McWade, Robert 142, 143
Meade, Julia 181
Meader, George 169, 172
Meadows, Audrey 180
The Meanest Gal in Town 61, 147
Medcraft, Russell G. 169, 170
Medina, Patricia 172
Meek, Donald 64, 146, 151
Meeker, George 143
Meet the Baron 60, 146
Meet the Mob 167
Meighan, Thomas 51, 127, 142
Meins, Gus 45, 112, 113
Melcher, Martin 176
Melendez, Bill 178
Melford, George 116, 160
Melton, Frank 147
Melton, James 74, 75, 157
Melton, Sid 175, 186
Men, Women, and Money 11, 116
Mendoza, David 135
Menjou, Adolphe 14, 20, 117, 120
Menzies, William Cameron 128, 132
Merande, Doro 102, 180
Mercein, Eleanor 134
Mercer, Beryl 42, 115, 130
Mercer, Frances 184
Mercier, Louis 131
Meredith, Charles 116, 172
Meredith, Cheerio 183
Meredith, Judi 184
Meredith, Madge (née Massow) 90, 105
Merkel, Una 47, 58, 136, 145
Merman, Ethel 178
Merrick, Leonard 117

Merrill, Martha 151
Merry Comes to Town 76, 158
Merry-Go-Round 26
Merton, John 160
Merton of the Movies 50, 140
Mescall, John 120, 132
Mesenkop, Louis 156
Messinger, Buddy 165
Messinger, Gertrude 110, 164
Mestayer, Harry 128
Metcalf, James 172
Methot, Mayo 133
Metty, Russell 158, 163, 165, 170, 176
Mexican Spitfire 165
Mexican Spitfire at Sea 82, 165
Mexican Spitfire Out West 165
Mexican Spitfire Sees a Ghost 165
Mexican Spitfire's Baby 81, 165, 166
Mexican Spitfire's Blessed Event 165
Mexican Spitfire's Elephant 165
Meyer, Fred S. 155
Meyer, Greta 146, 149
Meyer, Torben 137, 161, 163
Mickey the Kid 79–80, 160
Middleton, Charles 64, 147, 149, 151
Midgley, Fannie [Fanny] 14, 114, 116, 117, 121
Miehle, John 145
Mielke, Chad 121
Milasch, Robert 159
Miles, Vera 143
Milestone, Lewis 42, 129, 130
Miljan, John 131
Milland, Ray 133
Millard, Nancy 184, 185
Miller, Alice D.G. 122, 123, 128
Miller, Arthur C. 127
Miller, Christopher 181
Miller, David 143
Miller, Evelyn 154
Miller, Florence 148
Miller, Harold 141, 163
Miller, Henry 121
Miller, Joanna 181
Miller, Lester 183
Miller, Lucille 138
Miller, Mark 181
Miller, Marvin 181
Miller, Patsy Ruth 20, 40, 119, 127
Miller, Rolf 178
Miller, Seton I. 142
Miller, Sidney 136
Miller, Wesley C. 174
"The Million Dollar Mutt" 185
Mills, Billy 186, 187
Mills, Frank 140, 149, 150, 159, 163, 166
Mills, Harry D. 129, 130
Mills, Jackie 175
Milner, Martin 171
Milner, Victor 126, 130, 137
Miltern, John 157
Milton, Annette 101
Milton, Dave 167
Milton, Robert 126, 132, 139
Minardos, Nico 185

Mineo, Michael 172
Mineo, Ralph 172
Mintz, Sam 133, 140
Miracle 122
Misilagi, Falpava 182
Miss Polly 81, 95, 165
Miss Private Eye (play) 95
"Miss Wonderful" 127
Mr. and Mrs. Haddock Abroad 44, 133
"Mr. Belvedere" (television sketch) 96, 180
Mr. Deeds Goes to Town 102
Mister Ed 173
Mr. Skitch 60, 147
Mitchell, Claude 116
Mitchell, Frank 154
Mitchell, Geneva 135, 142
Mitchell, Grant 162
Mitchell, Howard M. 171
Mitchell, Irving 165, 167
Mitchell, Margaret 78
Mitchell, Norma 119, 169, 170
Mitchell, Thomas 129
Mitchum, Robert 97
Mix, Tom 49, 56, 137, 138
"Model Apartment" 183
A Modern Musketeer 9, 114
The Modern Wife 133
Moeller, Philip 136
Mohr, Hal 125, 135
Moler, Helaine 160
Molinari, Ernesto 175
Mollenhauer, William 121
Molnár, Ferenc 136
Monk, Thelonious 159
Monsieur Beaucaire 130
Montagne, Edward 120, 151, 164
Montague, Monte 145, 154, 156
Montana, Bull 120
Monte Carlo 31, 43, 123, 130
Montenaro, A.C. 181
Montgomery, Earl 118
Montgomery, Jack 173
Montgomery, Ray 182
Montgomery, Robert 43, 50, 131, 141
Montt, Christina 120, 148
Moody, Ruth 151
Moody, William Vaughn 121
Moore, Charles R. 142
Moore, Colleen 14
Moore, Dennis 158, 162, 183
Moore, Dickie 133, 134
Moore, Matt 31, 124, 129, 135
Moore, Milton 119
Moore, Robin 183
Moore, Roger 173
Moore, Scott 153
Moore, Tom 28, 122
Moorehead, Agnes 157
Moorhouse, Bert 141
Moraine, Lyle 158
Moran, Frank 145, 160
Moran, Lee 124
Moranti [Moranti], Milburn 9, 109, 110
Morden, Ethan 41

Moreland, Andria 169
Morgan, Bob 173
Morgan, Claudia 142
Morgan, Freddy 179
Morgan, Gene 143, 156
Morgan, Glenn 120
Morgan, Ira H. 116, 122
Morgan, Joe 116
Morgan, Ralph 64, 150
Mori, Toshi 140
Moriarity, Pat 148
Morley, James B. 145, 147
Morris, Carol 184
Morris, Chester 67, 152
Morris, Frances 149
Morris, Johnny 142
Morris, Reginald 124
Morrison, James 120
Mortimer, Edmund 115, 138, 141, 151, 159, 162
Morton, Arthur 154
Morton, James 112, 149
Morton, Michael 117, 118
Moss, Joel 170
Mother of His Children 17
"Mother Steps Out" 185
Mother's Helper 60
Motion Picture Almanac 154
Mougin, Madlyn 125
Moulton, Buck 138
Mowbray, Alan 186
Mower, Jack 156, 160, 163
Moyer, Ray 126
Moyer, Raymond 169
Mrs. Wiggs of the Cabbage Patch 64, 65, 89, 105, 107, 151, 152
Muhl, Edward 176
Muir, Esther 108
Mulhall, Jack 20, 40, 119, 126, 156, 167, 184
Müller, Hans 130
Mulligan, Edward 138
Mundin, Herbert 138, 154
"Murder in a Chinese Theatre" 156
Murder in the Gilded Cage 136
Murder on a Bridle Path 74, 157
Murder on a Honeymoon 74, 157
Murder on the Blackboard 74, 157
Murphy, Audie 49, 138
Murphy, Edna 119
Murphy, Maurice 130
Murphy, Ralph 135, 149, 152
Murray, Feg 186
Murray, John T. 149, 158
Murray, Tom 122
Muse, Clarence 136, 139
Mustin, Burt 176, 184
Musuraca, Nick 148, 157
Mutiny on the Bounty 154
My Heart Belongs 91
My Husband's Wives 17
"My Lover" 127
"My Northern Light" 132
My Square Laddie (record) 96
Myers, Carmel 11, 115
Myers, Harry 123
Myers, Henry 149

Nagel, Conrad 44, 122, 133
Naish, J. Carrol 100, 173, 175, 181
The Name's the Same 179
Nash, Brian 176
Natheaux, Louis 31, 120, 124, 129, 143, 153
National Recovery Administration see NRA
Naughty but Nice 79, 160
Naughty Girls 157
Navarro, Ramon 39
Nay, Frederic 169
Neagle, Anna 80, 161, 163
Nearing, Margaret 146
Negley, Howard 170, 173
Neilan, Marshall 45, 110, 111, 113, 114, 123
Neill, James 116
Neill, Noel 165, 169
Neilson, Lois 6, 11, 12
Nelson, David 181
Nelson, Frank 187
Nelson, Gene 185
Nelson, Harriet 181
Nelson, Karl 181
Nelson, Kirk 181
Nelson, Lori 93
Nelson, Mildred 181
Nelson, Nels P. 181
Nelson, Ozzie 181, 186
Nelson, Ricky 181
Nelson, Stuart 181
Nemo, Charlotte 111
Neptune's Casino
Nervig, Conrad A. 132, 136
Nesmith, Ottola 154
Neumann, Dorothy 176, 183
Neumann, Harry 163
Neumann, Kurt 155
Newall, Guy 158
Newcom, James E. 146
Newell, David 160
Newell, Marie 116
Newell, William 160, 164, 165, 170
Newlan, Paul 160
Newman, Alfred 144, 159
Newman, Anne 176
Newton, Mary 186
Niagara 149
Niagara Falls 81, 144, 149, 164
Niblo, Fred 46, 135
Nichols, Connie 178
Nichols, George 36, 119, 125
Nichols, George, Jr. 125, 126, 129
Nicholson, Kenyon 156
Nicholson, Paul 148
"Nicked in Naples" 182
Nigh, William 154
"A Night in Monte Carlo" 182
The Night of the Hunter 97
"The Nightcap" 120
The Nightcap 120
Niles, Ken 187, 188
Niles, Wendell 187
Niven, David 80, 88, 162, 171
Nixon, Julie 181
Nixon, Marian 30, 51, 123, 142

Nixon, Pat 181
Nixon, Richard 100, 181
Nixon, Tricia 181
"No Breaks" 127
"No Tears for the Captain" 185
"No, No Nanette" 163
No, No, Nanette (1930) 41, 128
No, No, Nanette (1940) 80, 163
Noisom, George 163, 169
Nolan, Tom 181
Nomis, Geraldine 144
Nordstrom, Clarence 138
Norman, Al 159
Norris, Charles G. 134
Norris, Frank 1, 21, 120
Norris, Kathleen 132
North, Robert 127
Northrup, Harry S. 116
Norton, Barry 38, 126, 165
Norton, Cliff 179
Norton, Edgar 120, 131
Norton, Fletcher 128, 139
Norton, Jack 153, 154, 155
Norton, S.S. [Stephen S.] 113
Norwood, Ralph 162
"Nostalgia" 135
"Not Quite Paradise" 180
"Not So Innocents Abroad" 184
Novak, Jane 30, 123
Novello, Jay 182
Novis, Donald 110, 111, 131
Nowell, Wedgwood 160
Noyes, Harold 151
NRA 60
Nugent, Edward 131
Nugent, Elliott 147
"Nugey, Come Home" 185
No. 13 Washington Square 125
Nurse Edith Cavell 80, 161
The Nut 17
Nye, Carroll 126, 132
Nyitray, Emil 163

O Mistress Mine 94
O-My the Tent Mover 9, 109
Oakie, Jack 39, 51, 126, 140, 142
Oakland, Vivien 143
Oakman, Wheeler 167
Oberon, Merle 96, 180
O'Boyle, Mickey 160
O'Brien, Dave 139, 141
O'Brien, Edmond 94, 173
O'Brien, Eugene 113
O'Brien, Margaret 118
O'Brien, Tom 117, 136
O'Brien, William H. 162
O'Brien, William J. 111, 112
O'Brien, Willis H. 178
O'Bryan, Carl 174
O'Byrne, Patsy 153
S.S. *Ocean Queen* 1, 97
O'Connell, Hugh 68, 142, 154, 155
O'Connell, L. William 154
O'Connor, Donald 92, 172, 173, 174
O'Connor, Frank 146, 150, 153, 159

O'Connor, Robert Emmett 158, 169
O'Connor, Una 162
O'Day, Dawn 120, 126
O'Dell, Georgia 154
Odell, Robert 151, 153
Odell, Rosemary 172
O'Donnell, Gene 167
O'Donnell, Spec 124
O'Farrell, Broderick 123, 137, 142, 162
O'Gatty, Jimmy 149
Oggle, Howard 151
Ogilvie, Jack 113, 167
Ogle, Charles 113, 116, 117, 119
"Oh Mary" 176
Oh, Promise Me 145, 146
Oh, Susanna!/The Gale Storm Show 1, 97, 98, 99, 105, 182
Oh, Yeah! 40, 127
O'Hanlon, James 118
O'Hara, Maureen 180
O'Higgins, Harvey J. 126, 127
O'Keefe, Dennis 81, 147, 156, 164, 166, 181
Okey, Jack 126
Oland, Warner 46, 50, 135
The Old Bull 50, 112
"An Old Chinese Custom" 185
Old Shoes 28, 122
"The Old West Per Contract" 113
Oliver, Edna May 60, 74, 80, 146, 157, 161, 170
Oliver, Guy 119, 120, 126, 129
Oliver, Roland 114
Olivier, Laurence 50, 139
Olmstead, Gertrude 31, 123
O'Loughlin, Charles 128, 132, 135
Olsen, Moroni 171
O'Malley, J. Pat 182
O'Malley, Pat 138
"On the Dot" 185
On the Loose 48, 111
Once in a Lifetime 51, 142
"One Captain Too Many" 185
"One Coin in the Fountain" 185
One-Round Hogan 30
One Track Minds 56, 106, 113
"One, Two, Ski!" 185
O'Neal, Anne 154
O'Neil, Barry 21
O'Neil, Nance 134, 135, 139
O'Neil, Nita 124
O'Neill, Alice 132
O'Neill, Eileen 176
O'Neill, Henry 126
O'Neill, Thomas F. 144, 155
Onyx, Narda 182
Orlamond, William 121, 140
Orlando, Don 183, 185
Ormonde, Eugene 114
Ornitz, Arthur J. 175
Orry-Kelly 151, 155
Orth, Frank 164
Osborne, Bud 113
O'Shea, Oscar 166
O'Shea, Ted 165
The Other Half 13, 116

Ottiano, Rafaela 157
"The Ouija Board" 184
"Our Dear Captain" 184
Out All Night 56, 57, 70, 144, 149
Overall-Hatswell, Donald 125
Overbaugh, Roy 129, 135
Ovey, George 169
Owen, Garry 153, 160
Owen, Reginald 176
Owsley, Monroe 133

P. Schulberg Productions 14
Padden, Sarah 141, 170
Padula, Vincent 182, 183
Page, Anita 43, 129, 131
Page, Gale 79, 160
Page, Mann 155
Pagel, Raoul 149
Paggi, M.M. 156
"Painted in Paris" 184
A Pair of Silk Stockings 143
Paiva, Nestor 184, 186
The Pajama Party 46, 111
Pall, Gloria 175
Pallette, Eugene 50, 60, 126, 139, 147
Palm [Palmer], Ernest G. 123
Palmer, Adele 161
Palmer, Ernest 124, 138
Palmer, Maria 184
Palmer, Stuart 74, 157, 158
Palmer, Tom 184
Pandora's Box 106
Pangborn, Franklin 46, 57, 81, 135, 145, 166, 186
Panzer, Paul 29, 122, 141, 155, 158
Papa Loves Mamma 136
Papa sans le savoir 129
Pape, Lionel 162
Papke, Billy 51, 142
"Pardon My Aunt" (television sketch) 95, 179
Paris 40, 127
Paris, Manuel 183
A Parisian Scandal 14
"The Parisian Touch" 183
Parker, Charlie 159
Parker, Dorothy 81, 165
Parker, Franklin 162
Parker, J.F. 110
Parker, Jack 158
Parker, Jean 61, 92, 148
Parker, Max 124, 160, 162
Parker, Suzy 182
Parks, Eddie 182
Parnell, Emory 169
Parrish, George 171
Parrish, Helen 134
Parrish, Robert 130
Parrott, Charles 113
Parry, Harvey 173, 178
Parsons, Kansas 3, 105
Parsons, Lindsley 167
Parsons, Louella 44, 50, 60
Partners in Time 166
Parton, Regis 178
Pasadena Playhouse 97, 100, 101, 102, 103, 104

Pasch, Reginald 133, 137
A Passage to Hong Kong 140
"Passenger Incognito" 182
Passion Flower 44, 132
Pasternak, Joe 174
"Pat on the Back" 183
Paterson, Pat 159
Patrick, Gail 186
Patrick, John 102, 119
The Patriots 39
Patsy 14, 117
Patten, Jane 165
Patterson, Elizabeth 136, 143
Paul, Jad 179
Pawley, Edward 159
Pawley, William 138, 155
Payne, Sally 163
Payson, Blanche 111, 154
Payton, Claude 162
Payton, Lew 159
Peacock, Herbert 187
Peacock, Lillian 9, 109, 110
Pearce, Alice 176
Pearce, George 113, 152
Pearce, Wynn 181
Pearl, Jack 60, 146
"Pearls Before Cecily" 124
Pearson, Humphrey 139, 146, 153, 187
Pearson, LaVerne 179
Pearson, Virginia 143
Peary, Harold 186, 187
Peattie, Elia W. 29, 122
Pederson, Carl 178
Pegler, Westbrook 51, 142
Peil, Edward, Sr. 115, 137
Pemberton, Margaret 139
Pembroke, George 165
Pendleton, Nat 62, 67, 136, 148, 152, 157
Penguin Pool Murder (movie) 74, 157
Penguin Pool Murder (novel) 74
Pennick, Jack 139
Pennington, Ann 122
Penrod 136
Penrod and Sam 46, 135, 136
Pepper, Barbara 159, 169, 179
Percy, David 131
Pereira, Hal 173
Perez, Paul 126
The Perfect Marriage 88–89, 170, 171
The Perfect Snob 135
Perkins, Frank 162
Perkins, Gil 142, 178
Perkins, Jack 178
Perkins, Voltaire 174
Perrin, Jack 162
Perrott, Ruth 184, 185
Perry Mason 181
Perry, Bob 138, 160
Perry, Harry 118
Perry, Jack 137, 149
Perry, Kathryn 31, 124
Perry, Linda 158
Perry, Paul P. 116
Perry, Sam 134, 136

Peters, Susan 83, 169
Petersen, Paul 175
Peterson, Dorothy 136, 159, 164
Petit, Albert 153
Petzoldt, Edward 181
Peyton, Larry 114
"The Phantom Valice" 183
Phelps, Buster 156
Phelps, Lee 139, 141, 145, 153, 163, 170
The Philco Television Playhouse 92, 179
Philips, Terry 176
Phillips, Andre 185
Phillips, Barney 181
Phillips, Bill 180
Phillips, Dorothy 11, 115
Phillips, Eddie 148
Phillips, Howard 138
Phillips, John 174
Phipps, Sally 142
Phipps, William 174
Picerni, Paul 182, 184
Pichel, Irving 139
Pickford, Jack 126
Pickford, Mary 9, 10, 17, 105, 113, 114, 172
Pidgeon, Walter 30, 40, 123, 133
The Pie Eyed Piper 9, 110
Pierce, Andrew 121
Pierce, Jack P. 143, 149
Pierce, James 138
Pierson, Leo 113
Pigott, Tempe 121
Pingree, Earl 152
Pinkard, Maceo 110
Pinte, Andor 134
The Pirate 94
"Pirate Treasure" 183
Pittack, Robert 164, 165, 180
Pitts, Rulandus 3, 5
Pitts, ZaSu 22, 109, 110, 111, 112, 113, 114, 115, 116, 117, 118, 119, 120, 121, 122, 123, 124, 125, 126, 127, 128, 129, 130, 131, 132, 133, 134, 135, 136, 137, 138, 139, 140, 141, 142, 143, 144, 145, 146, 147, 148, 149, 150, 151, 152, 153, 154, 155, 156, 157, 158, 159, 160, 161, 162, 163, 164, 165, 166, 167, 169, 170, 171, 172, 173, 174, 175, 176, 179, 180, 181, 182, 186, 187, 188
Pitts Film Festival 105–106
Pivar, Maurice 129, 130, 137
Planck, Robert H. 128, 136
Playing with Fire 136
The Plot Thickens 74, 157, 159
Plowright, Hilda 185
Plunkett, Walter 148, 155
Poe, Bonnie 52
Poff, Lon 113, 121
Pogany, Willy 151
Polglase, Van Nest 145, 146, 147, 148, 150, 157, 158, 165
Polito, Sol 126, 127, 128, 150
Pollard, "Snub" 140, 180
Pollock, Channing 40, 127
Poor Men's Wives 14, 16, 118

Poor Relations 13, 116
Popeye the Sailor 52
Poppe, Harry 180
Porter, Cole 84, 127, 175
Porter, Del 170
Porter, Don 181
Portman, Clem 145, 178
Portman, Richard 178
"Possibility" 175
Post, Robert 181
Post, Wiley 156
Post Road (play) 93
Potel, Victor 119, 140, 153
Potoker, Oscar 126
Potter, Peter 156
Povah, Phyllis 169
Powell 172
Powell, Dawn 144, 145
Powell, Dick 63, 79, 151, 160, 187
Powell, Paul 115, 117
Powell, Russ 122
Powell, William 90, 171
The Power and the Glory 39
Powers, Len 111
Powers, Pat 34, 35, 125
Powers, Tom 173
Pratt, Gil 111
Pratt, Jack 117
Pratt, Purnell 128, 134, 136, 146
Pratt, Thomas 127, 157
Prentiss, Eleanore 169
Prestidge, Mel 186
Pretty Ladies 28, 122
Previn, Charles 164
Prevost, Marie 43, 131, 156
Price, Evadne 158
Price, Hal 137, 139, 143
Price, Kate 117
Price, Stanley 154
Prima, Louis 159
Prince, John T. 120
Prince, William 180
Pringle, Jessie 129
Prinz, LeRoy 105
Prior, Herbert 133
The Prisoner of Zenda 17
Prival, Lucien 57, 111, 113, 161
Private Scandal 63, 149
Private Secretary 180
Professional Sweetheart 57, 58, 145
The Professor Steps Out 160
Prohaska, Janos 178
Promenade Deck 148
Protection Is a Tough Racket 175
Prouse, Peter 173
Prouty, Jed 129, 149
Provine, Dorothy 178
Provost, Jon 181
Provost, Marie 14
Pryor, Roger 83, 167, 187
Pudge 136
Puglia, Frank 163
Pullen, William 182, 183
Purcell, Irene 51, 139, 141
Purdy, Constance 166
Purdy, Philip 144
Purity Girl 145
Purviance, Edna 110

Pushkin, Alexander 179
Putnam, George 181
Pye, Merrill 123

The Quaker Party 186
Qualen, John 62, 80, 148, 149, 161, 185
Questel, Mae 52
Quillan, Eddie 146
Quillian Family 30
Quimby, Margaret 123
Quine, Richard 83, 169
Quinn, James 127
Quinn, Jimmie 122
Quinn, Tom 157, 163

Raboch, Alfred 168
Radecki, Anthony 174
Radin, Oscar 146
Raft, George 78, 159
Raguse, Elmer 110, 111
Railsback, Howard M. 163
Raksin, David 159
Ralph, Jessie 80, 154, 161
Ralston, Esther 117
Ralston, Howard 118
Rambeau, Marjorie 119
"Ramshackle Inn" 179
Ramshackle Inn (play) 84–87, 94, 188
Rand, Hal 169
Rand, Philip 118
Rand, Sally 31, 124
Randall, Bernard 122
Randall, William 164
Randolph, Isabel 182, 186, 187, 188
Rankin, Spike [Caroline] 118
Rapee, Erno 131
Rapf, Harry 121, 156
Raphaelson, Samson 137, 170
Ratcliffe, E.J. 120
Rathbone, Basil 43, 132
Ratoff, Gregory 51, 142, 145, 186
Rattenberry, Harry L. 113
Ravel, Sandra 131
Rawlins, John 123
Rawlinson, Herbert 157, 160
Ray, Allen 169
Ray, Joey 163
Ray, Terrance 54, 144
Raye, Martha 76, 186, 187
Raymond, Frankie [Frances] 116, 123
Raymond, Jack 160
Raymond, Robin 169
Rea, Mabel 181, 185
Reagan, Nancy 104–105
Reagan, Ronald 79, 104–105, 160, 180
Rebecca of Sunnybrook Farm 9, 113
The Re-Creation of Brian Kent 28, 121
Red Dice 135
Red Lamp in My Window (play) 92
Red Noses 49, 111
Redd, Ferrel 166
Redden, Arthur 116
Redmond, Granville 110

Redmond, Harry, Sr. 146, 148
Rée, Max 125, 126
Reed, Alan 182
Reed, George 151
Reed, J.T. 132
Reed, Phillip 81, 166
Reed, Tom 133, 149
Rees, William 155
Reeves, Alf 110
Regan, Phil 151
Regas, Robert 183
The Registered Woman 46, 135
Reicher, Frank 126, 134, 141, 161
Reicher, Hedwiga 134
Reid, Clara 172
Reid, Cliff 150, 165, 166
Reid [Davenport], Dorothy 173
Reid, Elliott 176
Reid, Wallace 17
Reilly, Tommy 162
Reiner, Carl 102, 176, 179
Reinhardt, Harry 125
Reis, Irving 122, 165
Reiser, Alois 128, 133
Reisner, Charles 110
Remarque, Erich Maria 41, 129, 130
Remisoff, Nicolai 164
Renavent, Georges 171
Renié 158, 165
Rennahan, Ray 125, 173
Renoir, Jean 54
"Repeal" 152
Repeal 153
Revela, Reta 121
Revier, Dorothy 129
"Revue" 187
Reynolds, Ben F. 120, 125
Reynolds, Craig 149
Reynolds, Debbie 102
Reynolds, John 100, 102, 105
Reynolds, Joyce 101
Reynolds, Lynn 178
Reynolds, Merrily Gay 180
Reynolds, Ralf 100, 105
Reynolds, Vera 31, 124
Reynolds, William 159
Reynolds Brothers Rhythm Rascals 100
Rhodes, "Little Billy" 140
Rhue, Madlyn 179
Ribardier, Susie 33
Riccioni, Enzo 129
Rice, Alice Hegan 151
Rice, Elmer 117
Rice, Frank 139, 145, 153
Rice, Grantland 51, 142
Rice, Jack 164
Rice, John 162
Richards, Addison 184
Richards, Cully 169
Richards, Lloyd 163
Richards, Thomas 160, 162
Richardson, Frank 114
Richardson, Jack 135, 155
Richman, Charles 158
Richmond, Kane 149
Richmond, Ted 173

Richmond, Warner 139
Ricketts, Tom 120, 122, 123, 158
The Riddle of the Dangling Pearl 157
The Riddle of the Forty Naughty Girls 158, 159
"Ride 'Em Cowgirl" 184
Ridgely, John 160
Riedel, Richard H. 172
Riesenfeld, Hugo 126, 132
Riffel, Jon 173
Riggs, C.A. 171
Riggs, Tommy 186
Riley, Thomas 110
Rinehart, Mary Roberts 83, 167, 169
Ring, Cyril 143, 146, 159, 163, 169
Rin-Tin-Tin 30, 40
Riordan, Robert 184
Risdon, Elisabeth 120, 165, 166, 171
Riskin, Robert 137
Risky Business 31, 124
River's End 43, 131
Rivkin, Allen 139, 140, 142, 146
Roach, Bert 127, 128, 133, 161
Roach, Hal 2, 45, 50, 56, 57, 80, 105, 110, 111, 112, 113, 149, 165
Roach, Hal, Jr. 44, 97, 164
Roach, Margaret 164, 165
Roar of the Dragon 50, 140
Robards, Jason 127
Robb, Cleora 147
Robb, Glorea 147
Robbins, Archie 154, 155
Robbins, Beverly 178
Robbins, Jess 122
Robby the Robot 184
Robeling, Albin 171
Rober, Richard 85
Roberts, Alan 185
Roberts, Arthur 148
Roberts, Charles E. 165, 166
Roberts, Florence 139, 140, 147
Roberts, Mark 181
Roberts, Roy 97, 99, 179, 182
Roberts, Stephen 185
Roberts, Theodore 114
Robertson-Cole Distributing Corporation 13
Robertson, John 134
Robertson, Stuart 163
Robertson, Willard 137, 148
Robin, Leo 130, 131
Robinson, Andrew 175
Robinson, Bertrand 145
Robinson, Casey 129, 139
Robinson, Dewey 149
Robinson, Edward G. 180
Robinson, George 142, 145
Robinson, James 135, 151
Robinson, W.C. 143
"Robot from Inner Space" 184
Robotham, George 178
Robson, May 80, 161
Rocco, Maurice 159
Roche, John 124, 128, 131, 132
Rock, George 179

Rockett, Ray 126
Roden, Molly 184
Roder, Milan 137
Rodgers, Richard 175
Roemheld, Heinz 133, 134, 149, 153, 162
Roerick, William 184
Rogers, Bogart 156
Rogers, Charles 82, 110, 121, 135, 142, 149, 165, 166
Rogers, Ginger 57, 145, 186
Rogers, Howard Emmett 128, 132
Rogers, Jean 151
Rogers, Kasey 173
Rogers, Roz 187, 188
Rogers, Stan 152, 156
Rogers, Walter Browne 130
Rogers, Will 60, 66, 147
Rogers, Will, Jr. 182
Rohrbach, G.M. 163
Romano, Nina 123
Romano, Tony 182
Romberg, Sigmund 125, 154
Romero, Carlos 184
Rominger, Glenn 137
Rondell, Ronald R. 141, 163
Rooney, LaVerne 125
Rooney, Mickey 63, 149, 173, 178
Roosevelt, Buddy 140, 156
Roosevelt, Franklin D. 60, 108
Roquemore, Henry 151, 153
Rorke, Hayden 176
Rosanova, Rosa 122
Roscher, Charles 131
Roscoe, Alan 139
Rose of Nome 17
Rose, Jackson 134
Rose, Tania 177
Rose, Wally 178
Rose, William 177
Rosen, Morris 178
Rosen, Phil 141
Rosenberg, Ruby 158
Rosenbloom, Maxie 79, 160
Rosener, George 143
Rosher, Charles 114
Rosher, Dorothy 114
Rosing, Bodil 122, 130, 157, 161
Rosley, Adrian 157, 158
Ross, Earle 187
Ross, Ishbel 148
Ross, Michael 184
Rosson, Hal 117, 132
Rostand, Maurice 137
Roth, Lillian 41, 128
Roy, Gloria 148
Roy, Rosalie 143
"Royal Welcome" 184
Royce, Lionel 161, 169
Royer 148
Rub, Christian 138, 141, 149
Rubens, Alma 29, 122
Rubin, Benny 163, 166
Rudie, Evelyn 184
Rudolph, Oscar 180
The Rudy Vallee Hour 186
Rued, Robert 85
Ruffner, Tiny 186

Ruggiero, Jack 175
Ruggles of Red Gap 66–67, 97, 105, 153, 154
"Ruggles of Red Gap" 187
Ruggles, Charles 66, 67, 140, 153, 171, 187
Ruggles, Wesley 128, 140, 144
Rugolo, Pete 175
Ruick, Melville 187
Ruman, Sig 154
The Runaway Express 19
Runyon, Damon 51, 142
Rush, Dick 165
Ruskin, Harry 144, 168
Russell, Andy 88, 170
Russell, Elizabeth 82, 159, 165, 167
Russell, John 181, 183
Russell, Rosalind 128, 172
Russell, Shirley 182
Russell, William G. 176
Ruth, Marshall 155
Ruth, Phyllis 169
Ruttenberg, Joseph 156
Ryan, Don 125
Ryan, Edward 170
Ryan, Mary 128
Ryan, Tommy 51, 80, 142, 161
Ryder, Eddie 179, 181
Ryerson, Florence 156

Sackin, Louis 136
"Sadie Green (the Vamp of New Orleans)" 175
Sage, Sally 160
Sainpolis [St. Polis], John 118
St. Angel, Michael 183
St. Clair, Malcolm 82, 166
St. John, Al 155
St. John, Howard 96, 180
St. Oegger, Joan 172, 174
St. Polis, John 134
Sale, Charles "Chic" 95–96
Sale, Virginia 95, 160, 165
Salt Water 145
Saltern, Irene 164
Sande, Walter 162
Sanders, George 80, 161
Sandford, Tiny 111
Sandrich, Mark 146
Sanford, Ralph 166
San Francisco Examiner 124
Santell, Alfred 126
Santina, Bruno Della 175
Santley, Joseph 156
Santschi, Tom 131
Sardo, Cosmo 176, 185
Sarecky, Barney 167
Sarracino, Ernest 182
Sartov, Hendrik 115
Satori, Peter 176
Satterfield, George 151
Sauber, Harry 157
Sauers, Joseph 158
Saulter, Dorothy 159
Saum, Cliff 131, 151, 158, 160
Saunders, Russell 135, 162
Savage, Archie 175

Sawtell, Paul 173
Sawyer, Gordon 178
Sawyer, Joe 84, 137, 148, 169
Sax, Arline 181
Saxe, Carl 178
Saxon, Hugh 116, 117
Sayles, Francis 139
Saylor, Syd 133, 165, 170
Scarborough, George 127
Scardon, Paul 169
"Scarlet" 43, 188
Schable, Robert 118, 128
Schaefer, Ann [Anne] 114, 119
Schaefer, Ed 156
Scharf, Walter 172
Schayer, Richard 137, 147
Scheid, Francis J. 160
Scheiwiller, Fred 178
Schenck, Harry 121
Schenck, Joseph M. 119, 132
Schertzinger, Victor 29, 122
Schiller, William 134
Schlom, Herman 160
Schmitt, W.R. 130
Schneiderman, George 122, 159
Schoedsack, Ernest B. 121
Schoenbaum, Emmett 132
Schoengarth, Russell F. 174
Scholl, John [Jack] 155
Schrock, Raymond L. 133
Schroeder, Charles 182
Schroeder, Doris 119
Schroeder, Edward 126, 127
Schulberg, B.P. 118, 125, 140
Schulberg, Budd 165
Schultz, Harry 111, 142
Schumann-Heink, Ernestine 126
Schumann-Heink, Ferdinand 125, 126
Schuster, Harold 154, 170
Scott, Charles 178
Scott, Derek 171
Scott, Fred 134
Scott, Leroy 125
Scott, William 139
Screen Directors Playhouse 96, 180
Scully, Mary Alice 121
Seabrook, Edward E. 165
Seal Skins 48, 111
Searl, Jackie 133
Seastrom, Dorothy 122
Seawright, Roy 164
Sebastian, Dorothy 135
"Secret Assignment" 184
The Secret Garden 114
The Secret Witness 47, 136
Secrets of the Night 20, 120
Sedan, Rolfe 112, 131, 133, 143, 146, 153, 184, 185
Seddon, Margaret 123
Seed 44, 134
Seeger, Miriam 139
Seeing It Through 13, 116
Segar, Elzie 52
Seider, Bill 99
Seidner, Irene 183
Seiler, Lewis 162
Seiling, Kenneth 134

Seiter, William A. 123, 139, 145, 148, 149
Seitz, George B. 156
Seitz, John F. 126, 133, 147
Selby, Sarah 182
Seldeen, Murray 161
Seller, Tom 167
Sellon, Charles 129, 136, 140, 149
Selwyn, Edgar 43, 131
Selwyn, Ruth 138
Selwynne, Clarissa 115
Selznick, David O. 27, 139, 140, 143, 146
Selznick, Lewis J. 27
Semels, Harry 137, 139, 147
Sennett, Mack 95
Sextet, Male 110
Seymour, Dan 183, 186
Seymour, Lew 155
Shamburger, Lucille 172
Shanahan, Dick 179
Shannon, Bill 178
Shannon, Ethel 118
Sharkey, Tom [Sailor] 51, 142
Sharp, Alex 178
Sharp, Henry 142, 164
Sharpe, David 110
Shaw, Al 151
Shaw, Brinsley 118
Shaw, C. Montague 141
Shaw, Wini 148
Shawlee, Joan 174
Shawn, Dick 178
Shay, Nellie 3
She Gets Her Man 68, 154
Shean, Al 159, 169
Shearer, Douglas 131, 132, 136, 141, 146, 152, 156, 169
Shearer, Norma 28, 66, 122, 128
Shears, Barbara 123
Sheehan, John 143, 164
Sheehan, Perley Poore 115
Sheehan, Winfield R. 53, 144
Sheffield, Reginald 182
Sheldon, E. Lloyd 126, 156
Sheldon, Gene 181
Sheldon, Kathryn 169
Sheldon, Lorraine 180
"She'll Love Me and Like It" 131
Shelley, George 159
Shelton, George 186
Shelton, Marla 159
Shepley, Ruth 129
Sherbett, Hazel 182
Sheridan, Ann 79, 80, 152, 158, 160, 162, 180
Sheridan, Anne 120, 124
Sheridan, Frank 137
Sherlock, Charles 179
Sherman, Lowell 128
Sherrod, Edgar 154
Sherwood, Bobby 160
Sherwood, John 172, 174
Sherwood, Lew 151
Shield, Leroy 110, 111, 112, 113
Shilling, Marion 44, 134
Shimada, Teru 156
Shipman, Helen 146

Shirley, Anne 120, 126
Shirley, Florence 170
Shirpser, Cliff 130, 151
Shopworn 49, 137
Shore Acres 39
Shore, Roberta 181
Shores, Byron 169
Shores, Jeanne 174
Short, Gertrude 114, 117, 129, 140, 149, 156
Shoulder Arms 9
Shoup, Howard 160, 162, 168
Shourds, Sherry 151
"Show Biz" 186
Show Business 50, 112
"Show Me" 176
Showalter, Max 96, 182
Shubert, Eddie 151
Shuken, Leo 159, 171
Shulter, Edward 129
Shumway, Walter 122
Shutta, Ethel 125
Shutta, Jack 173
Sidney, Sylvia 140
Siegler, Allen [Allan] G. 140, 146
The Sign 40
The Sign on the Door 127
"The Silent Partner" (television sketch) 96, 180
Siletti, Mario 183
Silk Stockings 144
Silver, Johnny 183
Silvera, Darrell 157, 163
Silvers, Louis 187
Silvers, Phil 178
Silvers, Sid 159
Simmons, Floyd 183
Simmons, Georgia 187
Simmons, Jean 100, 175
Simon, S.S. 121, 167
Simpson, Don 174, 175
Simpson, Russell 29, 122, 148
Sims, George 158
Sims, Milton 110
Sin Takes a Holiday 43, 132
Sing and Like It 62, 148, 149
Sing Me a Love Song 74, 75, 157
"Sing, Susanna, Sing" 183
"Singapore Fling" 183
Singh, Reginald 182
Singleton, Joseph 120
Singley, A.W. 149
Singley, Arthur 156
Sins of the Fathers 38, 126
Sistrom, Joseph 179
Sistrom, William 141, 155, 157, 158
Sitting Pretty 180
Skall, William V. 171, 172
Skelton, Red 140
Skinner, Frank 172
Skipworth, Alison 48, 136
Slade, Barbara 182
Sleeper, Martha 131
Sloan, Tod 142
Smalley, Phillips 119, 135
Smedley-Aston, E.M. [M.] 158
Smiley, Ralph 184
Smith, Barbara 174

Smith, C. Aubrey 80, 133, 143, 162
Smith, Charles 178
Smith, Danny 178
Smith, Ed W. 142
Smith, Eddie 179
Smith, Frank 178
Smith, Gerald Oliver 169
Smith, James 115
Smith, Lew 175
Smith, Oscar 133
Smith, Paul Girard 164
Smith, Stanley 128
Smith, Winchell 118
"Smokie, Part 2" 175
Sneak Easily 53, 106, 112
Snell, David 168
Snell, Earle 137, 145
Snowden, Alec C. 126
Snowden, Carolynne 126
Snowden, Eric 187
Snyder, Edward 143
So This Is Washington 166
"So You Won't Sing, Eh?" 148
"Social Pirates" 155
Social Pirates 155
A Society Sensation 11, 115
Soderling, Walter 165
The Soilers 51, 112
The Solid Gold Cadillac (television series) 97, 188
"Solid Potato Salad" 170
"Somebody Mighty Like You" 127
"Somebody Nobody Wants" 176
Somerset, Pat 138
Somerville, A.W. 127
Son of India 39
The Son of Wallingford 14
"Song of Napoli" 132
"Song of the Women's Army Corps" 174
Sonia, Countess 148
Sorel, George 157, 158
Sorenson, Buster 125
"S.O.S. Dad" 185
So's Your Aunt Emma (aka *Meet the Mob*) 82, 84, 166
Sothern, Ann 181
Soule, Olan 174
Souls for Sale 16, 18
Soussanin, Nicholas 126
Sowders, Edward 121, 125
Space, Arthur 169
Spagnoli, Genaro 153
Spalding, Harry 175
"Spanish Souvenir" 185
Sparks, Ned 63, 129, 148, 149
Sparkuhl, Theodor 156, 159
"The Specialist" (monologue) 95, 96
Spence, Ralph 141, 147, 155
Spencer, Dorothy 161
Spencer, Vicki 176
Spewack, Bella 152
Spewack, Sam 136, 152
Spielter, William 148
Spigelgass, Leonard 144, 170
Spike Jones and His City Slickers 88

The Spike Jones Show 95, 179
Spooner, F.E. 116
Sporting Blood 39
Sprague, Chandler 134, 166
"Spring Cleaning" 120
Spring Cleaning 20, 120
Spring in Park Lane 129
Spring Tonic 67, 68, 154
Springer, John 41
The Squall 40, 126
The Squealer 43, 129
Stader, Paul 178
Stafford, Hanley 181
Stahl, John M. 134, 143
Stand Up and Cheer! 39
Stand Up and Sing 161
Standing, Herbert 114
Standing, Joan 121, 137
Stanford, Anthony 186
Stang, Arnold 179
Stanley, Edwin 162
Stanton, Penny 182
Stanton, Will 140, 141, 144, 164
Stanwyck, Barbara 40, 49, 74, 128, 137
Starkey, Dewey 140, 145
Starling, Lynn 143
Starr, Fred 9
Starrett, Charles 62, 147, 148
Statter, Arthur F. 121
Staudte, Wolfgang 130
Staunton, Ann 181
Steady Company 49, 137
Stedman, Lincoln 117
Stedman, Myrtle 129
Steele, Tom 178
Steele, Vernon 117
Steers, Larry 141, 143, 158, 160, 162, 173
Stein, Paul L. 128, 132
Steiner, Max 139, 140, 146, 147, 148, 150, 171, 172
Stengler, Mack 167
Stephens, Marvin 137
Stephenson, Robert R. 160, 161
Steppling, John 114, 115
Sterling, Ford 124, 125
Stern, David 93, 172
Sternad, Rudolph 177
Stevens, Ashton 89
Stevens, Craig 183
Stevens, Edwin 116
Stevens, Landers 142, 148
Stevens, Louis 155
Stevens, Onslow 142
Stevens, W.L. 164
Stevens, William 181
Stevenson, Edward 133, 157, 161, 163, 165, 166
Stevenson, Robert 143
Stewart, Donald Ogden 44, 133, 171
Stewart, Eleanor 162
Stewart, James 49
Stewart, Leslie, Jr. 116
Stewart, Nick 171, 179
Stewart, Sophie 161
Stickney, Dorothy 126, 172

Stillman, Patricia 162
Stine, Harold 127, 134
Stockbridge, Henry 128
Stockdale, Carl 122, 160, 165
Stoll, Billy 175
Stoll, George 174, 175
Stollery, David 182
Stoloff, Ben 137
Stone, Arthur 140, 149, 155
Stone, George E. 164
Stone, John 148
Stone, LeRoy 126, 135, 140
Stone, Lewis 132
Stone, Mildred 156
Stone, Sandra 183
"Stop, Thief" 183
Storey, Edith 116
Storey, June 80, 161
Storm, Gale 1, 80, 97, 98, 99, 104, 106, 164, 182
Storm, Jane 151
Storm, Jerome 119
Storm, Rafael 153
Stothart, Herbert 132
Stowell, William 115
Stowers, Frederick 28, 122
Stradling, Walter 113, 114
Strange, Robert 141
Strangers of the Evening 49–50, 138
Stratton, Chet 180, 183
Strauss, Robert 176
"Streamline Feature" 149
The Street of Forgotten Men 106
Strictly Unreliable 449111
Strohback [Strohbach], William 167
Strong, Austin 118
Strong, Leonard 175
Stroud, Clarence 149
Stroud, Claude 149
Strudwick, Shepperd 94
Struss, Karl 118, 120
Stuart, Arlen 186
Stuart, Gloria 143
Stuart, Iris 124
Stuart, Leslie 116
Stuart, Marilyn 187
Stuart, Michael 135
Stuart, Nick 170
Stuart, Norman 176
Stubbs, Harry 128, 139, 142
Stumar, Charles J. 137
Stumar, John 122, 125
Sturgeon, Rollin S. 119
Sturges, Preston 143
Sturgis, Eddie 129
Sudden Riches 39
Sullavan, Margaret 143
Sullivan, C. Gardner 119, 127, 130
Sullivan, Charles 128, 143, 153, 155, 164
Sullivan, Frank 152
Sullivan, J. Maurice [John M.] 138
Sullivan, Liam 183, 185
Sully, Frank 161
Sully, Janet Miller 110
Summers, Hope 181, 185
Summers, Jay 187

Summerville, Slim 42, 43, 44, 48, 55, 56, 58, 63, 64, 80, 81, 129, 130, 133, 136, 143, 144, 145, 149, 150, 164, 165
Sunlight of Paris 20
Sunny Ducrow 31, 124
Sunnyside 11
Sunny Side Up 31, 124
Sunset Blvd. 54
Sunshine Inn 187
"Super Snoop" 182
"Susanna and the Pirates" 184
"Susanna Goes Native" 183
"Susanna Plays Cupid" 183
"Susanna Strikes Back" 182
"Susanna Strikes Oil" 183
"Susanna Takes a Husband" 184
"Susanna, the Babysitter" 185
"Susanna, the Chaperone" 183
"Susanna the Matchmaker" 184
"Susanna's Baby" 183
"Susanna's True Confession" 185
Sutherland, Ethel 133
Sutherland, Evelyn Greenleaf 130
Sutherland, Jack 130
Sutton, Grady 160, 166
Swain, Mack 124, 128, 133
Swan, William 182
Swanson, Gloria 54
Swanson, H.N. 145, 147
Swanton, Fred 4, 5, 6, 14, 117
Swartley, Raymond E. 163
"The Swedish Steward" 185
"The Sweepstakes Ticket" 184
Swerling, Jo 129, 137
Swift, Joan 183
"Swiss Miss" 182
Sylbert, Paul 175
Sylvester, Henry 172

Tabor, Joan 176
Tabori, Kristoffer 142
Tahbel, N. 110
"Take a Little One Step" 163
"Taking a Chance on Love" 175
"Taking Ways" 184
Talbot, Nita 175, 181
Taliaferro, Edith 113
The Talk of the Town 11, 115
Tallman, Chester 165
Tallman, Frank 178
Talmadge, Constance 11, 20, 114, 115, 119, 144
Talmadge, Norma 40
Talman, William 181
Tamara 163
Tamblyn, Eddie 113, 151
Tamiroff, Akim 145
Tannen, Julius 163
Tapps, George 159
Taranda, Anya 156
Tarkington, Booth 44, 46, 130, 133, 134, 135
Tashman, Lilyan 28, 30, 122, 128, 133
Tate, Cullen 128
Tatum, Art 159
Tatum, Jeanne 174

Tauber, Doris 110
Taurog, Norman 64, 133, 151
Tavares, Arthur 134
Taylor, Deems 26
Taylor, Dub 184
Taylor, Elizabeth 76, 90, 91, 101, 171
Taylor, Ferris 165, 166
Taylor, Forrest 173
Taylor, Helen 159
Taylor, Howard 76
Taylor, Joyce 183
Taylor, June 180
Taylor, Kent 140, 151
Taylor, Libby 153, 171
Taylor, Paul 186
Taylor, Pop 116
Taylor, Rex 124
Taylor, Ruth 128
Taylor, Sam 144
Taylor, Sara 76
Taylor, Stanley 122
Taylor, Stanner E.V. 115
Taylor, Vaughn 175
Taylor, William Desmond 11, 114
Tayo, Lyle 111
Tea for Two 128
"Tea for Two" 163
Tea: With a Kick! 14, 118
Tead, Phil 138, 146, 149, 151, 156
Tearle, Conway 28, 121
Teasdale, Verree 143, 145
"Teen-age Millionaire" 175
Teen-Age Millionaire 102, 175
Tell, Olive 149
Temple, Shirley 56, 66, 70–71, 74, 101, 114, 144
Templeton, [George] Dink 140
Templeton, Harry 173
The Ten Commandments 90
Tenbrook, Harry 137, 138, 140, 153, 160
Terror by Night 136
Terry, Alice 28, 121
Terry, Don 145
Terry, Ethel Grey 122
Terry, Jack 119
Terry-Thomas 178
A testör 136
Tetley, Walter 186
Tetzlaff, Ted 129
Tevis, Carol 142, 156
Texaco Star Theater 93, 179
Thalasso, Arthur 120
Thalberg, Irving 18, 26, 136
Thayer, Ernest Lawrence 124
Thayer, Tiffany 50, 138
Theby, Rosemary 118, 120, 122
Their Big Moment 64, 150
Their Mad Moment 46, 134, 135
"Them There Eyes" 110
There Shall Be No Night 94
There's Always Tomorrow 147
Thew, Harvey 127
They Had Faces Then 41
They Just Had to Get Married 55, 143
Thimble Theater 52

13 Hours by Air 70, 156
13 Washington Square 34, 35, 125
"This Could Be the Night" 174
This Could Be the Night 100, 174, 175
This Modern World 134
This Thing Called Love 41, 128
Thomas, A.E. 128, 129
Thomas, Alan 176
Thomas, Bill 177, 178
Thomas, Dolph 162
Thomas, Edward 149
Thomas, Frank M. 159
Thomas, Jameson 138
Thomas, Jay 187
Thompson, Al 139
Thompson, Bill 186, 187
Thompson, Charlotte 113
Thompson, Clifford 111
Thompson, Harlan 153, 187
Thompson, Lotus 124
Thompson, Nick 140, 149
Thompson, Stuart 180
Thompson, William 116
Thomson, Kenneth 31, 124
Thornley, William 116
Thorpe, Jim 159
The Three Musketeers 17
3 on a Honeymoon 62, 148
Three Stooges 60
Three Wise Fools 118
The Thrill of It All! 104, 176
Thunder 29
"Thunder" 122
Thunder Mountain 29, 122
Thurston, Helen 178
Tibbets, John 106
Tierney, Harry 139
Tilbury, Zeffie 148
Tillie of the Nine Lives 9, 109
Tillotson, David Leo 143
Tindall, Loren 172
Tinling, James 148
Tish 83, 85, 167, 169
Titus, Lydia Yeamans 115
Tobin, Genevieve 44, 133, 134
Todd, Arthur 123, 124, 157, 160
Todd, Harry 117, 118
Todd, James 172, 175
Todd, Thelma 1, 2, 40, 43, 45, 46, 48, 49, 50, 51, 53, 55, 56, 69–70, 106, 110, 111, 112, 113, 133, 186, 188
Toler, Sidney 50, 139, 141
Tollaire, August 125
Tom Breneman's Breakfast in Hollywood 170
Tombes, Andrew 84, 169
Toncray, Kate 113
Toney, Jim 164
Tong, Sammee 179, 181
Tonight at 8:30 83, 188
"Too Many Maharanis" 182
Tooker, William H. 135, 139
Toomey, Regis 49, 133, 137, 182
Toones, Fred "Snowflake" 146, 151, 153
Torrence, David 131

216 INDEX

Torrence, Ernest 119
Totheroh, Dan 147
Totheroh, R.H. 110
Tourneur, Christiane 155
Tover, Leo 139
Towers, Dick 172
Towne, Gene 129, 161
Towne, Rosella 163
Townley, Jack 157
Tracey, William 110
Tracy, Lee 146
Tracy, Spencer 178
Trail Street 90
Traxler, Valeria 115
Treacher, Arthur 67, 155
Treacy, Emerson 148
Treadwell, Laura 154, 155, 172
Tree, Dolly 146, 152, 156
A Tree Is a Tree 8
Trent, Jack 133
Trevor, Claire 67, 68, 154
The Trial of Vivienne Ware 49, 138
Tribby, John E. 140
Trifling Women 17
"Trimmin' the Women" 131
"A Trip for Auntie" 185
Triumph 20, 119
Troffey, Alex 148
"Trouble in Trinidad" 183
Trout, Dink 165, 187
Trowbridge, Charles 157, 160
Troy, Elinor 170
Truex, Ernest 126
"Trumpet Boogie" 174
"The Truth Machine" 184
Tryon, Glenn 149
Tryon, Tom 181
Tucker, Richard 118, 126, 134, 139, 146, 157
Tucker, Robert 174
Tuesday Night Party 187
Tugend, Harry 169
Turk, Roy 149
Turnbull, Hector 124, 126
Turner, F.A. 116
Turner, Florence 138
Turner, Frank 113
Turner, George 160
Turner, George Kibbe 140
Turner, Ray 147
Turner, Roscoe 156
Turner, William H. 122
Turpin, Ben 30, 50, 140
Tuttle, William 174
TV Hour of Stars 180
Tweddell, Frank 180
Twelvetrees, Helen 45, 50, 68, 134, 135, 139, 154
Twemlow, Mabel 158
The 20th Century–Fox Hour 180
The 20th Century Hourr of Stars 96
Twenty Hours by Air 156
Twerp, Joe 153
Twin Beds 40, 126
"Twistin' U.S.A." 176
Twitchell, Archie 160, 161
Two Alone 61, 147

Two Clucks 149
Two Weeks to Live 166
Tyler, Harry 127, 160
Tyler, Kim 180
Tyler, Lelah 187
Tynan, Brandon 162
Tynan, James J. 121
Tyrell, David 130
Tyron, Max 121
Tyrrell, Ann 181

Udell, Peter 176
Uitti, Betty 175
Ullman, E.G. 115
Uncle Joe 80, 163
Uncle Tom's Cabin 16
Underwood, Loyal 110
Uneasy Money 9, 109
The Unexpected Father 48, 136
Unger, Gladys 119
An Unmarried Father 129
Unsell, Eve 118, 122
Urecal, Minerva 146, 163, 170
Urson, Frank 119

Vacío, Natividad 186
Vague, Vera 184
Vajda, Ernest 130, 136, 137
Valentine, Joseph A. 148
Valentino, Rudolph 11, 106, 115
Valerie, Gertrude 172
Vallee, Rudy 76, 180, 186
Van, Beatrice 114, 128
Van, Frankie 160
Van Buren, Mabel 117
Vance, Jerry 176
Vanderveer, Ellinor 133
Van Doren, Mamie 93, 174
Van Dreelen, John 185
Van Dyke, Truman 115, 119
Van Enger, Charles 118
Van Eps, Robert 174
Van Every, Dale 136, 149
Van Haden, Anders 156
Van Hessen, Richard 163, 166
Van Horn, Buddy 178
The Vanishing Frontier 50, 141
Van Keuren, Sidney S. 180
Van Lent, Lucille 126
Van Rooten, Luis 185
Van Sickel, Dale 163, 178
Van Sickle, Raymond 148
Van Trees, James C. 114, 115, 127
Van Zandt, Philip 172
Varconi, Victor 119
Varden, Norma 76, 158, 185
Vaughn, Billy 185
Vaverka, Anton 120, 125, 137
Vavitch, Michael 131
Velez, Lupe 82, 165, 166
Venable, Evelyn 67, 68, 151
Verdugo, Elena 185
Vermilyea, Harold 186
Verne, Kaaren 182
Vernon, Bobby 140
Vernon, Dorothy 136
Vernon, Vinton 178
Verrill, Virginia 159

A Very Missing Person 157
Vickers, Harold 115
Victor, Henry 161
Vidor, Florence 116
Vidor, King 7, 8, 10, 13, 14, 20, 116, 118, 120
Vigran, Herb 162, 188
Villa, Alberto 182
Vincenot, Louis 155
Vincent, June 184
Vincent, Sailor 155
Vinton, Arthur 151
Vinton, Victoria 151
Virgil, Jack 134, 152
Virginia Sale's Americana 95
Vogan, Emmett 149, 155, 158
Vogel, Paul 168
"Volcano" 182
von Brincken, Wilhelm 125, 126, 153, 161
Von Eltz, Theodor [Theodore] 134, 139
von Haartman, Carl 126
von Morhart, Hans 130
von Ritzau, Erich 121
von Rue, Greta 170
von Seyffertitz, Gustav 114, 157, 161
von Sternberg, Josef 125
von Stroheim, Erich 1, 2, 21, 22, 25, 26, 27, 34, 35, 36, 38, 53, 54, 102, 105, 120, 121, 125, 126, 144, 145
Vosper, John 171
Votion, Jack William 166
Votrian, Peter 182
Vreeland, Robert 171
Vye, Murvyn 175

Wachner, Sophie 121
Wade, Russell 166
Wagenheim, Charles 175
Wages for Wives 30, 123
Waggner, George 127
Wagner, Max 165
Wagner, Rob 110
Wain, Bea 186
Waite, Malcolm 123
Waizmann, Max 135
Wakeling, Gwen 128, 132, 134, 135
Walburn, Raymond 80, 84, 88, 162, 169, 170
Wald, Jerry 157, 160
Waldridge, Harold 139, 149
Wales, Ethel 117
Walker, Clifford 186
Walker, H.M. 110, 111, 112, 143, 145, 149, 155
Walker, Johnnie 120
Walker, Joseph 137
Walker, June 131
Walker, Nancy 96
Walker, Nella 134, 139, 140, 155
Walker, Ray 175, 184
Walker, Vernon L. 161, 163
Walker, Walter 145, 151, 152
Walking Down Broadway 53, 144, 145

Index

The Wall Flower 14
Wallace, C.R. 122
Wallace, May 113
Wallace, Morgan 137, 147, 148
Waller, Fats 159
Wallflower 101
Walling, Will 134
Wallis, Hal B. 150, 157, 160, 162, 170
Walsh, Raoul 54, 144
Walters, Luana 162
Walters, Polly 140
Walton, Fred 120, 132, 135
Waltz, Patrick 181, 183
Wanamaker, Zoe 142
Wang, Jimmy 121, 141
Wanger, Walter 159, 161
Wanted! 76, 158
War Mamas 46, 111
War Nurse 43, 131
Ward, Alice 169
Ward, Edward 127, 164, 165
Ward, Kathrin Clare 140
Ward, Lucille 114
Ward, Tiny 112, 118
Warfield, Natalie 122
Wark, Colin 158
Warner, H.B. 45, 127, 135, 161
Warner, Jack L. 157, 162, 171
Warren, Bruce 156
Warren, Fred 128
Warren, Harry 160
Warren, Julie 166
Warrenton, Gilbert 120
Warth, Theron 165, 166
Warwick, Robert 127, 172, 182
Washington, Blue 149
Waterman, Willard 187, 188
Watkin, Pierre 183
Watkins, Maurine Dallas 144, 145
Watson, Adele 128
Watson, Bobby 153
Watson, Bobs 181
Watson, Delmar 159
Watson, Lucile 94, 188
Watson, Margaret 158
Watson, Waldon O. 176
Watson, William Wright 16
Watt, Nate 123, 130
Waxman, Franz 155
Way, Guy 183
"The Way I Am" 176
Wayne, Billy 162, 170
Wayne, Jesse 178
Wayne, Justina 187
Wayne, Robert 169
Weatherwax, Paul 125, 169
Weatherwax, William MacAllister 162
Weaver, Doodles 179
Weaver, Marjorie 169
Webb, Clifton 180
Webb, Richard 183
Webb, Roy 145, 146, 147, 158, 165
Webb, "Speed" 126
Webster, Franklin H. 146
Webster, Lucile 43
Webster, Paul Francis 175

"Wedding at Sea" 185
"Wedding in Majorca" 183
The Wedding March 2, 34, 35–38, 43, 105, 125
Weekend for Three 81, 165
Weeks, Al 163
Weidler, Virginia 65, 151
Weigel, Paul 143
Weinberg, Herman 26
Weinrib, Len 176
Weiss, Lurie 126
Welch, Jim 153
Welch, Niles 120
Welden, Ben 185
Welk, Lawrence 181
Wellesley, Alfred 158
Wellesley, William 119
Wells, George 186, 187
Wells, Gilbert 175
Wells, William K. 146
Welsh, William 153
Wendell, Howard 180
Wenstrom, Harold 150
Werker, Alfred L. 53, 54, 144
Wescoatt, Rusty 174
West, Clare 119
West, Claudine 136
West, Mae 61, 66
West, Pat 156
West, Vera 143
West of Broadway 39
West of the Water Tower 15, 119
Westcott, Gordon 155
Westerfield, James 166
Western Story Magazine 49
Westman, Nydia 61, 148
Westmore, Bud 172, 174, 176
Westmore, Perc 162, 171
Westmore, Wally 170, 173
Westward Passage 50, 139
What a Liar! 146
What Happened to Jones 30, 123
"Whatever It Is, It's Grand" 131
What's My Line? 179
What's Your Daughter Doing 20, 119
Wheeler, Charles [F.] 178
Wheeler, Gertrude 181
Wheeler, Glen 120
Wheeler, Leonard 129
Whelan, Tim 141
Whelan, Tom 144
"Where Has My Hubby Gone" 163
Where Ignorance Is Bliss 136
White, Billy 110
White, Huey 155
White, Jack 159
White, Jesse 179
White, Jules 50, 112
White, Leo 113, 119, 132, 146, 151, 155, 160
White, Merrill G. 130, 161, 163
White, Sammy 50, 183
The White Dragon 157
Whitehead, O.Z. 184
Whitehill, Morton 126
Whiting, Richard 128, 130, 131

"Who Killed Holly Howard?" (television episode) 104, 182
"Who Stole That Melody?" 185
Who's Your Wife? 9, 110
Whose Wife 162
Why Harry Left Home 109
Why Leave Home? 170
Why They Left Home 9, 109
Whytock, Grant 121
Wickes, Mary 180
Widrig, Clem 181
Wife Savers 34, 125
Wiggin, Kate Douglas 113
Wilcox, Frank 182
Wilcox, Harlow 186, 187
Wilcox, Herbert 80, 161, 163
Wild Bird 148
Wild Birds 147, 148
"Wild Wings" 156
Wilde, Cornel 89, 135
Wilde, Heather 171
Wiles, Gordon 138
Wilkey, Violet 113
Wilky, L. Guy 120
Willens, Marvin 178
Williams, Brock 158
Williams, Charles 111, 139, 141, 143, 149, 151, 158
Williams, D.J. 158
Williams, Elmo 161, 163
Williams, George 174
Williams, Gloria 160
Williams, Guinn "Big Boy" 46, 110, 111
Williams, Guy 181
Williams, Lawrence P. 161
Williams, L.P. 163
Williams, Lottie 117
Williams, Maston 136
Williams, Paul 71
Williams, Percy 119
Williams, Roy 181
Willis, Bill 134
Willis, Edwin B. 146, 152, 156, 168, 174
Willis, F. McGrew 126, 135
Willis, Jack 134
Willis, Leo 111
Willis, Matt 170
Willock, Dave 165, 169
Wills, Chill 92, 173, 174, 181
Willson, Meredith 181
Wilson, Carey 120, 123
Wilson, Charles 164
Wilson, Charles C. 160
Wilson, Charles J. 109
Wilson, Clarence 145, 149, 153, 154
Wilson, Harry 140, 141, 153, 187
Wilson, Jack 110
Wilson, Jackie 176
Wilson, Julie 174, 175
Wilson, Lois 14, 117, 134
Wilson, Lulee 126
Wilson, Marie 158
Wilson, Stuart 174
Wilson, Tom 110, 120, 155
Wilton, Eric 135, 182

Wimperis, Arthur 125
Windsor, Claire 14
Windsor, Marie 166, 170
Wine of Youth 20, 120
Winkler, Ben 128, 134
Winninger, Charles 44, 133
Winslow, Dick 133, 134
Winslowe, Paula 182, 184
Winter, Verne 117
Winters, Jonathan 178
Winwood, Estelle 120
Wirth, Sandra 184
Wisberg, Claude 163
Wisdom, Philip 153
Wise, Jack 147, 151, 158
Wise, Robert 100, 174
Wissler, Rudy 169
"The Witch Doctor" 182
Withers, Grant 183
Withers, Hildegarde 157
Witherspoon, Cora 85, 172
Witting, Martha [Mattie] 113
"Wob-a-ly Walk" 127
Wolcott, Earl A. 127, 139, 158, 166
Wolfe, Bill 165
Wolfe, Jane 116
Wolfe, Sam 184
Wolff [Wolfe], Jane 113
Wolfson, P.J. 142, 146
Wolheim, Louis 130
Woman Hungry 121
A Woman of Experience 45, 135
A Woman's Faith 29, 122
Wong, Victor 163
Wood, Dorothy 119, 122
Wood, Douglas 154, 162
Wood, Ernest 148, 160
Wood, Freeman 123
Wood, Judith 132
Wood, Sam 28, 121
Woodall, Edward 62
Woodall, John E. 55
Woodbury, Albert 178

Woodbury, Evelyn 162
Woodbury, Joan 159
Wooden, Earl 166
Woodruff, Frank 187
Woods, Walter 117, 123
Woodthorpe, Georgia 116
Woodward, Henry 116
Woodworth, Jane 165
Woodworth, Marjorie 81, 164
Woody, Sam 174
Woolery, Adrian 178
Woolf, Edgar Allan 156
Woolley, Monty 96, 180
Worthington, William 138, 151
Worthley, Althea 114
Wrangell, Basil 146
Wray, Fay 36, 125
Wray, John 130
Wren, Sam 95
Wright, George 148
Wright, Harold Bell 121
Wright, Lynn 174
Wright, Marbeth 138
Wright, Marvin 175
Wright, William H. 182
Wurtzel, Sol M. 53, 144
Wyatt, Jane 81, 166
Wyler, William 58, 145
Wyman, Irene 178
Wynn, Ed 61

Yamaoka, Otto 156
Yarbrough, Jean 166, 180
Yarde, Margaret 158
Yates, Hal 164
Yates, John, Jr. 183
Ybarra, Frank 121
Yellen, Jack 155
Yetter, William, Sr. 111
"Yogi" 176
Yong, Soo 157
York, Duke 164, 173
Yorke, Edith 118

You Can't Take It with You 78
"You Gotta Have Charm" 184
Youmans, Vincent 163
Young, Clarence Upson 157
Young, Frank 164
Young, Freddie 161
Young, Georgiana 163
Young, Harold 133, 159
Young, Howard Irving 154
Young, Loretta 80, 88, 126, 131, 162, 171
Young, Lucille 115
Young, Mary 184
Young, Robert 180
Young, Roland 46, 48, 67, 80, 133, 136, 143, 153, 163
Young, Tammany 143
Young, Waldemar 121, 135
The Young and the Restless 101
"Your Mother" 149
"You're an Angel" 132
Youth to Youth 14, 117
"Yubla" 132
Yurka, Blanche 126

Zamecnik, J.S. 125
Zanuck, Darryl F. 53
ZaSu Pitts Memorial Orchestra 107
"ZaSu Pitts — The Girl with the Gingersnap Name" 107
"ZaSu's Lullaby — or the Jazz Baby's Dream" 107
Zaza 39, 79
Zbyszko, Stanislaus 51, 142
Ziegfeld, Florenz 125
The Ziegfeld Follies 106
Ziegfeld Follies of the Air 146
Zimmer, Dolph 156
Zinnemann, Fred 130
Zuckert, Bill 181
Zukor, Adolph 118, 125
Zuro, Josiah 132

www.ingramcontent.com/pod-product-compliance
Lightning Source LLC
Chambersburg PA
CBHW080935020526
44116CB00034B/2887